MAVERICK GUIDE TO
HONG KONG, MACAU, and SOUTH CHINA

mav•er•ick (mav'er-ik), *n* 1. an unbranded steer. Hence [colloq.] 2. a person not labeled as belonging to any one faction, group, etc., who acts independently. 3. one who moves in a different direction than the rest of the herd—often a nonconformist. 4. a person using individual judgment, even when it runs against majority opinion.

The Maverick Guide Series

The Maverick Guide to Australia

The Maverick Guide to Bali and Java

The Maverick Guide to Berlin

The Maverick Guide to Hawaii

The Maverick Guide to Malaysia and Singapore

The Maverick Guide to New Zealand

The Maverick Guide to Prague

The Maverick Guide to Thailand

The Maverick Guide to Vietnam, Laos, and Cambodia

MAVERICK GUIDE TO
HONG KONG, MACAU, and SOUTH CHINA

Len Rutledge
Researched by Phensri Athisumongkol

PELICAN PUBLISHING COMPANY
Gretna 1995

Copyright © 1995
by Pelican Publishing Company, Inc.
All rights reserved

ISBN: 1-56554-071-9

The word "Pelican" and the depiction of a pelican are trademarks of Pelican Publishing Company, Inc., and are registered in the U.S. Patent and Trademark Office.

Information in this guidebook is based on authoritative data available at the time of printing. Prices and hours of operation of businesses listed are subject to change without notice. Readers are asked to take this into account when consulting this guide.

Maps by Len Rutledge

Manufactured in the United States of America
Published by Pelican Publishing Company, Inc.
1101 Monroe Street, Gretna, Louisiana 70053

Contents

	Preface	11
	Acknowledgments	12
1.	**Why Go to Hong Kong, Macau, and the Pearl River Delta of China?**	
	Tourist Hong Kong, Macau and the Pearl River Delta in Summary	18
	The Confessional	20
	Getting the Most Out of This Book	21
	Some Quick Comments	22
2.	**Happy Landings**	
	How to Get There	25
	Transportation Within Hong Kong, Macau, and the Pearl River Delta	26
	Travel Facts	27
	Metrics and Electrics	29
	Money and Prices	30
	Government Fiddle-Faddle	32
	Travellers' Guide	34
	Travel Tips	37
	Visit the Region	38

HONG KONG

3.	**The Land, Life, and People of Hong Kong**	
	Geography	45
	Climate	46
	History	46
	The Government	48
	The Economy	49
	The People	50
	Religion	52
	Language	54
	Culture and Lifestyle	56
	Food and Drink	58
	Festivals	60
	Accommodations	64
	Health and Safety	64
4.	**Hong Kong Island**	
	1. The General Picture	67
	2. Getting There	69
	3. Local Transportation	69

		4. The Hotel Scene	72
		5. Dining and Restaurants	80
		6. Sight-seeing	86
		7. Guided Tours	96
		8. Culture	98
		9. Sports	99
		10. Shopping	100
		11. Entertainment and Nightlife	109
		12. The Hong Kong Island Address List	111
5.	**Kowloon**		
		1. The General Picture	113
		2. Getting There	115
		3. Local Transportation	116
		4. The Hotel Scene	118
		5. Dining and Restaurants	128
		6. Sight-seeing	133
		7. Guided Tours	140
		8. Culture	141
		9. Sports	141
		10. Shopping	142
		11. Entertainment and Nightlife	148
		12. The Kowloon Address List	150
6.	**The New Territories**		
		1. The General Picture	151
		2. Getting There	153
		3. Local Transportation	153
		4. The Hotel Scene	154
		5. Dining and Restaurants	156
		6. Sight-seeing	157
		7. Guided Tours	164
		8. Culture	165
		9. Sports	165
		10. Shopping	166
		11. Entertainment and Nightlife	166
		12. The New Territories Address List	167
7.	**The Outlying Islands**		
		1. The General Picture	169
		2. Getting There	170
		3. Local Transportation	171
		4. The Hotel Scene	171
		5. Dining and Restaurants	172
		6. Sight-seeing	173
		7. Guided Tours	181
		8. Culture	183
		9. Sports	183

CONTENTS

10. Shopping	183
11. Entertainment and Nightlife	183
12. The Outlying Islands Address List	183

MACAU

8. The Land, Life, and People of Macau

Geography	187
Climate	188
History	188
The Government	189
The Economy	190
The People	190
Language	191
Culture and Lifestyle	191
Food and Drink	192
Festivals	192
Accommodations	193
Health and Safety	194

9. Macau—Mainland and Islands

1. The General Picture	195
2. Getting There	196
3. Local Transportation	197
4. The Hotel Scene	198
5. Dining and Restaurants	205
6. Sight-seeing	208
7. Guided Tours	220
8. Culture	221
9. Sports	223
10. Shopping	224
11. Entertainment and Nightlife	225
12. The Macau Address List	228

CHINA—THE PEARL RIVER DELTA

10. The Land, Life, and People of the Pearl River Delta

Geography	231
Climate	232
History	232
The Government	236
The Economy	237
The People	238
Religion	240
Language	240
Culture and Lifestyle	242
Food and Drink	243
Festivals	245

        The Arts 246
        Accommodations 248
        Health and Safety 249
11. Guangzhou and the Pearl River Delta
        1. The General Picture 251
        2. Getting There 253
        3. Local Transportation... 254
        4. The Hotel Scene 255
        5. Dining and Restaurants 261
        6. Sight-seeing 264
        7. Guided Tours... 280
        8. Culture 281
        9. Sports 282
        10. Shopping 283
        11. Entertainment and Nightlife 284
        12. The Guangzhou Address List 285
Index 287

LIST OF MAPS

Pearl River Delta, Macau, Hong Kong 10
The Region 14
Major Tourist Interest 19
How to Reach Hong Kong... 24
See the Region 39
Hong Kong 44
Hong Kong Island 66
Hong Kong Island Transport.. 70
Central Hotels... 74
Wanchai and Causeway Bay Hotels 78
Central... 87
Wanchai and Causeway Bay 92
Central Shopping and Nightlife 102
Wanchai and Causeway Bay Shopping and Nightlife.......... 104
Kowloon 114
Kowloon Transport.. 117
Tsim Sha Tsui Hotels 119
Mong Kok and Yau Ma Tei Hotels.. 126
Tsim Sha Tsui 134
Mong Kok and Yau Ma Tei.. 139
Tsim Sha Tsui Shopping and Nightlife 143
The New Territories 152
Outlying Islands 168
Cheung Chau 174

CONTENTS

Lamma	176
Lantau	178
Macau	186
Peninsula Hotels and Restaurants	199
Peninsula Macau	209
Central Macau	210
Taipa Island	216
Coloane Island	219
Guangzhou	252
Guangzhou Hotels and Restaurants	262
City Attractions	265
Shenzhen Special Economic Zone	273
Zhuhai Special Economic Zone	279

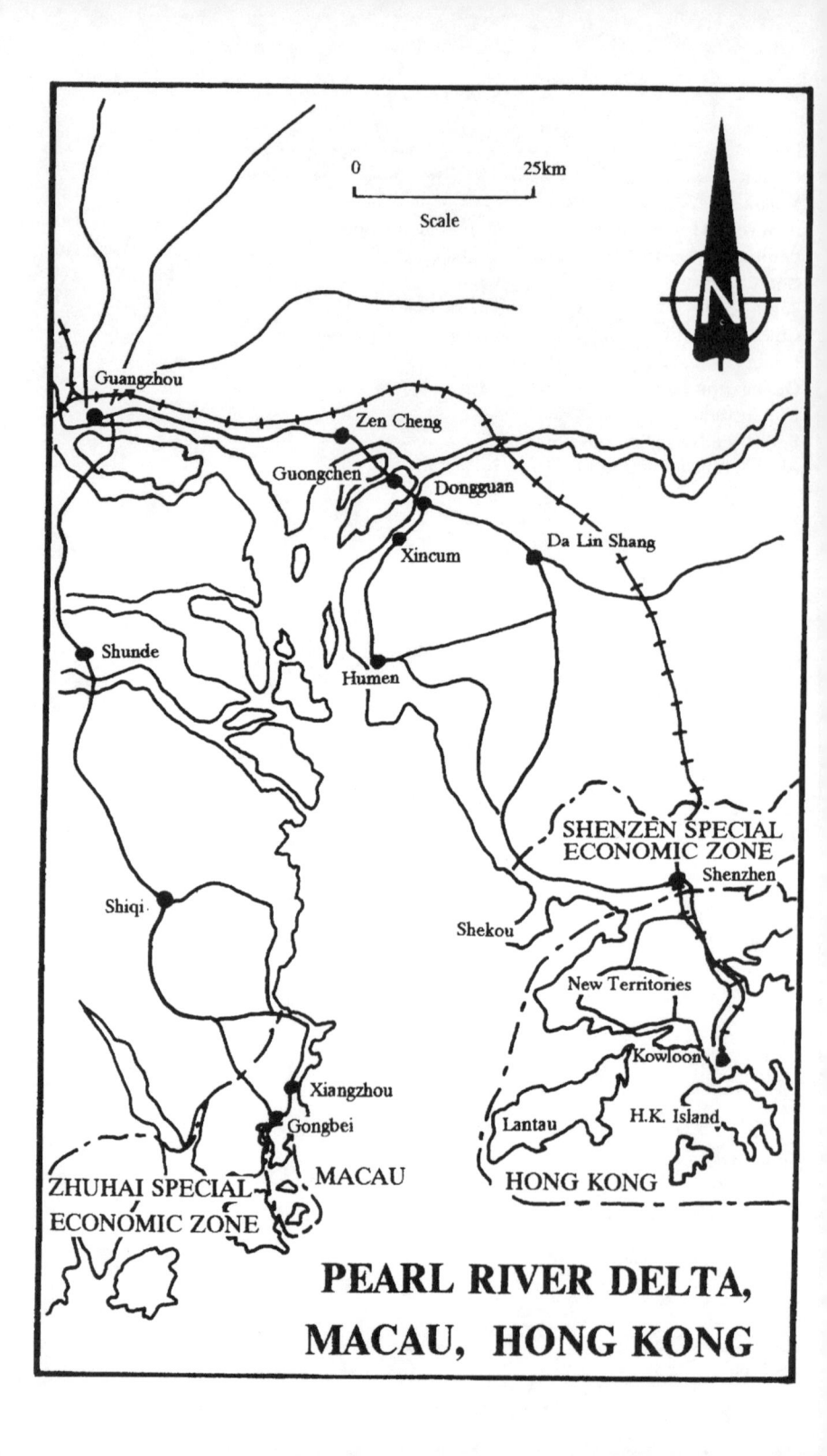

PEARL RIVER DELTA, MACAU, HONG KONG

PREFACE

Describing some of the specific areas covered in this book to someone who may be unfamiliar with the Far East poses a small problem. For this reason, the title of this guide is *The Maverick Guide to Hong Kong, Macau, and South China*. Yet given the scope of the area covered and the corresponding available information, the best all-encompassing phrase for what portion of southern mainland China is included is the Pearl River Delta region.

Because it may be helpful for some, here is a definition of the terms in regards to the region. Hong Kong is both a city and a country. Macau is both a city and a country. Guangzhou is a city, the capital of the Guangdong Province of China. Shenzhen and Shekou are cities within the Shenzhen Special Economic Zone. Gongbei and Xiangzhou are cities within the Zhuhai Special Economic Zone. All of these places are within the Pearl River Delta region, but in common usage this phrase is normally just used for the area within the borders of China.

ACKNOWLEDGMENTS

No guide book can be written without the help of many people on the ground. Meeting people is undoubtedly one of the joys of travel writing, and this book and the trips to sites provided me with many lasting memories and friendships. During the preparation of this book, I met hundreds of people who were helpful and friendly. The Hong Kong and Chinese people are often accused of being rude, selfish, and unhelpful. In a group situation this often seems to be the case. There are too many people everywhere, and courtesy seems to be forgotten. On a one-to-one basis, I find the situation is quite different and I would particularly like to acknowledge the following for help far beyond the normal expected of them:

Isabela Antunes, Eric Chang, Johanna Liefje Hung, Assunta Lei, Chan Lai Hoong, Christina Vong, Ken Morton, Sue Marsh, Helen Hawkins, Roger Henning, Florence Hui I Hang, William Marshall, Ricky Leung, Toni de Souza, Phensri Athisumongkol.

MAVERICK GUILTO
HONG KONG, MACAU, and SOUTH CHIA

THE REGION

1

Why Go to Hong Kong, Macau, and the Pearl River Delta of China?

China challenges travellers like few other places in Asia. It has thousands of years of tradition and culture, yet in the past 45 years these have been buffeted by ideologies and actions that the world has found hard to fathom. Meanwhile, a capitalist pimple on the great underbelly of the world's most populous nation has emerged as one of the world's most dramatic success stories.

Hong Kong has too many people, too little sentiment, no natural resources, and an unknown future; yet, it is a city vibrant with life that is enjoyed by seven million visitors a year. It has been described as more modern than anywhere in Europe, more electric than Manhattan, more efficient than Tokyo, and more fun than Bangkok. For many visitors it means one thing—shopping. The present money-obsessed community has been created by six million people who in many cases have thrust themselves towards prosperity by sheer hard work and an amazing level of purposefulness.

Macau remains a challenge and a mystery to many people. This was once a leading trade center but for hundreds of years it languished and rotted. Common sense said it should not exist but the 1980s saw Macau make a dramatic revival and now the new is learning to coexist with the old. There is a different ambiance here—one with a European flavor not found elsewhere in the region. You see it in the streets, taste it in the restaurants, and feel it in the people.

The region is a chaotic mixture of ideologies, cultures, political pressures, religions, and purposes. There are too many millionaires and far too many struggling poor. Governments interfere in people's lives yet generally fail to provide a safety net of support for those who need it most. Crowded urban areas and a feeling that the individual can never control his own destiny have bred people who en masse are uncaring and rude. There is an obsession with material wealth that has created a grabbing society with a cash register for a heart.

Hong Kong has long been proud of its juxtaposition of lifestyles, rich and poor, Eastern and Western, traditional and modern, fast and faster; and now Macau and adjacent China have jumped on the bandwagon, too. There is a headlong rush to modernization and development that sees vast areas in a chaotic state of concrete and mortar flux almost unknown elsewhere in the world. Traditions, environmental concerns, and plain good planning are taking a backseat to a build-build-build mentality. It is a valid question to ask why anyone would come to this region except to do business.

The mention of Hong Kong doesn't exactly evoke pictures of shady trees, rippling pools, and deserted beaches. When the world pictures Hong Kong, it conjures up images of Hong Kong Island's skyscrapers marching up the steep Peak (Victoria Peak) slopes and crowding the water's edge along a frenzied harbor. The picture may also include luxury high-rise living, Rolls Royces, shark's-fin soup, the world's finest hotels, and great shopping bargains.

The image probably doesn't extend to a different Hong Kong of crowded apartments, vast cramped public-housing developments, 15-hour peak traffic chaos, and a society hooked on work and achievement. Yet this is reality for most of Hong Kong's six million inhabitants. The outsider may wonder why this anomaly, this geopolitical aberration, doesn't just blow apart. There are too many crowds, too much noise, too little time. Surveys show that the locals rank money just after good health as the most important ingredient of happiness. It is not just for personal enjoyment, they want money for social status. Even people who are extremely successful feel a need to achieve even more.

The image also doesn't extend to the 400 square miles of New Territories, with the farms, forest parks, and marshlands. It forgets also the 235 other islands where you can still hike along a dusty trail, sun yourself on a quiet beach, or eat a vegetarian lunch at a hillside monastery. This book will show you that it is still possible to see a boat builder creating a working craft without plans or designs, watch fresh seafood being taken straight from boats to harborside restaurants, and know that here at last you have found a nonshopper's paradise.

Just why visitors find this chaotic region so fascinating may now be starting to emerge. It can be extremely visually stimulating and there are some excellent man-made attractions but these are just a small part of the total picture. The crowds, the excitement of change, the unknown future, the changing panorama of West superimposed on East, the political contradictions are all part of the lure. Just watching the world's most populous nation changing direction is a fascination in itself.

China is in the throes of another revolution but this has little to do with politics. Class struggle has been supplanted by the struggle to get rich. It is a revolution not based in the hills or the slums but in the glitzy office towers and thriving commercial districts of Guangzhou and the Special Economic Zones. The spectacular economic growth has decentralized power much more than the Communist Central Committee would wish and it has created an emerging elite of youthful entrepreneurs and power brokers who increasingly control the vigorous economy. This generation of leaders has no stated goals, no formal organization, but it relies on political stability to succeed. The exuberant kind of capitalism that they are pursuing still doesn't officially exist in China and many of these new leaders have disdain towards the Communist party, but they do not want to unseat it.

They know that they must keep the bureaucracy running while letting an older generation fight for political control. At the same time they have to forge institutions that can handle a wealth-producing economy and meet the ambitions of the newly wealthy. The spectacular corruption and greed that has emerged in the past few years are seen as a danger to the survival of both the country and the Party, and people are at last thinking about it.

China today is in search of a new soul. Religion, Confucianism, traditional culture, and century-old beliefs have been actively destroyed by 45 years of communism; but now the social ideals that were force-fed to a whole generation have been eradicated in the economic explosion of the past few years. No new set of values has emerged except the pursuit of profit, so the difference between right and wrong has blurred. Guangzhou and the Pearl River Delta area are the seedbed for all this. Many people see this region destroying itself in the pursuit of quick riches. Making money seems to be all that counts. Without consistent building, zoning, or environmental codes, it is even hard to define corruption. The end results can be seen, however, in the Mercedes and BMWs with military, police, and government license plates that fill the lots in front of the region's plush hotels and restaurants. Shops are bursting with smuggled goods. Prostitutes openly work the karaoke bars and coffee shops. Bulldozers, driven by workers who earn around US$1 a day, plow up hillsides for the construction of lavish villas selling for US$300,000.

All of this is obvious to even a casual visitor, and reactions range from amazement to sadness. There is no doubt, though, that we are witnessing a massive moment in history and one that may influence the world for many decades to come. It is a wonderful opportunity to be part of a revolution without running the risk of losing your life. You can be part of the excitement, then within 10 minutes be cocooned in a Western-style highrise hotel with all its safety and comfort—if this is what you need.

When visiting this area, do not fail to see the obvious but make time, too, for exploration. There is both a sense of timelessness and a sense of urgency. You have the chance to mix and match the experience in the way you wish. Visual impact is constantly there no matter where you are; and you will find that much of the region is a place of frenetic, almost psychotic, energy and drive. If that is all too much, give yourself a meal at a 16-seat Macanese restaurant, watch dawn through a swirling mist at Hong Kong's Mai Po marshes, or sit in Foshan's Ancestors' Temple, and you will find that your soul can be soothed enough for you to face another day in one of the world's most fascinating regions.

Tourist Hong Kong, Macau, and the Pearl River Delta in Summary

The official tourism authorities of China's Guangdong Province, Hong Kong, and Macau have begun a major initiative for the region's tourism industry—the joint marketing of the "Pearl River Delta" (PRiDe) region. This is a new era for the tourism industries involved, signifying a new cooperative marketing approach designed to maximize the tourism potential of the entire area. Each destination will continue its own marketing activities, but the Pearl River Delta is being offered as a new tourism product for all three destinations.

Each of the three areas offers its own special attractions. Here are some of my favorites:

• A Hong Kong visit can be a rewarding but overwhelming experience. The city and its people are constantly striving for more, bigger, better, and richer everything. It has a reputation as a shopper's "paradise," and you can almost be crushed to death by the millions in search of a bargain.

• Hong Kong has its soft side, too. Take a ferry to one of the Outlying Islands or walk through a park in the New Territories and you can find peace and tranquility close to nature.

• Enjoy one of Asia's premier entertainment and leisure centers by visiting Ocean Park, Water World, and Middle Kingdom near Aberdeen.

• Explore the fascinating and inexpensive transport options on Hong Kong Island. The double-decker trams, the mass transit railway, the Peak tram, and the hillside escalator are all visitor experiences not to be missed. Finish off with a ride on the Star Ferry to Kowloon.

• Enjoy the facilities of some of the best hotels in the world. Take "tea" in the lobby of the Peninsula Hotel, a drink in the Regent Hotel's Lobby Bar with its panoramic views of the harbor, a buffet dinner in the revolving

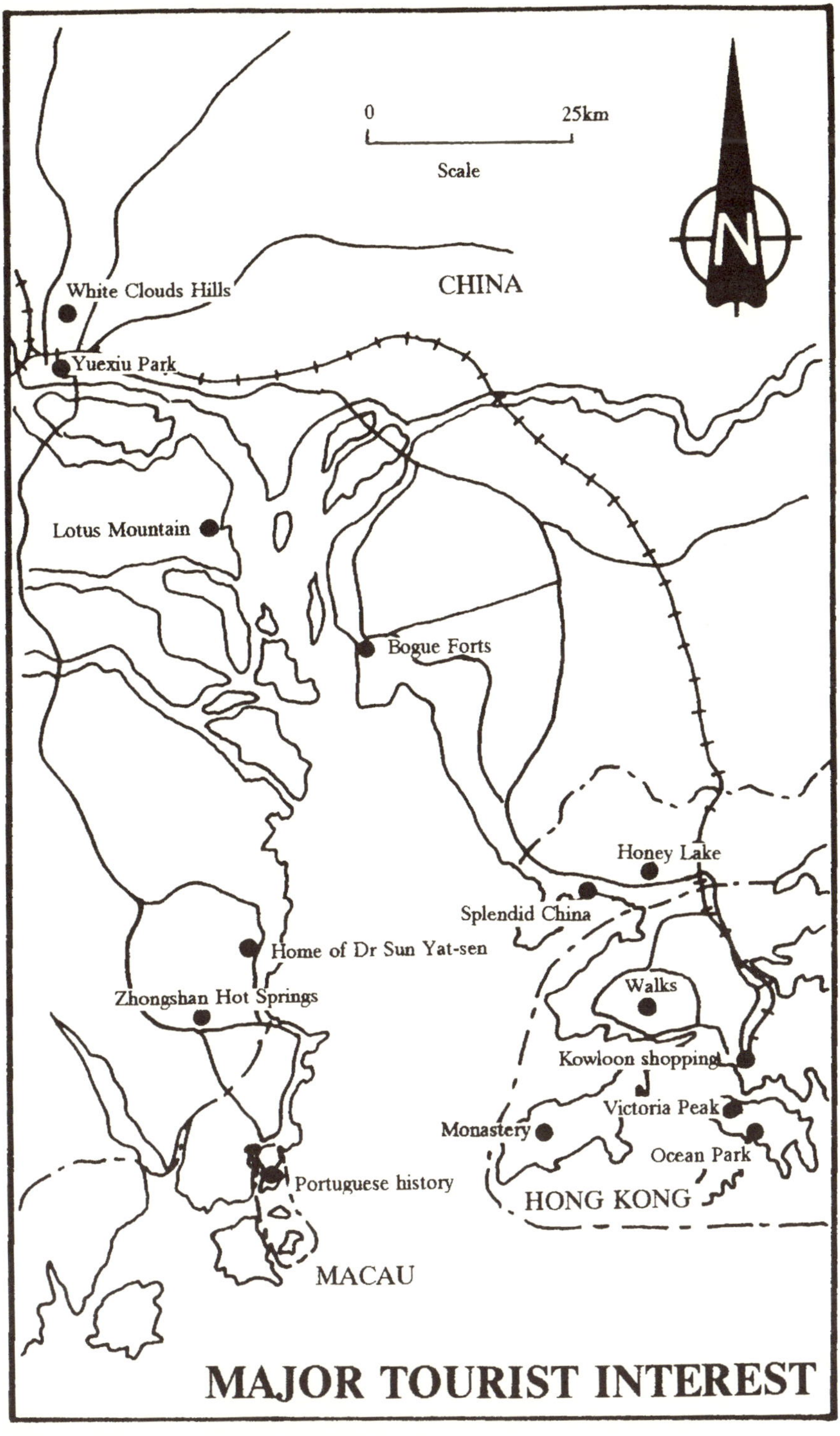
0
25km
Scale
N
CHINA
White Clouds Hills
Yuexiu Park
Lotus Mountain
Bogue Forts
Honey Lake
Splendid China
Home of Dr Sun Yat-sen
Walks
Zhongshan Hot Springs
Kowloon shopping
Victoria Peak
Monastery
Ocean Park
Portuguese history
HONG KONG
MACAU
MAJOR TOURIST INTEREST

restaurant at the Furama Kempinski Hotel, or a nightcap at the Captain's Bar at the Mandarin Oriental hotel.
- Don't miss a visit to the Happy Valley racecourse to smell the passion for gambling. The amount of money bet here is simply staggering.
- Take the ferry to Lantau Island to visit the monastery at Po Lin with its giant Buddha and its interesting vegetarian meals. Walk part way along the Ridge Path or laze on the beach at Tung Fuk.
- Visit Macau's A-Ma Temple and the nearby Maritime Museum then walk across to A Lorcha Restaurant for an excellent Macanese meal.
- Consider a night at the Bela Vista in Macau or, if that is too expensive, have a drink in the bar or on the verandah of this treasure.
- Walk around the ruins of St. Paul's Church and through the Cidadel of Sao Paulo do Monte in Macau then plunge into the maze of cobblestone streets to discover a European China from earlier in this century.
- Marvel at the Chinese economic miracle at the Shenzhen Special Economic Zone or around Zhuhai. In Shenzhen, visit the excellent China Folk Cultural Villages and the adjacent Splendid China.
- Enjoy some legacies of the past in Foshan near Guangzhou. The city's ancestral hall is well maintained and contains some remarkable art. In nearby Siwan, watch craftsmen working on ancient crafts.
- Live history at the Bogue Fort at Humen, where the destruction of seized opium took place before the infamous Opium Wars of the 1800s and the subsequent establishment of Hong Kong.
- Visit Guangzhou, southern China's largest city and attractive capital of Guangdong Province. See remains of a 2,800-year history and the new image of modern China that is emerging from the drab and gray. Walk in Yuexiu Park, through Shamian Island, and on the White Cloud Hills.

The Confessional

Unlike many other guidebooks, this one contains neither overt nor covert advertising. We do this quite deliberately because we believe we must be totally free to express an opinion about any hotel, restaurant, shop, tour, night spot, and so on. The opinions in this book are entirely mine. You may not always agree with them, but you will know that they are based on personal experience and are given openly and honestly.

I first visited this region in 1972 and I have been drawn back many times since. During the writing of this book, I have visited four times over an eight-month period. During these visits, I deliberately stayed in a wide range of accommodations, ate at a variety of restaurants and street stalls, experienced some guided tours, investigated the shopping opportunities, and tried some of the nightlife. I travelled by plane, train, car, bus, ferry, jetfoil, taxi, tram, escalator, and by foot. I visited temples, monasteries, museums, parks, national monuments, markets, tourist traps, cities, villages, and open countryside. I talked with government officials, business people, housewives, tourists, shopkeepers, tour guides, beggars, prostitutes, and monks. I was taken advantage of, treated like a valued guest, lied to, made to feel like a "king," and left to fend for myself. The sum of these experiences has become something unique in my life.

It was not possible for me to stay in every hotel that a visitor can use, but the book covers a good range from luxurious to basic; likewise with restaurants, night spots, shops, and attractions. You will end up eating at or visiting some places not mentioned in this book. Some may not have existed when I did my last inspection or perhaps time did not permit me to visit during open hours. If they are particularly good, friendly, interesting, or a good value; or if you think they should be avoided at all costs, please let me know about them, so that I can visit before completing the next edition of this guide.

Travel writing has been my life for 25 years now, and it has provided me the opportunity to travel throughout the world. I am sure that my travel experiences have made me a more aware, tolerant, and appreciative person, and they have helped to keep me young at heart. If you approach travelling in an enquiring, positive way, you too will receive the same benefits. Don't visit Hong Kong, Macau, or China expecting everything to be a duplication of things at home. If you do, you will surely be disappointed. Go with the knowledge that this region has a very long history and an unusual relationship with the West. It has been something of a love-hate relationship and even today there is some debate about some elements.

Understand that you are entering a different culture in this region. Do not be fooled by first impressions. Hong Kong's Central district may look like Manhattan but it doesn't think like Manhattan. Entrepreneurs in Guangzhou may drive imported luxury cars and make million-dollar decisions but they are working within a system that still does not officially recognize what they are doing. Try to melt into the surroundings rather than fight with what you find. Accept that the locals may find your ways as disconcerting as you find some of theirs. See these things as a broadening of your experience and benefit from them.

Getting the Most Out of This Book

This guide is arranged in a pattern similar to that of the other Maverick Guides. It is a format that has been tried and tested since 1977. It enables you to get a good feel for the region and its peoples, while at the same time getting the specifics that are so necessary when you are travelling.

There is a chapter on how to travel to and within Hong Kong, Macau, and the Pearl River Delta region, and how to minimize the potential hassles brought on by climate, government, and logistics. I have then split the book into three sections—one covering each of the three areas. Within each section, there are chapters on the land, life, and people of that area and specific chapters covering the main areas of interest to a visitor.

Each of these area chapters is divided into twelve numbered sections. After you become familiar with them in one chapter, you will know where to look for these same subjects in each of the other chapters. The categories are as follows:

1. **The General Picture**
2. **Getting There**
3. **Local Transportation**
4. **The Hotel Scene**
5. **Dining and Restaurants**
6. **Sight-seeing**
7. **Guided Tours**
8. **Culture**
9. **Sports**
10. **Shopping**
11. **Entertainment and Nightlife**
12. **The Address List**

The book has been set up to be used two ways. First, you should read it thoroughly before you finalize any plans for your trip. Decide where you would like to visit and what you would like to do when you are there. Consider the choice of hotels. Decide if there are any specific restaurants, museums, or night spots that you will visit. Make a list of the things you would like to buy while you are away. Then go talk to your travel agent.

Remember that although travel agents are well qualified to advise on airfares and some package tours, it is unrealistic to expect them to be familiar with the details of all destinations around the world. A good agent will appreciate you making informed suggestions, and I know of several who have used the contact names and telephone numbers found in all Maverick Guides to help with the detail planning and booking for their clients.

The book is also designed to be used while you are travelling. You will find that the recommendations on tours, hotels, restaurants, and shopping will smooth your travels and save you time. The information on sight-seeing, culture, and sports will help broaden your horizons and encourage you to explore things that most visitors miss. All of the sections are geared towards helping you save money and effort.

Some Quick Comments

This book is a good source of information on Hong Kong, Macau, and the Pearl River Delta region of China. I also hope that you find it an enjoyable read. The descriptive chapters are designed to give you a good appreciation of the area, the people, and the cultures. You will find that after reading through this book you will know more about this area than many tourists who have actually been there on a brief, fully escorted package tour.

There is considerable tourist information available on Hong Kong but less on Macau and much less on China. Your travel agent will be able to give you some and you should try your local library. Because the region is changing so rapidly, much of the available information is out-of-date and some will be downright misleading. Apart from history, geography, and cultural information, if it is more than three years old it should be disregarded. The political and economic situation is in a state of flux and so is travellers' information. Please bear this in mind when you are planning your trip. Make sure that the agent gives you current details and use this rather than anything else you have read.

Prices in this book are quoted in either U.S. dollars or local currency. You should work in local currency wherever possible but particularly in China you will often be quoted prices in U.S. dollars or Hong Kong dollars and you will only be able to pay in those currencies. When this happens just grin and bear it. You will not be able to buck the system.

Collecting information for this guidebook has been an expensive and at times difficult and frustrating experience. Despite nine months of work, it has not been possible to visit every place and experience every aspect of Hong Kong, Macau, and the Pearl River Delta region of China. Serious travellers and some business visitors to the region will find that they are eating, shopping, or staying in places that I have not mentioned. I would love to hear about these places, so that the next edition of the book can be improved for future readers. Please write to me (care of the publisher) and tell me about your experiences.

Use either the enclosed letter/envelope form, or if that is not enough space, copy the address onto your own envelope and include as many pages as you like. Your reactions to both the book and the destinations are earnestly solicited and will be warmly appreciated.

Good Travelling!
LEN RUTLEDGE

Please note: As of January 1, 1995, all existing seven-digit Hong Kong telephone numbers and fax numbers were amended; the number 2 was added as a prefix. The numbers in this guide reflect that change. Be aware that all Hong Kong pager numbers will be amended at some point in the middle of the year.

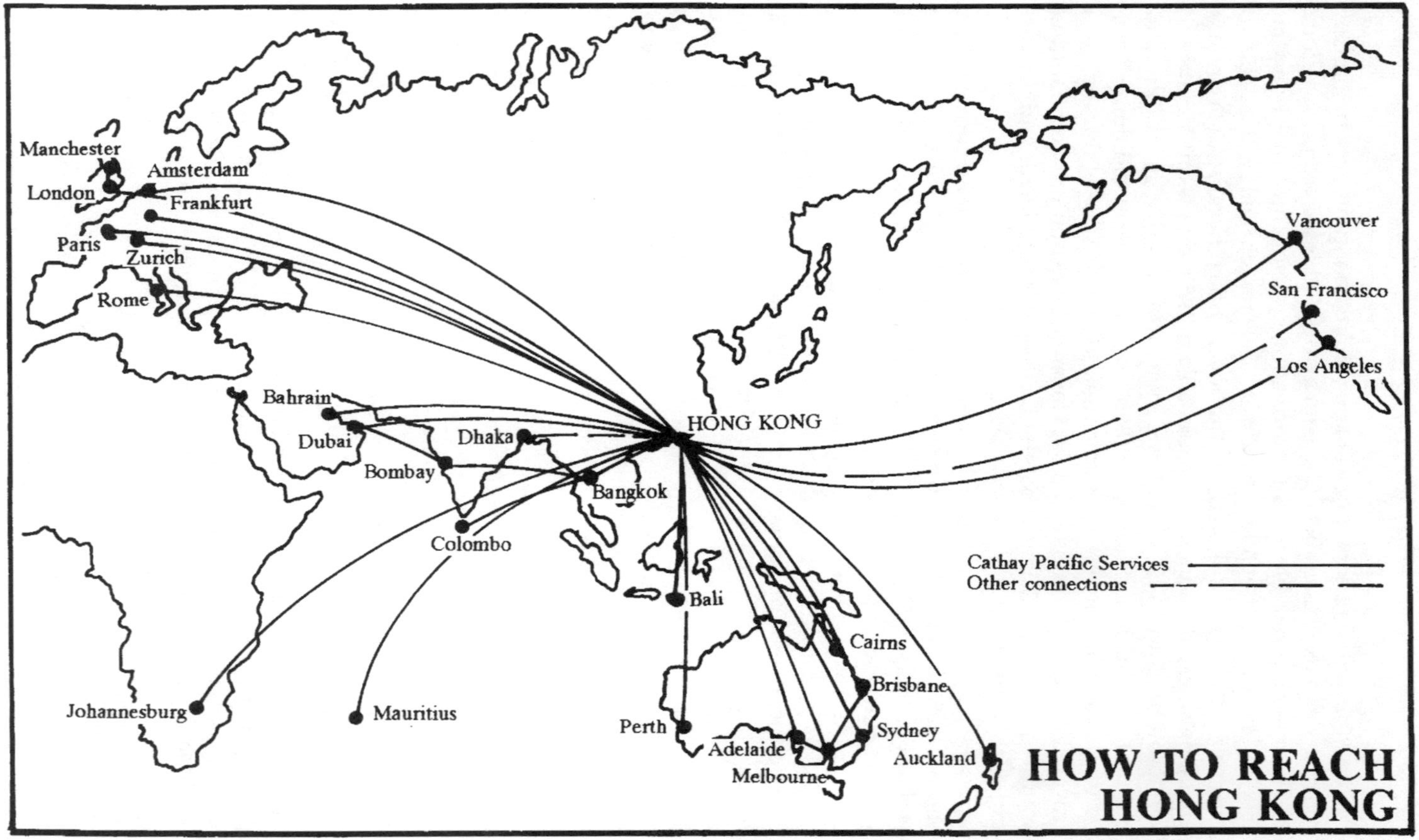
Manchester
Amsterdam
London
Frankfurt
Paris
Zurich
Rome
Bahrain
Dubai
Dhaka
Bombay
Bangkok
Colombo
HONG KONG
Vancouver
San Francisco
Los Angeles
Bali
Cairns
Brisbane
Sydney
Auckland
Perth
Adelaide
Melbourne
Johannesburg
Mauritius
Cathay Pacific Services
Other connections
HOW TO REACH
HONG KONG

2

Happy Landings

How to Get There

Hong Kong is one of the most important airline hubs in Asia, so there are direct services from many places in the world. Macau has no airport at the time that I am writing this, but the new international facility is scheduled to open in 1996. Guangzhou has an important airport with a growing number of international flights; however, there are few major intercontinental flights at present. Both Shenzhen and Zhuhai have newly developed airports. For most visitors, Hong Kong remains the gateway to the region.

From the United States and Canada, there are daily, Boeing 747, direct services on Cathay Pacific Airways from Los Angeles and Vancouver to Hong Kong. Cathay Pacific is based in Hong Kong and it is consistently rated as one of the best airlines in the world. It undoubtedly has the best connections from Hong Kong to the rest of the world and this could be useful if you plan to see more of the eastern Asian region as part of your trip.

Hong Kong has direct services from many points in Europe and Australia. Cathay Pacific has nonstop connections with London, Paris, Frankfurt, and Zurich; and one-stop connections with Rome, Amsterdam, and Manchester. There is growing traffic between Australia and New Zealand and Europe via Hong Kong, as the benefits of a stop-over in one of the most exciting areas of Asia becomes better recognized. Increasingly these passengers are also seeing some other parts of the Pearl River Delta region. There is a similar situation developing between North America and south and southeast Asia.

Cathay Pacific 747-400 landing at Hong Kong airport.

Transportation Within Hong Kong, Macau, and the Pearl River Delta

Hong Kong, Macau, and the Pearl River Delta area of China form a compact region that is rapidly becoming integrated. Transport links are extensive and significant improvements are occuring, particularly with surface connections.

Air. Hong Kong remains the major international hub for the region. There are services from here to Guangzhou and to many other points within China. Helicopter services operate from Hong Kong to Macau but at present these arrive and depart from the international ferry terminals rather than the airport. When the Macau International Airport opens in 1996, it is anticipated that there will be air links to Guangzhou and possibly also to Huangtian Airport near Shenzhen. Helicopter links may be established between Macau Airport and the huge, new Chek Lap Kok Airport in Hong Kong.

Ferry. This remains one of the most important links between the various areas. There are major services between Hong Kong and Macau that are used by millions of people each year, and there are growing services between Hong Kong and various points in China. Services between Macau and China have diminished as road connections have improved but there may be additional services established in conjuction with the new Macau airport.

In Hong Kong, there are two major international ferry terminals and some other minor ones. The major Macau terminal is at the Shun Tak Centre on Hong Kong Island in the Central district. From here there are jetfoils, jumbocats, and high-speed ferries to Macau at regular intervals. There are also services from here to Jiuzhou pier in Zhuhai and to Shekou in Shenzhen. The other major terminal is the China Ferry Terminal in Tsim Sha Tsui on the Kowloon peninsula. From here there are services to Guangzhou; to Zhongshan Harbour near Shiqi; and to Shekou, Jiuzhou, and Macau. The options are coastal ferries, hydrofoils, and a few jetfoils.

Rail. The Kowloon-Canton Railway provides several services a day between Hong Kong and Guangzhou and many more between Hong Kong and Shenzhen and between Shenzhen and Guangzhou. The international services are improving all the time with little delay at the border, so these have become a popular way to travel. The local services from Shenzhen to Guangzhou can be very crowded. There is a rail connection under construction from China to Macau but this will probably be used primarily for freight.

Bus. There are daily connections between Hong Kong and Guangzhou and between Guangzhou and Macau. As the road connections improve, so do these services; however, most international visitors still prefer to travel from Hong Kong to Guangzhou by train. Border formalities are still slow at times so some bus travellers prefer to take a bus to the border; walk across; then take another bus, train, or taxi on the other side. Note that when you enter the Special Economic Zones, you will need to go though the equivalent of a border check, by producing your passport to the authorities.

Rental Cars. There are no facilities to take self-drive rental cars across the border.

Travel Facts

Climate. The high tourist season is from October to late December for very good reason. The weather is usually pleasant with sunny days and comfortable evenings. The other favored time is April through May when there is somewhat similar weather. Average daily temperatures are in the 70s (24 degrees Celsius) while minimums can be in the 60s (18 degrees Celsius).

At other times of the year, the weather is less kind. January, February, and early March can be cold with long periods of overcast skies and drizzle. At this time the average temperature range is 64-55 degrees (18-13 degrees Celsius.) The rest of March and April can still be cool and overcast but there will also be some sunny periods. June to September is the hot and sticky time. There is lots of rain and the occassional typhoon (hurricane or cyclone). Temperatures climb to over 86 degrees (30 degrees Celsius) and rarely fall below 79 degrees (26 degrees Celsius).

Macau's summers are slightly cooler and wetter than Hong Kong; and Guangzhou has slightly more temperature variation, but generally the climate throughout the area is similar.

Visitors should be aware of the dangers of a typhoon. Winds can reach very high speeds, hurl debris around, cause buildings to be damaged, and sink ships in the harbor. Typhoons often bring heavy rain so there could be widespread flooding. The locals treat typhoons with respect; and in Hong Kong and Macau, you will receive good warnings and information if a storm is approaching. When a number 8 signal is posted, Hong Kong and Macau close down completely so you should immediately head for your hotel and stay there. In Guangzhou you will be less well informed due to language and cultural difficulties; but if you sense a typhoon is near, return immediately to your hotel.

Packing. If ever there were a place where the advice "travel light" was appropriate, it would be Hong Kong. Even the most uninterested shopper will be seduced into buying in this shopper's paradise. No matter how little you bring, you are sure to leave with a bulging suitcase. That is not necessarily because Hong Kong is cheap, it's more because you find it almost impossible to avoid someone trying to sell you something.

You will never need large quantities of warm clothing, so leave most of that at home. During the winter months a raincoat will be useful and a sweater is a must. A folding umbrella comes in handy most times. Dress in these parts is fairly informal. All visitors should, however, pack a lightweight jacket; and business people will need classical business dress on some occasions. Men are required to wear a tie in some hotels and restaurants in the evenings. In summer, take a swimsuit and high-protection suntan lotion. Lightweight cotton or linen clothes are most suitable for this time of the year.

The Chinese tend to be less conservative than some other Asian races in their dress but a foreigner in a micromini on the beach will draw a crowd and many stares; and tight shorts and bare midrifts are not recommended. Temples require conservative dress similar to what would be acceptable in your local church.

In mainland China, it is more difficult to get basic supplies so you should consider taking with you some English-language reading material, a flashlight (torch) with batteries, a small first-aid kit, and a few small gifts for people you may meet. If necessary, you can buy these in Hong Kong or Macau.

Mail and Telephone Service. Hong Kong has a reliable mail service for local and overseas articles. Airmail letters usually take about five days to Europe and Australia and six days to the United States and Canada. Surface letters and packages are slow. Allow about 10 weeks for delivery to North America and Europe. The service in Macau is also good but until the international airport opens in 1996, overseas mail has to pass through Hong Kong, thus adding a day or more to the delivery time. The Chinese mail service is considered to be less efficient and reliable. Some companies operating in China hand-carry mail for posting in Hong Kong.

The Hong Kong General Post Office is located adjacent to the Star Ferry Concourse on Hong Kong Island. This has the full range of services that you would expect at home. It is open from 8 A.M. to 6 P.M. weekdays and until 12:30 on Saturdays. Stamp machines are available at other times. On the Kowloon side, there is a post office at 10 Middle Rd. In Macau, the General Post Office is on Leal Senado and it is open from 9 A.M. to 8 P.M., Monday to Saturday. In Guangzhou, the GPO is adjacent to the railway station on Huanshi Xilu. Letters can be sent to any of these post offices by labeling them *Poste Restante* then the post office address. They will be held for two months.

Telephone services in Hong Kong and Macau are good but China still has some way to go. The Hong Kong and Macau services are geared to the needs of an internationally oriented business community so there are reasonable bilingual services. In China it is extremely difficult to get English language information so where international direct-dialing is available, you should use this. Some rural systems shut down at night so you could be isolated.

Local calls within all areas are free from private telephones but most hotels charge for the service. Payphones are available in Hong Kong, in most parts of Macau, and in some places in China. Calling between Hong Kong, Macau, and China involves an international call and international charges. You can direct-dial from most Hong Kong public telephones but you will need several HK$5 coins.

In Hong Kong there are two public offices of Hong Kong Telecom that are open 24 hours a day. These are at Exchange Square, Connaught Place, Central, Hong Kong Island; and at Hermes House, 10 Middle Rd., Tsim Sha Tsui, Kowloon. In Macau, the telephone office at the General Post Office on Avenida Almeida Ribeiro opens 24 hours a day.

Metrics and Electrics

The metric system of weights and measures is used officially throughout Hong Kong, Macau, and China; however, in practice, traditional Chinese weights and measures are still common in shops and markets. These include the "leung," a weight of about 38 grams (a bit less than 1.4 ounces), and the "catty" or "jin," a weight of about 600 grams (a bit over 20 ounces). If you are not familiar with the metric system, you can quickly learn a few conversions that will help you make sense of the strange terms. Temperature and distance are probably the two most important measures for the short-term visitor.

Temperature. In the Celsius system, zero degrees is the freezing point of water, and 100 degrees is the boiling point. From a climatic point of view, 10 degrees Celsius is cold, 20 degrees is temperate, 30 degrees is quite warm, and 40 degrees is extremely hot. In Fahrenheit, these are equivalent to 50 degrees, 68 degrees, 86 degrees, and 104 degrees respectively.

Distance. "Is it close or far away?" is what most travellers wish to know. All distances shown on signboards are in kilometers. To do a rough conversion to miles, remember that 5 kilometers is approximately 3 miles. Therefore, 10 kilometers equals 6 miles and 100 kilometers is roughly 60 miles. For small distances, remember that 5 centimeters equals 2 inches, 30 cm equals one foot, and a meter and a yard are roughly equal.

Electricity. Voltages, amperages, and cycles are a total mystery to most people, so don't worry too much about that. What you need to know is that Hong Kong, Macau, and China all use 220 volt, 50 Hz AC power. That means that European/Australian/Asian electrical appliances will work OK, but North American ones will not. A further problem, however, is that there are different types of electical outlets. In Hong Kong and Macau, three-pin round plugs are almost standard; while in China, three flat prongs are most common but a few places use the two round-prong European type. The message is: leave your electical appliances at home or buy an adapter (and a transformer if needed) in Hong Kong.

The standard of electrical wiring is good in Hong Kong and Macau and reasonable in new buildings in China. In old buildings it can be very bad. Many modern hotels have a razor outlet in the bathroom that is dual-voltage. This cannot be used for hair dryers.

Money and Prices

Money. The currency in Hong Kong is the Hong Kong dollar. This has a fixed exchange rate of 7.8 to the U.S. dollar. There are bank notes in denominations of HK$1000, $500, $100, $50, $20, and $10. Coins are HK$5, $2, $1, $0.5, $0.2, and $0.1.

The currency in Macau is called the *pataca* but this is normally written as M$. One pataca is divided into 100 *avos*. There are bank notes in denominations of M$500, $100, $50, $10, and $5. Coins are M$5, $1, $0.5, $0.2, and $0.1. The M$ is worth slightly less than the HK$. In Macau they are interchangable but M$'s are not generally accepted in Hong Kong.

The Chinese currency is the *yuan* (Y). There are 10 *jiao* in one yuan and 10 *fen* in one jiao. China once had a difficult dual currency system but this has been abandoned. The yuan in practice floats against other currencies.

At the time of writing there were around 13 yuan to the US$. Yuan can be converted back to other currencies at the Bank of China offices in China only if you have retained the original exchange documentation from when you bought yuan. Yuan is generally not accepted outside China.

In Hong Kong, you are best to pay for everything in HK$. There are no currency restrictions and money changers and banks are readily available. Banks give the best exchange rates but are mostly not open on weekends. Money changers at the airport give poor rates so only change enough for your immediate needs. For all money changers, always check the rates before handing over your foreign money and ask if there is a commission on top of the quoted rate. Banks and money changers will accept a wide range of currencies in both cash and travellers' checks. Hotels will change money but rates are generally very poor.

In Macau, you are best to pay in M$ although HK$ are accepted on par everywhere. Most banks in Macau will give you around M$104 for HK$100. You need to change any balance back to HK$ before you leave, because M$'s are not readily accepted elsewhere.

In China, you are best to pay for what you can in yuan, but in Guangzhou and the Special Economic Zones, you will often find that payment can only be made in US$ or HK$. Foreign currency and common travellers' checks can be exchanged at the border crossings, the main branches of the Bank of China, and at tourist hotels. A few money changers operate on the streets but these should be avoided because they have a bad reputation as thieves.

Prices. Hong Kong is not cheap for the visitor. The main problem is accommodation costs but other costs are also rising as the economic boom continues. Hong Kong has even lost its competitive edge with shopping as shop rents soar. The street markets are the only places that have good prices and that is only after heavy bargaining. Fortunately some basic food is still cheap if you eat at the local Chinese food shop or buy from the street vendors. Upmarket Western and Chinese restaurants, however, can be very expensive.

Apart from a few hostels and guesthouses, it is difficult to get a room in Hong Kong under HK$400 a night. Budget hotels start at around HK$600 and even self-contained rooms with organizations such as the YMCA and the Salvation Army start at around the same price. Often a 10 percent service charge and 5 percent government tax are added to the price. Four and five-star hotels are charging from around HK$1,500 for a room.

Small restaurants sometimes have a bowl of noodles and Chinese tea on the menu for around HK$10. A plate of rice and a small portion of meat costs around HK$15, while portions of dim sum cost around HK$6. You should be able to get a beer in these places for under HK$15. The same things in a hotel or large restaurant will be double those prices and a three-course steak meal could easily be HK$300.

The luxury shopping centers have some wonderful imported and local goods but prices are by no means inexpensive. Most goods are duty-free in Hong Kong so I fail to see the advantage of the duty-free stores. Nevertheless, many people still shop in these and apparently come away happy. It's a good idea to check the prices in a fixed-price department store before you start bargaining in the markets. The stories of people paying twice the home price or twice the normal Hong Kong price are legendary.

Macau accommodation is considerably cheaper than Hong Kong but other prices are on a par. Guangzhou and the Special Economic Zones are slightly cheaper again for accommodation but food and shopping prices vary enormously and it is more difficult to establish a fair price. Some of the smaller towns and cities within the Pearl Delta are much cheaper if you have yuan.

Tipping. Hotels and major restaurants hit you with a standard 10 percent service charge and a few places are now raising this even further. I find it difficult to tip further if the service has been less than excellent but many waiters and hotel-room staff are now expecting more. It is inferred that the Japanese are encouraging this practice. That is unfortunate. Bellboys, doormen, and taxi drivers expect a small tip for service. The Chinese never had the custom of tipping before Westerners introduced it, but now everyone is caught up in the practice. Please tip wisely and don't encourage the practice of heavy tipping.

Government Fiddle-Faddle

Passports and Visas. You need a passport to enter almost any foreign country and get back into your own country. You should ask your travel agent or the relevant government department about how you get a passport. First-time applicants should apply well in advance of their departure dates to allow ample time for processing.

Additionally, you will need a visa to enter some countries. The rules vary depending on your citizenship and the country you are visiting. Nationals of Britain, Commonwealth countries, and some European and Latin American countries do not require visas for a visit of less than three months to Hong Kong. United States nationals and those from many Central and South American countries and some European countries do not require visas for a visit of less than one month. On arrival in Hong Kong, visitors have to satisfy immigration officers that they possess an onward ticket and that they have adequate funds to cover the duration of their stay without work; however, this appears to be rarely applied. Visitors are not allowed to get a job, establish a business, or enroll as a student.

To enter Macau, visas are not required for citizens of the United States, Canada, Australia, New Zealand, and most Western European countries. Many other citizens can get a 20-day visa on arrival. Nationals of countries that do not maintain diplomatic relations with Portugal cannot obtain a visa on arrival. It would be best to apply to the Portuguese Consulate in Hong Kong (Tel: 2523-1338).

Note: Until recently, all visitors were required to have a visa to enter China. Now, revised regulations allow foreigners on group tours to make three-day trips to Shenzhen, China, without visas. A minimum of three tourists must register for a visit under these regulations, and must be part of a tour organized by authorized travel agents in Shenzhen. It is likely that the regulations will be revised before the end of 1995 and might allow individuals the opportunity to tour Shenzen without a visa. *Be sure to check with your travel agent for the current regulations at the time of your trip.*

Visas are readily available in Hong Kong and Macau and processing only takes two days. The application requires a photograph and you must hand over your passport while it is being processed. The visa will normally be a single-entry one valid for one month. You can go to the visa office yourself (in Hong Kong at 26 Harbour Rd., Wanchai) or ask a travel agent to do it for you.

Consulates. These consulates may be useful while you are in Hong Kong.

Australia—25 Harbour Rd., Wanchai	Tel: 2827-8881
Canada—Exchange Square, 8 Connaught Place	2810-4321
China—Visa Office. 26 Harbour Rd., Wanchai	2827-9569
Germany—United Centre, 95 Queensway	2529-8855
Japan—12 Harcourt Rd., Hong Kong Island	2522-1184
New Zealand—Jardine House, Connaught Road	2522-5044
Portugal—Tower Two, Exchange Square	2522-5789
Singapore—18 Harcourt Rd., Central	2527-2212
Thailand—8 Cotton Tree Dr., Central	2521-6481
U.S.A.—26 Garden Rd., Central	2523-9011

Travel Restrictions. These days there are few restrictions on where a visitor can go in this region. Apart from a few border areas, there are no obvious "no-go" areas. China still has a system that licenses hotels to accommodate foreigners. Because of this, some hotels will refuse to accept you no matter what the circumstances are.

Customs. Hong Kong is a duty-free port so customs are not very worried about what you bring in. There are restrictions on the amount of alcohol, cigarettes, and perfume that you can carry; and guns, drugs, and other illegal weapons are strictly forbidden. The situation with Macau is similar. In theory, China has many more restictions but in practice, I have never had a problem. You are still asked to list how many cameras, electronic gear, watches, and so forth you are carrying and you are supposed to show that you leave with the same number. I have never been queried or had my bags searched. Drugs, weapons, pornographic material, and some political literature are bad news in China. Don't tempt fate.

Airport Taxes. Hong Kong keeps changing its tax rate. In 1994, it had the highest departure tax in the world at the rate of HK$150. There was much criticism of this and the government slashed it to HK$50. The departure tax when you depart by boat to Macau or China is built into the ticket price. In China there is a Y$40 tax if you leave by plane but nothing if your departure is by land or boat.

Travellers' Guide

Safety. I have never encountered any personal safety problems in the region, and with a little common sense you should not either. Visitors should be aware, however, that there are pickpockets and confidence tricksters operating in all three countries. As capitalism takes over in China and expectations rise, petty crime is increasing. Beggers are on the streets and a small number of children can be a nuisance to foreign visitors. My advice—be sensible, but don't become paranoid.

Each country is generally free of major hassles for female travellers although again a word of caution. There are apparently some Chinese men and couples who are prepared to pay big money to spend time with young Western women. This encourages middle-men to seek out such women so you could be offered modeling work, escort work, film work, or even tour guide work, all as a front for sex. The situation is probably worst in Hong Kong but the temptation is also available in China.

Travellers should be aware that prostitution occurs in some cheap, and a few expensive, hotels throughout the region, and this has the potential for being a problem for the visitor.

Business Hours. Office hours in Hong Kong are generally 9 A.M. to 5 P.M. Monday to Friday and 9 A.M. to noon on Saturday. Lunch is usually from 1 P.M. to 2 P.M. and some offices close their doors during this time. Banks generally open 9 A.M. to 4:30 P.M. Monday to Friday and 9 A.M. to 12:30 on Saturdays. Most shops and stores open longer than this but exact hours depend on the locality and the type of shop. In the tourist areas of Kowloon and Causeway Bay, shops open until around 9 P.M. and stay open seven days a week. There are night markets in some areas.

In Macau, government offices open weekdays from around 8:45 A.M. to 1 P.M. and from 3 P.M. to 5 P.M., then on Saturday morning from 8:45 A.M. to 1 P.M. Banks normally are open weekdays from 9 A.M. to 4 P.M. and Saturday from 9 A.M. to noon. Shops in the city center and other tourist areas open until around 8 P.M.

In China, most offices open six days a week and close on Sunday. Hours seem to vary between areas and offices but many are open between 8 A.M. and about 5:30 P.M., with a two-hour break in the middle of the day. Some shops open Sunday morning and many stay open until around 8:30 at night. Ticket offices at railway stations and bus stations open around 5 A.M.

Tourist Information. Both Hong Kong and Macau have efficient and effective tourist organizations that produce a wealth of useful information for the visitor. Information on China is much more difficult to get and it is less reliable and up-to-date.

The **Hong Kong Tourist Association (HKTA)** will provide several brochures free of charge through its overseas offices or at various locations in Hong Kong. It also operates a hotel booking office at Kai Tak Airport for people with no accommodation bookings. You can also call the HKTA Hotline (Tel: 2801-7177) for information and help. If you want more information after reading this book, contact one of the following HKTA offices:

Australia—55 Harrington St., The Rocks, Sydney .... Tel: 02-251-2855
Canada—347 Bay St., Toronto, M5H 2R7 416-366-2389
France—38 Avenue George V, 75008 Paris 01-4720-3954
Germany—Wiesenau 1, 6000 Frankfurt/Main 069-722-841
Japan—1-5-2 Yurakucho, Chiyoda-ku, Tokyo 03-3503-0731
    —3-5-13 Awaji-machi, Chuo-ku, Osaka 05-229-9240
New Zealand—P.O. Box 2120, Auckland 09-521-3167
Singapore—Ocean Bld., 10 Collyer Quay 532-3668
South Africa—P.O. Box 9874, Johannesburg 011-339-4865
Taiwan—18 Chang An East Rd., Sec 1, Taipei 02-581-2967
U.K.—125 Pall Mall, London SW1Y 5EA 071-930-4775
U.S.A.—333 North Michigan Ave., Chicago 312-782-3872
    —590 Fifth Ave., New York 10036-4706 212-869-5008
    —10940 Wilshire Blvd., Los Angeles 310-208-4782

The **Macau Government Tourist Office** also produces some valuable brochures and these can be obtained from overseas offices and from outlets in Macau. I suggest you contact one of the following overseas offices as a starting point.

Australia—449 Darling St. ....Tel: 02-555-7548
    Balmain, Sydney
Canada—13 Mountalan Ave., Toronto M4J1H3 416-466-6552
    —10551 Shellbridge Way, Richmond BC 604-231-9040
Europe—See the Portuguese National Tourist Offices
Hong Kong—Shun Tak Ctr., 200 Connaught Rd. 2540-8180
Japan—1-5-2 Yurakucho, Chiyoda-ku, Tokyo 03-3501-5022
Singapore—PIL Bld., 140 Cecil St. 225-0022

Thailand—150/5 Sukhumvit 20, Bangkok 258-1975
U.K.—6 Sherlock Mews, Paddington St., London....................071-224-3390
U.S.A.—P.O. Box 350, Kenilworth, Illinois 708-251-6421
  —999 Wilder Ave., Honolulu, Hawaii...........................808-538-7613
  —77 Seventh Ave., New York, NY 10011 212-206-6828
  —3133 Lake Hollywood Dr., Los Angeles, CA 213-851-3402

The **China National Tourist Office** has opened several overseas offices and it has some information available on the more well known parts of China. Due to rapid changes within the Pearl Delta region, much of the current literature is well out-of-date. These are the important overseas offices:

Australia—55 Clarence St., Sydney...Tel: 02-299-4057
France—51 rue Sointe-Anne, 75002 Paris................................01-4286-9548
Hong Kong—75 Mody Rd., Tsim Sha Tsui..2732-5888
Japan—1-27-13 Hamamatsu-Cho, Minato-ku.....................03-3433-1461
U.S.A.—60 East 42nd St., New York, NY 10165.........................212-867-0271
  —333 West Broadway, Glendale, CA...............................818-545-7504

The other major source of information is **Cathay Pacific Airways**. There are offices around the world but these are likely to be of most value to readers:

Australia—28 O'Connell St., Sydney......................................Tel: 02-931-5500
  —30 Collins St., Melbourne 03-653-2022
Canada—650 West Georgia St., Vancouver..............................604-682-9747
France—267 Blvd. Pereire, 75017 Paris 4068-9899
Germany—Feuerbachstrasse 26 6000 Frankfurt.......................7100-8221
Japan—5-2-1 Yurakucho, Chuyoda-ku, Tokyo..........................03-3404-1531
New Zealand—191 Queen St., Auckland 09-379-0861
South Africa—Freedman Drive, Sandown, J'bg. 011-883-9226
Switzerland—Todistrassa 44 8039 Zurich.................................01-202-8156
Taiwan—129 Min Sheng East Rd., 3, Taipei 02-712-8228
U.K.—52 Berkeley St., London..071-930-4444
  —Parsonage Gardens, Manchester M2 3LF 061-833-0126
U.S.A.—360 N Michigan Ave., Chicago, IL................................800-233-2742
  —590 Fifth Ave., New York, NY 10036 800-233-2742
  —300 N Cont. Blvd., El Segundo, CA..............................800-233-2742

News Media. There are more than sixty newspapers and six hundred periodicals registered in Hong Kong. The Territory boasts one of the highest newspaper-reading ratios in the world. There are two English-language dailies (*The South China Morning Post* and *The Hong Kong Standard*) and many weekly and monthly magazines. Most notable are *The Far Eastern Economic Review* and *Asiaweek*. Hong Kong's printing industry is one of the most technically advanced in the world. Three international newspapers produce Asian editions printed in Hong Kong (*The Asian Wall Street Journal, The International Herald Tribune,* and *USA Today*), and both *Time* and *Newsweek* also publish here.

Hong Kong has 15 radio channels, 7 operated by the government-funded Radio Television Hong Kong and the others by commercial companies. Some channels broadcast in stereo FM and some are 24-hour operations. There are two commercial television companies, each producing one program in English and one in Cantonese. The government's educational service and documentary programs are also shown on these channels. A territory-wide cable service also operates.

Macau has no English-language newspapers but the Hong Kong and international papers are readily available. There are three radio stations—two in Cantonese and one in Portuguese—but you can pick up Hong Kong broadcasts. There is a government-run TV station that has two channels. One shows mainly English-language programs and the other mainly Portuguese. You can also receive stations from China and Hong Kong.

In China, *The China Daily* is an English-language newspaper readily available in the Pearl Delta region. English-language international newspapers are available in hotels and some other places. Western weekly news magazines are also available. In the Delta region, it is easy to pick up Hong Kong television, although this is not encouraged by the authorities. Some Guangzhou hotels have satellite receivers for a wide range of programs. Chinese TV in the Delta area is broadcast only in Mandarin or Cantonese.

Travel Tips

Before you go

• Consider the airline options. Comfort and safety are very important and the lowest-priced bargain airfare is not always the cheapest in the long run.

• Travel insurance is a "must" for overseas travel. Get a comprehensive policy covering all eventualities.

• Arrange unlimited medical insurance and if you plan extensive China travel, get a policy that provides for your evacuation to Hong Kong if major medical treatment is required.

• If you are travelling with someone, make sure both of you have some traveller's checks, a credit card, and cash.

• Travel light. Cool, casual clothes will be the most useful for eight months of the year.

- Get your timing right. Try to avoid the peak of the tourist season and the middle of the summer and winter.
- Don't be late at the airport. Airlines often overbook to compensate for "no-shows." If too many people turn up, it is often the last arrivals who suffer.
- Watch out for excess baggage charges as you travel around Asia. You are allowed two checked pieces between North America and Hong Kong; but within Asia there is a 20-kilo limit in economy and a 30-kilo limit in business class. Try to carry small, heavy items in your hand baggage if you know you are overweight. Most airlines impose hand-carry size restrictions and I strongly support this. There is nothing worse than baggage spilling into aisles or your neighbor stuffing huge quantities under his seat then expecting you to share your legroom.

While you are away

- Always confirm onward flights as early as possible.
- Understand what your money is worth, and try to buy things using the local currency.
- Report lost credit cards promptly. If necessary, make an international call back to your home country. Your liability is then small.
- Always carry your travel documents, money, and medical items with you, just in case the airline, busline, railway, ferry company, or hotel misplaces your main bag.
- In restaurants, do not order items that are not clearly priced on the menu. Always ask the price of a drink before ordering.
- Always put your valuables in a hotel safe or safety deposit box.
- Don't tip unnecessarily. Look at each situation as it occurs.
- Don't wear new shoes while you are away. Comfort is essential when travelling and blisters can be a nightmare.
- Accept that you will get overcharged on occasions simply because you are a visitor. At times there will be nothing you can do about it and getting annoyed will not help the situation or your well-being.

Visit the Region

Hong Kong is the hub of east Asia so it is convenient to include some other countries in the region as part of your trip. There are comprehensive air services to all adjacent countries and it may be possible to incorporate some ground arrangements so that you can do a circuit. Consider some of the following.

Taiwan has been occupied by the Chinese, Portuguese, Spanish, Dutch, French, and Japanese over the centuries. In 1949, two million mainland Chinese arrived, bringing with them their culture, artistic skills, commercial

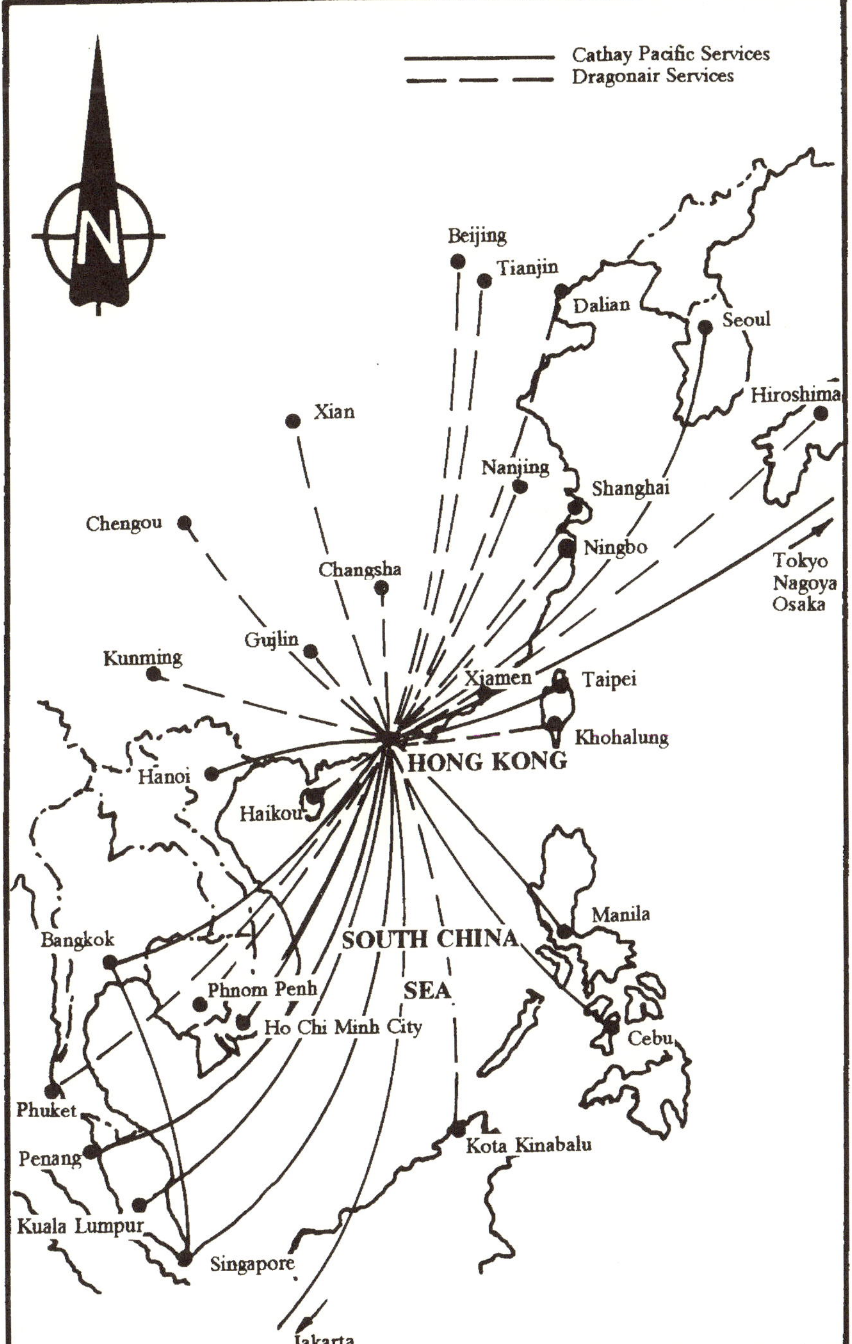

SEE THE REGION

abilities, and antique treasures. The island has some spectacular scenery; and the capital, Taipei, has temples, shrines, parks, and the magnificent National Palace Museum, which contains the world's finest collection of Chinese antiques and art treasures. Taiwan has become a major investment force in Asia.

The Philippines is an English-speaking nation where visitors can see the strong influences of Malay, Chinese, Spanish, and American periods of history as well as the considerable achievements of the modern independent nation. The archipelago of 7,000 islands has a great diversity of ethnic, cultural, and geographic features. There are some excellent beaches, dramatic mountain scenery, and a strong urban culture. The Filipinos are a warm race that love color, music, dancing, and enjoying themselves. There is a strong spirit of friendship towards visitors.

Vietnam is a new frontier for visitors but the country is rapidly opening to the world. Vietnam is an unusual and interesting destination reflecting an ancient history and great creative traditions, with a later French colonial period still visible in places. There is a growing infrastructure that means travel and accommodation are much less trying than in recent times. See *The Maverick Guide to Vietnam, Laos, and Cambodia* for further details.

South Korea is a varied and attractive country with a stormy history but a thriving present. There are subtropical beaches, seascapes, superb mountain scenery, and a well-developed snowskiing industry. Seoul, the capital, is a bustling, clean, modern city with luxurious hotels, shopping centers, and other facilities. Transportation around the country is good and visitors are welcomed by the people.

Thailand has sun, sea, sand, mountains, national parks, forests, walled cities, and ancient ruins. You will find peace and solitude as well as adventure. Bangkok, the capital, has great shopping opportunities, fabulous restaurants, museums and art galleries, and a nightlife scene that is almost legendary. All this is supported by one of the most friendly and attractive people on earth. See *The Maverick Guide to Thailand* for futher details.

Singapore is a bustling city-state with some similarities to Hong Kong but also with many great differences. High-density living is the norm in much of Singapore, yet this country is one of the cleanest, safest, and most orderly cities in the world. There are dramatic skyscrapers, quaint old Chinese shop houses, quiet back lanes, massive expressways, and bustling bazaars. The population is predominantly Chinese, with significant Malay and Indian minorities. See *The Maverick Guide to Malaysia and Singapore* for more details.

Malaysia has palm-fringed beaches, coral reefs teeming with fish, tropical forests, highland resorts, tea and rubber plantations, and interesting cultures. Kuala Lumpur, the federal capital, is a modern city of tall buildings, gold-domed mosques, and lush gardens. The islands of Penang, Langkawi, and Tioman offer excellent facilities for visitors in idyllic surroundings. See *The Maverick Guide to Malaysia and Singapore* for more details.

Central and North China provide a complete contrast to the Pearl Delta region. It is potentially the most interesting destination in Asia and although it is still a little rough around the edges, there is plenty of interest for most visitors. China has some unmatched cultural and scenic attractions ranging from the Great Wall to the Terracotta Warriors to the scenic wonders of Guilin. These will prove to be irresistible lures for many people.

Hong Kong

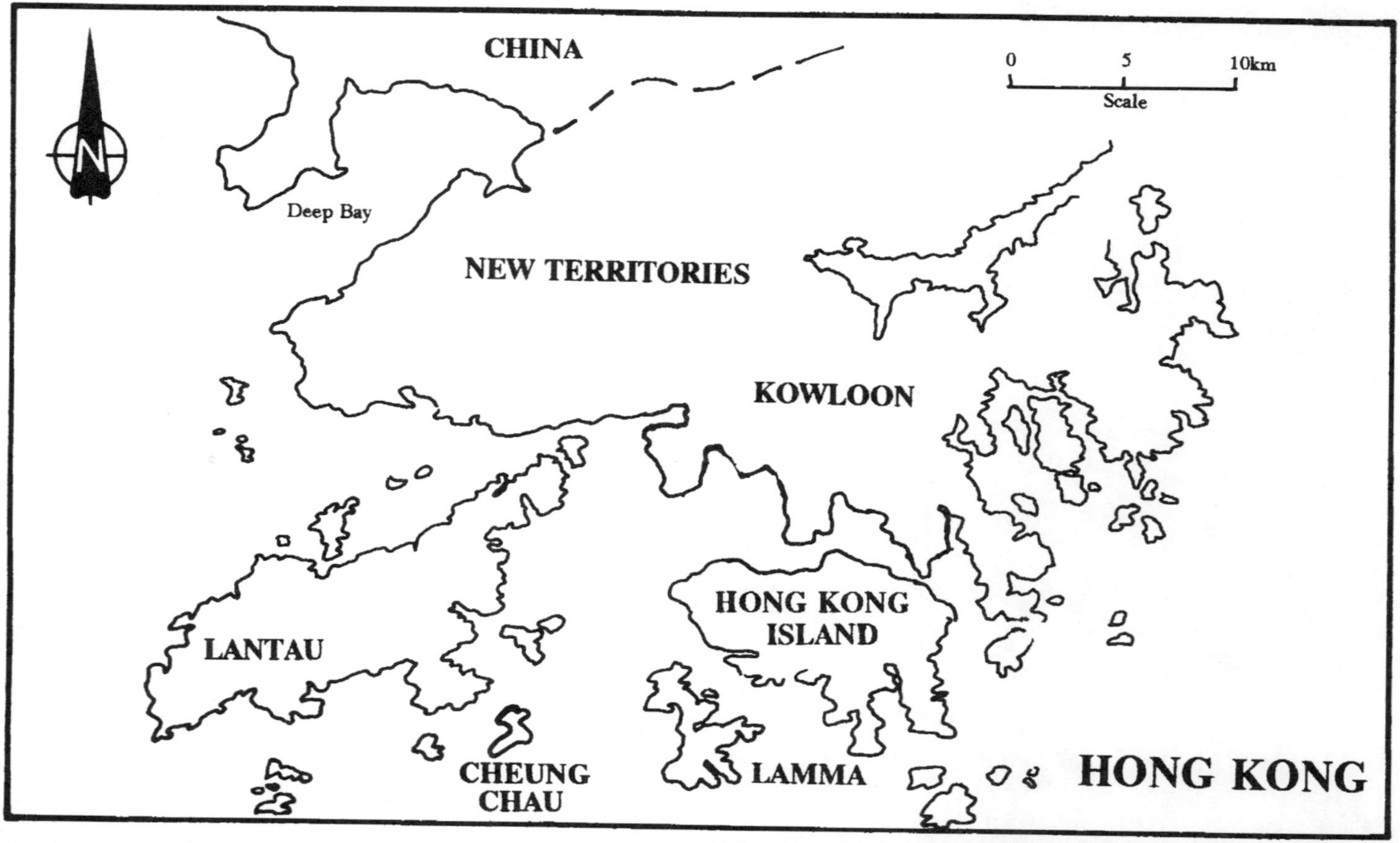
CHINA
0
5
10km
Scale
N
Deep Bay
NEW TERRITORIES
KOWLOON
LANTAU
HONG KONG
ISLAND
CHEUNG
CHAU
LAMMA
HONG KONG

3

The Land, Life, and People of Hong Kong

Geography

Hong Kong naturally divides into four areas—Hong Kong Island, Kowloon, the New Territories, and the Outlying Islands.

Out of a total land area of around 1,070 sq km, Hong Kong Island covers around 80 sq km or 7 percent of the total, Kowloon covers about 12 sq km or 1 percent of the total, the New Territories cover about 760 sq km or 70 percent of the total, and the 235 or so Outlying Islands make up the rest.

Hong Kong Island is the main business center and is home to the spectacular skyscrapers that are a feature of the southern side of Hong Kong Harbour. There are many hotels, shopping centers, tourist attractions, and sight-seeing locations on the island. This is home to the central business district, to the Wanchai nightlife area, to Causeway Bay and its convention center, to Happy Valley and its popular racecourse, to the Peak and the Peak tram, to Aberdeen with its thousands of junks, to Ocean Park and its associated attractions, and to Repulse Bay and Stanley.

Kowloon forms the northern side of the harbor. This is the site of the airport, several museums, and Tsim Sha Tsui, which is the premier tourist area. Interestingly very few tourists get to use the name Tsim Sha Tsui, preferring to use Kowloon instead. There are more tourist hotels in this area than any other in Hong Kong.

The New Territories are north of Kowloon and south of the border with China. There is no distinct change when you cross Boundary Road from

Kowloon but large sections of the more distant areas are rural in character or have been preserved as parks.

The Outlying Islands are actually part of the New Territories. The largest is Lantau Island and this is twice the size of Hong Kong Island but is sparsely populated. Cheung Island is the only Outlying Island that is densely populated but even here the development is only a fraction of that found in many other areas of the city.

Climate

Hong Kong falls just within the tropic zone but anyone who has been there midwinter would know that it can be far from tropical. In summer the monsoon brings hot, humid tropical air from the south and many visitors find it too hot for extensive sight-seeing. Heavy thunderstorms can occur. Winter is cold and requires some warm clothing. This is not a problem for visitors, but it is also frequently windy and cloudy and there can be a drizzling rain so this is not my favorite time.

Fall, from late September to early December, and spring, from the end of March to the end of May, are the best weather times to visit. It is usually sunny and fine. June and August are the wettest months with more than 350 mm of rain falling in each. July is officially the hottest month.

Typhoons are a feature of the July to October period. These can bring very strong winds and torrential rain. They are not much fun even if you are in a relatively safe hotel room. In a severe typhoon you cannot leave the hotel, most businesses will close, and you may be without electricity. If you happen to be out on the water it can be fatal. In Hong Kong's 1937 typhoon, 260 km-per-hour winds caused the drowning of about 2,500 people and the grounding of many ships.

History

Although Hong Kong's past is often dated back only to the British arrival in 1841, the area has a long history as part of the San On district of Imperial China, and the town of Tsuen Wan was in 1277 the seat of a Sung emperor.

The later history of Hong Kong is linked closely to European trade with China. Regular Chinese contact with the European trading nations began in 1557 when the Portuguese settled in Macau, a tiny peninsula south of Canton on the outer edge of China. It was not, however, until about 1685 that Canton itself was opened for trade. This encouraged the British and French to open trade contacts and these nations were followed in the next one hundred years by the Dutch, the Danes, the Americans, and others.

In these early days, China placed little importance on this trade because Europeans were seen as being of little importance. As far as the official Chinese government was concerned, only the Chinese empire was civilized, and the people beyond its borders were barbarians. As time went on, though, the importance of trade became more accepted and in 1757, a Canton merchants' group was given exclusive rights to China's foreign trade.

The Canton group immediately imposed numerous restrictions on the Western traders. They could not live in Canton for more than six months of the year, they were restricted to a small area of the city, they could not bring their families with them, they were forbidden to learn the Chinese language, and they could trade with no one other than the merchants' group. This caused considerable resentment and led to a different trading attitude on the European side.

Despite these problems, trade florished because of the great demand for Chinese tea and silk. The Chinese bought little in return. The British believed they could change this situation by introducing the Chinese to opium and they landed a large shipment in Canton in 1773. It was immediately successful. Chinese demand grew rapidly to the point where the emperor Dao Guang became alarmed and issued an edict in 1796 banning the drug trade. The foreign traders and the Canton merchants were making large profits from the trade, however, so they strongly resisted the decree and the trade continued and grew.

Forty years later, opium was still the cornerstone of British trade with China but it was causing the situation within the country to deteriorate. The Chinese emperor decided to stamp out the opium trade once and for all and he appointed Lin Zexu to do this. Lin surrounded the British enclave in Canton and demanded the surrender of all the opium. The British originally resisted but after six weeks they handed over 20,000 chests. Lin destroyed this in a public ceremony. The British Superintendent of Trade, Capt. Charles Elliot, then unsuccessfully tried to negotiate with Lin.

The British government reacted by sending a naval force to China under the command of Captain Elliot's cousin, Rear Adm. George Elliot. This arrived in 1840 and set about blockading Canton and many other ports up the coast. Lin was replaced by Qi Shan as the emperor's representative and he negotiated for the British to withdraw. The outcome of all this was the signing of the Convention of Chian Bi, which was immediately slammed officially by both governments. Qi Shan was dragged back to the Chinese court, the British landed on Hong Kong Island and claimed it for Britain, then they laid seige on Canton and extracted a large monetary payment and various concessions from the Cantonese merchants.

Shortly afterwards, Sir Henry Pottinger arrived with a powerful force and attacked China. This force was later supplemented by re-inforcents from India and by the middle of July, Nanking (Nanjing) was under threat. The Chinese were forced to accept the Treaty of Nanking. One of the terms of the agreement was that Hong Kong Island was ceded to the British "in perpetuity."

An uneasy truce persisted until 1856, when fighting broke out again. This time the French, Russians, and Americans joined the fighting. The result of this was the Treaty of Tientsin, which allowed the British to establish a diplomatic mission in China. But even this caused further problems. When the British representative arrived off the coast of China, he refused to abide by a Chinese request and the ship was fired upon. The British and French then invaded China and marched on Peking. This time the Treaty of Peking was forced on the Chinese. From this the British gained the area now known as Kowloon plus Stonecutters Island just off the coast.

Perhaps the most significant land acquisition of all was achieved under the Second Treaty of Peking when Britain was presented with the New Territories on a 99-year lease ending in 1997. Although Britain didn't realize it at that time, this spelled the ultimate end of Hong Kong as we know it.

For the next 95 years Hong Kong flourished and it became a conduit from China to the rest of the world. During the 1920s and 1930s, Chinese capitalists fled with their money to the British colony. When the Communists came to power in China in 1949, many thought Hong Kong would soon be taken over. But while the Communists denounced the old treaties, they made no military moves. During the Cultural Revolution of 1967, the colony's future again looked bleak. At one point a militia unit crossed the border and killed a number of people before pulling back.

With the New Territories lease problem hanging over its head, the British government in 1984 agreed to hand the entire colony back to China in 1997. It was argued that to retain just Hong Kong Island, Kowloon, and Stonecutters Island after the expiry of the New Territories lease would not be viable.

The agreement known as the Sino-British Joint Declaration will, in theory, allow Hong Kong to retain its present social, legal, and economic systems for at least fifty years after the Chinese takeover. In 1997, Hong Kong will cease to be a British colony and will become a Special Administrative Region of China. What the ultimate result will be, only time will tell. Its future will be decided by politics in China.

The Government

Hong Kong is currently a British colony with only a touch of democracy. Heading Hong Kong's administration is a governor appointed by the British prime minister. The main policy-making body of the government is the

Executive Council. This is composed of top-ranking officials and other members who are appointed either by the governor or the British government. The council is presided over by the governor.

Then there is the Legislative Council, which frames legislation, enacts laws, and controls government expenditure. Below these bodies are the Urban Council and the Regional Council, which are in control of the day-to-day operations of the city; and the District Boards, which have some degree of control over the local areas. The British government is belatedly trying to make reforms to this system and attempting to introduce some additional democracy, but this is being resisted by the Chinese government.

The Hong Kong civil service is a large and powerful body that controls all government departments in the city. It presently contains several thousand expatriates in senior positions but these are being slowly replaced by Chinese. The government is perceived as being generally efficient and free of major corruption.

This system is under some pressure at present and will likely change in the time leading up to 1997 and beyond.

The Economy

Hong Hong started as a trading support center and it largely remains that today. Business dominates the economy and it has produced a hard-working, money-oriented society with low taxes, free trade, and minimal social security systems. Because of its trade orientation, Hong Kong has developed a modern and efficient seaport and a modern but crowded airport, excellent communications with the rest of the world, and a sophisticated banking industry.

In contrast to most of its neighbors, Hong Kong has only a small agricultural base. Less than two percent of the population is engaged in agriculture and fishing and while these industries are efficient, Hong Kong imports most of its food requirements.

Manufacturing remains the dominant part of the economy and in recent years there has been a shift from labor-intensive industry to capital-intensive. Despite this, Hong Kong suffers from a labor shortage. This has caused a rise in labor costs and has been a contributing factor in inducing investors to establish new factories across the border in China where labor and land costs are cheaper. China's per capita income is still less than US$500 (although the new economic zones are much higher) compared with Hong Kong's of around US$12,000.

While Hong Kong has most of the benefits of capitalism, it also displays many of the problems. There are great extremes in living conditions and you can see this in the contrasts in housing between an area such as the

Peak and the slums of northern Kowloon. There is still some shanty-town housing but the government has built vast areas of subsidized housing in areas such as the New Territories to overcome this.

Hong Kong depends on imports for most of its requirements and increasingly these are being provided by China. The Chinese have long provided foodstuffs, raw materials, and fuel. In more recent years, water, manufactured goods, and tourist handicrafts have been added to the list. China has progressively invested in property, manufacturing, and service industries and is now the largest foreign stakeholder in Hong Kong and Macau.

Tourism has been a significant foreign-exchange earner and employee of labor and this is still the case. Textile production dominates Hong Kong's foreign-exchange earnings with a contribution of around HK$90 billion a year. Tourism has pushed into the number-two spot with a contribution of around HK$60 billion in 1993/94. The industry has learned, however, that it is becoming increasingly reliant on a stable relationship with China. Hong Kong has become the largest transit point for China visitors and there are now good facilities for organizing your China visit from here. Interestingly, Hong Kong has become a favorite destination of visitors from China so now there is two-way travel. It has also become the major contact point between China and Taiwan with visits and trade being conducted through the colony.

In recent years, a sizable number of Hong Kong Chinese have been discreetly shifting some of their personal fortunes out of the Territory to houses in London and on the French Riviera, to apartments in Australia and Singapore, and to businesses around the world. Children have been placed in American and Australian universities while the business people themselves have been busy making more money in Hong Kong and cultivating contacts in China, just in case. This freedom to make money with a minimum of official restrictions has made the city a brutally insensitive place for many. Empty of political life until very recently, it is a society where objects are of supreme importance.

The People

When the British first landed on Hong Kong Island, it was basically unoccupied. The Tankas, a nomadic boat people, had fished the area for centuries but had not established any major form of settlement. The New Territories were a different situation. Here the Hakkas, who had moved from northern China, were well established as farmers. Their numbers, however, were relatively small.

Most of Hong Kong's six million or so inhabitants have origins in China's Guangdong Province. They have arrived mostly this century; in fact only

Hong Kong—Children at play. (Courtesy of the Hong Kong Tourist Association)

about sixty percent of the present population was born in the colony. The collapse of the Qing dynasty in China in 1911 and the various wars that followed caused Chinese close to the border to flee to the safer confines of Hong Kong. By 1930 there were 850,000 people living there. After Canton fell to the Japanese in 1938, another 700,000 fled to the city.

The Japanese attacked Hong Kong on December 8, 1941, and occupied it for three-and-a-half years. During this time mass deportations of Chinese were carried out until the population had fallen to 600,000. Most of these deported people returned to the colony once the Japanese had left and there was a further influx of 750,000 when Chiang Kai-shek was defeated by the Communists in 1949. By 1950 the population had risen to about two-and-a-half million. During the past four decades there has been continued migration (much of it illegal) so that the population has jumped to the present six million.

Today 98 percent of the population is ethnic Chinese. The other 2 percent is mainly made up of Westerners and other Asians. The largest foreign groups are the British, the Americans, the Filipinos, and the Indians.

About 60 percent of the population lives on Hong Kong Island and Kowloon, but the major growth area is the New Territories. The overall population density is about 5,000 people per sq km but there is wide variation between areas. Some of the urban areas have extremely high densities with high-rise government apartment blocks squeezed into every space. In contrast, some of the Outlying Islands are uninhabited.

Religion

The bulk of the population would call itself Buddhist although Taoism, Confucianism, Buddhism, ancester worship, and ancient animist beliefs have become somehow intertwined. There are around 350 temples and monasteries in Hong Kong and a Western visitor should visit at least one of them. Two of the most well known are the Po Lin Monastery on Lantau Island and the Temple of 10,000 Buddhas at Shatin in the New Territories.

BUDDHISM

This ancient religion was established in the sixth century B.C. by an Indian prince named Siddhartha Gautama. At age 30 he became disillusioned with the material world and sought "enlightenment" on the meaning of life. It is said that one evening after many failures he slipped into deep meditation and achieved his goal. The name Buddha means "the enlightened one." Buddha founded an order of monks and preached his ideas for the next forty years until his death. He didn't write anything, however, and what exists today came from a time about 150 years after his death.

At some time Buddhism split into two major arms—*Theravada* (also sometimes called *Hinayana*), which is the Buddhism of Thailand, Laos, Myanmar, and Sri Lanka; and *Mahayana*, the school popular in China, Hong Kong, Japan, and Korea. Buddhism is an emperical way of life rather than a strict religion. It is free of dogma and is a flexible moral, ethical, and philosophical framework within which people find room to fashion their own salvation.

Buddhism reached China before the birth of Christ and it spread rapidly in the north of the country, but it was much slower to spread in the south. There were several periods when Buddhists were persecuted and their temples destroyed but the religion survived. Its appeal lay in the doctrines of reincarnation and enlightenment, which provided hope for the peasants.

TAOISM

Taoism is a Chinese philosophy that has evolved into a religion. It is second only to Confucianism in its influence on Chinese culture. The philosophy originated with Laotse, who lived in the 6th century B.C. He left behind a record of his beliefs and this was developed into a formal religion by Chang Ling some three hundred years later.

Live and let live is the basic philosophy of Taoism. Great patience and harmony with nature are essential features. Taoists believe that often the best results are obtained by doing nothing. This of course runs completely counter to the Western notion of action to achieve quick results. Taoism has become involved with the supernatural over time including self-mutilation, witchcraft, fortune-telling, ghosts, and magic. Stark evidence of this can be seen at certain religious festivals.

CONFUCIANISM

Confucius is regarded as China's greatest philosopher and teacher. He never claimed to be a religious leader but his influence has been so great in China that his thoughts are treasured by many as a religion. Confucius lived through a turbulent period of Chinese history about five hundred years before Christ. He emphasised peace, education, reform, loyalty to friends, devotion to family, and humanitarianism as a way of overcoming the period's problems. His most famous quote was "do not do unto others what you would not want them to do to you."

Confucius also spoke about the evils of corruption, war, and excessive taxation. He was the first teacher to make education available to students on the basis of their interest in learning rather than their noble birth.

During the 400 years of the Han dynasty, Confucianism effectively became the state religion. It was made the major discipline for training government officials and effectively remained so for the next 2,000 years.

In Hong Kong today, no house or shrine is built until an auspicious date for the start of construction is chosen and incence is burned, gifts presented, and prayers said to appease the spirits. On a daily level, however, the people are much less concerned with the high-minded philosophies than they are with the pursuit of worldly success and money, and the seeking of knowledge about the future.

You can find Taoist, Buddhist, and Confucian temples in Hong Kong but there is also considerable mixing in some temples. Taoist temples tend to be bright and colorful, Buddhist are more sedate, while Confucian are very quiet and do not have monks living at them. In all the temples there is no set time for prayers or services. Worshippers simply enter the temple when they wish and make offerings and pray in their own way.

OTHER RELIGIONS

All other religions are comparatively small but Christianity probably has about 500,000 adherents. About half are Roman Catholic but there is also a strong Chinese Methodist community. There are churches in all areas and services are advertised in the Saturday edition of *The South China Morning Post*.

Islam has about 50,000 followers and these include people from India,

Pakistan, Malaysia, and Indonesia. For Jews, there is a synagogue on Robinson Road, Hong Kong Island. There are also communities of Sikhs and Hindus, mainly from India, and representatives of most other faiths.

Language

Hong Kong has two official languages: English and Cantonese. The latter is a southern Chinese dialect, which is different from Mandarin, the official language of China. Cantonese is used in everyday life while English is the main language of law, banking, and commerce. You can get along reasonably well in Hong Kong without speaking Cantonese but you will find that many local people cannot speak or understand English.

Unless you are planning on a long stay it is unlikely that you will wish to learn Cantonese. All the Chinese languages are tonal and Cantonese has more tones than most. It is very difficult for most Western ears to distinguish all the tones. Mandarin has become more common in recent years and this trend will continue, so it would probably be better to learn this. While this is still difficult, it is significantly easier than Cantonese.

Written Chinese has about 50,000 characters but only 5,000 are in common use and you probably only need 2,000 of these to read most newspapers or magazines. All Chinese dialects use more or less the same characters, but the Cantonese have invented some which are not understood by Mandarin speakers. To make matters worse, Hong Kong has not adopted the simplified characters that were introduced in China in the 1950s so many characters appear differently in the two countries. In Hong Kong, characters can be read from left to right, from right to left, or from top to bottom. In China, they are usually read left to right.

It is easy to get an English map in Hong Kong and this will assist you in finding your way around. Unfortunately the romanized names are not necessarily a good indication of how they should be pronounced in Cantonese so you will find that a Chinese speaker may not be able to understand you if you ask for directions. If all this sounds very frustrating then just remember that the differences you find are one of the joys of travel. If you persist and do it with a smile you will always find someone who can help, often in perfect English.

Here is a selection of words and phrases that you will find useful in Hong Kong.

Numbers

one	—yat
two	—yee
three	—saam
four	—sei

THE LAND, LIFE, AND PEOPLE OF HONG KONG

five	—ng
six	—lok
seven	—chut
eight	—baht
nine	—gau
ten	—sup
eleven	—yat sup yat
twelve	—yat sup yee
one hundred	—yat but
one thousand	—yat cheen

Useful Words and Phrases

hello	—nay ho
good morning	—joe sahn
excuse me	—mmgoi
thank you	—doh jeh
yes	—hai
hotel	—jau deem
ferry	—ma tau
road	—doh
street	—gai
alley	—hong
bus	—ba see
taxi	—dik see
left	—joh
right	—yau
straight on (straight ahead)	—cheek hoi
slower	—man dee
stop here	—hai doh teng, mmgoi
I want to go	—Ngo seung hoi
I am looking for	—Ngo seung wun
I am an American	—Ngo seung mei gwok yan
Can you speak English?	—Lei sik gong ying man?
What time is it?	—Gay deem-a?
What is your name?	—Lei gu mei meng?
How much is it?	—Gay doh cheen?
Too expensive	—Ho gwai
Can we order please?	—Ngo day dem choi?
Menu	—choi dan
Bill	—mai dan

Locations

Kowloon	—gau loong

New Territories —sun gai
Central —chung wan
The Peak —san deng
Nathan Road —lei dun doh

Culture and Lifestyle

In the 1990s, most of the Hong Kong culture seen by many tourists is the potted, easily digestible variety; but if you look for it, there is much more. Enjoy the packaged after-dinner entertainment of folk singing and dancing but venture out into the New Territories or the back streets of Western District and there are still glimpses of traditional China. Such scenes were once Hong Kong's greatest attraction; but with easy access to China now available, this aspect of Hong Kong has less significance.

I have covered some aspects of traditional Chinese culture in chapter 10, "The Land, Life, and People of Guangzhou." Here are just a few snippets from modern Hong Kong culture.

The Hong Kong business community would shrivel and die without a massive supply of business cards. These are an essential part of all business dealings and any visitor to Hong Kong will need an ample supply. But it is also important to know how to use them. You must present your name card with two hands and receive them likewise. Then you should look at it for several seconds. It is considered the height of bad manners to deal a card across a table with a casual flick.

Taxis regularly use the traffic tunnels between Hong Kong Island and the mainland. You will find, however, that some taxis will not want to know you and other taxis will welcome you with open arms. To indicate that you wish to cross the harbor, make a dipping motion with your hand at a passing taxi. Those that wish to get back to their normal area will screech to a halt for you.

Hong Kong has had a local pop music scene for many years but until recently this was built on a slavish imitation of Western forms. It has now discovered its own sense of identity and has come up with a curious homegrown hybrid that is part Frank Sinatra, part Madonna, and all gloss; it is called Cantopop. This has taken root in the hearts and minds of Hong Kong youth and is being exported to Taiwan, China, and throughout Asia via MTV Asia. Cantopop now has more than 50 percent of all Hong Kong sales of recorded music, a market worth around US$1,000,000,000 in retail terms.

Perhaps the most visual expression of modern Hong Kong is in its architecture. The building boom of the past fifteen years or so has given rise to a number of buildings of real architectural significance. Among the most successful, and certainly one of the most distinctive, is the Hongkong &

Hong Kong's Central district is dominated by sparkling skyscrapers, which overlook Victoria Harbour. Among the tallest is the Bank of China Tower. (Courtesy of the Hong Kong Tourist Association)

Shanghai Bank Building, which seems to display its insides to the world. Another is I. M. Pei's 70-story Bank of China Tower, which is topped by 63-meter twin masts and was Hong Kong's tallest building for some time. Now that title belongs to Central Plaza, a 314-meter, high-tech, neoclassical masterpiece that is currently the tallest building in the world outside of New York and Chicago. Under construction at the moment is a building that is destined to become another Hong Kong landmark. The new Peak Tower is deliberately unconventional and from its commanding position it will be seen from miles around. The previous building to occupy this site was not quite twenty-two years old when it was demolished. That is a fitting cultural statistic for where Hong Kong is today.

Food and Drink

Love of food is almost on a par with Hong Kong's enthusiasm for gambling and making money. A visit to any food market will demonstrate that buying right is taken very seriously. Housewives and chefs can be seen poking, sniffing, and squeezing the produce, including livestock, which is kept very much alive until purchase to ensure freshness. Freshness is a fetish that accounts in part for the city's reputation as a gastronomic showcase for regional styles of Chinese cooking.

Dining out in Hong Kong can be a great experience. Most major cuisines are represented in some of Asia's finest restaurants. At the same time it is possible to have an inexpensive meal at many food stalls and restaurants in most parts of the city. Hong Kong diners are very demanding and chefs are careful to preserve the true tastes of Chinese food, but they also produce the authentic flavors of other Asian countries and the best that the West has to offer.

China can be divided gastronomically into four main regions: Guangzhou (Canton), Beijing (Peking), Shanghai, and Sichuan (Szechuan). These cuisines are all well represented in Hong Kong. Other styles of cuisine include Fujian (Fukien), Kejia (Hakka), Chiu Chow, Hunan, and Hangzhou—each with its own distinctive flavor.

With literally thousands of Chinese restaurants, teahouses, and noodle shops, Hong Kong offers a great opportunity to experience the variety and subtlety of Chinese cuisine at its best. Frankly it is much better than eating in China.

It is a Chinese belief that eating should be enjoyed in a friendly atmosphere but that the food itself should always be the center of attraction. You will find that some of the finest food can be found in restaurants that may seem rather austere by Western standards.

Chinese people in Hong Kong usually go out to dine in groups. Eating

Among the tempting dishes shown here are Beggar's Chicken, deep-fried fillet of fish, sweet and sour prawns, and braised chicken with soya beans. (Courtesy of the Hong Kong Tourist Association)

Chinese-style is a communal affair, with the dishes placed in the middle of the table and shared by everyone. You will normally be greeted with a hot towel and a refreshing cup of tea. This will often be repeated at the end of the meal.

Be warned that some restaurants charge extra for this even though you didn't order it. Also note that your bill will usually show all "food" items as a lump sum so it is impossible to check. Don't be afraid to ask for an itemized bill if you have doubts about the total. Remember, too, that water is usually only served on request and bottled water will be charged to the bill.

As the great majority of Hong Kong residents originated in Guangdong Province, of which Guangzhou is the major city, Cantonese cuisine is by far the most popular in the city. This is the style of Chinese food with which most people around the world are familiar. It is known for its fresh, delicate flavors. Fresh ingredients are used and cooked, just before serving, with a minimum of oil or spicy seasonings.

Another part of Cantonese cuisine that you will discover is *dim sum*. This means "light snack" and it forms part of the Chinese tradition of drinking tea. Tea is in fact drunk right throughout the meal.

You can enjoy a wide variety of dim sum from early morning to midafternoon in Cantonese restaurants that specialize in this kind of food. Often the steaming baskets of food are paraded past on carts, so you can look before choosing. In other places you fill in a card on the table and hand it to the waiter.

As for drinks, San Miguel beer still ranks at the top with the locals. Many Hong Kong drinkers also enjoy brandy—neat and in a tumbler filled to the brim. Per capita consumption is higher here than in France. In the winter, some locals drink snake bile wine—a heady cocktail of rice wine, snake blood, and snake gall bladder, all blended and knocked down in one shot.

Festivals

Hong Kong has the best of both worlds when it comes to festivals. It has embraced Christmas and Easter from the West, but it also enthuiastically celebrates many Chinese traditional festivals during the year. Here are the most important.

New Year—The first weekday in January is a public holiday but generally the celebrations are subdued.

Lunar New Year—This festival in late January or early February is the most important of all Chinese celebrations. It is a time for spring cleaning, buying new clothes, settling debts, visiting friends and relatives, and exchanging gifts. Most businesses close for three days or more. On Lunar New Year's

Assorted cakes, both sweet and savory, are sold in large quantities prior to Chinese New Year. Most of these are fried before they are eaten; and although they can be purchased all year round, they are most popular at Chinese New Year.

Eve, the entire family gathers for a reunion dinner to eat symbolic food to bring good luck and prosperity in the new year. After dinner, many people visit a flower market to buy peach and plum trees, which signify good luck. Strips of red paper containing greetings of longevity, good luck, and wealth are pasted on doors. The evening culminates in a great fireworks display over the harbor.

On Lunar New Year's Day, people visit temples and hand out lucky money to children and unmarried men and women.

Arts Festival—In late January and early February, Hong Kong has its annual culture fest. Renowned orchestras, dance companies, drama groups, opera companies, and jazz ensembles are invited to perform alongside talented local artists.

Spring Lantern Festival—This marks the fifteenth and final day of the Lunar New Year. It is sometimes known as Chinese Valentine's Day.

Food Festival—Restaurants, clubs, pubs, and whole districts gear up for this annual culinary event of the year held in March or April. It has been organized since 1988 by the HKTA and American Express. There are food fiestas; a dinner-date offered by some of the top restaurants; theme parties; waiters' races; and outdoor food stalls, games, and entertainment.

Easter—Several public holidays make this a popular time for many people to get away.

Ching Ming Festival—This is observed by the visiting of ancestral graves and by making offerings of meat, fruit, wine, and flowers. Gold and silver "money" is burned and graves are washed and repainted. The festival occurs in early April.

Tin Hau Festival—Temples, dedicated to the Goddess of the Sea, burst into life on the deity's birthday in early May. There are colorful parades, Chinese opera, and the sailing of hundreds of decorated junks and sampans.

Birthday of Lord Buddha—This festival commemorates the birth of Prince Siddhartha Sakyamuni, the founder of Buddhism. A major Buddha-Bathing Ceremony takes place at the 10,000 Buddhas Monastery near the Sha Tin railway station.

Tam Kung Festival—A procession is held from the Tam Kung Temple at Shau Kei Wan on Hong Kong Island in May.

Cheung Chau Bun Festival—Takes place over seven days on Cheung Chau Island and is held to placate the spirits that are said to roam the island. Paper houses, cars, and money are burnt; food is offered to the ghosts; and the people eat no meat or fish during this time.

Dragon Boat Festival—This commemorates the third-century B.C. death of national hero and poet, Ch'u Yuen, who drowned himself in protest against a corrupt government. The celebrations are held in June and they have spawned the popular International Dragon Boat Races, which involve teams from many countries. The best viewing position is the Tsim Sha Tsui East waterfront in Kowloon.

Birthday of Lu Pan—Lu Pan was born in 507 B.C. and is the Taoist patron saint of carpenters and builders. He is remembered as a brilliant architect, engineer, and inventor and is regarded as the Chinese equivalent of Leonardo da Vinci. Lu Pan is credited with inventing many common items such as the ladder, the drill, the saw, the lock, and the shovel. His wife is said to have invented the umbrella. Celebrations take place in July and are centered on the Lu Pan Temple at Kennedy Town at the western end of Hong Kong Island.

Maiden's Festival—Unmarried men and women burn joss sticks and make offerings to this ancient Chinese legend at Lover's Rock, Bowen Road on Hong Kong Island in mid-August.

Hungry Ghosts Festival—This takes place to placate the ghosts who have become dispossessed and thus could become dangerous to the earthly world. Paper offerings of cars, furniture, and money are made. Chinese opera performances take place in public areas on the day of the festival in late August.

Mid-Autumn Festival—Thousands of paper lanterns are sold and throngs of people make their way to parks and public places, where they light them and watch the moon. This is also the time for mooncakes. This legend goes back to the fourteenth-century revolt against the Mongols, who held a particular walled city. A revolutionary entered the city dressed as a Taoist priest and handed out mooncakes containing messages about the revolt. The revolt succeeded and formed the basis to create the Ming dynasty. Victoria Park and the Peak are two good places to see the celebrations in mid-September.

Birthday of Confucius—This festival, which is held in early October, is no longer widely celebrated. Confucius is regarded as one of the most influencial Chinese philosophers and his teachings are still widely followed. Filial devotion and ancestral worship, observed at both the Ching Ming and Chung Yeung festivals, continue to be a cornerstone of Confucianist practice today.

Chung Yeung Festival—This Confucian holiday is another time to visit family graves to make offerings and pray. All the cemeteries in Hong Kong are alive with people during this time in mid-October.

In 1995, there will be the first **Hong Kong Festival,** a happening planned for every November. It will feature, amongst many activities, carnivals, fireworks, floats and parades, open-air concerts, and exhibitions.

Christmas—This is a two-day holiday and although few of the population are Christian, the commercial aspects of the festival are embraced with enthusiasm.

Accommodations

Hong Kong hotels are now running at close to 90 percent occupancy so there is little pressure to discount. In fact, at some times of the year visitors are being turned away. Current economics are such that developers can make more money from office buildings than hotels so few new hotel rooms are likely to be added to stock in the near future.

Hong Kong is not the best place in the world to find budget accommodation; however, at the other end of the scale you will find some of the world's best hotels. New hotels are being built all the time; but at popular times of the year such as Chinese New Year or Easter, accommodation can be extremely hard to find.

Luxury hotels are mainly clustered in Tsim Sha Tsui and Tsim Sha Tsui East in Kowloon; and in Central, Wanchai, and Causeway Bay on Hong Kong Island. You can make reservations through your local travel agent or by telephone or fax. The Hong Kong Tourist Association has a hotel guide that lists all the main places. If you arrive at the airport without a booking, the HKTA desk will help you. A luxury hotel will cost at least HK$1,400. Many are much more.

Midrange hotels start at about HK$600. They are not so easy to find but in fact there is a large amount of accommodation in this category. Some of these properties are listed by the HKTA and many can be booked from the airport. Hotels in this category are in most areas except Tsim Sha Tsui East.

Guesthouses are the next category down from here. A self-contained room is likely to cost around HK$350 while a dormitory bed will be about HK$80. Most guesthouses are in old buildings in Tsim Sha Tsui and on Hong Kong Island, and the standard of accommodation varies considerably. It is very wise to see the room before agreeing to stay.

The Hong Kong Youth Hostels Association has several hostels in the colony that are available to those with an IYHF card. The association can be contacted on Tel: 2788-1638 and they also sell cards to those without them. Dormitory beds are available for HK$35.

Health and Safety

Hong Kong is considered to be a very safe place to visit but travellers are advised to take the usual precautions. The government says the water is safe to drink and because most Chinese cooking relies on fresh ingredients, this should be safe as well. If the worst happens, Hong Kong has some excellent private hospitals at fairly high prices or public hospitals that charge significantly lower fees. Private doctors are available, but you should inquire about the fees before going too far. There is no national health scheme so all medical treatment must be paid for at the time of service. Travel insurance comes in very handy at times like this.

As well as traditional medicine, Hong Kong is an excellent place to try some herbal medicine. There is debate in the West about the value of this treatment and I cannot contribute to that; however, I have met several people who claim they have been cured of migraine headaches, asthma, and other complaints that did not respond to Western treatment. You will find traditional herbal pharmacies in Hong Kong that have English speakers in attendance and they will be happy to discuss a problem.

Because Hong Kong can be very hot and humid at times, it is not uncommon for visitors to develop minor skin complaints. These can be very frustrating but they can generally be cured by careful hygiene. Prickly heat rash is caused by excessive sweating. You need to bathe often, then dry and cool the skin before using talcum powder. The same treatment applies to fungal infections but you should also add treatment with an antifungal powder or cream. Your own doctor will be able to give you helpful suggestions to avoid these conditions.

There is some tuberculosis and hepatitis around but at rates far below most other Asian countries. Again, seek your doctor's advice. Malaria does not appear to be a major problem.

Sexually transmitted diseases exist in Hong Kong as they do in all other countries. Abstinence is the only sure preventative. Effective treatment is available for many of these; however, there is currently no cure for herpes or AIDS.

Women travellers should not experience any particular problems in Hong Kong but I am told that there is a demand for young foreign women by older local men. In this case it is likely that the usual scams are taking place. It would be wise to avoid all offers of modeling, photographic, and escort work.

Street crime in the tourist areas is much less than in many cities and generally it is safe to walk around at night. Pickpockets are known to operate in the crowed areas, so you should be careful with your valuables.

One minor problem that is often encountered by visitors is the rudeness and take-it-or-leave-it attitude that is displayed by many shop assistants and even some people in the hospitality industry. There are periodic campaigns to try to improve the situation.

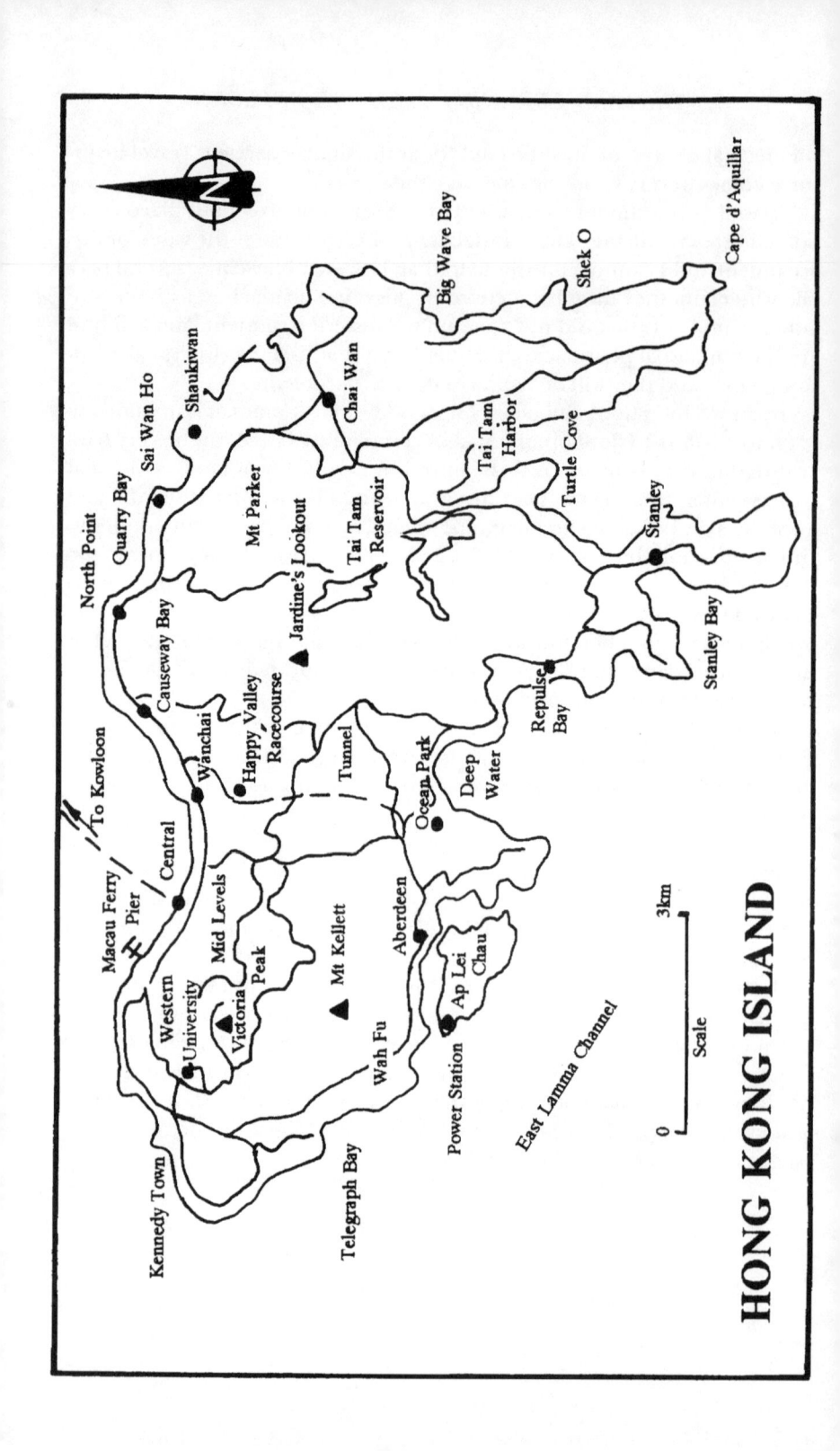

HONG KONG ISLAND

4

Hong Kong Island

1. The General Picture

A visitor to Hong Kong soon realizes that the city is actually many very different places all rolled into one. You see this best on Hong Kong Island, where there is a delightful diversity of communities. A successful visit to Hong Kong Island will be a patchwork of personal experiences involving many of these.

Hong Kong Island was the first area settled by the British, and even today it remains the financial and corporate center of the city. The British first developed the area now known as Western; but Central, the home of sober-suited stockbrokers, accountants, and megatraders, is now considered to be the heart of the city.

The difference between the two areas is amazing. Central has sleek, complacent office towers; Western has squat, crumbling warehouses. Central shops sell French handbags and Italian fashions while those in Western sell funeral offerings, incense, snake bile, and crushed pearls. In Central, business is conducted over mobile telephones, in the backseats of limousines, or on computer display terminals. In Western, it is conducted with abacuses, in back rooms, and over packing cases stacked high on the dockside.

Most of the development on Hong Kong Island is on the northern coast between Kennedy Town and Chai Wan. This stretch of waterfront is a place of blood, sweat, and tears for many, but it is where it is all happening—it is the heart and soul of the Territory.

This ragged, raucous, coastal strip is very crowded with new towering

Hong Kong Island—Hong Kong's Central district is the heart of the Territory's financial and business activity. (Courtesy of the Hong Kong Tourist Association)

banks, office blocks, hotels, apartment blocks, and shopping centers fighting with older low-rise commercial and residential development for the precious, dwindling space. Development has moved up the slopes of the Peak and there is a constant program of reclamation that adds some valuable waterfront land at regular intervals, which literally changes the map of the city. A small sign fixed to the wall of a building in Central informs passersby that the sea once reached this point. Now the building is 300 meters inland.

This strip is well served by transport facilities. A mass transit underground railway runs its full length, while on the surface there are new road systems, an extensive network of buses, and the slow but appealing double-decker tramway. The area is always busy and is often noisy and polluted. The raw commercialism you find here can numb the spirit of the newcomer and the visiting business person.

The south side of the island is a complete contrast. Repulse Bay and Stanley have been developed as spacious and relatively quiet upmarket residential areas. These centers even have nice beaches that are clean enough for swimming. Expensive houses are perched on the hillsides, giving spectacular seaviews. It is more like being on the Mediterranean than in

Asia. Farther east, Big Wave Bay and Shek O beaches provide good swimming in relative isolation.

It is worth mentioning that, despite its crowded urban appearance, Hong Kong Island has many rural areas. Most notable are the five country parks that form a green blanket through the center of the island. There is a fifty-kilometer Hong Kong Walking Trail traversing the parks from Victoria Peak to Shek O that provides spectacular views of Victoria Harbour and the South China Sea islands, as well as interesting forest and grassland vistas.

Hong Kong Island has some of the city's best hotels, restaurants, tourist attractions, shopping centers, and nightlife facilities. It is connected to the mainland by road and rail tunnels and by the famous Star Ferry, which provides a cheap but wonderful view of the harbor and the island. The island is an essential part of a Hong Kong visit.

2. Getting There

If you are arriving in Hong Kong from anywhere else but Macau, or ferry from Shekou, you will arrive in Kowloon rather than on Hong Kong Island. The international airport, the international cruise terminal, the main China ferry terminal, and the station for the China railway are all on the mainland.

From the international airport to Hong Kong Island, you have a choice of taxi or airport coach, called **Airbus**. (For more details on the airport, see the Kowloon section.) Taxis are numerous and readily available. Most drivers speak some English, but it is wise to have the full address of where you wish to go written in Chinese characters. I have found that even some of the large hotels are not known by some drivers. Fortunately, they are in radio contact with a base and you can speak to the base in English and let them translate for the driver. Taxis have meters and you should pay only the fare that is shown plus any additional authorized charge. Extra charges include HK$5 for each piece of luggage and a HK$20 surcharge for cross-harbor tunnel trips. The taxi fare to most Hong Kong Island hotels will be HK$80-90.

The Airbus operates on a 15-20 minute frequency, daily from 7 A.M. to midnight. There are two routes serving Hong Kong Island—one to Central and Wanchai (A2) and the other to Causeway Bay (A3). The fare is HK$16. The Airbus does not travel to Western, Happy Valley, or North Point, or to the hotels at Pacific Place.

3. Local Transportation

Public transportation is excellent on Hong Kong Island, so most visitors do not even consider car rental. There are taxis, buses, minibuses, the excellent mass transit railway (MTR), and trams. For access to Victoria Peak,

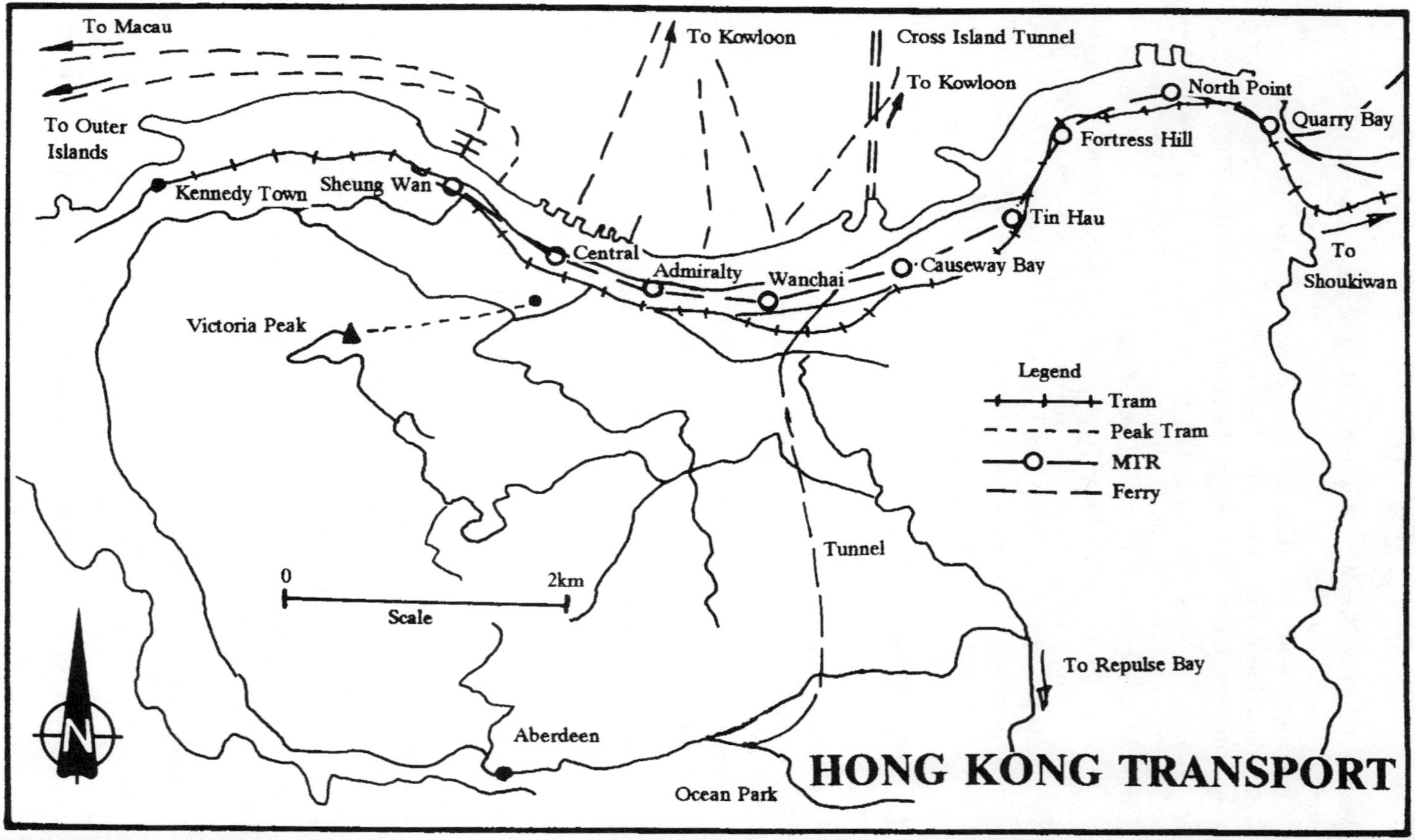
To Macau
To Outer Islands
To Kowloon
Cross Island Tunnel
To Kowloon
North Point
Quarry Bay
Fortress Hill
Kennedy Town
Sheung Wan
Tin Hau
Central
Admiralty
Wanchai
Causeway Bay
To Shoukiwan
Victoria Peak
Legend
Tram
Peak Tram
MTR
Ferry
Tunnel
0
2km
Scale
To Repulse Bay
Aberdeen
Ocean Park
HONG KONG TRANSPORT

there is the Peak tram, while the lower reaches of the hill are served by a unique Hillside Escalator link. There are still a few rickshaws but these are for tourist photo opportunities rather than local transport. Contrary to popular belief, rickshaws were not a Chinese invention, but a Japanese one. They were introduced to Hong Kong in the nineteenth century.

Taxis serving Hong Kong Island and Kowloon are red with a silver top. They are available outside hotels, tourist attractions, railway stations, shopping centers, and so forth; and they may be hailed on the streets. During normal conditions, they are readily available but there can be a problem at peak periods or when it rains. Rates start at HK$9 on flag fall plus HK$0.90 for every 200 meters after the first two kilometers. Taxi drivers need not be tipped. The English language ability of most drivers is quite limited, so it is wise to have an address written in Chinese characters. If you have any complaints, note the taxi's number and call the 24-hour Police Hotline (Tel: 2527-7177).

The **Mass Transit Railway (MTR)** is fast, clean, and safe. Trains run along the north shore of Hong Kong Island and connect to Kowloon and the New Territories. For short trips, the MTR is more expensive than buses or trams but it is air conditioned so it is often more pleasant to ride. Fares are from HK$3.50-9.00. The MTR is fully automated and is easy to negotiate. There are good English language signs to help visitors. Note that ticket machines do not give change. There are separate change machines to help you get the correct coins. The ticket is encoded when you pass through the turnstile, so do not lose it because you will need it to exit at the other end. You only have 90 minutes to complete the journey before the ticket runs out of time. You cannot buy round-trip tickets but there are "stored value tickets" for making multiple journeys. These are useful if you plan to use the MTR frequently and they have the added advantage that the last ride can be made to anywhere, regardless of how much is left on the ticket. The HK$25 "Tourist Ticket" is only worth HK$20 in travel but does give you a souvenir.

Smoking, eating, and drinking are not permitted in the MTR stations or on the trains. A free MTR pamphlet is available from station information booths. Trains cease operation around 12:30 at night. The MTR carries some 2.3 million passengers a day, with a highest train frequency of 31 trains per hour. Statistics show that more than half of the seven million international visitors to Hong Kong each year travel on the MTR.

The **tram** is slow, fun, and a great experience. The best view is from the front of the upper deck but any seat is great to watch your fellow passengers going about their daily business. There is a single route from Kennedy Town in the west to Shaukiwan in the east, with a small loop through Happy Valley. Trams operate from 6 A.M. until 1 A.M. but you should note that many do not serve the full route. There is a flat fare of HK$1, which you pay as you leave the tram. No change is available.

There is an extensive **bus** network but it is not as easy for the visitor to use as the MTR or the tram because it can be difficult to decide which bus goes where and from where. The blue-and-cream buses are operated by the China Motor Bus Company (Tel: 2565-8556). These run from around 6 A.M. until midnight. Fares range from 70 cents to HK$25.50 and you pay the exact fare into a box as you enter. There are some English signs at bus stops listing the common fares. Then there are the orange air-conditioned Citybus services. These generally go nonstop between two points and can be a useful, quick way to travel. The yellow-and-red **minibuses** are also good if you know which one goes where. There are small English signs on most of them but they are difficult to see and understand as the bus approaches you. In theory, minibuses stop whenever you hail them but no-stopping zones can make that a bit of a gamble. They are a useful way of travelling between Central and Causeway Bay. Fares range from HK$2 to HK$6, depending on the distance—but they can rise in peak periods and on rainy days. You pay as you exit. **Maxicabs** are the green-and-yellow versions of the minibuses and they run on a fixed route. From the Star Ferry, maxicabs go to Bowen Road and Ocean Park, and from City Hall you can catch one to the Peak. Prices are fixed and range from HK$1 to HK$8. You pay as you enter.

The **Peak Tram** is primarily a visitor attraction that takes tourists up 397 meters to Victoria Peak. From the lower terminus on Garden Road, trams run every 10-15 minutes from 7 A.M. to midnight. Fares are HK$10 one-way and HK$16 roundtrip for adults, and HK$4 and HK$6 for children under 12. A free shuttlebus operates from the Star Ferry concourse in Central to the lower terminus from 9 A.M. to 7 P.M. daily.

The newest transport mode on the island is the **Hillside Escalator.** The system consists of a series of escalators and moving walkways that are linked together with elevated walkways. It starts at the side of the Central Market on Des Voeux Road, Central, and eventually reaches Conduit Road about 800 meters from the start. I first rode the system in November 1993 shortly after it opened and there were a few teething problems but these have since been eliminated. It is a great boon if you wish to visit the smart residential areas of the Middle Level but is also fun to use for short sections. It is primarily designed to ease commuters' journeys to and from work, but the escalator passes some interesting and historical sites that are easily accessible by the frequent "stopping off" points along the route.

4. The Hotel Scene

There has always been competition between Hong Kong Island and

Hong Kong Island—The Peak tram carries visitors to Hong Kong's highest spot, where they can enjoy a magnificent panoramic view of Hong Kong and Kowloon. (Courtesy of the Hong Kong Tourist Association)

Kowloon as to which offers the visitor the best facilities and location. Kowloon has tended to win with tourists but the Island has snared many business visitors. Today the battle continues to be waged but it has become less important since the opening of the MTR railway and the cross-harbor tunnels.

In the past few years, several new luxury hotels have opened on Hong Kong Island and these are doing very well, although current economics are such that further hotel development is unlikely in the near future. There is also good choice in the medium-price hotel sector but there are fewer options at the budget end of the market. I have classified those hotels that have standard rooms at prices above HK$1,500 as expensive, those with standard rooms between HK$600-1,500 as medium-priced, and those below this as budget. This is a clear indication that Hong Kong is an expensive place for accommodation.

EXPENSIVE HOTELS

The **Mandarin Oriental** (Tel: 2522-0111) is regarded by many as the Island's top hotel. The 542-room property is in a great location in the Central district and it offers excellent facilities and superb service. You are

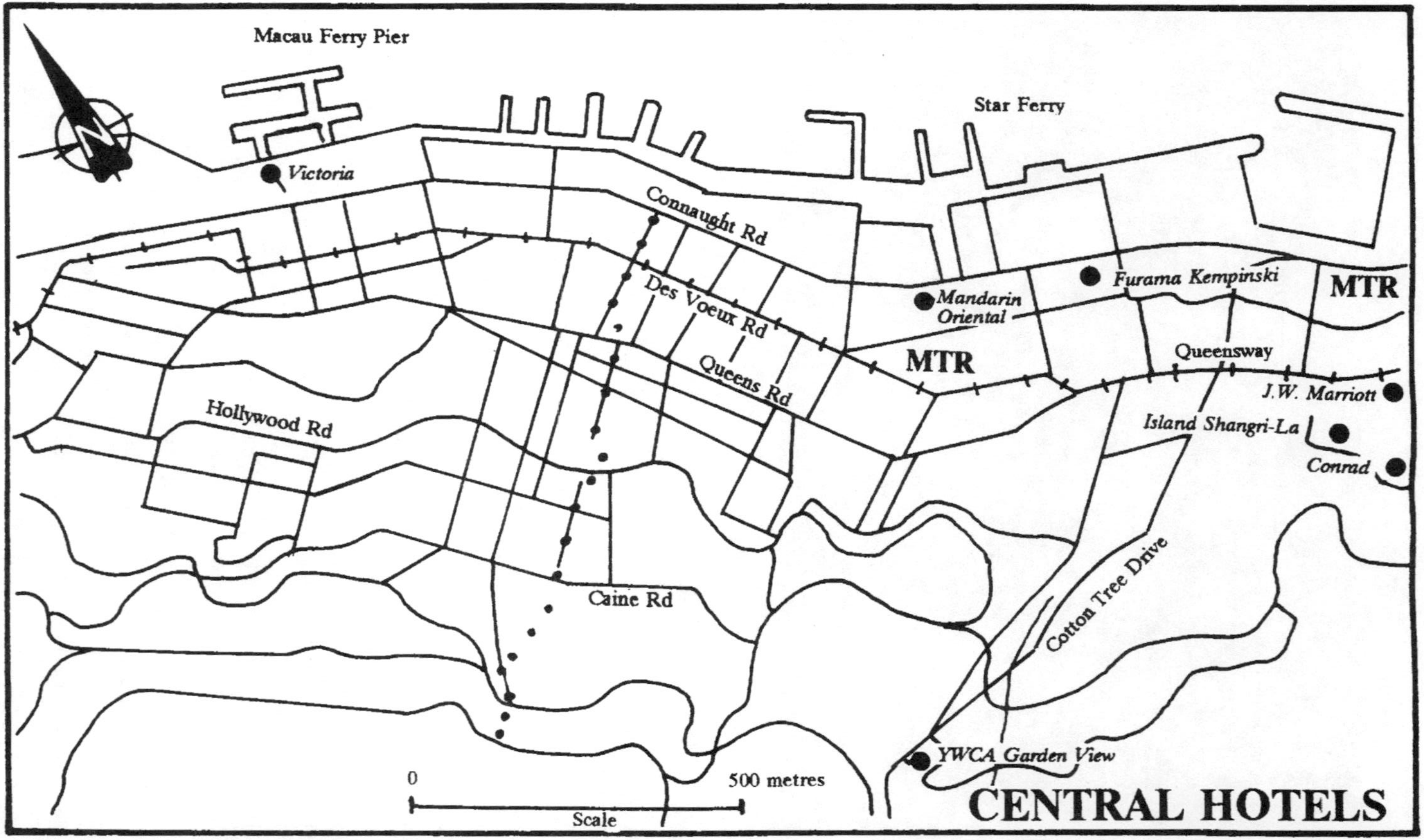
Macau Ferry Pier
Star Ferry
Victoria
Connaught Rd
Des Voeux Rd
Queens Rd
Hollywood Rd
Caine Rd
MTR
MTR
Mandarin Oriental
Furama Kempinski
Queensway
J.W. Marriott
Island Shangri-La
Conrad
Cotton Tree Drive
YWCA Garden View
0
500 metres
Scale
CENTRAL HOTELS

welcomed to the hotel in a lobby decked in Chinese antiques and subdued elegance. This same ambiance is continued through the other public areas and into the guest rooms and suites. Rooms are not huge or grand but they have been furnished with attention to detail and a warmth that is immediately inviting. Most rooms have a balcony but it is doubtful if many guests find this useful as a place to relax.

As you would expect, there is a fully equipped business center and a fine fitness center. Guests can also relax in the penthouse Roman pool, and with acupressure and massage specialists. You can mingle with the city's business elite in the Chinnery Bar, dance at the lively Captain's Bar, or enjoy celebrated French cuisine at Pierrot Restaurant. Mah Wah is one of the city's best Cantonese restaurants, while the Mandarin Grill is almost like a private club for those in the know. Some of Hong Kong's most exclusive shopping can be found within the hotel. The flower shop on the mezzanine floor is always worth a visit. (Book in the United States and Canada on 1-800-526-6566; in Australia on 1-800-222-011; in the United Kingdom on 0-800-181-307; or direct with the hotel at 5 Connaught Rd., Central, Hong Kong; Fax: 852-2810-6190.)

The **Hotel Furama Kempinski** (Tel: 2525-5111) is another property that has been a favorite for quite some time. This is a classic hotel in the Continental tradition that affords every comfort in its 468 guest rooms and 55 suites. The renowned La Ronda revolving restaurant commands spectacular views of the harbor and city, while four additional restaurants indulge guests with superb international and Asian cuisine. The Lau Ling Bar is a popular meeting point, while the exclusive Wine Room serves choice vintages from around the world. There are grand-scale fitness facilities and a fully equipped business center. (Book in the United States and Canada on 1-800-426-3135 or contact the hotel at 1 Connaught Rd., Central, Hong Kong; Fax: 852-2845-9339.)

The huge Pacific Place development has been a great boost for Hong Kong Island, and the three new hotels in the development have added almost 1,700 new luxury rooms. The **Island Shangri-La** (Tel: 2877-3838) is perhaps the most glamorous of the three. The 531 rooms and 34 suites are all lavishly decorated and are claimed to be the most spacious on the island. The building is the tallest hotel on Hong Kong Island at 775 feet, so most rooms have great views through panoramic windows. There is a choice of French, Chinese, and Japanese restaurants; the Lobster Bar; Island Cafe; the Poolside snack bar; and several lounges.

Recreational facilities include a swimming pool and a health club with gymnasium, sauna, Jacuzzi, steam bath, solarium, and massage service. There is a 24-hour business center, 24-hour room service, fax and personal computer outlets in the rooms, same-day laundry and valet service, and all the other facilities you would expect. (Book in the United States or Canada on 1-800-942-5050; in the United Kingdom on 81-747-8485; in Australia on 1-800-222-448; or direct with the hotel at Supreme Court Road, Central, Hong Kong; Fax: 852-2521-8742.)

The 605-room **J. W. Marriott Hotel** (Tel: 2810-8366) is the second hotel in this complex. This is another fine hotel where perhaps the emphasis is on the business market. Room facilities include electronic safes, hair dryers, bathrobes, bottled water, tea/coffee-making heater, and continuous CNN and BBC news broadcasts. There are three executive floors with their own check-in facilities, and guests staying here receive free breakfasts and cocktails together with access to study and work areas.

Dining options include the Marriott Cafe for all-day dining with a view of the harbor; JW's California, where Western dishes are blended with the flavors of Asia; and Man Ho, where you can sample dim sum and regional Chinese delicacies. There is a professionally run health club and an outdoor heated pool. (Book in the United States and Canada on 1-800-228-9290; in the United Kingdom on 71-439-0281; in Australia on 1-800-251-259; or direct with the hotel at 88 Queensway, Hong Kong; Fax: 852-2845-0737.)

Then there is the **Conrad Hotel** (Tel: 2521-3838) with its 467 rooms and 46 suites. I have never stayed here but on several brief visits to the hotel I have been impressed by the decor and service. The rooms are large and friendly, while the bathrooms are awash in marble. The lobby and the public areas have a feeling of quality. The top-level suites are grand. There are four floors of executive rooms, each with three telephones, a facsimile machine, and international direct-dialing facilities. Guests in these rooms receive complimentary breakfast and evening cocktails.

Each of the restaurants has a very distinct decor and feel. Nicholini's has a bright, modern atmosphere with class and authentic northern Italian cuisine. The Brasserie On The Eighth offers traditional French provincial fare in a casually elegant atmosphere. The Golden Leaf has traditional Cantonese cuisine served amid hand-painted silk screens and delicate Yiching teapots. The Garden Cafe offers the flavors of southeast Asia and a wide range of Western dishes.

The hotel has a 24-hour business center with telex, fax, photocopying, secretarial, translation, and courier services. There is a health club with gymnasium, sauna, solarium, steam bath, outdoor heated pool, Jacuzzi, and massage. (Book with the Hilton Reservation Service or direct with the hotel at 88 Queensway, Hong Kong; Fax: 852-2521-3888.)

The final hotel that I wish to recommend in this category is the **Grand Hyatt** (Tel: 2588-1234). This has a waterfront location adjacent to the Hong Kong Convention Center in Wanchai. In its public areas, the hotel is reminiscent of the grand old European hotels of 100 years ago, while most of the 575 guest rooms and suites have spectacular views and a feeling of space.

There are seven floors of Regency Club accommodations with extra services and facilities.

Dining and entertainment are not forgotten. Grissini specializes in authentic Milanese cuisine. One Harbour Road, a split-level Cantonese restaurant, captures the spendor of a taipan's Peak home from the 1930s. The Grand Cafe has a theatrical quality, while the Tiffin Lounge takes high tea to new heights. Take cocktails in the Parisian-style Champagne Bar or late-night entertainment in JJ's, a multitheme nightclub and restaurant. (Book in the United States and Canada on 1-800-233-1234; in the United Kingdom on 345-581-666; in Australia on 1-800-222-188; or direct with the hotel at 1 Harbour Rd., Hong Kong; Fax: 852-2802-0677.)

MEDIUM-PRICE HOTELS

The largest hotel in Hong Kong, **The Excelsior** (Tel: 2894-8888), heads this list. The 913-room hotel is in the popular Causeway Bay area, a few kilometers east of Central. This is part of the Mandarin Oriental Group, so guest expectations are high. Most people are satisfied. Facilities and service are good and the rooms are attractive. There is a range of dining from the Excelsior Grill, to Cammino with its Italian cuisine, to the casual atmosphere of the Coffee Shop. A selection of lively bars has earned the hotel a good reputation as an entertainment venue.

There are three executive floors, where there is a higher level of service and accommodation, and the hotel has 22 suites. The business centers provide everything from secretarial services to a library and meeting rooms. The hotel has indoor tennis courts, while right outside the front doors are cinemas, restaurants, nightclubs, boutiques, and six department stores. (Book in the United States and Canada on 1-800-526-6566; in the United Kingdom on 345-581-442; in Australia on 1-800-222-011; or direct with the hotel at 281 Gloucester Rd., Causeway Bay, Hong Kong; Fax: 852-2895-6459.)

The **China Merchants Hotel** (Tel: 2559-6888) is to the west of Central, in the Western district. The location explains why this good quality hotel has double rooms starting from around HK$750. It appears most tourists want to stay in other areas. I have no argument with the fact that some other areas are more exciting; but after staying here for two days, I found it quite interesting and there are good tram and bus connections to the other parts of the island. The 285 rooms are fairly ordinary but they will be adequate for most people and I have no complaints about the public areas, restaurants, and bars. Shopping within the hotel is not great but there are good-priced options on nearby streets. (Book with the hotel at 160 Connaught Rd. West, Hong Kong; Fax: 852-2559-0038.)

China Harbour View Hotel (Tel: 2838-2222) is in many ways similar to the China Merchants Hotel. The 316-room hotel is in a slightly out-of-the-way

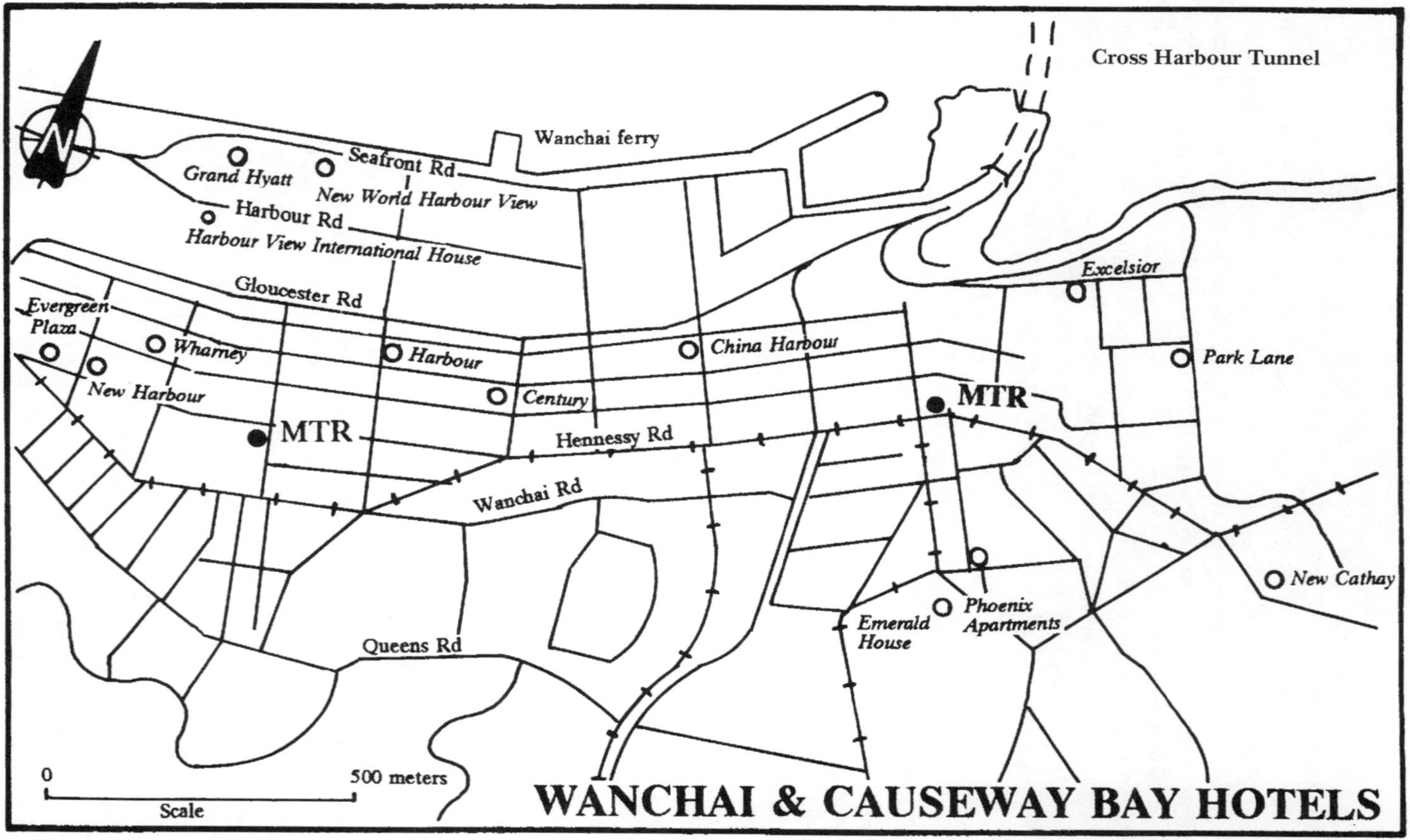

WANCHAI & CAUSEWAY BAY HOTELS

area of Wanchai. Rooms are adequate and some have harbor views, but the public areas are a little cramped. The Chrysanthemum Chinese Restaurant serves Cantonese and seafood, and the Harbour View Restaurant offers an array of Western and Asian specialties. The Supernova Lounge has live entertainment while the Supernova Karaoke Club has eight rooms with karaoke facilities. (Book with the hotel at 189 Gloucester Rd., Wanchai, Hong Kong; Fax: 852-2838-0136.)

Wharney Hotel (Tel: 2861-1000) is a nice property in one of the better areas of Wanchai. The 335 guest rooms are spacious and well equipped and the public areas are smart. The Fontana Restaurant serves international cuisine in nice surroundings with floor-to-ceiling windows letting you gaze down on a cascading fountain to the lobby area two floors below. Nickeby's Bar and Lounge has a light-hearted atmosphere, snacks, and live music. There is a business center and a health club with modern gym equipment, a steam room, a sauna, and an open-air plunge pool. The hotel is within walking distance of the Convention Centre, the Arts Centre, the MTR station, and ferries to Kowloon. (Book with the hotel at 57 Lockart Rd., Wanchai, Hong Kong; Fax: 852-2529-5133.)

The **Harbour View International House** (Tel: 2520-1111), is a gleaming, modern facility operated by the YMCA. The 320 guest rooms are air conditioned and have private bathrooms, TVs, radios, and IDD telephones. Many rooms have good harbor views. Rates are from HK$650. The location near the Hong Kong Arts Centre and the Convention and Exhibition Centre is not the best in town but there are a growing number of facilities in the immediate area. There is a restaurant serving Chinese and Western dishes and a coffee lounge for light snacks and drinks. Staff can assist with sightseeing and travel arrangements. (Book at 4 Harbour Rd., Wanchai, Hong Kong; Fax: 852-2865-6063.)

The **New Cathay Hotel** (Tel: 2577-8211) is one of a growing number of properties owned by the Guangdong government of China. The 230-room hotel is modern, economical, and well run. Rooms are average and have all the necessary facilities. Each has a floor-to-ceiling window but there are no spectacular views. For HK$600 for a single and a double beginning at HK$820, the rooms are good value. The New Cathay Seafood Restaurant on the first floor is attractive and it offers dim sum and a tempting selection of Asian specialities. The Wah Yuen Coffee Shop is a relaxed place serving Chinese and Western food and snacks for breakfast, lunch, and dinner. (Book with the hotel at 17 Tung Lo Wan Rd., Causeway Bay, Hong Kong; Fax: 852-2576-9365.)

BUDGET ACCOMMODATION

Garden View International House (Tel: 2877-3737) is operated by the

YWCA. The modern high-rise building is situated up the hill above the Botanical Gardens, Government House, and the Peak tram station. It is quite a walk from the Star Ferry Pier, but when you reach the site there are some great views from the 130 rooms. Rooms are self-contained with wall-to-wall carpeting, television, and direct-dial telephones. There are 24 family suites that are equipped with kitchens for longer-stay visitors. The standard is as good as some of the medium-price hotels. A restaurant serves Chinese and Western dishes, and an outdoor swimming pool and a fitness center are available. While it just scrapes into the budget category on price, it is highly recommended. (Book at 1 Macdonnell Rd., Central, Hong Kong; Fax: 852-2845-6263.)

Noble Hostel (Tel: 2577-9406) is one of the few other places where you will find reasonable budget accommodation on the island. The check-in area is Flat C1, 7th Floor, Paterson Building, 37 Paterson St., Causeway Bay. There are locked metal gates and security guards; it is generally safe and it is also clean, so it is deservedly popular. The rooms are spread out over several locations. Rooms with a shared bath are from HK$250, while rooms with a private bath are from HK$350.

The **Phoenix Apartments**, at 70 Lee Garden Hill Rd., has a number of options but you need to check them out before you decide to stay. The 15-room **Phoenix Yuen Guest House** (Tel: 2890-5868) has clean, air-conditioned rooms with TV at HK$450. **Manor Inn** (Tel: 2577-5513) has 12 rooms with circular beds for HK$350 on weekdays and HK$450 on weekends. **The Sunset Inn** (Tel: 2576-2419) has rooms at HK$300. All these are on the first floor. There are other options on higher floors.

5. Dining and Restaurants

Hong Kong Island has some of the best restaurants in the city. Some of these are very expensive but it is also possible to have a memorable meal at a quite reasonable price. As well as restaurants, though, you should also eat at some of the roadside stalls, the small, one-dish local diners, and at the markets. This is an equally enjoyable side of Hong Kong dining that can broaden anyone's experience. Watch as flames roar and the oil in a row of woks starts to sizzle. Listen to the unmistakable sounds, the scrape-scrape-scrape of stir-frying. Smell the ginger, garlic, soy sauce, and rice wine in the humid night air. That is something you rarely get in an upmarket restaurant.

You should also make some effort to track down some of the culinary "shows." The best is seeing Peking noodles made by hand. Starting with a long rope of wheat flour, the chef tosses and twirls the dough, slaps it against the tabletop, and rolls it until, almost magically, it separates into strands. The process is repeated again and again until there are dozens of thin, two-meter-long strands. It is real theater.

The following are some of my own favorite restaurants and they cover a wide price range. No doubt you will discover other places that are equally good. If any of the listed restaurants disappoint you, please let me know so I can re-evaluate them on my next visit to Hong Kong.

HOTEL RESTAURANTS

There are some great Cantonese restaurants in the luxury hotels. Most will cost more than HK$200 per person. For sheer splendor and luxury, it is hard to go past the **One Harbour Road Restaurant** at the Grand Hyatt Hong Kong (Tel: 2588-1234). The decor is built around a taipan's home from the 1930s and there are great views over Victoria Harbour. It opens daily for lunch and dinner and there is a separate street entrance and private elevator. Dim sum is served Sundays and public holidays.

The **Man Wah Restaurant** at the Mandarin Oriental (Tel: 2522-0111) is another classic. This rooftop restaurant provides an elegant setting for some traditional favorites. The restaurant often has some seasonal specialties as well as regional dishes such as Peking duck. It opens daily for lunch and dinner.

At Pacific Place, you will find the **Man Ho Restaurant** at the J. W. Marriott Hotel (Tel: 2810-8366). This open-plan restaurant serves fine seafood and some excellent seasonal dishes as well as the usual favorites. Take note of the place settings and furniture. It opens daily for lunch and dinner. Dim sum is served each lunchtime.

One of the longtime favorites is the **Eagle's Nest** at the Hong Kong Hilton (Tel: 2523-3111). The combination of position, view, and distinguished menu keeps bringing people back time after time. The restaurant has some interesting vegetarian specialties. It opens daily for lunch and dinner and you need to book if you want a table with a harbor view. Dim sum is served daily from noon until 3 P.M. While at the Hilton, you may wish to check out the elegant Japanese basement restaurant called **Genji**. There are teppanyaki tables, private rooms, and a sushi bar. Set meals and classic à la carte dishes are served. Grape and rice wines are available.

The other classic Japanese restaurant is the **Nadaman** at the Island Shangri-La Hotel (Tel: 2877-3838). This elegantly simple suite of rooms linked by stone pathways serves traditional set courses, and there are separate teppanyaki and sushi counters. Lobster is a specialty at both lunch and dinner.

I hesitate to select my favorite Western restaurant because the choice is wide. The **Bocarinos Grill** at the Hotel Victoria (Tel: 2540-7228) is an outstanding Mediterranean restaurant. There is a real stylishness here complemented by fine cuisine and strolling musicians. Carts parade salads, breads, cheeses, fruits, and cakes. It opens for lunch Monday through Saturday and for dinner daily.

Equally appealing in a different way is **Pierrot Restaurant** in the Mandarin Oriental (Tel: 2522-0111). This sophisticated dining room has some of the finest French cuisine in the city and service that is almost theatrical in its efficiency. It opens for lunch Monday through Friday and for dinner nightly. Also worth mentioning is the **Mandarin Grill** at the same hotel. This relaxed yet formal dining room has a clublike atmosphere and wonderful grills. Try the beef rib provencale and I almost guarantee you will be delighted. It opens daily for breakfast, lunch, and dinner.

Another great French restaurant is the **Restaurant Petrus** at the Island Shangri-La (Tel: 2877-3838). The restaurant is spacious, has fine harbor views, and offers modern French cuisine. The medallions of veal with bellpepper sauce is outstanding and there is a vintage wine list to match. It opens for lunch Monday through Saturday and daily for dinner.

A wide selection is available at the **Banyan Grill** at the Hotel Conrad Hong Kong (Tel: 2521-3838). This is a light and spacious setting for great steak dishes, a wide choice of seafood including fresh lobster, and a well-stocked salad bar. It opens daily for lunch and dinner. Also opening daily in the same hotel is **Nicholini's,** a fine restaurant for northern Italian cuisine's subtly herbed simplicity and great homemade pasta. Check out the extensive wine cellar for some unusual offerings.

There is still a great deal of choice. I have had some outstanding meals at the luxurious **Excelsior Grill** within the Excelsior Hotel (Tel: 2894-8888), at the handsome **Grill** in the Hong Kong Hilton (Tel: 2523-3111), and at the slightly cheaper **The Rotisserie** at the Hotel Furama Kempinski (Tel: 2525-5111) and the even cheaper **Harbour View Restaurant** at the China Harbour View Hotel (Tel: 2838-2222).

OTHER RESTAURANTS

Cantonese restaurants again dominate the wide choice of offerings. At the top end of the market there are two recommendations. The **Sun Tung Lok Shark's Fin Restaurant** (Tel: 2574-8261) is at 376 Lockart Rd., Wanchai. As the name suggests, the Chinese delicacy of shark's fin is the specialty here. Waiters will explain the shark's fin gradings and consequent price differences. If you are unimpressed, try some of the fresh seafood or the seasonal game dishes. The other top choice is the **Fook Lam Moon Restaurant** (Tel: 2866-0663) at 35 Johnston Rd., Wanchai. This long-established restaurant is justly famous for its seafood creations. The pan-fried lobster balls is one of the popular choices. Both these restaurants open from late morning until late evening.

There is a small step down in price to the next three options. The **Harbour View Tsui Hang Village Restaurant,** (Tel: 2827-5755) in the Great Eagle Centre, 23 Harbour Rd., Wanchai, has market-fresh food, superb harbor views, and excellent service. In the cooler months, the game dishes and the casseroles are very popular. The **Guangzhou Garden Restaurant** (Tel: 2525-1163) is a chic diner in Two Exchange Square, 8 Connaught Place, Central. Lotus leaves and pine nuts add sparkle to many dishes, with spiced chicken and casseroles among the favorites. **The Sunning Unicorn** (Tel: 2577-6620) is stylish. Here in Sunning Plaza, 1 Sunning Rd., Causeway Bay, there is a chic lobby bar and a big selection of "new-style" cuisine. Drunken prawns are a popular early choice and there is an extensive dessert menu.

A further drop in price brings us to a wide choice of good-value restaurants. Among these, the following have appeal to me. The **Yung Kee Restaurant** (Tel: 2522-1624) at 36 Wellington St., Central, has been owned by the Kam family for more than half a century. They must be doing something right because the restaurant now has more than 1,000 seats on five floors. Roast goose is the house specialty. Deep-fried boneless duck with mashed taro is one of the top choices at the **Pepper Garden Restaurant** (Tel: 2802-0006) at the Hong Kong Arts Centre, 2 Harbour Rd., Wanchai. You can enjoy a meal here before or after a show or call in for lunch daily. The black mushroom soup is another suggestion. Out at Repulse Bay, the **Hei Fung Terrace Restaurant** (Tel: 2812-2622) is situated within the Repulse Bay Shopping Arcade. The palatial restaurant has an extensive menu featuring both common and unusual specialties. Try stuffed sea whelk in Portuguese sauce or scented-herb roast pigeon.

At the other end of the island, the **Cityplaza Harbour Restaurant** (Tel: 2884-4188) at 1111 King's Rd., Quarry Bay, is one of a kind. You step over the gangway to be seated on the deck of the full-scale model of a luxury cruiser that dominates this restaurant. It is a pleasant surprise to find that the food is excellent. Try the fresh crab in chilli sauce in a clay pot, or the lobster salad with caviar. Another option is the **East Ocean Seafood Restaurant** (Tel: 2827-8887) in the Harbour Centre, Wanchai. The set menus offer good value and there is a good choice of seafood and other dishes. The **Luk Yu Tea House and Restaurant** (Tel: 2523-5464) is an unofficial historical monument. This sixty-year-old restaurant is a living museum, stocked with memories of a bygone age. The food here at 26 Stanley St., Central, would be worth experiencing even without the extraordinary character of the building.

Consistently good cuisine at low prices is what is offered by the **Jade Garden Restaurants.** There are several of these on the island in both Central and Causeway Bay. A favorite dish of mine is the duck with parsley, but you should also inquire about the daily specials because these are usually an excellent value. The **Broadway Seafood Restaurant** (Tel: 2529-9233), at 73 Hennessy Rd., Wanchai, is another good-value place. The house specialty is crispy chicken, but the many seafood dishes are good alternatives. The crab fried with ginger and shallots is good. Finally, there is the **Tsui Hang Village Restaurant** (Tel: 2524-2012) in the New World Tower, 16 Queens Rd., Central. This is a glass-walled tribute to the home village of Dr. Sun Yat-sen. The menu includes some delightful soups, chicken, and fried milk fritters.

I would be remiss in not mentioning the Aberdeen floating restaurants. The huge **Jumbo Restaurant** (Tel: 2553-9111) is a landmark and almost a symbol of Hong Kong. In fact, this is still my favorite because it offers good value for the money and it has two essential ingredients for this type of restaurant—good, fresh seafood and a great harbor vista from its roof garden. It is open daily from 7:30 A.M. to 11:30 P.M.

If you are not happy going nowhere, the **Hong Kong Harbor Tour Night Club** (Tel: 2541-6026) may be the answer for you. The boat leaves Wanchai and offers the chance to dine and dance the night away amid the dramatic setting of Hong Kong Harbour. There are other cruises that just offer a buffet meal—either Chinese or Western.

Of course, other cuisines are also available. Peking-style food is popular, particularly in the cooler months because it tends to be more substantial than some of the other regional dishes. Peking duck is the most well known dish, but there are some sizzling plates of seafood, meat, or chicken that also can be highly recommended. Look out for the chain of **Peking Garden Restaurants** in Central, Causeway Bay, and Quarry Bay if you wish to try this cuisine. These restaurants stage nightly noodle-making displays, and sometimes there are Peking duck carving exhibitions. Another popular Peking establishment is the **King Heung Restaurant** (Tel: 2577-1035) at 59 Paterson St., Causeway Bay. This brightly decorated place specializes in Peking duck, which you can combine with bean paste dumplings.

There are two favorite Sichuan restaurants that should not be missed by lovers of this spicy Chinese food. The **Red Pepper Restaurant** (Tel: 2577-3811), at 7 Lan Fong Rd., Causeway Bay, is a family-run establishment that loves peppercorn flavor in many dishes. The garlic-chillied sliced pork is quite outstanding. The **Sze Cheun Lau Restaurant** (Tel: 2891-9027), at 466 Lockhart Rd., Causeway Bay, is one of those comfortable old-fashioned places with almost a club atmosphere. The spiced perfumed chicken is a favorite here.

The **Wishful Cottage Vegetarian Restaurant** (Tel: 2573-5645), just down the road at 336 Lockhart Rd., is the place to head for surprising vegetarian dim sum dishes. This is a gloriously old-fashioned Chinese Buddhist restaurant where the atmosphere is as good as the food. In the evening an à la carte menu offers just as many surprises.

The **Ashoka Restaurant** (Tel: 2525-5719), at 57 Wyndham St., Central, is my favorite dining place for Indian food. The set meals are attractive and very well priced, yet the atmosphere is classy. The **Benkay Japanese Restaurant** (Tel: 2521-3344), at the Landmark, 11 Pedder St., Central, also qualifies as being elegant and classy, but the price is considerably higher. Kyoto-style cuisine is featured in the à la carte menu. Then there is the **Supatra's Thai Gourmet** (Tel: 2522-5073) at 50 D'Aguilar St., Central. This is one of the most authentic Thai restaurants in town. The roast duck curry with fresh lychees is a personal recommendation.

When it comes to Western restaurants there are two elegant choices. The **Amigo Restaurant** (Tel: 2577-2202) is housed in a Spanish-style mansion at 79A Wong Nei Chong Rd., Happy Valley. This French restaurant has set meal lunches at acceptable prices, then at night you get the full treatment as you dine upstairs in an intimate timbered setting. Atmosphere is also big at the **Verandah Restaurant** (Tel: 2812-2722) at 109 Repulse Bay Rd., Repulse Bay. Wooden ceiling fans and elaborate candelabra create a spacious period atmosphere that complements the fine food. The desserts are a particular favorite.

Another place out this way is **Stanley's Restaurant** (Tel: 2813-8873) in the main street at Stanley. As expected in this location, the restaurant is very strong on seafood. You can dine inside, on the terrace, or on the rooftop. Another top place for seafood is **Bentley's Seafood Restaurant and Oyster Bar** (Tel: 2868-0881) at 10 Chater Rd., Central. High quality seafood specialties are served in stylish surroundings.

There are a series of theme restaurants that offer atmosphere and good food at reasonable prices. American food lovers will gravitate to **Dan Ryan's Chicago Grill** (Tel: 2845-4600), at 88 Queensway, Central, for barbecued ribs, Maryland crab cakes, and so on, served in an atmosphere of photographs and old prints. An alternative is the **Texas Rib House and Lounge** (Tel: 2566-5560), at Victoria Centre, 15 Watson Rd., North Point, which has an early Texas timbered decor and prime rib, choice steak, and seafood on the menu.

If your need is English food, then the **Gallery and Pier One** (Tel: 2526-3061), with its timber beams, beer kegs, lively music, and dart board, will be the place for you. It is situated in the basement of Jardine House, 1 Connaught Place, Central. The **Mozart Stub'n Restaurant** (Tel: 2522-1763), at 8 Glenealy, Central, has pine panelling, Austrian bric-a-brac, and scrumptious strudels; while the **Prince's Tavern** (Tel: 2523-9352), at 19 Chater Rd., serves Cajun and Creole delights.

Two of my favorite Continental eateries are **Jimmy's Kitchen** (Tel: 2526-5293), at 1 Wyndham St., Central, with its club-style atmosphere and fifty-year history; and the **Houston Restaurant** (Tel: 2577-9110), at 1 Cleveland St., Causeway Bay, with its cozy, candlelit grill-cum-bistro serving such delicacies as garoupa fillet with almonds.

Finally, I should mention the **Revolving 66 Restaurant** (Tel: 2862-6166) on the Hopewell Centre, 183 Queens Rd. East, Wanchai. Seafood and steak dishes are a popular choice in this romantic candlelit venue.

6. Sight-seeing

Hong Kong Island provides a wealth of sight-seeing options that can be enjoyed by everyone. My suggestion is to start with a walking tour of the Central district then work outwards from there. You will be surprised how much you can see in four hours of walking; then, when you get tired, just hop onto some public transport and you will be back where you started in a matter of minutes. First impressions of Hong Kong Island are of a contemporary metropolis, but amid the chrome, concrete, and steel, gems of Colonial period architecture still survive and we pass many of these on the suggested walk.

CENTRAL DISTRICT

This is the business and financial hub of the Territory. It is a glistening collection of mirrored towers, luxury hotels, and designer shops. It is a place of action. Commuters jostle in line for the ferries and hydrofoils that zip across to the Kowloon mainland. Rows of gray, pinstripe suits pour in and out of the offices. You can also see the dockers loading the monstrous moored barges, camera-happy tourists, reckless seaside skateboarders, hustlers, tour guides, touts, pickpockets, policemen, and bar girls. Three tiers of pedestrians bustle around this anthill and crowd the streets, the overhead walkways, and the underground concourses of the smart, efficient Mass Transit Railway. This is where you may decide that Hong Kong has too many people and too little sentiment. On closer inspection, however, you will discover a different aspect: one that has charming reminders of Hong Kong's colonial past, unexpected corners of greenery, and a soul that is still truly Chinese.

A good place to start a walking tour is the **Star Ferry** concourse. Immediately to the east is **City Hall,** which contains a fine concert hall and theater. Alongside City Hall is the pick-up point for a free shuttle bus to the lower terminal of the Peak tram.

A pedestrian underpass leads under Connaught Road to Chater Road, the Cenotaph, and Statue Square. **Statue Square** is named after Sir Thomas Jackson, an early manager of the Hongkong Bank. His statue is one of several that stand in the square. Hong Kong's war dead are remembered at the Cenotaph across the road. Immediately to the east is the handsome late-Victorian style, former supreme court building, now the home of the Legislative Council.

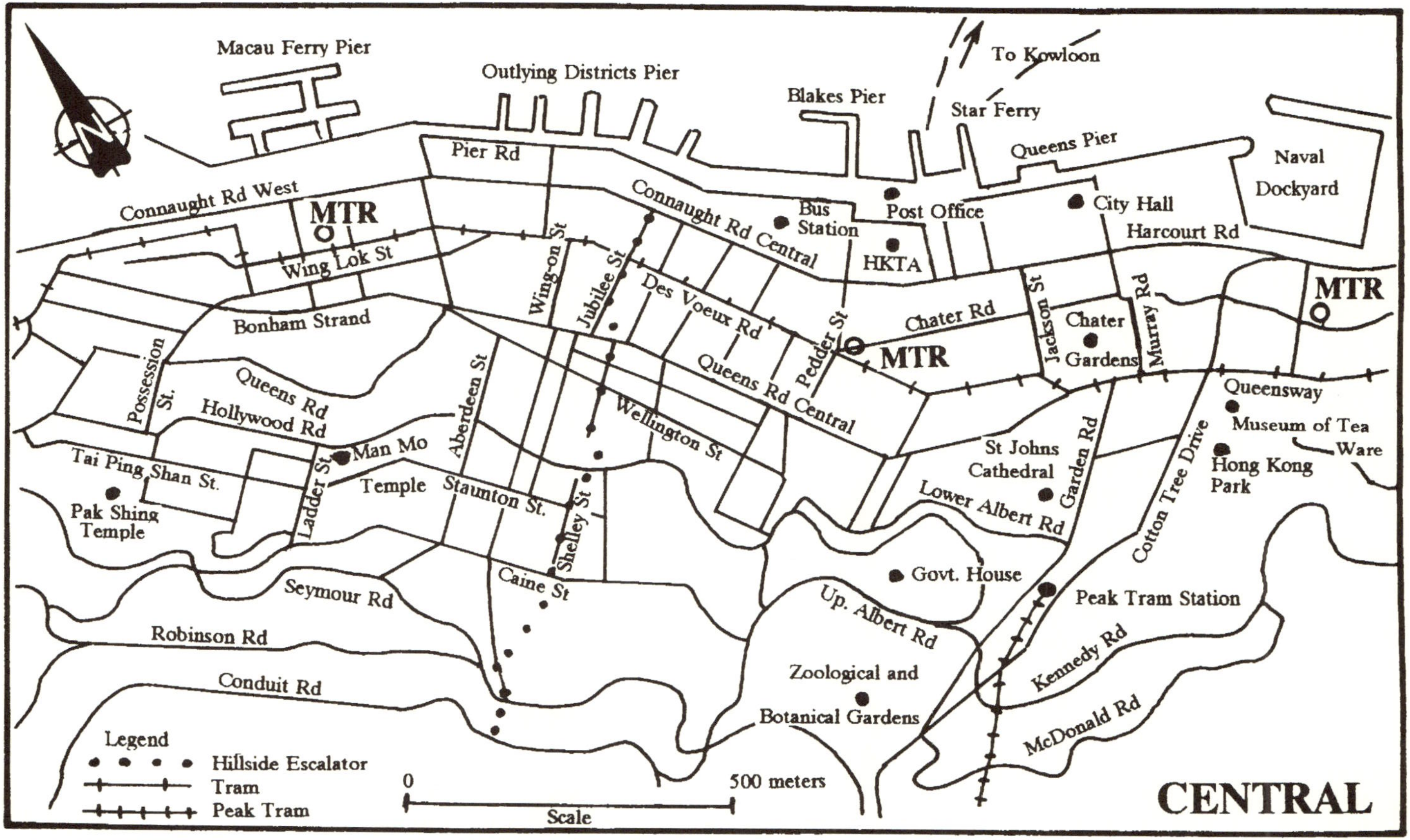
CENTRAL
Macau Ferry Pier
Outlying Districts Pier
Blakes Pier
To Kowloon
Star Ferry
Queens Pier
Naval Dockyard
Pier Rd
Connaught Rd West
MTR
Connaught Rd Central
Bus Station
Post Office
City Hall
Harcourt Rd
HKTA
Wing Lok St
Wing-on St
Jubilee St
Des Voeux Rd
Bonham Strand
Chater Rd
Jackson St
Chater Gardens
Murray Rd
MTR
MTR
Possession St.
Queens Rd
Hollywood Rd
Aberdeen St
Pedder St
Queens Rd Central
Queensway
Museum of Tea Ware
Hong Kong Park
Man Mo Temple
Wellington St
St Johns Cathedral
Garden Rd
Cotton Tree Drive
Tai Ping Shan St.
Ladder St
Staunton St.
Lower Albert Rd
Pak Shing Temple
Shelley St
Govt. House
Caine St
Peak Tram Station
Seymour Rd
Up. Albert Rd
Robinson Rd
Kennedy Rd
Zoological and Botanical Gardens
Conduit Rd
McDonald Rd
Legend
Hillside Escalator
Tram
Peak Tram
0
500 meters
Scale

Hong Kong—A crowded street in the Central district.

    This area is often thronged with people. You would expect to find it quiet on Sunday morning but an 8 A.M. visit will reveal trams flooding the streets with passengers, rickshaw men aggressively trying to solicit business, and Hong Kong's Filipino domestic workers scrambling for the best sitting positions for their day of music and talking. The Legislative Council building is a minor work of Aston Webb—one of the leading European architects of public buildings in the late-nineteenth and early-twentieth centuries. Webb was responsible for such grandiose Victoriana in England as the facade of Buckingham Palace and the Victoria and Albert Museum.

The **Hongkong and Shanghai Bank Building** is a marvelous contrast in style to the buildings across the street. This is very much a building of the late-twentieth century just as the old court is from the nineteenth century. Although the bank does not actively encourage sightseers, they come anyway. Escalators and elevators provide easy access to upper levels.

You can now walk up the stone steps on the other side of the road to Battery Path and **St. John's Cathedral.** The cathedral was inaugurated in 1849 and is probably the oldest Anglican church in the Far East. It was the founding church of the newly created Anglican diocese of Victoria, which at that time also included, with enormous optimism, all of China and Japan. The tower was added in 1852 and the choir in 1872. During the Japanese occupation of Hong Kong, the cathedral was converted into a club and considerable damage was done to the building. Fortunately, it has since been restored. You can get an informative booklet on its history from the Old Hall within the grounds. Here you will also find an elegant red-brick building that was once the French Mission.

Nearby are the **Duddell Street Lamps and Steps,** an obscure but charming antiquity. The steps date from between 1875 and 1889 and feature four original gas lamps in working condition—the only public gas lamps surviving in this part of the world. The local gas company maintains them and lights them nightly as a concession to history.

It is now a short walk to the east to **Hong Kong Park** with its fountains, waterfalls, lakes, and walk-through aviary. The **Museum of Tea Ware** is housed in the city's oldest surviving Colonial-style building, Flagstaff House. It is open daily except Wednesday, and admission is free. This was the former residence of Hong Kong's garrison commanders, and the building now suffers in its ignoble new role.

You now walk past the Peak tram terminal and along Upper Albert Road to the **Zoological and Botanical Gardens.** These were established in 1864 and have all the formal Victorian features you would expect. There is a good aviary section that has a very successful breeding program for species on the verge of extinction. The gardens are a popular spot in the early morning for devotees of *t'ai chi* to practice this ancient form of exercise. There are good views of the 1855 Government House, which is the residence of Hong Kong's Governor.

Close-by is the start of **Hollywood Road,** a well-known street that links Central district with Western district. A short distance along here is a cluster of Victorian buildings that are more than 100 years old. You find the Central Police Station here and also the *L*-shaped cobblestone lane called **Lan Kwai Fong,** which is home to a group of chic restaurants that spring to life once the sun goes down. Later in the evening the trendy, young set congregate in the fashionable discos.

WESTERN DISTRICT

Like a forgotten sleeper in a quiet corner of a well-trampled beach, Western is a historic and now neglected dockside area, dozing gently under a mantle of faded glamour. The farther west you go, the more local color you will find. The shopping malls give way to street markets and alleyways, crammed with bargain clothing and numerous items of unknown use. Western provides visitors who care to look with an incomparably convenient living, natural, outdoor folk museum. It is an unstructured museum, of course. In and around the balconied, pillared shop houses, or up steep and winding lanes, the sights and sounds, the aromas and activity are haphazardly blended. It is best to explore here on foot. You can reach Western by taxi, by MTR to Sheung Wan Station, or by tram.

If you continue your walk along Hollywood Road, you will pass under the **Hillside Escalator,** consisting of twenty moving sidewalks and staircases, which snakes its way up to the prime residential area of the midlevels. You are now entering an area long famous for its many antique and curio shops. These are a brower's paradise—but do not assume that all the prices are bargains. It was at the western end of Hollywood Road that British naval officers first hoisted the British Union Jack in 1841. You will see a sign that reads **"Possession Street"**—this was once the waterfront.

Back on the corner of Ladder Street, you will find the **Man Mo Temple,** named after its two principal deities: Man, the god of literature, and Mo, the god of war. The building dates from the early British years, and the interior is notable for its many brass and pewter incense burners, which waft fragrant smoke spirals towards the ceiling. If you are interested in what the future holds for you, try shaking the "fortune sticks" out of a bamboo cylinder. You can read an English translation of the old sayings on the sticks in a book called "Man Mo Temple" that is on sale here. This is also the area of **Cat Street,** once famous for its seamen's lodging houses, brothels, and hideouts for various criminal activities. Today it serves as a flea market. An adjacent area houses the Cat Street Galleries, a shopping emporium devoted to the sale of antiques and art.

Farther west again in Queens Road West, there are exotic sights, smells, and sounds to satisfy everyone, right there on the street. It is a little world of its own that is to be enjoyed slowly. You will see long-apprenticed herbalists dispensing tonic recipes drawn from 4,000 years of experience. Inside their grandly old-fashioned dispensaries, they dart from one antique stack of drawers to another as they prepare their magic brews from roots, twigs, barks, leaves, flowers, and dried insects.

While it is a little out of the way, the **Fung Pin Shan Museum,** which is housed in the University of Hong Kong, will appeal to some visitors. Its most prized possession is a collection of bronze Nestorian crosses from the Yuan dynasty, about 800 years ago, but there are numerous other objects to be seen. The museum is open daily from 9:30 A.M. until 6 P.M. and admission is free.

As you head back towards the waterfront you will pass **Bonham Strand,** which is known for its snake wholesalers; **Man Wah Lane,** which has some unique souvenirs; and **Wing Sing Street,** which will introduce you to the world of eggs. You pass bubbling cauldrons of cooked meats, beancurd combinations, and deep-fried pasteries, all scenting the air. The local wok-wielding wizards fan their gas-stove flames with bravado as they weave their magic with simple ingredients available to everyone.

WANCHAI

While parts of Western district have not changed in a hundred years, much of Wanchai did not exist twenty years ago. This area has changed faster than perhaps any other part of the entire Territory. Huge reclamation schemes have created new land; and modern shopping malls, revolving restaurants, exhibition and concert halls, and traffic flyovers have appeared in recent years. Fortunately not all of the old has been lost, so there are many reasons for visiting here. It is a hotchpotch district—part office, part commercial, part entertainment, and a baffling jumble of inhabitants from the British Council and the Methodist Church to the Popeye Lounge and the Pussycat Bar. There is a direct ferry service from Kowloon, and the Wanchai MTR station is convenient to most of the area. From Central you can take a tram.

The **Hong Kong Convention and Exhibition Centre** dwarfs everything else in the area. The complex houses two hotels, an office and trade mart, an apartment tower, two huge exhibition halls, a state of the art convention hall, two theaters, and a variety of other facilities. It is currently being enlarged further. The seventh floor provides a great panoramic view of the harbor and Kowloon and this can be reached by public escalators or elevators. Along the promenade outside the Centre, you will find dozens of couples filling every available inch of seating space. Privacy is a rarity in overcrowded Hong Kong and this is probably the most seclusion some lovers will ever get.

Also in the same area, is the **Academy for the Performing Arts,** where there are often public performances in the fine venues. The nearby **Hong Kong Arts Centre** has exhibition galleries and further performing venues. Getting to these areas in so-called "Wanchai North" can be a pedestrian's nightmare. A bewildering network of footpaths and walkways link this area

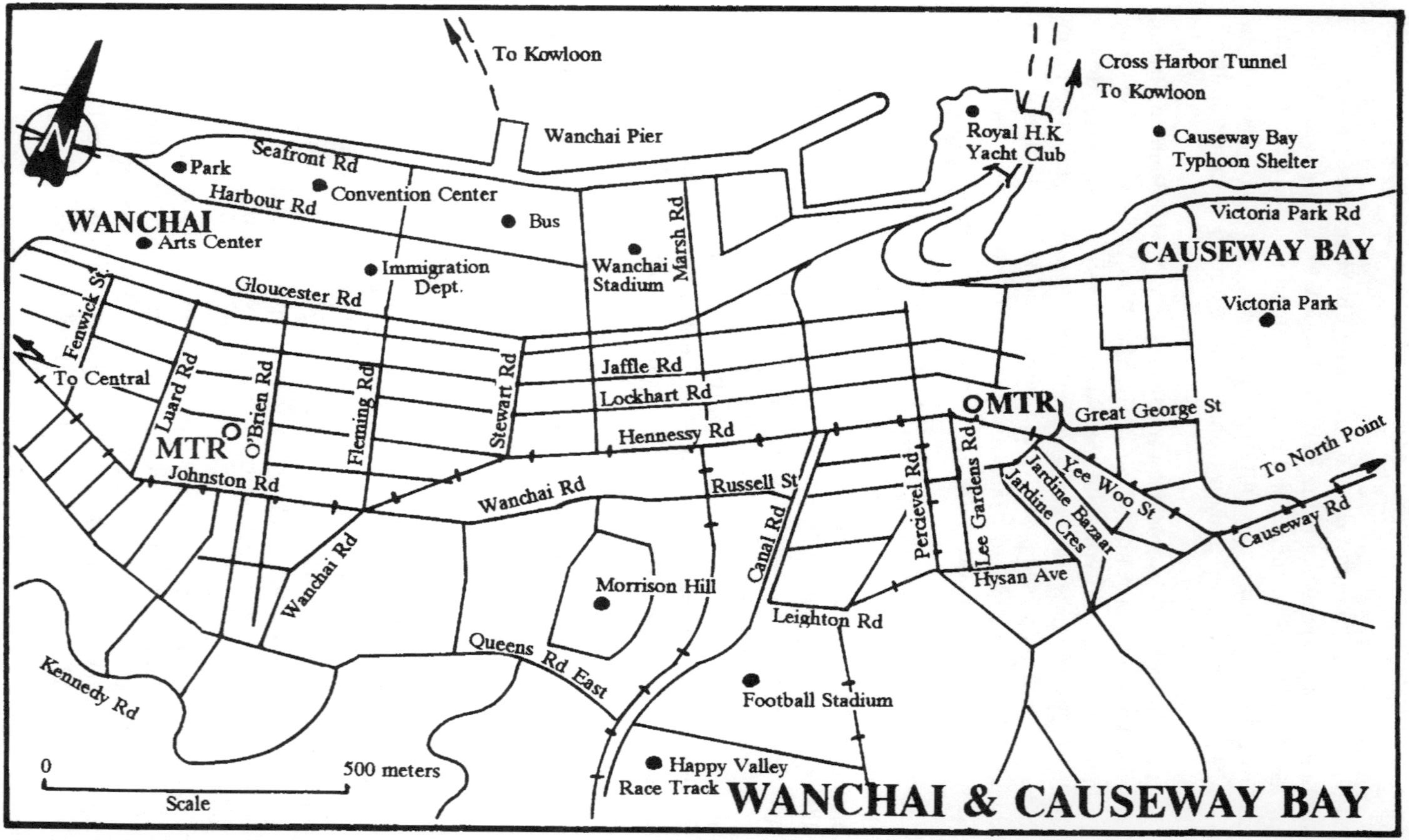
To Kowloon
Cross Harbor Tunnel
To Kowloon
Wanchai Pier
Royal H.K
Yacht Club
Causeway Bay
Typhoon Shelter
Park
Seafront Rd
Convention Center
Harbour Rd
Bus
Victoria Park Rd
WANCHAI
Arts Center
Immigration
Dept.
Wanchai
Stadium
Marsh Rd
CAUSEWAY BAY
Gloucester Rd
Victoria Park
Fenwick St
To Central
Luard Rd
O'Brien Rd
Fleming Rd
Stewart Rd
Jaffle Rd
Lockhart Rd
MTR
Great George St
MTR
Hennessy Rd
To North Point
Johnston Rd
Russell St
Percievel Rd
Lee Gardens Rd
Jardine Bazaar
Jardine Cres
Yee Woo St
Causeway Rd
Wanchai Rd
Canal Rd
Hysan Ave
Wanchai Rd
Morrison Hill
Leighton Rd
Queens Rd East
Kennedy Rd
Football Stadium
0
500 meters
Scale
Happy Valley
Race Track
WANCHAI & CAUSEWAY BAY

with Admiralty MTR station, but it is hit and miss whether you reach your destination by the most direct route.

Queens Road East, which retraces the old waterfront, is known for its fine cabinet makers. You can also visit the **Tai Wong Temple** and maybe have your fortune told. Spring Garden Lane and nearby Wanchai Road are traditional market areas packed with shops and stalls.

CAUSEWAY BAY

Immediately east of Wanchai is Causeway Bay. This is a popular shopping and entertainment area that is best accessed through the Causeway Bay MRT station, tram, or bus from Central. For some reason, virtually every major Japanese retailer has taken a liking to Causeway Bay and has opened a department store here.

Forty years ago, most of Causeway Bay did not exist—it was literally a bay. In 1841, when the British took possession of Hong Kong Island, Causeway Bay only had one significant building. It was a temple perched high on a knoll, facing the sea and the coastal swamplands. To the left, a rocky promontory thrust into the harbor and crookedly pointed to a small offshore island. The British called them **East Point** and **Kellett Island.** Now 155 years later, Causeway Bay is almost totally reclaimed land, East Point and Kellett Island are joined, and the temple lies more than a mile inland.

One of the well-known attractions is the **Noon Day Gun,** which has been fired for many years, each midday. The gun is located in a small garden opposite the Excelsior Hotel. Also popular is **Victoria Park,** which is almost opposite the Park Lane Hotel. There are sporting facilities, a popular aviary, and nice greenery. This is the venue of one of the largest Chinese New Year flower fairs. A pedestrian bridge links the park with the **Causeway Bay Typhoon Shelter.** The waterfront is lined with boats, some occupied by several generations and assorted cats, dogs, and potplants.

Food Street, and the adjacent area, is famous for its many Japanese, Vietnamese, Korean, Taiwanese, and regional Chinese restaurants. Jardine's Bazaar has stalls selling various fashion items, while adjacent Jardine's Crescent has old-fashioned shops selling all sorts of traditional produce and medicinal herbs. There are several temples and the faded **Aw Boon Haw Gardens.** The gardens were built sixty years ago by the philanthropist who became a millionaire through his formula for **Tiger Balm®,** that pungent ointment that has many reputed illness-curing properties. They are open 10 A.M. to 4 P.M. and admission is free.

A little inland is **Happy Valley,** Hong Kong's oldest horseracing course, which was originally established in 1846. Today's sophisticated racetrack can be glimpsed from aboard a tram, or you may wish to visit on a Wednesday evening or weekend afternoon.

VICTORIA PEAK

A visit to the Peak by tram is a must for all Hong Kong visitors. Select a clear day and you will be enthralled by the ride and the panoramic view from the top. As you climb the hill, you will pass by some of the city's most exclusive residential properties.

A convenient free shuttle bus runs between the Star Ferry and the lower tram terminus on Garden Road. At the top, a new Peak Tower is under construction. Located directly opposite the upper tram terminal is the 460-seat Cafe Deco Bar and Grill, faithfully recreating the Art Deco style of the 1920s and 1930s. Nearby is the **Victoria Peak Markets,** specializing in Hong Kong memorabilia. If you feel like walking around the top, Harlech and Lugard roads offer a flat circular route of about one hour in length, while the energetic can reach the highest point by walking up Mount Austin Road. Close to the summit, you can rest in the lovely **Victoria Peak Gardens,** which at one time surrounded the summer residence of the early Hong Kong governors.

You can return to the real world by tram or, for a change, take a double-decker bus to the Central Bus Station at Exchange Square.

ABERDEEN

This housing and factory center on the southside of Hong Kong Island is another area that has been dramatically changed in recent years and the result is not particularly attractive. The area is popular with visitors, however, because of Aberdeen Harbour and the floating restaurants that offer seafood in a novel atmosphere. The harbor can be explored by sampan and you will see hundreds of people who live out their entire lives on boats. Guided tours are available from 9 A.M. until 5 P.M. from the main seawall.

It is not far from here to **Ocean Park,** one of mainland Asia's largest entertainment and leisure centers. The park attracts more than three million visitors a year and offers a dramatic cable car ride; a coral atoll, where the fish gaze at a never-ending stream of people who parade in front of them; a glass-sided wave cove with seals and penguins; a huge aviary; a butterfly house; a sophisticated fun fair; and shows by killer whales, dolphins, and high-divers. The Atoll Reef is currently being extended and enhanced, and a Killer Whale breeding pool and underwater viewing gallery is scheduled to open mid-1996.

You can reach Ocean Park by a special citybus that leaves Admiralty MTR station at half-hourly intervals from 9:30 A.M. each day, or by the No. 6 minibus that leaves the Star Ferry terminal each day except Sunday. The park is open 10 A.M. to 6 P.M. everyday. The current admission price is HK$140.

Adjacent to Ocean Park, and under the same management, is **Water**

Visitors to the Middle Kingdom at Hong Kong's Ocean Park can stroll through 5,000 years of Chinese history. (Courtesy of the Hong Kong Tourist Association)

World, a fun park incorporating every imaginable way of staying wet. The kids will love it. Also adjacent is **Middle Kingdom,** which provides a trip back through 13 Chinese dynasties and 5,000 years, via the medium of living history. This is open 10 A.M. to 6 P.M. daily and admission is HK$140. There are also tours that include lunch.

FARTHER SOUTH

There are several good beaches south from here. Some such as Deep Water Bay are easily accessible while others such as Big Wave Bay are more remote. On weekdays all are quiet but on Sundays they can be crowded. **Repulse Bay** is the most popular of all. This is a popular residential area for expatriates and there are good shopping and restaurant facilities. The beach here is good for lazing or people-watching and the Life Guard Club provides beach patrols. Repulse Bay is reached by bus 6 or 61 from the Exchange Square central terminus. It is worth a trip anytime.

Farther still, you come to **Stanley,** one of Hong Kong's oldest settlements. There is some modern development here but this is still basically a fishing village nestling on the sandbar and cliffsides of Stanley Peninsula. In the past, it was noted for its pirates and smuggling activities but now people visit for the atmosphere and the popular market. Here you will find designer

Repulse Bay Beach is one of Hong Kong's most popular summer attractions. (Courtesy of the Hong Kong Tourist Association)

denim, upmarket T-shirts, mohair sweaters, silk, leatherware, porcelain, and souvenirs. I am told there are still bargains to be found if you persist. To reach here from Central, take bus 6 or 260.

The south side of Hong Kong Island provides a good opportunity to explore some of the country parks that preserve much of the island in its natural state. There are four interconnected parks that provide a 50-kilometer walking trail, but this is not recommended for the casual visitor because some of the sections are very rugged and should only be tackled by well-equipped, experienced hikers. Most of the paths through the parks are very ancient and even a short walk can be worthwhile. All parks have route maps at their entrance points and there are picnic facilities, rain shelters, and barbecue pits. Some have information centers. Further information can be obtained from the Country Parks Division, Agriculture and Fisheries Department, 12/F, 393 Canton Rd., Kowloon; Tel: 2733-2132.

7. Guided Tours

There is a surprising number of tours around Hong Kong. Most are half-day land or water journeys. Some are operated by the Hong Kong Tourist Association and others by private operators. In addition, there are daily one-

HONG KONG ISLAND

day tours to Macau and to mainland China, and also some two- and three-day offerings to these places as well.

In this chapter I cover tours of Hong Kong Island and the harbor. Kowloon tours, New Territories tours, and Outlying Islands tours are covered in their respective chapters.

There are many half-day **Hong Kong Island** tours. They range in price from HK$120 to HK$150 for adults. Routes vary, but most include a visit to Victoria Peak for a panoramic view of the Territory, the Stanley Market, beautiful Repulse Bay, and the waterborne population of the Aberdeen typhoon shelter. Some tours include a trip on the Peak tram. Tours operate both in the morning and the afternoon.

The morning **Ocean Park Tour** costs HK$260-280. It visits one of the world's largest oceanariums and allows you to ride the cable car and the longest covered single escalator in the world. Other attractions include the Wave Cove, Ocean Theater, Atoll Reef Shark Aquarium, and several fun and thrill rides. It is optional to stay behind to explore Middle Kingdom at your own cost in the afternoon.

The **Come Horseracing Tour** operates on Saturday or Sunday afternoons, and Wednesday evenings from September to June. Visitors must be over 18 years old and have arrived in Hong Kong less than 21 days before raceday. The tour visits either Happy Valley or Shatin racecourses. The tour price includes entry to the members' enclosure, transfers, guide service, buffet lunch or dinner, and printed material to help you pick a winner.

The **Discover Stanley** afternoon tour costs HK$155 for adults. A coach is taken through the Eastern Corridor and Aberdeen Tunnel to the Aberdeen typhoon shelter. This is followed by a visit to a jewelry factory and a walk through Stanley Market for bargain shopping.

The **Dim Sum Tour** can be fun. There are morning and afternoon departures on this two-hour tour. You ride an open-top bus from Central to the tram depot, then board an antique tram for a tour past Western, Central, Wanchai, and Causeway Bay. Dim sum and soft drinks are served on the tram.

Harbor cruises start with one-hour morning and afternoon departures for around HK$100. They visit or pass Western anchorage, the Macau ferry wharf, Wanchai, Central, North Point, the airport runway, Tsim Sha Tsui East, and the Causeway Bay typhoon shelter. Beer and soft drinks are included in the price. The two-hour tour (cost: HK$130) goes farther afield. There is a five-hour **Grand Tour** (cost: HK$330) with a morning departure that goes to some of Hong Kong's western islands and Aberdeen. It returns via Sulphur Channel with a Chinese set lunch served on board.

There is a **China Sea Happy Hour Cruise** that departs before sunset and includes unlimited free drinks on board. It lasts for two hours and costs around HK$240. A variation of this is the four-hour **Sunset Cruise** that stops in Aberdeen for one hour for an optional Chinese dinner aboard a floating restaurant. The **Lei Yue Mun Seafood Dinner Cruise** does a similar thing but stops at the Lei Yue Mun fishing village for a meal. You can enjoy a two-hour Western buffet with live music and dancing aboard the *Pearl of the Orient* for HK$300.

Wan Fu Cruises go to Aberdeen, Clearwater Bay, or Repulse Bay with various cruises that include snacks or lunch served on board. There are similar offerings in the evening with either hot and cold hors d'oeuvres or a barbecue dinner.

As well as these, there are various offerings that include land and water travel. One is the **City and Harbour by Night** tour, which takes you to the midlevels of Victoria Peak before you have dinner at a revolving restaurant. This is followed by a visit to one of the open-air markets and a leisurely harbor cruise by junk, with drinks on board. The **Aberdeen and Harbour Cruise** substitutes a seafood dinner on a floating restaurant for the revolving restaurant.

There are whole-day Hong Kong with Lunch Tours (HK$220) and a combined Ocean Park/Middle Kingdom Tour (HK$415). One-day tours are available to Macau by Jetfoil (HK$ 650), to Macau and Zhongshan in China by jetfoil and bus (HK$860), to Shenzhen in China (HK$720), and to Canton (Guangzhou) by ferry, train, or bus (HK$1,050). It is possible to extend the Macau or China tours to two, three, or four days.

8. Culture

Hong Kong is indeed a remarkable marriage of East and West, uniting Western technology competence with the support of an Eastern civilization that dates back thousands of years. You do not have to go looking for evidence of this. You come face to face with it everywhere you go, whether you are carrying out business or enjoying a vacation. Chinese traditions, thoughts, activities, and character are part of almost all Hong Kong actions. You do not visit some tourist show to see what the culture once was; in parts of Hong Kong you live that culture on the streets, in the temples and markets, and even in the ultramodern shopping centers and high-rise apartment blocks.

While living a frantic twentieth-century life, for most people there are still evil spirits to be guarded against, unlucky numbers to be avoided at all costs, and dragons to be accorded due respect.

Major festivals offer excellent opportunities to sample the many deep-rooted Chinese customs and traditions that still affect daily life in Hong Kong. For further information see chapter 3, "The Land, Life, and People of Hong Kong."

Free one-hour **Chinese Cultural Shows** are staged by the Hong Kong Tourist Association every Thursday at Cityplaza, Taikoo Shing (out past North Point and Quarry Bay), and by the New World Centre Management every Friday at New World Centre, in Kowloon. Each show features one cultural performance, such as Chinese instrumental music, puppet theater, acrobats, or martial arts. Local musicians often hold concerts at St. John's Cathedral in Central on Wednesdays at 1:20 P.M. with a light lunch available. Call 2523-4157 for details.

Museums are a way to record and study history and culture, and Hong Kong does this well. These museums on Hong Kong Island are worth visiting if you have an interest in any of the activities that they cover.

The Flagstaff House Museum of Tea Ware, off Cotton Tree Drive, in Hong Kong Park, has tea ware from various dynasties. The building itself, built in 1844, is the oldest Colonial building in Hong Kong.

The Fung Ping Shan Museum, at Hong Kong University, Sai Ying Poon, has bronze and ceramic collections including a display of Nestorian crosses from China.

The Museum of Chinese Historical Relics, in the Causeway Centre, Wanchai, displays short-term exhibitions of both Chinese paintings and handicrafts.

The Law Uk Folk Museum, at 14 Kut Shing St., Chai Wan, is a 200-year-old Hakka village house that has been converted into a furnished period house museum. On display are rural furniture and farm implements.

The Police Museum, on the site of the former Wanchai Gap Police Station, showcases the history of the Royal Hong Kong Police Force from its inception in 1844 up to the present day.

9. Sports

Gambling is the true national sport, whether it is four people locked in conflict around a mahjong table or thousands roaring a horse home at the Happy Valley or Shatin racecourses.

Nevertheless, Hong Kong people are keen on regular sport and fitness. You will see them in the parks early morning going through their *t'ai chi ch'uan* routines. Others are found pounding the pavement in Victoria Park, Causeway Bay, or along Bowen Road between Wanchai and Central, where there are spectacular views of the city and harbor. Then any weekend there are thousands of walkers on the paths of the country parks. In fact, sport in the Territory is growing by leaps and bounds.

Public **tennis courts** are available at several places on Hong Kong Island. You could try Victoria Park, Causeway Bay (Tel: 2570-6186); Bowen Road, Wanchai (Tel: 2528-2983); or the Hong Kong Tennis Center, Wong Nei Chong Gap Road, Happy Valley (Tel: 2574-9122). Squash is not a big sport but there are courts at Victoria Park at around HK$30 an hour (Tel: 2570-6186). Its also worth trying the Hong Kong Squash Centre (Tel: 2521-5072).

Hong Kong has many **beaches** but quite a few are suffering from major pollution. Repulse Bay, where there are lifeguards, showers, and changing facilities, is the most popular beach on the island. Shek O, on the southeast coast, is probably the best easily accessible beach. Waterskiing is popular at some of the beaches. The Deep Water Bay Speedboat Co. (Tel: 2812-0391) rents skis and a boat with driver for around HK$400 an hour. A windsurfing center is situated on Stanley Main Beach (Tel: 2723-6816). Public **swimming pools** are also popular. Try the Victoria Park swimming pool or Water World, a fun park with a variety of pools. Members of yacht clubs with reciprocal privileges should contact the Royal Hong Kong Yacht Club, Causeway Bay (Tel: 2832-2817).

There is a nine-hole **golf course** at Deep Water Bay operated by the Royal Hong Kong Golf Club. It is open to the public Monday to Friday for around HK$250 a round (Tel: 2812-7070).

Horseracing is held at the Royal Hong Kong Jockey Club course at Happy Valley from September to May. The seductive smell of easy money hangs in the air every horse race day. This get-rich-quick city is obsessed with making millions so the promise of quick gambling returns provides an almost irresistible lure. The sumptuously appointed track at Happy Valley and its modern twin at Shatin in the New Territories, with their electronic tote boards, monster live-action television screens, computerized betting, and luxurious boxes are the true temples of Hong Kong, dedicated to the twin deities of cash and chance.

Horseback riding is available through the Jockey Club stables in Pookfulam (Tel: 2550-1359). The best **bowling alleys** are at the South China Athletic Association on Caroline Hill Road, Happy Valley. This is also a good place to learn the martial arts of *t'ai chi ch'uan* and *judo*. Iceskating and roller skating are both available at Cityplaza, Taikoo Shing, Quarry Bay (Tel: 2567-0391).

A major international Rugby Sevens competition is held each year at Easter. For details contact the Hong Kong Rugby Football Union, 4 Watson's Rd., North Point (Tel: 2566-0719). This is held at the ultramodern, 48,000-seat Hong Kong Stadium.

Details of major sporting events can be obtained from the Sporting Promotion Program, Queen Elizabeth Stadium, 18 Oi Kwan Rd., Wanchai (Tel: 2557-6793).

10. Shopping

Seven million visitors go to Hong Kong each year and, for most of them, shopping is high on their list of priorities. Some arrive with little more than the clothes they are wearing, but they leave weighed down with excess baggage. Hong Kong Island fosters the sin of greed and no matter where you are, temptation is only a few steps away. Only God knows how many people have gone bankrupt saving money by shopping in Hong Kong.

The Territory has long been famous for its shopping facilities, variety, efficient service, and price. There are designer boutiques, department stores, huge shopping complexes, factory outlets, sidestreet specialty shops and stalls, and open-air street markets. Most shops are open seven days a week, except during the Lunar New Year holidays. In Central, the normal trading hours are 10 A.M. to 6 P.M. and at Causeway Bay and Wanchai, hours are 10 A.M. to 9:30 P.M.

There are some obvious things to do when shopping in Hong Kong but it is surprising how many visitors forget them in the excitement. *Don't you do the same!* Remember to shop around and compare prices before making a major purchase. Bargaining is expected in all outlets except department stores and a few fixed-price shops. There are no hard and fast rules for how much you can get off a price, but 20 percent is possible off jewelry and clothing, and between 5 and 10 percent on electronic goods when you buy in regular shops. I have bargained for 50 percent off at some markets and I have still probably paid far too much. The secret is in knowing what the price should be. You can gauge this by seriously bargaining in one shop without actually buying, or you can check prices at home before you leave for Hong Kong.

As a general rule, goods sold in Hong Kong are not refundable unless they are faulty. Because of this, it is wise to consider making major purchases at shops that are members of the Hong Kong Tourist Association. These have a red junk logo on the window. The Association cannot vouch for every member, but it is prepared to put a certain amount of pressure on the retailer if there is a dispute. It is nice to have someone on your side. If this does no good, you should contact the Consumer Council (Tel: 2736-3322) with the complaint.

Both cash and credit cards are widely accepted in Hong Kong. Personal checks are usually not accepted. You may find that the price in shops is a few percent higher when you pay with a credit card.

For goods such as cameras, electronic equipment, and watches, make sure you get a worldwide guarantee that carries the name of the Hong Kong sole agent. Some shops will try to give you a guarantee that is only valid in Hong Kong or at that particular shop. The guarantee should have a complete description of the item including the model and serial number, the date of purchase, the name and address of the store, and the store's official stamp. Remember to ask for a detailed itemized receipt that includes a

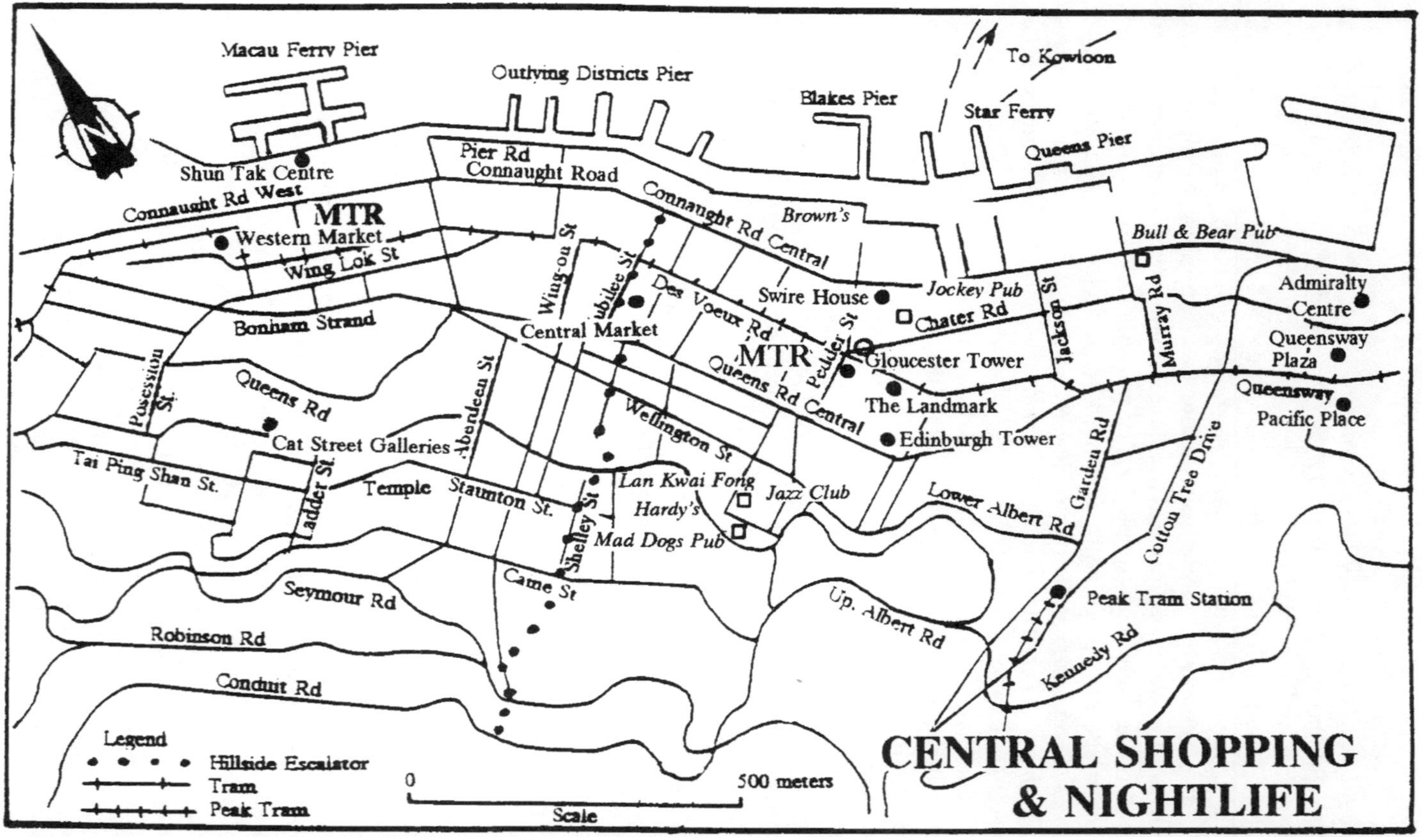
CENTRAL SHOPPING
& NIGHTLIFE
Macau Ferry Pier
Outlying Districts Pier
Blakes Pier
To Kowloon
Star Ferry
Queens Pier
Shun Tak Centre
Pier Rd
Connaught Road
Connaught Rd West
MTR
Western Market
Wing Lok St
Connaught Rd Central
Brown's
Bull & Bear Pub
Wing-on St
Jubilee St
Des Voeux Rd
Swire House
Jockey Pub
Chater Rd
Jackson St
Murray Rd
Admiralty Centre
Queensway Plaza
Queensway
Pacific Place
Bonham Strand
Central Market
MTR
Pedder St
Gloucester Tower
The Landmark
Edinburgh Tower
Queens Rd Central
Possession St.
Queens Rd
Aberdeen St
Wellington St
Cat Street Galleries
Tai Ping Shan St.
Ladder St
Temple
Staunton St.
Shelley St
Lan Kwai Fong
Jazz Club
Hardy's
Mad Dogs Pub
Lower Albert Rd
Garden Rd
Cotton Tree Drive
Caine St
Seymour Rd
Up. Albert Rd
Peak Tram Station
Kennedy Rd
Robinson Rd
Conduit Rd
Legend
Hillside Escalator
Tram
Peak Tram
0
500 meters
Scale

description of the goods purchased. If you are shipping things home, it is advisable to take out an extra "all-risks" insurance policy to cover damage in transit because most stores will only insure against loss.

DEPARTMENT STORES

These cover the range from expensive to reasonable. At sale time, you can pick up some real bargains. **Lane Crawford** was the original store and it is still going strong. It is stylish and upmarket. There are outlets at 70 Queens Rd., Central (Tel: 2526-6121); The Mall, Pacific Place, Central (Tel: 2845-1838); and Windsor House, 311 Gloucester Rd., Causeway Bay. A bit downmarket from here is **Marks and Spencer (UK),** the well-known British store. This has outlets at Cityplaza, King's Road, Quarry Bay (Tel: 2567-2102); Excelsior Plaza, Causeway Bay (Tel: 2577-8318); The Mall, Pacific Place; and The Landmark, Pedder Street, Central.

There are several locally controlled stores that have a mixture of local, Chinese, and Western goods at attractive prices. **Wing On** has two outlets at 211 and 26 Des Voeux Rd., Central (Tel: 2852-1888); and another at Cityplaza, Quarry Bay (Tel: 2885-7588). **Dragon Seed** is at 39 Queens Rd., Central (Tel: 2524-2016); and **Sincere** is at 173 Des Voeux Rd., Central (Tel: 2544-2688).

Then there are the big Japanese department stores. **Daimaru** is at Great George Street, Causeway Bay (Tel: 2576-7321). **Matsuzakaya** is in the Hang Lung Centre, Paterson Street, Causeway Bay (Tel: 2890-6622); and at Queensway Plaza, 93 Queensway, Central. **Isetan** is in the Aberdeen Centre, 6 Nam Ning St., Aberdeen (Tel: 2814-7406). **Sogo** is in the East Point Centre, 555 Hennessy Rd., Causeway Bay (Tel: 2833-8338).

SHOPPING MALLS

The most fashionable center is **The Mall** at Pacific Place, 88 Queensway, Admiralty. This 800,000-square-foot complex has hundreds of shops and several department stores on three levels. Attached to it are three major hotels, numerous restaurants, and a food court so you can spend all day brousing around. Prices are not cheap. Pacific Place is connected by a footbridge to other shopping centers such as Queensway Plaza, United Centre, and Admiralty Centre to give almost unlimited shopping opportunities.

The Landmark on Des Voeux Road, Central, is similar. There are fountains, chrome, glass, escalators, boutiques, a department store, art galleries, and high prices. Hong Kong people flock there. Not far away is Swire House and Worldwide Plaza.

Out at Causeway Bay there are several major centers. The **Excelsior Centre** in Paterson Street is one of the best known. Also in this street there are the **Island Shopping Centre,** the **Hang Lung Centre,** and the **Paterson Plaza;**

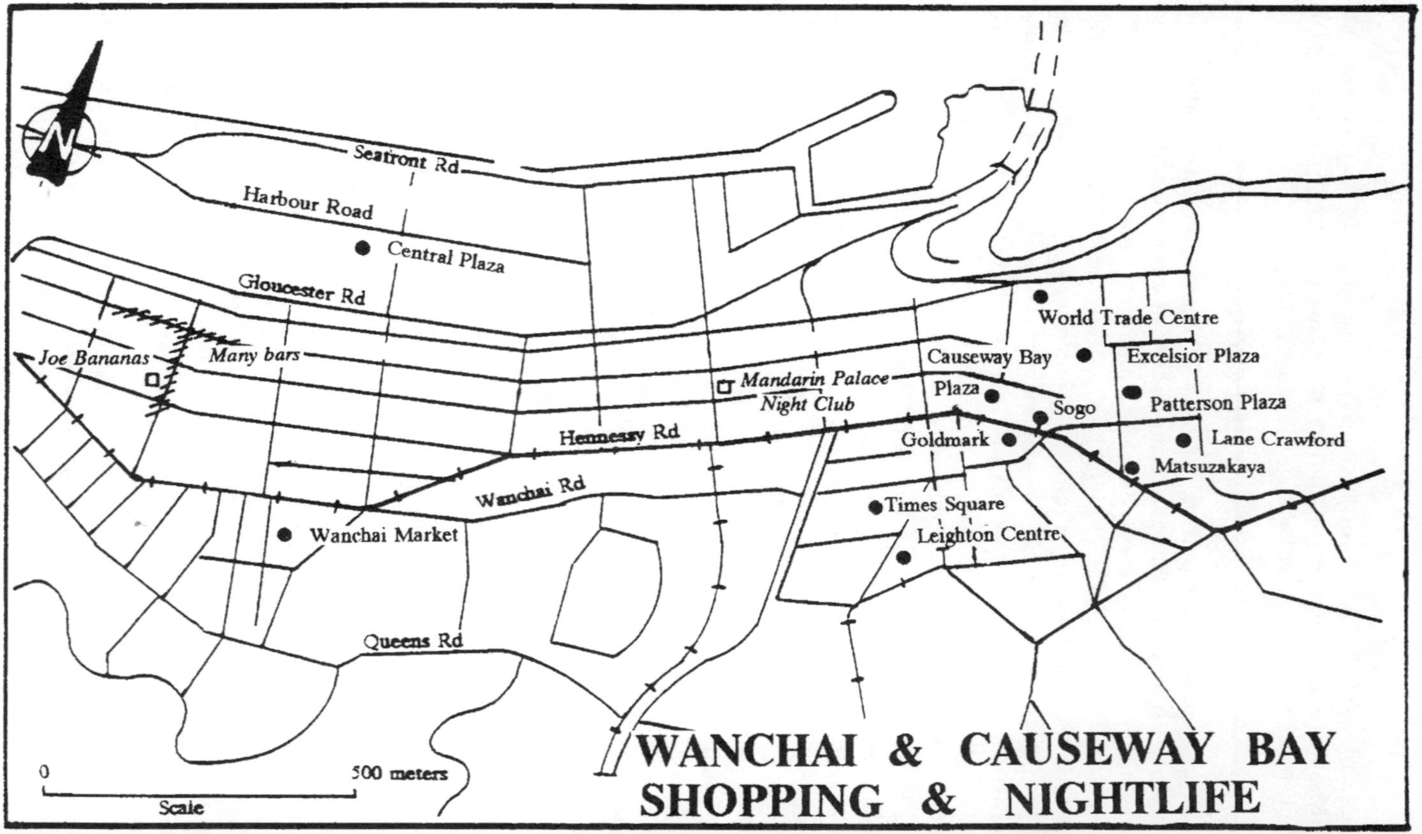
N
Seafront Rd
Harbour Road
Central Plaza
Gloucester Rd
Joe Bananas
Many bars
Mandarin Palace
Night Club
Hennessy Rd
Wanchai Rd
Wanchai Market
Queens Rd
World Trade Centre
Causeway Bay
Plaza
Excelsior Plaza
Patterson Plaza
Sogo
Goldmark
Lane Crawford
Matsuzakaya
Times Square
Leighton Centre
0
500 meters
Scale
WANCHAI & CAUSEWAY BAY
SHOPPING & NIGHTLIFE

while around the corner in Hennessy Road there are the Sogo store, the **Goldmark Centre** and the **Causeway Bay Plaza.** The newest attraction is **Times Square,** which is built on the site of the former tramways depot. The complex incorporates more than a million square feet of commercial space and it offers a 14-story retail podium and a 6-level basement, 4 cinemas, and 17 restaurants. The shopping atrium boasts the first spiral escalators in Hong Kong and the largest video wall in the Territory.

The huge new **Cityplaza Center** opened a couple of years ago on Tai Koo Shing Road, Quarry Bay. This has rapidly developed into a very popular place for both locals and visitors. There are fashions for all the family, department stores, restaurants and entertainment, and attractive prices.

INTERESTING SHOPPING AREAS

Apart from the modern centers, Hong Kong Island has some other areas that you should not miss if you want to catch a bargain or find something different. Here are a few suggestions:

Li Yuen Street East and West, in Central, have stalls with everything from dress fabrics and leather accessories to sweaters and children's wear. You can also pick up some fake brand fashion but be aware that these have been manufactured illegally and should not be patronized. Opening hours are usually from 10 A.M. to 7 P.M.

Cat Street, off Hollywood Road in Central, was once notorious for its women and criminals, but now it is a flea market offering inexpensive trinkets and bric-a-brac. The surrounding area, however, is the antique area of the city and you will find traditional furniture, wall scrolls, paintings, and more at prices that reach from inexpensive to amazing.

Wanchai is a good place for street markets. In the area between Wanchai Road and Spring Garden Lane, you will find locally made designer jeans, children's wear, and a variety of other things. In Queens Road East there are many outlets for rattan and rosewood furniture.

Farther out at Causeway Bay, **Jardine's Bazaar,** which runs from Yee Woo Street, is good for ladies' and children's wear, cosmetics, and accessories. Farther down the street, you will find flower stalls and a fruit and vegetable section. The best time to visit is between 11 A.M. and 6:30 P.M.

A final favorite is **Stanley Market** on the south side of the island. This is well known for sports and casual wear but there is also a good range of linen, tablewear, silk, and leather goods. It is a nice trip in the bus. Opening hours are 10 A.M. to 7 P.M.

BEST BUYS

Liquor, perfume, and tobacco are about the only things that attract a duty in Hong Kong so most merchandise is potentially at good prices.

Antiques, cameras, clothing, computers, cosmetics, electrical equipment, furs, jewelry, jade, leather goods, optical goods, toys, and watches are all popular buys.

Antiques and Asian Handicrafts can be purchased in all the main shopping areas. There are original and reproduction Qing and Ming dynasty furniture, prints, scrolls, statues, and other items. You can buy puppets from Indonesia or Myanmar, embroidery from the Philippines, and porcelain from Thailand.

Chinese handicrafts are found in the Chinese product department stores. You could also try: Chinese Arts & Crafts in Shell House, Central (Tel: 2522-3621); at 26 Harbour Rd., Wanchai, and Pacific Place.

Hobbs & Bishops Fine Art at 81 Hollywood Rd. (Tel: 2548-0632).

Amazing Grace Elephant Co. in the Excelsior Centre, Causeway Bay (Tel: 2890-2776), and at Cityplaza, Quarry Bay.

Tong's Sheets and Linen Co. in the main street Stanley (Tel: 2813-8326).

Cameras and Photographic Equipment. Unless you are absolutely certain about what you want, it is a good idea to contact one of the sole agents in Hong Kong to get information on the latest models and prices. I have quickly looked at equipment from time to time and come away totally confused because the range and models have been different from what I looked at back home. With video cameras, it is important to select a camera that is compatible with the broadcasting system in your home country. Here are some of the agents:

Canon—Jardine Consumer Electronics. Tel: 2529-7921.
Fuji—Fuji Photo Products Co. Tel: 2406-3226.
Hanimex—Hanimex Vivatar HK. Tel: 2363-6313.
Kodak—Kodak Far East Limited. Tel: 564-93333.
Minolta—Minolta HK, Ltd. Tel: 2565-8181.
Nikon—Shriro (HK), Ltd. Tel: 2524-5031.
Olympus—Kingstone Development Co. Tel: 2730-5663.
Pentax—Jebson & Co., Ltd. Tel: 2873-7923.

Don't forget to check the serial numbers against the guarantee and unpack and check all the parts before you leave the shop.

Computers and Software can be excellent buys but again it is worthwhile checking with the sole agents. Here are some of them:

Apple—Gilman Business System. Tel: 2893-0303.
AST & Canon—Jardine Office Systems. Tel: 2565-2011.
Digital—Digital Equipment HK, Ltd. Tel: 2805-3111.
IBM—IBM China/HK Corporation. Tel: 2825-6222.

My experience with retail outlets is very limited but the HKTA recommends Continental Computer Systems at 199 Des Voeux Rd., Central (Tel:

2854-2233); and Master Technology in Cityplaza, Quarry Bay (Tel: 2886-3678).

Furs. Hong Kong is the world's largest exporter of fur garments and prices for top quality garments are said to be as much as 50 percent lower than in the United States. The most popular buys are ranch-bred mink and fox that come mainly from the United States and Scandinavia. They are available in a wide range of colors and you should look at the fur in daylight as this will have a different color than when seen under florescent light. Two popular outlets are Camay Fur Company in the Landmark, 12 Des Voeux Rd. (Tel: 2523-5279), and Broadway Fur Company at 12 Pedder St., Central (Tel: 2810-0388).

Clothing. Hong Kong designers have received international recognition in recent years so now these join the "world" names in boutiques and designer-label shops. The leading designer shops are found in the smarter malls, while chain boutiques cater to the younger and less wealthy by putting the emphasis on rapid turnover. The majority of the factory outlets sell clothes originally destined for the export market, so there are plenty of Western sizes available. This brings its own problem, however, because the labeled size will vary depending on where the export market was to be. Ladies dress sizes for an "average" size vary as follows; U.S.A. 8, U.K. 10, Japan 11, Australia 12, Germany 36, France 38, Italy 42. That's rather confusing. Even shoe sizes vary. An American 7 is the same as a British 5.5 and a European 39. Note that many of the factory outlets and chain shops have no changing facilities. Here are a few designer boutiques for ladies' wear:

Boutique Christine Dior—2 Ice House St., Central. Tel: 2537-1079.
Chanel Boutique—3 Des Voeux Rd., Central. Tel: 2810-0978.
Hermes Boutique—The Galleria, 9 Queens Rd. Tel: 2525-5900.
Joyce Boutique—The Landmark, Des Voeux Road. Tel: 2523-5236.
Laura Ashley—Prince's Bld., Des Voeux Road. Tel: 2524-5041.

These are popular factory outlets:

The Silkware House—12 Pedder St. Tel: 2877-2373.
—Paterson Plaza, Causeway Bay.
GAT Design, Ltd.—8 Lan Kwai Fong, Central. Tel: 2524-9896.
Vigo Fashion Co.—458 Hennessy Rd., Causeway Bay. Tel: 2574-9729.

These are exclusively for men:

Alfred Dunhill—Chater Road, Central. Tel: 2524-3663.
—The Mall, Pacific Place. Tel: 2848-9475.
Gentleman Givenchy—The Landmark, Pedder St. Tel: 2525-7586.
Hugo—The Landmark, Pedder Street. Tel: 2877-8357.
—Cityplaza, 1111 King's Rd., Quarry Bay. Tel: 2885-3440.
The Swank Shop—The Mall, Pacific Place. Tel: 2845-4929.

Cosmetics and Perfumes. Since they are tax-free, you will probably find it is worth your while to pick up your favorite brand. Department stores, pharmacies, boutiques, and specialty shops all stock many of the brand names. If you need to contact the importer, here are a few popular names:

Chanel—New Asia Import and Export. Tel: 2526-6461.
Christian Dior—Perfumes Christian Dior. Tel: 2837-3382.
Givenchy—Hagemeyer (HK), Ltd. Tel: 2563-6221.
Guerlain—Guerlain (Asia Pacific), Ltd. Tel: 2524-6129.
Guy Laroche, & Lacome—Scental, Ltd. Tel: 2828-1300.
Hermes—Siber Hegner Marketing. Tel: 2529-9110.
Nina Ricci—Nina Ricci (FE), Ltd. Tel: 2735-6303.

Men's Tailoring. Forget the 24-hour suit if you want to be proud of the finished product. Most reliable tailors will wish to take three days and have at least two fittings. Custom tailoring still offers good value for the money compared to many other countries and some of the results are excellent. Remember though, that you generally get what you pay for. Some of the best tailors are in the major hotels, and as you would expect, their charges and standards are in line with this location. Most tailors request a nonrefundable 50 percent deposit. Kwun Kee Tailor has the biggest operation in Hong Kong with outlets at Queensway Plaza (Tel: 2527-2530), 128 Queens Rd., 28 Yun Ping Rd., Causeway Bay; Cityplaza, Quarry Bay; and several other locations in Causeway Bay and Wanchai.

Jewelry is a priority purchase for many people. Hong Kong is the world's third-largest diamond trading center and imported gem stones from all over the world are available either set or loose. Prices vary enormously according to design, workmanship, the amount of precious metal used, and the number and quality of the gemstones. Location plays some part in this, too. Under Hong Kong law, gold and platinum jewelry must be marked with the accurate content. You should always obtain a receipt that states this and the number and weight of the stones. There are more jewelry shops in Hong Kong per square meter than any other city in the world, so you have an amazing choice of outlets. I do not make any recommendations.

Leather Goods. Items from around the world are available, but of special interest are the goods made in Hong Kong and China. An excellent source of quality leather is the factory outlets, many of which stock designer labels at good prices. Some of the more exclusive outlets are:

Louis Vuitton—The Landmark, Des Voeux Road. Tel: 2523-2915.
    —The Repulse Shopping Arcade. Tel: 2812-7780.
Great Wall Leather—14 Lyndhurst Terrace, Central. Tel: 2815-0126.
Jamson Luggage—10 Chater Rd., Central. Tel: 2523-7901.
a.testoni—The Landmark, Des Vouex Road. Tel: 2523-8303.

Millie's Co., Ltd.—24 Lan Fong Rd., Causeway Bay. Tel: 2890-6606.

Optical Goods. Take your lens prescription to Hong Kong and get some new glasses at almost unbeatable prices. Single lenses will take only a day to make. Prescription lens sunglasses and contact lenses are also available. There are many places from which to select. The Optical Shop chain of stores in the Landmark, The Mall at Pacific Place, Cityplaza, and many other locations is by far the largest chain.

Watches. You can pay almost whatever you want for a timepiece in Hong Kong. All the world's best brands are available, but there are cheaper varieties as well. At the markets, you will often be offered fake watches at very low prices. If you want to buy an expensive watch, it is best to go to an authorized dealer of the brand you seek. The relevant sole agent will advise you on this. Here are some of the better known names:

Baume & Mercier, and Piaget—PBM (HK), Ltd. Tel: 2522-0139.
Cartier—Les Must de Cartier (Far East), Ltd. Tel: 2532-0333.
Citizen—Sun International Trading Co., Ltd. Tel: 2722-6868.
Longines, and Swatch—SMH (HK), Ltd. Tel: 2510-5100.
Omega, and Tissot—Omtis, Ltd. Tel: 2527-7622.
Rolex—Rolex (HK), Ltd. Tel: 2525-6156.
Seiko—Thong Sia Co., Ltd. Tel: 2730-2081.

11. Entertainment and Nightlife

If your ideas of Hong Kong nightlife are still colored by images of "Suzie Wong," you will be in for a shock. Sure the daughters of Suzie Wong can still be found, but these days the nighttime scene is much wider and far more expensive than those old days, with one exception. One of the greatest spectacles in Hong Kong is the transition from day to night—and it is still free. Stand on the waterfront, find a vantage point on Victoria Peak or take an elevator to the top of one of Hong Kong's many skyscrapers, and you will get a mind-blowing experience.

Tropical dusk does not linger. Darkness falls like a shutter, and soon the sun is locked away again for another twelve hours. The night emerges with its hundred smells, thousand sounds, and billion lights. Small wonder that the human beings who dominate every part of the day fade to pale at night. Hong Kong shimmers with high-intensity excitement as a million lights bounce off hard surfaces, multiplied by water, reflective glass, and thousands of diamonds worn around silken, smooth necks. There is an excitement, intensified by an urgency caused by the knowledge that people, politics, and lifestyles will be different tomorrow.

Other activities are far from free. Many of Hong Kong's hotels offer a range of drinking, listening, and dancing options. You can choose between small, elegant club-style bars, more lively lounges with a band and vocalist, or trendy discotheques that are the latest in sophisticated technology. Some of the small bars are excellent and they are not necessarily expensive. Some of the best in the first category are the **Noon Gun Bar** at the Excelsior Hotel, Causeway Bay (Tel: 2894-8888), where the resident piano player welcomes requests; **Dickens Bar** in the same hotel, where there is often jazz on a weekend; the clubby, tiny **Chinnery** or the **Harlequin Bar** at the Mandarin Oriental hotel (Tel: 2522-0111); and the **Lobby Lounge Bar** at the J. W. Marriott Hotel, where a pianist combines with immense picture windows to set an appealing scene.

The lounge/band/dance scene is everywhere. Some of my favorites are the nautical **Admiral's Bar** at the City Garden Hotel, North Point (Tel: 2887-2888); the **Gallery Bar and Lounge** with its large show band featuring music from the sixties to the present at Park Lane, Causeway Bay (Tel: 2890-3355); **Interlude** at the Hotel Victoria (Tel: 2540-7228), where you can mix conversation with music; the **Clipper Lounge** with its soothing music at the Mandarin Oriental, Central (Tel: 2522-0111); and the **Lau Ling Bar** at the Hotel Furama Kempinski, Central (Tel: 2525-5111). **JJ's**, at the Grand Hyatt (Tel: 2588-1234), is an entertainment center all rolled into one place. The disco can be very popular. So too can **Oasis** at the New World Harbour View Hotel, Wanchai (Tel: 2802-8888).

Outside the hotels, the scene is even more varied. There are three excellent pubs that have all the atmosphere that you could possibly want. The Tudor-style **Bull and Bear**, at 10 Harcourt Rd., Central (Tel: 2525-7896), was one of the first in Hong Kong but it is still going strong. **Mad Dogs**, at 33 Wyndham St., Central, has a particularly lively, and at times very noisy, atmosphere, and there is British football on Saturdays. **The Jockey**, at 11 Chater Rd., Central (Tel: 2526-1478), has a more refined Edwardian atmosphere of red velvet, etched glass, and timber.

The disco scene is alive and well. The Lan Kwai Fong area below the Botanic Gardens is one of the most popular spots. Here you will find such places as **Club 1997** at 8 Lan Kwai Fong, Central (Tel: 2810-9333). This is part of a complex that has a 24-hour cafe, a Middle East-style restaurant, and the disco. Club 1997 is open from 11 P.M. until 5 A.M. with a cover charge. At number 24 you will find the **California** (Tel: 2521-1345), a trendy restaurant that turns into a vibrant disco bar late in the evening. **DD 11** is just around the corner at 38 D'Aguilar St., Central (Tel: 2524-8809). It has been popular for a decade and is going as strong as ever. It opens from 9:30 P.M. until 4 A.M. and is a good place to see the latest fashion scene. Out at Wanchai, **Joe Bananas**, at 23 Luard Rd. (Tel: 2529-1811), is another cafe that has a nighttime party atmosphere helped along by a resident deejay.

There are several more places worth visiting. **Brown's** at Exchange

Square, Central (Tel: 2523-7003), is the best wine bar in the city. **The Champagne Bar** at the Grand Hyatt (Tel: 2588-1234) is an intimate, very upmarket corner with the most extensive champagne list in Hong Kong. **Lord Stanley's Bistro and Bar** at 92A Main St., Stanley, combines the atmosphere of a British pub and a European bistro so you can have a full meal or just drop in for a drink. The **Supernova Karaoke Club** at the China Harbour View Hotel (Tel: 2838-2222) is currently one of the best places for this craze. **The Jazz Club** in D'Aguilar Street, Central (Tel: 2845-8477), has a house band and the occasional visiting international act. It is well worth while checking out. Close-by at number 35, **Hardy's** (Tel: 2522-4448) has live folk music nightly.

Bars with girls are an expensive "con" in Hong Kong. There is neither the excitement nor fun of a Bangkok or Manila bar and the cost can be horrific. If you would like to see what remains of the "Suzie Wong" scene, you can safely walk through the former redlight district of Wanchai. There are still some bars there but I find they have little appeal. The same can be said for the Chinese hostess clubs that exist in Wanchai. You need to be a big spender to enjoy this atmosphere of nonstop music, amazing decor, cute hostesses who will talk and dance with you for a price, and sky-high drink prices. Budget HK$500-1,000 if you want to investigate this scene. Places to try are the **New Tonnochy Night Club** at 1 Tonnochy Rd. (Tel: 2575-4376); the **Mandarin Palace Night Club** at 24 Marsh Rd. (Tel: 2575-6551); and **Club Celebrity** at 175 Lockart Rd. (Tel: 2575-7161).

There are several cinemas showing English language films. The UA Queensway at Pacific Place, Admiralty (Tel: 2869-0322); Columbia Classics at 23 Harbour Rd., Wanchai (Tel: 2827-8291); and the Palace at 280 Gloucester Rd., Causeway Bay (Tel: 2895-1500) are three good complexes that you could try. You should also check the entertainment pages of the newspapers.

Other nighttime offerings of a different kind can be found in the concert halls and theaters. Try the following for information on what is currently available;

The Fringe Club—the name says it all. Tel: 2521-7251.
City Hall Concert Hall and Theatre—Tel: 2522-9928.
Hong Kong Academy for Performing Arts—Tel: 2584-1500.
Hong Kong Arts Centre Booking Office—Tel: 2582-0230.

12. The Hong Kong Island Address List

Airlines—Cathay Pacific, Swire House
        Reservations   Tel: 2747-1888
        Flight Information   Tel: 2745-1234

         —Dragonair
            Reservations   Tel: 2590-1188
            Flight Information   Tel: 2769-7728
Ambulance—St. John's   Tel: 2576-6555
Churches—St. John's Anglican Cathedral, 4 Garden Rd.   Tel: 2523-4157
         —St. Joseph's Roman Catholic, 37 Garden Rd.   Tel: 2522-3992
         —Methodist, 271 Queens Rd. East, Wanchai   Tel: 2575-7817
         —Union, 22A Kennedy Rd.   Tel: 2523-7247
         —Jewish Synagogue, 70 Robinson Rd.   Tel: 2801-5440
Consulates—Australia   Tel: 2827-8881
         —Canada   Tel: 2810-4321
         —Germany   Tel: 2529-8855
         —Japan   Tel: 2522-1184
         —Malaysia   Tel: 2527-0921
         —New Zealand   Tel: 2525-5044
         —Singapore   Tel: 2527-2212
         —United States   Tel: 2523-9011
Credit Cards—American Express
            Hotline   Tel: 2885-9366
            Global Assistance   Tel: 2528-3476
Emergency (Police, fire, ambulance)   Tel: 999
Hong Kong Tourist Assoc.—General Information   Tel: 2801-7177
                        —Shopping advice   Tel: 2801-7278
Hospitals—Queen Mary, Pokfulam Road   Tel: 2819-2111
         —Queen Elizabeth, Wylie Road   Tel: 2710-2111
         —Adventist, 40 Stubbs Rd., Happy Valley   Tel: 2574-6211
Immigration—7 Gloucester Rd.   Tel: 2824-6111
Police—Crime hotline & taxi complaints   Tel: 2527-7177
Post Office—Next to Star Ferry Terminal   Tel: 2523-1071
Public Transport—China Motor Bus   Tel: 2565-8556
                —Citybus   Tel: 2873-0818
                —Hong Kong Ferry Co.   Tel: 2542-3082
                —Hong Kong Tramways   Tel: 2559-8918
                —Mass Transit Railway   Tel: 2750-0170
                —Peak Tramways Co.   Tel: 2522-0922
                —Star Ferry Co.   Tel: 2366-2576
Samaritans—A friend in need.   Tel: 2834-3333
Telephone Information—   Tel: 1081
Typhoon Information—   Tel: 2835-1473

5

Kowloon

1. The General Picture

Kowloon was a barren wasteland when Governor Nathan first proposed development here in 1904. Now it is seen by many as the shopping mecca of Asia. Kowloon is a small, 12-square-kilometer area of intense development at the southern end of a mainland peninsula that juts out towards Hong Kong Island. The southern end is known as Tsim Sha Tsui and the northern extreme is Boundary Street. North of here is an area known as New Kowloon that is actually part of the New Territories but is commonly thought of as Kowloon because it is indistinguishable from the real thing.

Kowloon has the widest and best selection of shops, hotels, and restaurants in Hong Kong. It has very few historic points of interest but there are several cultural attractions, including a science museum, a space museum, a history museum, and a cultural center smack on the waterfront where you can view one of the world's most important collections of Chinese art, calligraphy, and ceramics. There are several temples, a mosque, some churches, and some of the best day and night markets in the city. Some areas are also depressingly crowded with apartment blocks festooned with acres of washing.

This part of Hong Kong has excellent transport facilities. It is linked to Hong Kong Island by the Star Ferry, by the Cross Harbour Tunnel, and by the Mass Transit Railway. Kowloon also contains the southern terminal of the KCR railway that links Hong Kong to China and it has the major ferry terminal for trips to Canton (Guangzhou). Some ferries to Macau also leave

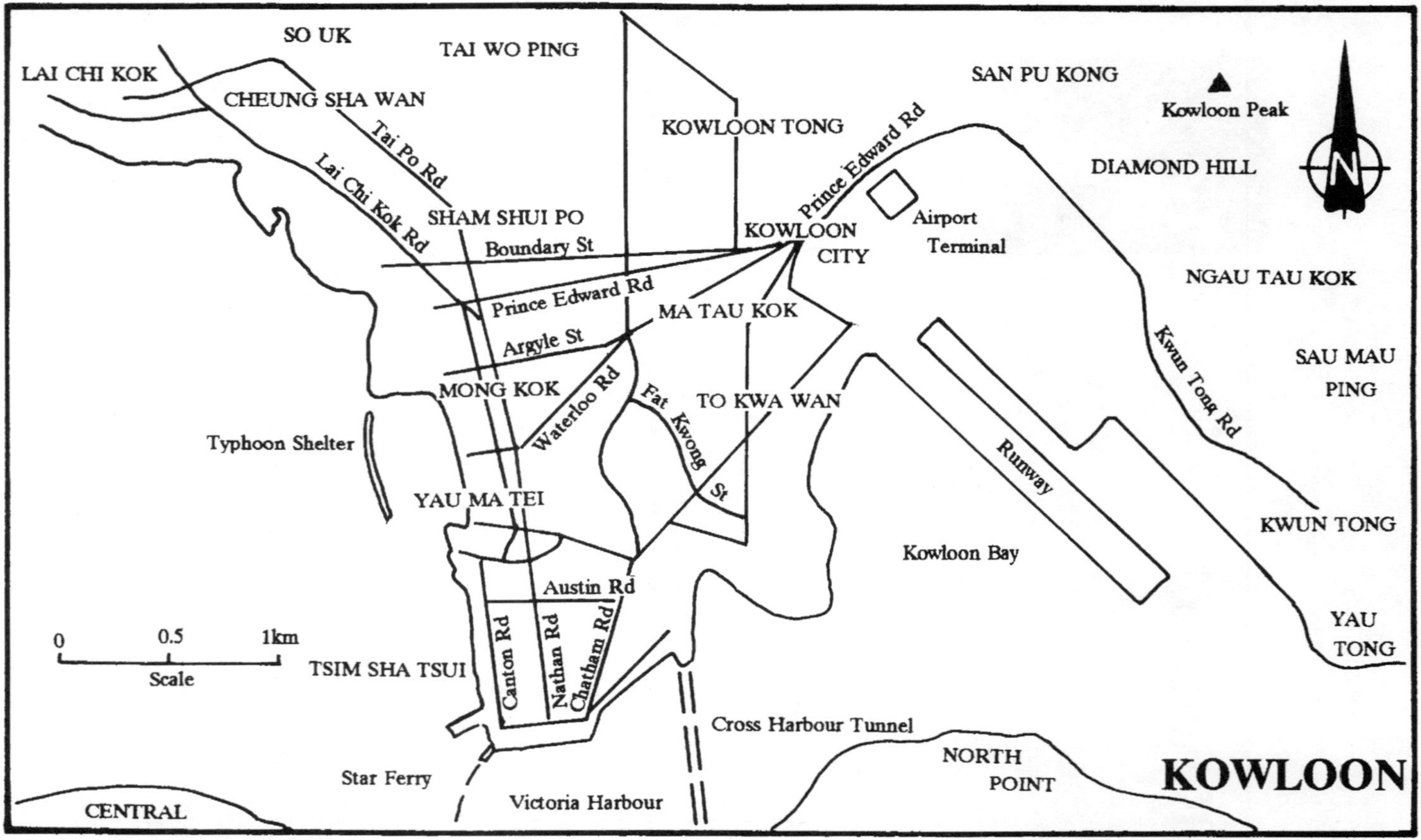
SO UK
TAI WO PING
LAI CHI KOK
CHEUNG SHA WAN
Tai Po Rd
Lai Chi Kok Rd
SHAM SHUI PO
Boundary St
KOWLOON TONG
Prince Edward Rd
KOWLOON
CITY
Airport
Terminal
SAN PU KONG
Kowloon Peak
DIAMOND HILL
NGAU TAU KOK
Prince Edward Rd
MA TAU KOK
Argyle St
MONG KOK
Waterloo Rd
Fat Kwong St
TO KWA WAN
Kwun Tong Rd
SAU MAU
PING
Runway
Typhoon Shelter
YAU MA TEI
KWUN TONG
Kowloon Bay
Austin Rd
0
0.5
1km
Scale
TSIM SHA TSUI
Canton Rd
Nathan Rd
Chatham Rd
YAU
TONG
Cross Harbour Tunnel
NORTH
POINT
Star Ferry
Victoria Harbour
CENTRAL
KOWLOON

from here. Then, of course, there is the international airport and the international cruise ship terminal, which connect Hong Kong with the rest of the world.

Whether you arrive by rail from China, drop through the clouds at rooftop height, or sail in out of the sunset from Macau or the blue Pacific, arriving involves a face-to-face encounter with striking Victoria Harbour. The trip from the transport terminal to your accommodation is through a high-rise forest. There is no way to sneak up on Hong Kong. You are thrown into it, and the decision to like it or loathe it is generally made on that brief first encounter.

2. Getting There

Hong Kong International Airport (Kai Tak Airport) is not one of the highlights of the city. It is to be replaced by a completely new high-tech airport to be called Chek Lap Kok International, in 1997. The new facility will handle 35 million passengers a year in relative comfort and will be one of the best airports in the world. The existing site is cramped and the facilities have not kept up with the rapid development in passenger traffic passing through the terminal. There is a limited number of aircraft parking bays at the terminal so you will often find that you will be bused from the plane to the terminal.

No matter how many times you fly into Hong Kong, however, the experience always creates a ripple of excitement. The aircraft banks steeply over Kowloon rooftops, the undercarriage caressing the forest of television aerials, before plonking down on the narrow concrete strip that dares to intrude into Victoria Harbour. Pilots still rely on the human eyeball to steer the big jets to a landing where no computer system can put them safely. As you taxi towards the terminal, you are surrounded by the overweening monuments to one of the world's most dramatic success stories.

Once inside, there are often long lines at immigration and long waits at the six baggage carrousels before you pass through customs. You now enter a buffer hall where there are banking facilities, a hotel booking office, a desk manned by the Hong Kong Tourist Authority, another with representatives from the Macau Government Tourist Office, luggage storage, telephones, and rest rooms. From here you enter the chaos of the public greeting area and through this to the transport areas. From this point on, Hong Kong is about rush and noise. There is no escape.

The airport is about 20 minutes from most Kowloon hotels and you can reach many of them by taxi or air-conditioned Skybus. If you have no local currency on arrival, change only enough at the airport to get you to your hotel because rates here are poor. A taxi will cost around HK$50 and the

Skybus HK$11. The Skybus operates on a 15- to 20-minute schedule from 7 A.M. to midnight and serves most of the Tsim Sha Tsui hotels. It does not serve the Tsim Sha Tsui East hotels or those in Mong Kok.

If you have arranged hotel transfers as part of your bookings you should exit the Buffer Hall through the Hotel Transport exit and look for the hotel representative waiting outside to greet you. You do not pay the driver because the charge will be on your hotel bill.

If you are arriving by boat from Canton (Guangzhou), you will arrive at the **China Ferry Terminal** at the far northern end of Harbour City. For some reason I find this a most confusing place but at least you are within striking distance of accommodation and shopping facilities. It is also possible to get connections from Macau that arrive at the same terminal and this can be useful if you have Kowloon accommodation or need to go to the airport.

If you are coming by train from China, you will find yourself at the **Kowloon Railway Station** in Hung Hom. This is close to the Cross Harbour Tunnel, but unfortunately there is no connection to the mass transit railway at this point. Most hotels are a taxi ride away.

3. Local Transportation

The transport options here are fairly similar to those on Hong Kong Island (see preceding chapter). Red-and-silver **taxis** are readily available at most times and are a good way to travel longer distances. Walking is a good option for short distances because there is always plenty of interest in the streets and at times traffic congestion and one-way streets can slow the alternatives to the walking pace.

There are two **Mass Transit Railway (MTR)** lines in Kowloon. One starts at Central on Hong Kong Island and travels through Tsim Sha Tsui on its way to the New Territories. The other starts at Yau Ma Tei in Kowloon, where there is an interchange with the first line, then it winds its way north, then east, and eventually south to link up with the Hong Kong Island line at Quarry Bay. This second line also has an interchange with the Kowloon-Canton Railway at Kowloon Tong station.

The **Kowloon-Canton Railway** is the only overground system in Hong Kong. It goes from the Kowloon Station in Hung Hom, near the entrance to the Cross Harbour Tunnel, up to the border with China at Lo Wu. The journey takes about half an hour and costs around HK$7.50 ordinary-class and HK$15 first-class. Trains operate about every 10 to 15 minutes. The route, after you clatter past the people-boxes of Kowloon, is quite scenic and surprisingly rural, and there are such attractions as Shatin Racecourse, the Chinese University, the Hong Kong Railway Museum, and various temples and monasteries.

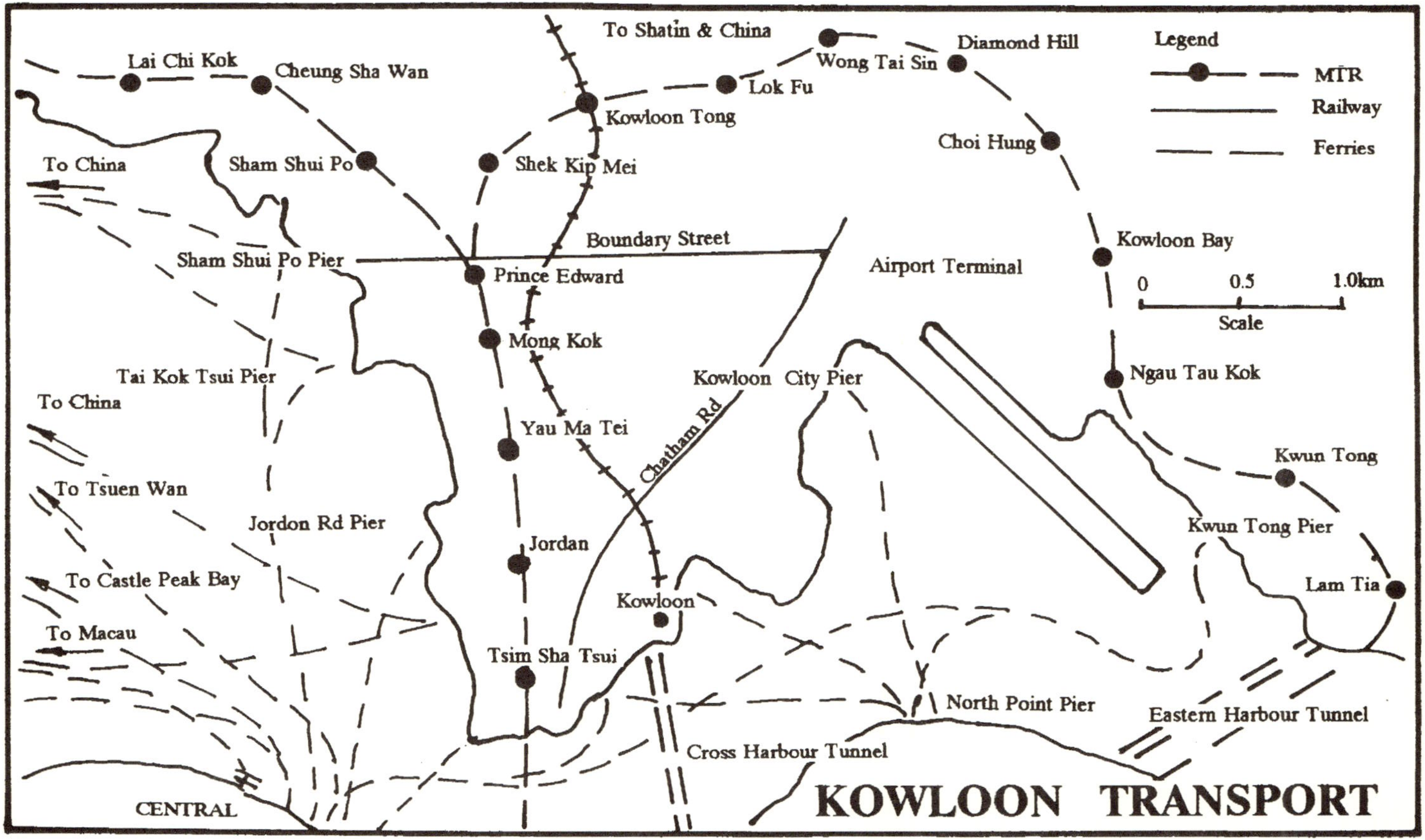
KOWLOON TRANSPORT
Legend
MTR
Railway
Ferries
0
0.5
1.0km
Scale
To Shatin & China
Lai Chi Kok
Cheung Sha Wan
Sham Shui Po
Shek Kip Mei
Kowloon Tong
Lok Fu
Wong Tai Sin
Diamond Hill
Choi Hung
Kowloon Bay
Ngau Tau Kok
Kwun Tong
Lam Tia
Kwun Tong Pier
Boundary Street
Prince Edward
Mong Kok
Yau Ma Tei
Jordan
Tsim Sha Tsui
Kowloon
Chatham Rd
Airport Terminal
Kowloon City Pier
North Point Pier
Eastern Harbour Tunnel
Cross Harbour Tunnel
Sham Shui Po Pier
Tai Kok Tsui Pier
Jordon Rd Pier
To China
To China
To Tsuen Wan
To Castle Peak Bay
To Macau
CENTRAL

The **Star Ferry** is probably Hong Kong's most well known form of transportation because it seems to feature in every film and television program ever made about Hong Kong. The green-and-white ferries have connected Kowloon with Hong Kong Island since 1898. A single journey from Tsim Sha Tsui to Central costs HK$1.50 for the upper deck and HK$1.20 for the lower deck. There are also services from Hung Hom to Central and from Tsim Sha Tsui to Wanchai.

4. The Hotel Scene

Kowloon has traditionally been the favorite for tourists visiting Hong Kong and although accommodation options have improved elsewhere, it still retains the premier position.

Business travellers also have some excellent alternatives in this part of the city and there is a growing number of hotels that are targeting this market with good corporate rates and special facilities to meet the needs of this market sector.

Kowloon has at least sixteen hotels that are in the luxury and expensive categories, a huge range of midmarket hotels, and a growing range of upper-level budget accommodation. It is fairly difficult to find acceptable low-budget accommodation, however. The whole city is too expensive for that.

You will find that all hotels within the luxury, expensive, and medium-price categories have air-conditioned rooms with attached bathrooms, a selection of bars and restaurants, direct-dial local and international telephone facilities, safe-deposit boxes or room safes, and room service. Many of the cheaper hotels also have some of these facilities.

The following is a personal selection that is by no means complete, but I have been satisfied with my visit to these places and I can discuss them from first-hand experience.

LUXURY HOTELS

For tradition, facilities, service, and top price there is one outstanding property. **The Peninsula** (Tel: 2366-6251) has been a Hong Kong institution since 1928. In 1994 there was a major change in the hotel when a high-rise wing was grafted on to the original structure. This has increased the original 137 rooms and 19 suites to 300. The Peninsula has always been a meeting place. Its celebrated lobby has seen heads of state, royalty, celebrities, and acclaimed artists pass through the splendid interior.

Every thing about the Peninsula is top quality. The rooms are large and well appointed. The bars and restaurants are some of the best in the city. The hotel has a tradition of service that is the envy of most other establishments. The opening of the new wing has allowed the hotel to dramatically

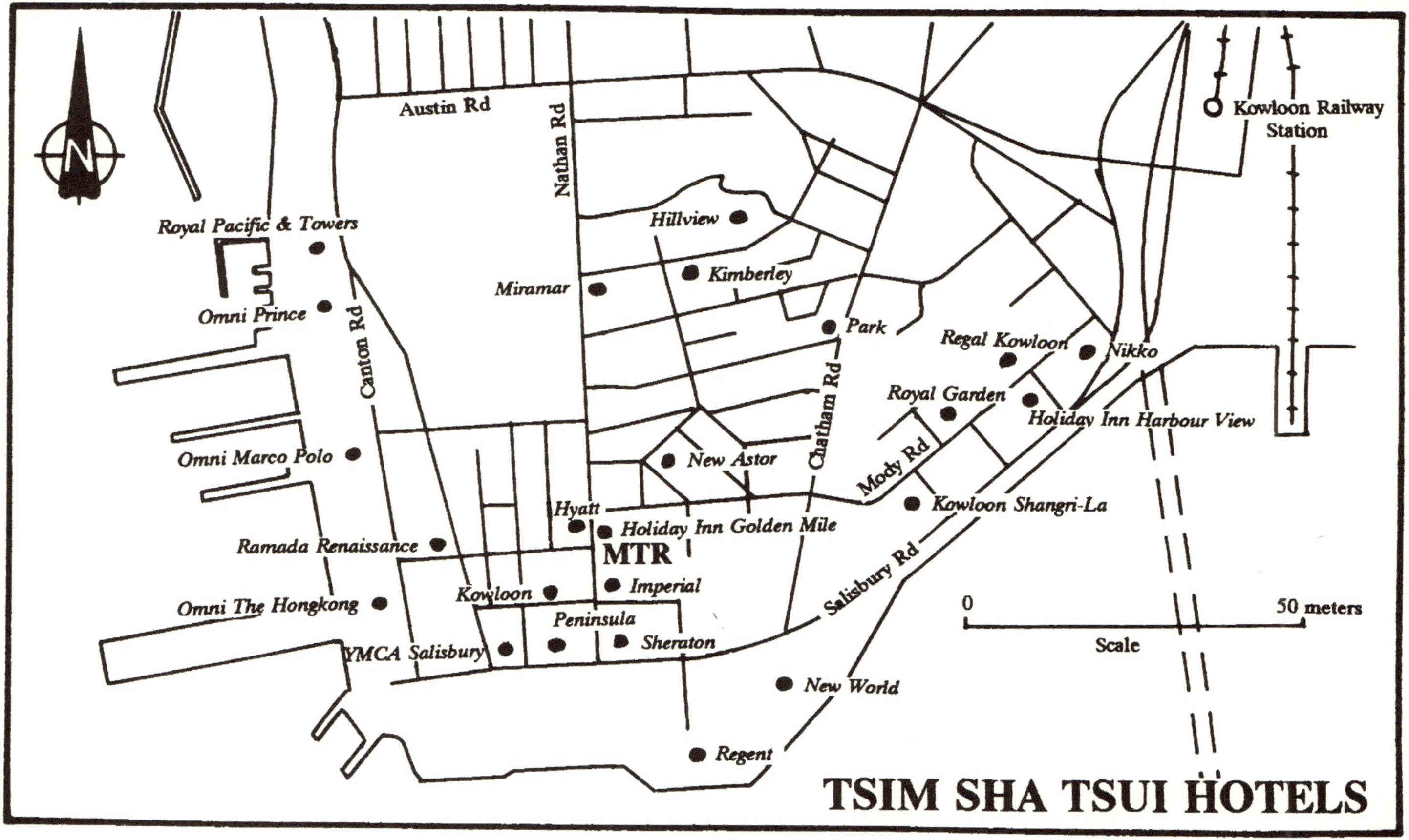
TSIM SHA TSUI HOTELS
N
Austin Rd
Nathan Rd
Canton Rd
Chatham Rd
Mody Rd
Salisbury Rd
Kowloon Railway Station
Royal Pacific & Towers
Omni Prince
Omni Marco Polo
Ramada Renaissance
Omni The Hongkong
YMCA Salisbury
Kowloon
Peninsula
Sheraton
Imperial
MTR
Hyatt
Holiday Inn Golden Mile
New Astor
Miramar
Kimberley
Hillview
Park
Regal Kowloon
Nikko
Royal Garden
Holiday Inn Harbour View
Kowloon Shangri-La
New World
Regent
0
50 meters
Scale

improve facilities. A striking double-story rooftop restaurant incorporating a seafood and caviar bar and a contemporary-style lounge has been added to the long established Gaddi's, Chesa, The Verandah Grill, and Spring Moon. A palatial, indoor-and-outdoor pool in the Roman style with a spacious sundeck and a health club and spa with Jacuzzis, saunas, steam and massage rooms, cold tubs, and a beauty salon are on the 7th and 8th floors of the new block.

A state-of-the-art business center has the facilities to do business anywhere in the world, at any time. The hotels fleet of green Rolls Royces stand ready for airport transfers, appointments, or excursions, while twin helipads will enable guests to connect with destinations throughout the Territory within minutes. The shopping arcades feature the world's most renowned brand names and some specialty boutiques. (Book with the hotel in the United States and Canada on Tel: 1-800-462-7899; in the United Kingdom on Tel: 071-730-0993; in Australia on 02-261-4322; or direct with the hotel at Salisbury Road, Kowloon, Hong Kong; Fax: 852-2722-4170.)

EXPENSIVE HOTELS

This is the category where Kowloon excels. The following is a selection of hotels that offer standard rooms in the HK$1,400-2,000 price bracket. Special rooms and suites will be higher.

The Regent (Tel: 2721-1211) is my favorite in this category. The hotel has 514 rooms and 88 suites in a magnificent harborside location that will take your breath away. The guest rooms and public areas make full use of the site. The informal Harbourside coffee shop, the leathered Steak House, and the exquisite Plume Restaurant all have added magic because of one of the world's finest urban views.

Away from the view, Oriental art treasures can be seen on the walls and extensive landscaping provides a feeling of warmth and homeliness. Complete privacy is available in the health spa where marble walls enclose a hot tub, steam bath, sauna, and solarium that is yours alone. Three outdoor spa pools offer a choice of temperatures, while close-by a swimming pool may tempt you in. (Book with the hotel at Salisbury Road, Kowloon, Hong Kong; Fax: 852-2739-4546.)

Omni The Hongkong Hotel (Tel: 2736-0088) is another great choice. The hotel opened in 1969 and it was given a lavish renovation in the early 1990s. Crystalline glass, black granite, marble, and polished wood give an effect of resplendent sophistication. The hotel has 665 rooms and 44 suites and is located in one of Asia's largest shopping and commercial complexes—Harbour City. It is on the waterfront with easy access to the Star Ferry, so it is popular with business guests who have a need to visit all areas of the city.

All rooms are spacious and well appointed. Some offer spectacular harbor views and others look out over Kowloon. There is a small price differential. The 117 rooms and suites on the 17th and 18th floors are named the Omni Continental Club. These have a range of special facilities and services aimed at the discerning business market, such as private reception and lounge, complimentary breakfast, complimentary use of the board room with full meeting facilities, and a packing and unpacking service with shoe shine and clothes pressing.

The hotel has an excellent range of bars and restaurants. The Tai Pan Grill is the premier restaurant, but others will enjoy the fine Japanese cuisine in Nishimura, the Chiu Chow style Chinese cuisine in the Eastern Palace, or the more reasonable prices in the Coffee Shop. Gripps Restaurant and Piano Bar has a business lunch and afternoon tea, then at night it offers live entertainment. There is an outdoor heated swimming pool, a barbershop, a beauty salon, a flowershop, car rental and limousine service, nonsmoking floors, and just about every other facility you would need. (Book with an Omni regional sales office—United States Tel: 310-568-0000; United Kingdom Tel: 606-767-090; Singapore Tel: 472-3323; or contact the hotel direct at Harbour City, Kowloon, Hong Kong; Fax: 852-2736-1136.)

Adjacent to the Hongkong Hotel is the **Omni Marco Polo Hotel** and the **Omni Prince Hotel**. Both fit into the lower end of the expensive category and both have a level of facilities and service that would please most people. Booking arrangements are similar to the Hongkong Hotel.

Several people have told me that the **Ramada Renaissance Hotel** (Tel: 2375-1133) should be my next choice; but frankly, I find this to be a property that offers so much but on occasions just does not quite deliver like it should. Perhaps it all stems from the street entrance and the sometimes off-handed attitude at reception. Certainly the rooms are attractive and functional, and the suites with their Jacuzzi and fax machine are very popular with business people. The new executive rooms are a further level higher while the Renaissance Club offers special facilities and complimentary breakfast.

The restaurant offerings are also good. Cantonese cuisine is served in elegant surroundings at the T'ang Court; Italian cooking is featured at the Capriccio; and American specialties are offered at the Bostonian Restaurant. On the top floor of the hotel there is a comprehensive health club with squash court, gym with sauna, massage and solarium, and an outdoor pool. The concierge desk will take care of entertainment bookings, airline ticketing, and sight-seeing. (Book through the Ramada International system, Utell International, or direct with the hotel at 8 Peking Rd., Kowloon, Hong Kong; Fax: 852-2375-6611.)

I stayed at the **Royal Garden Hotel** (Tel: 2721-5215) about two months after it opened and I was as impressed with it then as I am impressed with it now. This is one of the hotels in the Tsim Sha Tsui East area and when it opened, you felt a bit isolated and away from the action. In the fifteen years since then, the surrounding area has developed all types of facilities and it is now an acceptable area for everyone.

The hotel has 375 rooms and 45 suites, which makes it smaller than most of its competition and gives it a slightly more personal feel. The rooms are large and well appointed. Each one opens off an open balcony overlooking the "hanging gardens" of the 110-foot atrium. The Greenery is a lush setting where you can enjoy a meal or a snack anytime of the day or evening, while The Balcony is a cosmopolitan terrace lounge for a buffet lunch or an evening cocktail. In the basement, the Falcon Pub and Discotheque, with its English Victorian decor, provides a good backdrop for a roast beef lunch or an evening of music and fun. There is a business center and several function rooms. (Book with the hotel at Mody Road, Tsim Sha Tsui East, Kowloon, Hong Kong; Fax: 852-2369-9976.)

The **Kowloon Shangri-La** (Tel: 2721-2111) is close-by. This was opened at the same time as the Royal Garden and has been there for almost fifteen years longer than the Island Shangri-La. The hotel has matured with age and is a lovely place to stay. There is an elegance and sophistication that is missing from some of the new hotels. The 716 guest rooms and suites are light and spacious. Some have great views over Victoria Harbour. There are eight restaurants and bars. Margaux serves fine European food; the Shang Palace has Cantonese specialties; Nadaman serves Japanese delicacies, while the Coffee Garden and the Steak House have less formal menus. Evening choices are the intimate rooftop Tiara Lounge, the Music Room, or the Lobby Lounge. There is a health club with a pool, exercise equipment, sauna, solarium, whirlpool, and massage. (Book in the United States and Canada on Tel: 1-800-942-5050; in the United Kingdom on Tel: 81-747-8485; in Australia on 1-800-222-448; or direct with the hotel at 64 Mody Rd., Tsim Sha Tsui, Kowloon, Hong Kong; Fax: 852-2723-8686.)

The **Holiday Inn Crowne Plaza** (Tel: 2721-5161) is the third hotel in East Tsim Sha Tsui East that I can recommend. Perhaps this is slightly downmarket from the Shangri-La, and the room rates reflect this. It is good value for a top hotel in Hong Kong. The 593 rooms and suites are large in the Holiday Inn tradition and about half have harbor views. Executive floors cater for the needs of the travelling business executive. The Belveder is a French gourmet restaurant and The Mistral has regional Italian flavors. Cafe Rendezvous is the coffeehouse, the Harbour View Lounge is a Victorian cocktail lounge, and the Golden Carp Bar has a dance floor and nightly live entertainment. There is a business center and a sauna and health spa. (Book with the Holiday Inn organization in the United States and Canada on Tel: 1-800-HOLIDAY; in the United Kingdom on Tel: 722-7755; in Australia on Tel: 02-261-4922; or direct with the hotel at 70 Mody Rd., Tsim Sha Tsui East, Kowloon, Hong Kong; Fax: 852-2369-5672.)

In fact there are two Holiday Inn hotels in Kowloon. The other is the **Holiday Inn Golden Mile** (Tel: 2369-3111), which is, as its name suggests, in the middle of the Nathan Road action strip. If you want to be in the center of things, this is the place to be. The downside to the hotel is that it has been here for quite some time and it is suffering from not having enough space both inside and out. A recent refurbishment has raised the standard of the rooms and facilities.

Right across the road is the **Hyatt Regency** (Tel: 2311-1234). The comments about position apply equally here. This is an extremely popular hotel and despite its 723 rooms and suites, it is often booked out. The building is showing its age somewhat but there have been several refurbishments and the facilities are equal to any in this price range. The rooms are done in earthtone colors, which have a warmth and comfort and there are some exquisite antiques in the public areas. The Regency Club floors provide extra facilities. The Chinese Restaurant has received many awards and rave reviews, and Hugo's remains one of the top European restaurants in Kowloon. Nathan's and the Cafe restaurant both offer popular local and Western food in a bright atmosphere. (Book with the Hyatt organization in the United States and Canada on Tel: 1-800-228-9000; in Australia on Tel: 1-800-222-188; or direct with the hotel at 67 Nathan Rd., Kowloon, Hong Kong; Fax: 852-2739-8701.)

The final recommendation is the largest hotel in Kowloon. The **Sheraton Hotel and Towers** (Tel: 2369-1111) has 922 rooms and suites on a great site on the corner of Nathan Road and Salisbury Road. Some rooms have good harbor views. There are some excellent dining options: Bukhara has Indian tandoori cuisine, Unkai has fine Japanese cuisine from Osaka, The Grandstand Grill boasts U.S. prime rib and seafood, and the Celestial Court Cantonese Restaurant has the best from China. There is a good business center and a health club and rooftop pool. (Book with the Sheraton organization in the United States and Canada on Tel: 1-800-325-3535; in the United Kingdom on Tel: 0-800-353-535; in Australia on Tel: 1-800-073-535; or direct with the hotel at 20 Nathan Rd., Kowloon, Hong Kong; Fax: 852-2739-8707.)

MEDIUM-PRICE HOTELS

I have defined these hotels by the HK$600-1,400 price bracket for a standard room. This means that there is a considerable difference in standard within this group, so you must take price into consideration when making a choice.

Near the top of the range is the **Kowloon Hotel** (Tel: 369-8698). I must confess when I first checked in here I was surprised by the apparent small size of the room, but after two days I was captivated by the facilities and realized that there is sufficient space for all your needs. This is a high-tech hotel with a shimmering mirrored exterior; a chrome, glass, and marble lobby; and sophisticated computer equipment in every room. The telecenter allows you to access information such as location maps of the city, weather reports, messages, room accounts, tourist and business guides, stocks and shares, up to 99 TV channels, and so forth. A built-in fax machine with individual number serves as a photocopier, printer, and fax receiver. The telephone message system allows you to leave a recorded message or talk to the operator, and guests can retrieve messages from outside the hotel. Rooms have tea- and coffee-making facilities, safes, and outside temperature and humidity readouts. There is a choice of restaurants on the second floor, and the Wan Loong Court Chinese Restaurant, with its cheerful atmosphere and Cantonese specialties, in the second basement. Guests have access to the Peninsula and Repulse Bay restaurants. (Book with the hotel at 19 Nathan Rd., Kowloon, Hong Kong; Fax: 852-2739-9811.)

The **Park Hotel** (Tel: 2366-1371) is an old favorite. The hotel has been kept modern, however, and it offers a certain elegance at a more affordable price than the expensive hotels. The 333 double and twin rooms are surprisingly large, while the 31 suites would suit even the most discerning of tastes.

There is a choice of Cantonese food in the Park Chinese Restaurant, Western dishes in the Poinsettia Room, and well-priced fare in the Coffee Shop. The Marigold Bar is a popular afternoon and evening hangout. Do not look for swimming pools or too many other facilities, but most Hong Kong visitors are not wanting these. At HK$1,000 for a standard double room, the Park is good value in Kowloon. (Book with the hotel at 61 Chatham Rd. South, Tsim Sha Tsui, Kowloon, Hong Kong; Fax: 852-2739-7259.)

The 205-room **Ramada Hotel** (Tel: 2311-1100) is one block from the Park. In many ways this is an undistinguished property with a small lobby, bar, coffee shop, and business center, but little else. Even the rooms are predictable. After I have said all this, though, the Ramada is a property that I like. It has the feel of a professional operation and you see that the hotel is getting everything it can out of its building and location. In reality, it provides all the facilities that many visitors need from a hotel and it does it in the Ramada International tradition. A stay here can be very pleasant. (Book in the United States on Tel: 1-800-228-9898; in the United Kingdom on Tel: 0-800-181-737; in Australia on Tel: 1-800-222-4331; or contact the hotel at 73 Chatham Rd. South, Tsim Sha Tsui, Kowloon, Hong Kong; Fax: 852-2311-6000.)

KOWLOON

The Salisbury (Tel: 2369-2211) is at the bottom end of this price range, yet the hotel has a location envied by many. It is situated next to the Peninsula, it has rooms with harbor views, and the 366 rooms have all-modern facilities. The reason for the excellent price is that this hotel is operated by the YMCA of Hong Kong and is partly provided as a service. Families, women, men, and groups are all welcome here.

Single rooms are around HK$600 and standard doubles are around HK$700. You pay HK$900 for harbor-view rooms and HK$1,200 for suites. There are also some dormitory beds for HK$150. All rooms have satellite television, international telephone, room safe, card key security, and refrigerator with minibar. Amenities include two swimming pools, a fitness center, squash courts, hair salon, business center, tour counter, convenience shop, and book shop. The Dining Room has an international menu and great views of Victoria Harbour, while the ground-floor Cafe provides a cafeteria-style menu. (Book with the hotel at 41 Salisbury Rd., Tsim Sha Tsui, Kowloon, Hong Kong; Fax: 852-2739-9315.)

BP International House (Tel: 2376-1111) is a more modern version of what the Salisbury is providing. It opened late 1993. This hotel is owned by the Scout Association. It has 536 rooms ranging from twins at HK$880, suites at HK$1,400, and 4-bedded bunk rooms at HK$1,000. All rooms have a private bathroom, air conditioning, IDD telephone, and color television. There are no porters or laundry service, but there is a coin-operated laundry room for guests. The hotel has a Chinese restaurant and a coffee lounge. A cocktail lounge and health club is planned. (Book with the hotel at 8 Austin Rd., Tsim Sha Tsui, Kowloon, Hong Kong; Fax: 852-2376-1333.)

The **Regal Airport Hotel** (Tel: 2718-0333) falls into this category. The hotel is directly connected to the terminal building by a walkway, and the best rooms face the airport. The 400 rooms are sound-proofed and each provides arrival and departure information. Restaurant choices are the Seafood Restaurant for Cantonese food, the Five Continents Restaurant for Western Cuisine, and La Plantation Coffee Shop. Entertainment options are the Flying Machine Bar with its great airport view, the warm atmosphere of the China Coast Pub, the China Coast Karaoke, or the Lobby Lounge. There is a modern business center. (Book in the United States on Tel: 1-800-222-8888; in Canada on Tel: 1-800-233-9188; in the United Kingdom on Tel: 081-577-9888; in Australia on Tel: 02-956-8988; or direct with the hotel at Sa Po Road, Kowloon, Hong Kong; Fax: 852-2718-4111.)

BUDGET ACCOMMODATION

There are some good options under HK$600 but below HK$300 you are beginning to struggle.

My choice here would be the **Caritas Bianchi Lodge** (Tel: 2388-1111).

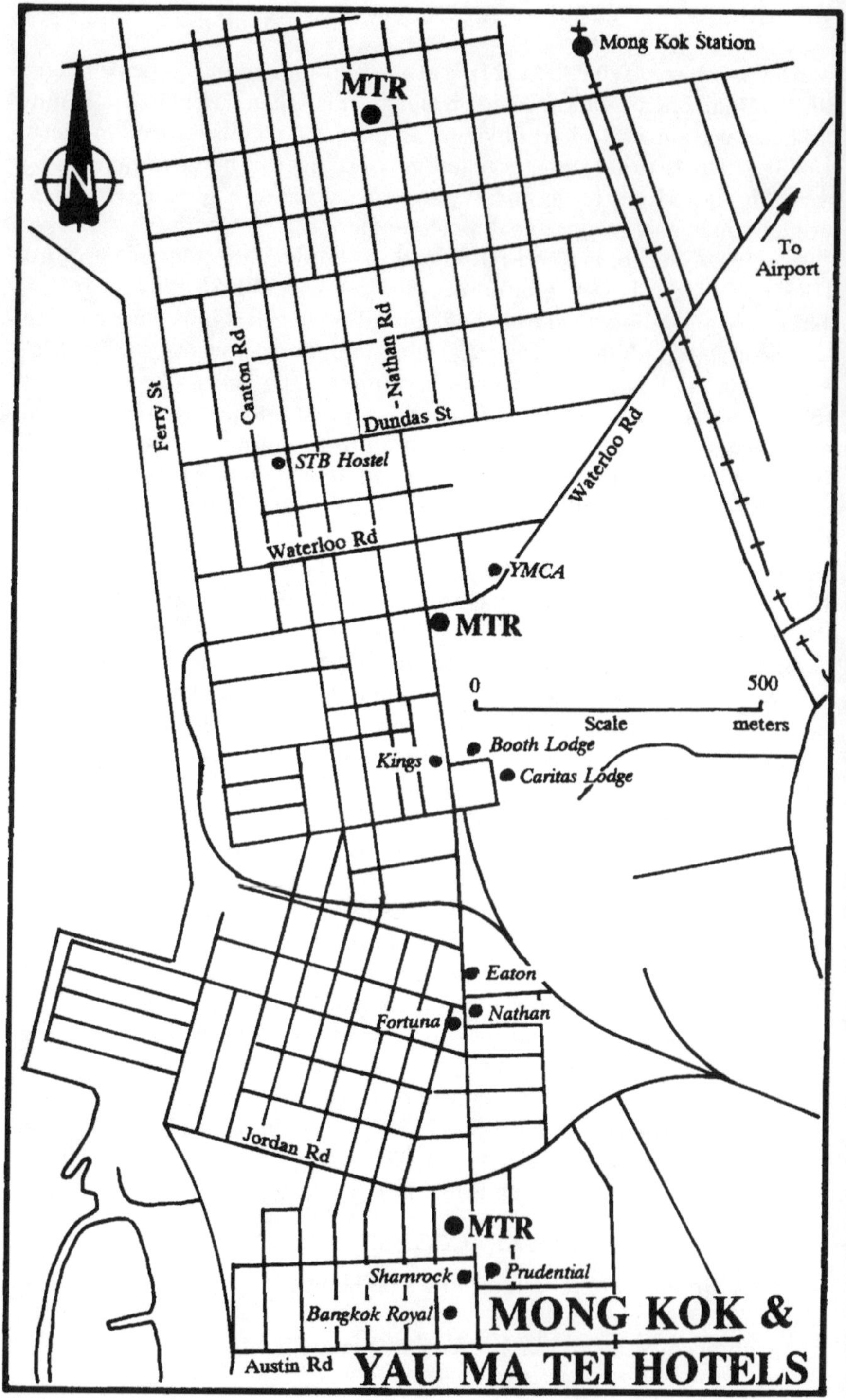

Mong Kok Station
MTR
N
To Airport
Canton Rd
Nathan Rd
Ferry St
Dundas St
STB Hostel
Waterloo Rd
Waterloo Rd
YMCA
MTR
0
500
Scale
meters
Booth Lodge
Kings
Caritas Lodge
Eaton
Nathan
Fortuna
Jordan Rd
MTR
Shamrock
Prudential
Bangkok Royal
Austin Rd
MONG KOK &
YAU MA TEI HOTELS

This is a little away from the main Kowloon tourist area but there are plenty of transport and shopping options close-by. The Lodge is operated by the Roman Catholic Church in Hong Kong, and with single rooms at around HK$500 and doubles at HK$550 including breakfast, it is a good value. The 90-room lodge was opened in 1980 so it is reasonably modern. The lobby is attractive and the rooms are a good size and are equipped with telephone, refrigerator with minibar, music, and TV. The restaurant is fairly basic but the food is good. (Book with the hotel at 4 Cliff Rd., Yau Ma Tei, Kowloon, Hong Kong; Fax: 852-2770-6669.)

Another excellent alternative is close-by. **Booth Lodge** (Tel: 2771-9266) is a modern building run by the Salvation Army. The 54 rooms offer adequate space and facilities, and at HK$420 for a standard and HK$540 for a superior, they represent an excellent value. Breakfast is served each morning, and hot and cold drinks are available from vending machines 24 hours a day. The whole operation lacks a little sophistication, but this is compensated for by the friendliness. There are facilities for making overseas telephone calls, tour arrangements, storing luggage, and car rental. A small gift shop provides a range of travel essentials. (Book with the hotel at 11 Wing Sing Lane, Yau Ma Tei, Kowloon, Hong Kong.)

The **Bangkok Royal Hotel** (Tel: 2735-9181) is a pleasant surprise. This hotel is one street removed from Nathan Road in the Yau Ma Tei area. The 70 rooms are reasonably neat and clean and have telephone, refrigerator, and television. The ground-floor restaurant has a good atmosphere and serves some of the best Thai food in Hong Kong. The service is friendly. Single rooms start at around HK$400 and doubles are from HK$500. (Book with the hotel at 2 Pilkem St., Kowloon, Hong Kong; Fax: 852-2730-2209.)

King's Hotel (Tel: 2780-1281) is older and not as good as the previous choices but it does have single rooms from HK$380, which makes it attractive to some. The doubles, at around HK$500, are not particularly recommended. The 72 rooms have telephone, television, and refrigerator. There is a bar, a small Thai restaurant, and a dining room serving Western and Chinese food. (Book with the hotel at 473 Nathan Rd., Kowloon, Hong Kong; Fax: 852-2782-1833.)

The **Star Guest House** (Tel: 2723-8951) is a step down from here in some respects, but there will be some travellers who will enjoy it more. This is one of several relatively newly created small guesthouses that are aiming at the backpacker market. You will find them on the upper levels of old office buildings and you reach them via ancient elevators that grind upwards. Once you reach the guesthouse, it is clean, bright, and friendly; and you are likely to meet other young travellers from around the world. The 13 rooms are very small, but they have a telephone and television. You can choose between a room with private shower from HK$350 or without a shower for

HK$280. (Book with the guesthouse at 21 Cameron Rd., Kowloon, Hong Kong; Fax: 852-2311-2275.) The 16-room **Lee Garden Guest House** (Tel: 2367-5972) at 36 Cameron Rd. is run by the same management and has rooms from HK$440.

The **City Guest House** (Tel: 2730-0212) is a similar establishment in another part of Kowloon. The 16 rooms are adequate and have telephone, television, and minibathroom. Prices are HK$300 for a single and HK$350 for a double. (Book with the guesthouse at Cumberland House, 227 Nathan Rd., Kowloon, Hong Kong.)

Excellent dormitory accommodation is available at **The Salisbury** (Tel: 2369-2211). This hotel is described in the medium-price hotel section. The HK$150 price is high but it is safe, clean, and well managed; and you can use all the other hotel facilities. If price is a major consideration, then **Victoria Hostel** (Tel: 2312-0621) may appeal. This is at 33 Hankow Rd., and beds in an air-conditioned dorm will cost HK$80 and in a non-airconditioned one around HK$60. (Book by fax to 852-2730-0336.) A further choice in this price range is the **STB Hostel** (Tel: 2710-9199) where there are 70 dormitory beds and 19 rooms at about HK$300. This is operated by the Hong Kong Student Travel Bureau and is clean and well managed. (Book with the hostel at 255 Reclamation St., Mong Kok, Kowloon, Hong Kong; Fax: 2385-0153.)

5. Dining and Restaurants

Kowloon has an astonishing range of restaurants. If you ever doubted that the Chinese were food mad, a quick spin through this area will soon put you right. Some are exclusive and wildly expensive, others are well priced and suitable for anyone. I readily admit that I have only eaten in a fraction of the hundreds of restaurants to choose from, so the following is very much a personal choice. You will find that prices will range from more than HK$700 for two, to under HK$100. Some of the fast-food-type places can cut this cost to less than HK$50.

HOTEL RESTAURANTS

My two favorite Cantonese restaurants are poles apart in style yet they are equally good at producing that "never to be forgotten" experience. Both are expensive, so do not go if the funds are tight. **Lai Ching Heen** at the Regent Hotel (Tel: 2721-1211) is discreetly elegant while making full use of its great harbor view. Table settings are apple-green, and antiques line the room. The à la carte menu is justly famous but there are monthly specialties to add variety. The **Chinese Restaurant** at the Hyatt Regency Hotel (Tel: 2311-1234) is a high-ceilinged 1920s teahouse with traditional booth seating. It has an ambiance that I find particularly appealing and the food is excellent.

Fresh seafood is a strong recommendation. Both restaurants open daily for lunch and dinner.

The **Spring Moon Restaurant** at the Peninsula (Tel: 2366-6251) is another favorite. Specialties include shark's fin, bird's nest, and Peking duck. Dim sum is featured at lunchtime. **Wan Loong Court** at the Kowloon Hotel (Tel: 2369-8698) is downmarket from the others mentioned to date and it is difficult to find, but the large restaurant is often full, so many must agree that it is doing something right. What that is could be the delightful combination of exciting tastes, good service, and reasonable prices.

Tang Court at the Ramada Renaissance Hotel (Tel: 2375-1133) is distinctly luxurious and the cuisine is stylish. This ranks with the **Shang Palace** at the Kowloon Shangri-La Hotel (Tel: 2721-2111) with its red and gilt decor, and the **Golden Unicorn** at the Omni The Hong Kong Hotel (Tel: 2730-6565) for sophistication. All have excellent menus and a fine selection of Chinese teas.

The **Yat Tung Seafood Restaurant** at the Eaton Hotel (Tel: 2782-1818), the **Regal Seafood Restaurant** at the Regal Kowloon Hotel (Tel: 2722-1818), and the **Yee Garden Seafood Restaurant** at the Windsor Hotel (Tel: 2739-5665) are three places that show what Cantonese chefs do best—turn fish into a unique gourmet experience.

When it comes to other cuisines the hotels have it all. The **Bukhara Tandoori Restaurant** at the Sheraton Hotel and Towers (Tel: 2369-1111) is my favorite Indian restaurant. There are sandstone walls and open-to-view clay ovens for atmosphere and tiger prawns, vegetarian dishes, and leg of lamb marinated in dark rum for the palate. **Nadaman** at the Kowloon Shangri-La (Tel: 2721-2111) is arguably the best Japanese restaurant in town with its impeccable service and elegant restraint. Another favorite is **Sagano** at the Hotel Nikko (Tel: 2739-1111), where an elegant restaurant is highlighted by a harbor-facing glass wall and a menu featuring 11-course dinners. The **Thai Restaurant** at the Bangkok Royal Hotel (Tel: 2735-9181) is bright, well priced, and deservedly popular.

There are so many good Western restaurants that it is difficult to choose a "best." **Gaddi's** at the Peninsula (Tel: 2366-6251) has had a great reputation for years, so who am I to argue with that. It is the supreme social setting and is a great restaurant as well. The menu is comprehensive, but you do not have to spend hours looking through pages of options. The wine list is superb. **Plume** at the Regent Hotel (Tel: 2721-1211) is another outstanding restaurant. The brilliant European cuisine and superb service is complemented by the magnificent view of Hong Kong by night. Plume only opens for dinner.

The **Tai Pan Restaurant** at the Omni The Hong Kong Hotel (Tel: 2736-0088) is notable for its contemporary decor with Oriental accents and its excellent menu, while just down the road **The Chalet** in the Royal Pacific

Hotel and Towers (Tel: 2736-1188) features timber and brass, brick and stone, and wooden shutters to create a cozy Swiss restaurant with traditional dishes such as fondues. If German food is what you are after, then it is hard to go past the **Baron's Table** at the Holiday Inn Golden Mile (Tel: 2369-3111). You get excellent service and superb cuisine in a rustic atmosphere. **Margaux** at the Kowloon Shangri-La Hotel (Tel: 2721-2111) is, as the name suggests, a fine French restaurant with classical cuisine. Lunches are popular when the atmosphere is more casual.

All the Western restaurants mentioned to date are in the "expensive" category. The following are somewhat less expensive while still providing a memorable meal. **The Bostonian** at the Ramada Renaissance Hotel (Tel: 2375-1133) is designed for lovers of zesty Californian or New Orleans-style cuisine. There is a seafood bar and a menu of spicy Cajun and Creole dishes. **Lalique** at the Royal Garden Hotel (Tel: 2721-5215) is a relaxed French restaurant set amid brilliantly etched glass panels from the famed French Lalique glassmaker. **The Grandstand Grill** (Tel: 236-1111) at the Sheraton Hotel and Towers is the place for U.S. prime rib but the menu offers many other choices, including some fine desserts. Another grill room worth considering is the **Poinsettia Room** at the Park Hotel (Tel: 2366-1371). There are lunchtime roasts from the wagon and daily dinner buffets at good prices.

OTHER RESTAURANTS

While many of the hotel restaurants tend to be expensive, it is still possible to eat reasonably cheaply in an outside restaurant. Here are some Chinese restaurants where you will get change from HK$100. Seafood favorites are the attraction at **Tai Woo Restaurant** (Tel: 2369-9773), 14 Hillwood Road, Tsim Sha Tsui. Set meals provide good value. The **Chicken Inn Restaurant** (Tel: 2739-0889) at 86 Canton Rd., Tsim Sha Tsui, is a casual place highlighting a variety of chicken dishes. A favorite is the double-boiled ginseng and black chicken soup. The **Can Do Restaurant** (Tel: 2721-8183) at 37 Cameron Rd., Tsim Sha Tsui, opens daily from 7 A.M. with special "congees," and continues with other dishes such as sweet and sour won ton. It is unpretentious and inexpensive. The **Jade Garden Restaurants** provide consistently good cuisine. The one in the BCC Bank Building at 25 Carnarvon Rd. (Tel: 2369-8311) is open from 7:30 A.M. to midnight. There is another outlet in Star House.

At the other end of the market there are some classic restaurants that rival anything produced by the hotels at similar prices. In this category, I recommend the **Fook Lam Moon Restaurant** (Tel: 2366-0286) at 53 Kimberley Rd., Tsim Sha Tsui, for outstanding seafood creations, and the **Sun Tung Lok Shark's Fin Restaurant** (Tel: 2730-0288), at shop 63 Ocean Galleries, Harbour City, 17 Canton Rd., for that distinctly Chinese delicacy.

In the intermediate category, the **Siu Lam Kung Seafood Restaurant** (Tel: 2721-6168), at 17 Manden Ave., Tsim Sha Tsui, is a long-established favorite; the elaborately decorated **North Sea Fishing Village** (Tel: 2723-6843) in the basement of Auto Plaza, 65 Mody Rd., Tsim Sha Tsui East, is great for giant lobsters; while the **Flourishing Restaurant** (Tel: 2384-0358), at 504 Canton Rd., Yau Ma Tei, blends traditional hotpots with a stylish brass and mirror decor.

Of course, other styles of Chinese cooking are also available. Chiu Chow cuisine is featured at the **Chiuchow Garden Restaurant** (Tel: 2368-7266) at 66 Mody Rd., Tsim Sha Tsui East. Shark's fin dishes are excellent as is the ricefish hotpot. Try the "Ku Fu" tea, prepared at your table. A home-style version of this cuisine is available at the unpretentious **New Golden Red Chiu Chau Restaurant** (Tel: 2366-6822) at 13 Prat Ave., Tsim Sha Tsui. Roast goose is a specialty but it is also worth trying the cold cuts.

Beijing cuisine tends to be more substantial and flavored than Cantonese and you get a good example of this at the **Peking Restaurant** (Tel: 2730-1315) at 227 Nathan Rd., Yau Ma Tei. This is a cheerful old-style place with shrimp and beancurd dishes among the menu choices. For something a little different, try the **Sun Hung Cheung Hing Restaurant** (Tel: 2367-7933) at 45 Kimberley Rd., Tsim Sha Tsui. You gather around a chimneyed table for the fun of a Mongolian-style hotpot barbecue. For Shanghai cuisine, try the **Great Shanghai Restaurant** (Tel: 2366-8158), a long-time favorite at 26 Prat Ave. The food is substantial and you can try heated Shanghainese wines. An alternative is the **Wu Kong Shanghai Restaurant** (Tel: 2366-7244), which is established in an Art Deco style in the basement of Alpha House, 27 Nathan Rd. The braised eggplant with hot garlic sauce is very good. The **Prince Court Szechuen Restaurant** (Tel: 2730-3100), at Sutton Court, Harbour City, 9 Canton Rd., allows you to try this cuisine in a wood-panelled atmosphere. Dancing prawns, scallops with eggplant, and crab dishes are some of the menu choices.

The food from other parts of Asia is also available. The clublike **Koh-I-Noor Indian Restaurant** (Tel: 2368-3065), at 16C Mody Rd., Tsim Sha Tsui, offers the chance to try the subtleties of Mughlai cuisine. There are finely spiced meat dishes and vegetarian favorites. The **Woodlands International Restaurant** (Tel: 2369-3718) is an unpretentious green-tiled place at 8 Minden Ave., Tsim Sha Tsui, offering some good-value dishes. The bistro-style **Java Rijsttafel Restaurant** (Tel: 2367-1230), at 38 Hankow Rd., Tsim Sha Tsui, has Indonesian satays, Malay curries, salads, and desserts.

The **Kotobuki Restaurant** (Tel: 2368-2711) is one of the most authentic Japanese restaurants in town. It is located at 176 Nathan Rd. and has sushi, sashimi, shabu shabu, and some interesting exotica on the menu. The **Restaurant Matsuzaka** (Tel: 2724-3057), at 75 Mody Rd., Tsim Sha Tsui East, starts the day with business lunches then continues until 5 A.M. with seafood set dinners, a sushi bar, sashimi, tempura, and teppanyaki. The **Arirang Restaurant** (Tel: 2730-3667), in Sutton Court, Harbour City, 19 Canton Rd., provides a simple setting for Korean barbecue and mildly spiced Seoul-style cuisine; while the spacious **Golden Elephant Restaurant** (Tel: 2735-0733), at Barnton Court, Harbour City, Canton Road, serves floating-market style Thai buffet lunches and well-priced dinner specials. The **Golden Bull** (Tel: 2369-4617) in the New World Center, 18 Salisbury Rd., has French-influenced, Chinese-style Vietnamese food. The grilled prawns in garlic butter are a recommendation.

When it comes to Western restaurants, there is a great choice. The **Au Trou Normand** (Tel: 2366-8754), at 6 Carnarvon Rd., is a superb, intimate French restaurant with provincial cuisine and an excellent wine list. Leave space for a mousse because they are excellent. A meal for two will be around HK$500. The **Palm Restaurant** (Tel: 2721-1271), at 38 Lock Rd., Tsim Sha Tsui, is in the same price bracket. This bistro, decorated with graffiti and film stars' photos, serves Macau-style Portuguese food along with other dishes. The **San Francisco Steakhouse** (Tel: 2735-7576), at Barnton Court, Harbour City, 7 Canton Rd., is my final choice in this price category. There is turn-of-the-century elegance with San Francisco memorabilia; U.S. beef and seafood are favorites.

Two Italian restaurants are worth trying. **Valentino Ristorante** (Tel: 2721-6653), at 115 Chatham Rd. South, Tsim Sha Tsui, has a romantic, nostalgic atmosphere with sculpture, photographs, and fashion designs combining with the best cuisine from Venice, Milan, and Rome. The Italian-owned **La Taverna** (Tel: 2369-1945), at 34 Ashley Rd., is a popular bistro favored for its comprehensive menu and regular, special seasonal dishes. **Jimmy's Kitchen** (Tel: 2368-4027), at 29 Ashley Rd., Tsim Sha Tsui, combines Italian with a wide range of other European cuisines in a timbered club-style restaurant that has been popular for fifty years.

At the cheap end of the market, there are good choices. I like the **Patisserie** (Tel: 2736-1818) in Ocean Galleries, Harbour City, Canton Road. It has soups, sandwiches, snacks, desserts, and many coffee and tea specialties. For something more filling, the **Italian Garden** (Tel: 2724-1936) on the rooftop terrace at the Kowloon Park Swimming Complex, 22 Austin Rd., has pizza, spaghetti, and fettucine served in an indoor garden setting. The **Boulevard** (Tel: 2730-3377), in the Ocean Terminal, Harbour City, 3 Canton Rd., is different again. This is a most attractive and informal restaurant in a conservatorylike indoor garden that opens for breakfast then has a buffet dinner at night.

The **Ruby Restaurant** (Tel: 2712-9147), at 65 Waterloo Rd., Ho Man Tin, is an unusual place. Japanese, French, Italian, and Hawaiian influences combine in this Tokyo-style brasserie. Inexpensive set meals are served all day. The **Jouster Restaurant/Pub** (Tel: 2723-0022), at 19 Hart Ave., Tsim Sha Tsui, has a decor of timber beams, mock stone walls, and knights' suits of armour. There are set meals and an à la carte menu. Then there is **Maxim's Restaurant** (Tel: 2366-8635) at 66 Mody Rd. It has a good range of old favorites and some new dishes at affordable prices. Australians will not be able to resist the **Windjammer Restaurant** attached to the Kangaroo Pub. There is wood panelling, a casual atmosphere, and typical Australian pub food. Finally there is the **Spaghetti House** chain of restaurants. These have good-value pizzas, sandwiches, chicken, and spaghetti dishes and are very popular. There are six or seven outlets scattered around Kowloon.

6. Sight-seeing

Many people do not agree, but I do not find Kowloon as interesting for sight-seeing as Hong Kong Island. There are, however, several places of interest and three areas worth exploring on foot.

The first area is the tourist province of **Tsim Sha Tsui**. Many visitors will be staying in this area and others can easily reach here by the Star Ferry. The ferry terminal is a good place to start a walk through the area. Just outside, you will see a clock tower. This is all that remains of the original Kowloon Railway Station that was used until 1975, when a new station was built at Hung Hom.

Heading east along the waterfront, you come to the **Hong Kong Cultural Centre** occupying one of the most spectacular city sites in the world, yet apparently not using it to any advantage. The windowless building with its "skislope" roofline houses a concert hall, a theater, and a range of exhibition spaces. There are restaurants, bars, and other facilities. The Hong Kong Philharmonic Orchestra performs here regularly, and the Hong Kong Museum of Art is within the complex. The museum has a collection of oil paintings, drawings, and etchings, as well as lithographs of old Hong Kong. There are also galleries with Chinese antiquities, fine arts, and contemporary Hong Kong art. The museum is open Monday to Wednesday and Friday and Saturday from 10 A.M. to 6 P.M., and Sunday from 1 P.M. to 6 P.M. Admission is HK$10 for adults and HK$5 for children.

The **Space Museum** (Tel: 2734-2722), which is next door, houses one of the world's largest planetariums, the Space Theatre, where Omnimax and Sky shows are presented. Simultaneous translation in English, Cantonese, Mandarin, and Japanese is available. The museum also houses the Hall of Space Science and the Hall of Astronomy. The exhibition halls are open weekdays, except Tuesday, from 1 P.M. until 9 P.M. and on Saturday and Sunday from 10 A.M. until 9 P.M. Admission is HK$10 for adults and HK$5 for children. You pay extra for the shows.

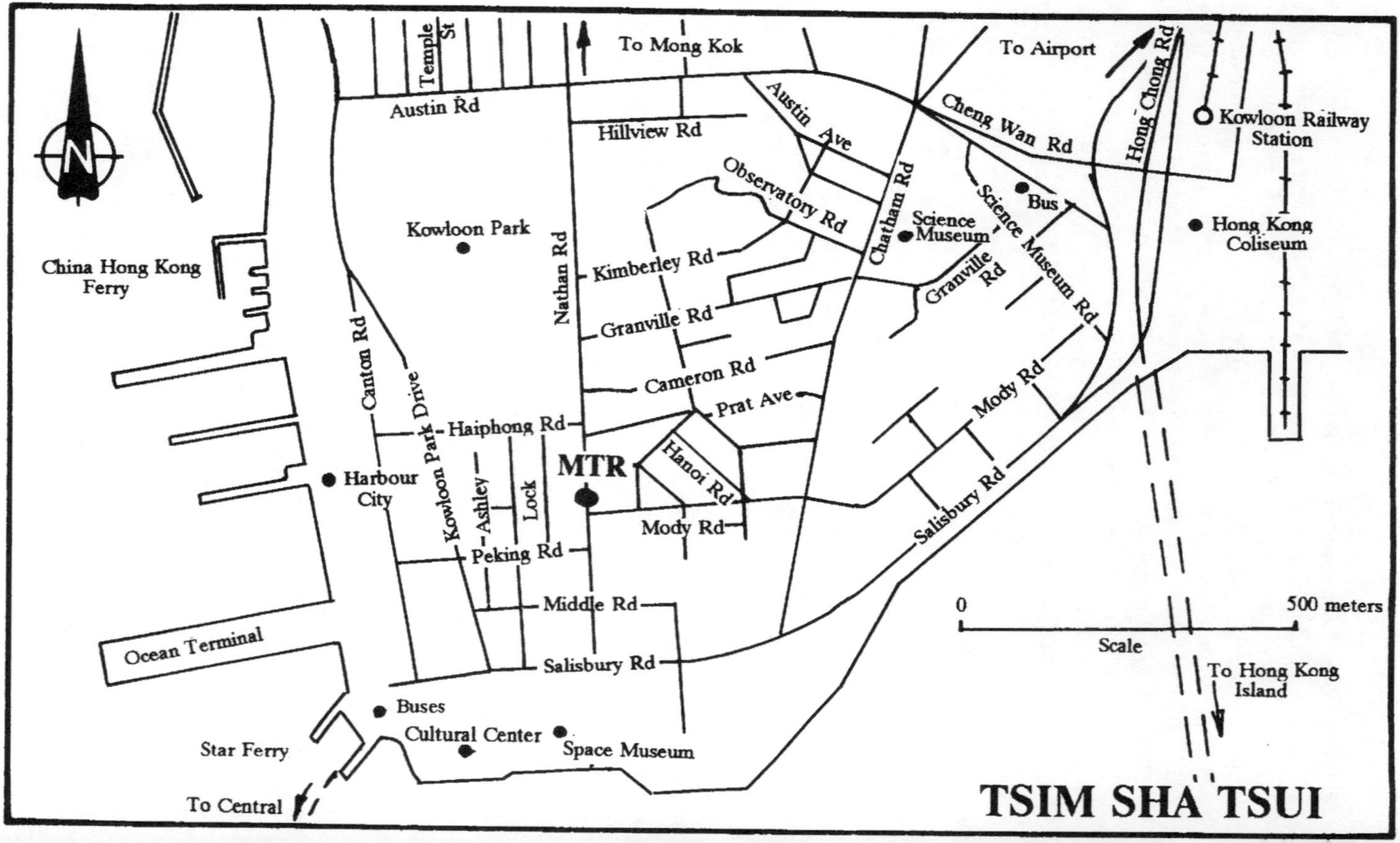
TSIM SHA TSUI
To Mong Kok
To Airport
Temple St
Austin Rd
Hillview Rd
Austin Ave
Cheng Wan Rd
Hong Chong Rd
Kowloon Railway Station
Hong Kong Coliseum
Observatory Rd
Chatham Rd
Science Museum
Bus
Science Museum Rd
Kowloon Park
China Hong Kong Ferry
Nathan Rd
Kimberley Rd
Granville Rd
Granville Rd
Cameron Rd
Prat Ave
Mody Rd
Canton Rd
Kowloon Park Drive
Haiphong Rd
MTR
Hanoi Rd
Harbour City
Ashley
Lock
Mody Rd
Salisbury Rd
Peking Rd
Middle Rd
Salisbury Rd
Ocean Terminal
Buses
Cultural Center
Space Museum
Star Ferry
To Central
0
500 meters
Scale
To Hong Kong Island

Across the road from here is the **Peninsula Hotel,** one of Hong Kong's most prestigious landmarks. The lobby is a great place to have tea or coffee in a rarefied atmosphere and do some people watching. The Peninsula is on the corner on Nathan Road, which is now often called the "Golden Mile," but was originally known as "Nathans Folly." The price of land along here is astronomical, as are some of the prices in some of the "name" shops. The area is crowded with hotels, shopping arcades, and restaurants. It is worth exploring some of the side streets because rents are lower and some prices more economical. Tsim Sha Tsui MTR Station is right at the center of all this activity. After you walk a few blocks north, you will see the white marble **Jamia Masjid,** a lovely mosque built in 1984 along traditional lines. Behind this, but now almost hidden from view, is Kowloon Park. The park was once a leafy retreat but now it is crowded with "improvements" that have given it buildings, concrete plazas, and swimming pools. The Sculpture Walk is worth a visit, as is the Bird Lake and Chinese Garden. Also within the park, is the Hong Kong Museum of History, which has some interesting exhibits housed in old barracks buildings. It is open Monday to Thursday and on Saturday from 10 A.M. to 6 P.M. and on Sunday from 1 P.M. to 6 P.M. Admission is HK$10.

Hong Kong's Nathan Road has been dubbed the "Golden Mile" because of the vast number and selection of shops that line both sides of the street. These shops are surmounted by hundreds of signs in both Chinese and English, in all colors. (Courtesy of the Hong Kong Tourist Association)

If you exit the park on the opposite side from Nathan Road, you will be close to the China Ferry Terminal and the new China Hong Kong City. This is now a major marine entry point from Canton and Macau. Immediately to the south of here is the huge Harbour City complex that houses Hong Kong's largest shopping mall and several major hotels. It would be possible to spend the rest of the day here as you slowly wend you way back to the Star Ferry Terminal through a maze of interconnected buildings.

The next area worth exploring on foot is **Tsim Sha Tsui East.** If you start at the Peninsula Hotel at the corner of Nathan Road and walk along Salisbury Road to the east, you will be heading in the right direction. It is worthwhile to cross the road and visit the lobby of the Regent Hotel for a good example of how to use a spectacular site. If shopping is your need, head into the adjacent New World Centre. But if you are more into sight-seeing, check out the Waterfront Promenade, which runs in front of the Regent then all the way to Hung Hom. The views of Victoria Harbour and Hong Kong Island can be stunning.

Inland from here, are a group of luxury hotels—the Kowloon Shangri-La, the Royal Garden, The Regal Kowloon, the Holiday Inn Harbour View, and the Hotel Niko. There are also shopping centers, restaurants, and nightclubs. Back behind these, on the corner of Chatham and Granville roads, is the **Hong Kong Science Museum.** This is Hong Kong's best museum and is one of the most advanced in the world. It is packed with more than 500 exhibits on four floors and more than half of them are "hands-on." Four major themes are represented—orientation, science, life science, and technology. The Museum opens Tuesday to Friday from 1 P.M. to 9 P.M., and on weekends from 10 A.M. to 9 P.M. Admission is HK$25 for adults and HK$15 for students under 25 and seniors over 60.

For those who are not tired, you can now walk farther to the northeast to the **Hong Kong Coliseum,** a 12,500-seat stadium used for sports events, concerts and exhibitions, and then on to the Kowloon Railway Station. Beyond here are the Hung Hom factory outlets where you can buy low-priced, ready-to-wear fashions. Here you will also find the large Hong Kong Place shopping center and its well-known musical fountain. Almost as well known is the nearby fullsize concrete, luxury cruiser. The 100-meter-long ship sits in the middle of a high-rise housing estate and contains shops, a restaurant, a cinema, and a children's playground. It is a fitting place to finish this walking tour.

The third area to walk is **Yau Ma Tei.** This is north of Tsim Sha Tsui and it contains some of the least changed streets in Hong Kong. It is also one of the most densely settled areas in the city (read this as the world) so there is always plenty to see. The best place to start is the Yau Ma Tei MRT station where you take the Man Ming Lane/Central Post Office exit to Nathan Road. You emerge in the center of a busy shopping thoroughfare and could be tempted to head into the emporiums and arcades. Resist this temptation and walk two blocks south to Public Square Street. Here you will see a small park with some temples and big banyan trees. The park is often filled with men playing Chinese chess and other games. The largest temple is dedicated to Tin Hau, the Goddess of the Sea. Inside the green-roofed temple, you will find incense coils, carved spirits, memorial tablets, a man who interprets the bamboo fortune sticks, and a blind fortune-teller. It is open from 8 A.M. to 6 P.M.

Now walk three blocks down Public Square Street to Shanghai Street and turn right. Walk slowly down here because this street is packed with interest. On your right you will see a shrine shop selling household shrine cupboards and ancestral shrines. If you look carefully you will find that almost every business has such a shrine for worship and to ward off evil spirits. Next door is an incense shop. Incense is burned inside temples, in front of ancestral shrines and at the entrance to homes. Farther along, there is a roasted meat shop with display racks of glazed ducks and chickens, while nearby is a sausage shop. The shop at number 302 has mainland Chinese wine made from herbs, fruits, flowers, and animals. These are taken as a tonic and many of them are claimed to have almost magical properties. Near the corner of Man Ming Lane, there is an old Chinese teahouse that serves dim sum. It is a great place to join the locals—just smile and point.

Keep walking until you reach Waterloo Street then turn left. You will pass a cluster of cheap food stalls, the area's ancient cinema, and the huge wholesale fruit market. Ahead is the Yau Ma Tei typhoon shelter, which is a maze of cargo lighters, sampans, and dwelling boats. Now head south along Ferry Street until you come to the Kansu Street flyover. Here you will find Hong Kong's jade market. The market has been in existence for about 25 years, first in Canton Road, then here since 1984. There are some 450 stall holders and buying and selling is a very serious business. Many Chinese attribute magical and medicinal powers to the cold green stone. The market operates from 10 A.M. to 3:30 P.M. Bargaining is very much part of the action. A little farther to the east, you will find a retail fruit market. All the streets south from here have places of interest. You could wander around for several hours. Canton Road has a marble factory and a mahjong tile painter. Reclamation Street has a typical Cantonese open-air market with a profusion of fresh vegetables. Shanghai Street has jewelry shops, a lovely embroidery store, and a Chinese bakery. Saigon Street has an herbal tea shop and a pawn shop on the corner of Shanghai Street. It is said that fisherwomen used to pawn their babies here. There is still a letter-writer on Woosung Street, and near Ning Po Street there is an herbalist who will examine your tongue and pulse before prescribing a range of herbs, flowers, and insects to be made into a tea and drunk slowly.

This area is also well worth visiting at night because of the Temple Street

Market. Stalls start setting up from around 6 P.M. but the best time to visit is after 8 P.M. Here everything is cheap, if you bargain properly. You will find sweaters, brand-name T-shirts, jeans, jogging gear, bags, cassette tapes, C.D.'s, watches, and so forth. Some are factory over-runs, some are seconds, and others are counterfeit copies. There are also many seafood stalls that sell and serve clams, shrimp, mussels, and crabs at less-than-restaurant prices. Under the flyover, you will see fortune-tellers, professional chess players, and vendors of magic cures clustered around kerosene lamps.

OTHER AREAS

North from Yau Ma Tei is **Mong Kok.** This was once considered to be the world's most densely populated area and it was associated with crime and secret societies. While it remains crowded, it has taken on a different appearance in recent years and some visitors are choosing to stay here because it is cheaper but still quite convenient. The Bird Market on Hong Lok Street is a good insight into Chinese thought. Birds are a favorite pet in many traditional Chinese families and here you will see hundreds of birds for sale at prices that seem astronomical. Singing ability is favored over appearance but the intricately fashioned wood and bamboo cages are works of art. Note the bags of live grasshoppers that are for sale as bird feed. The market is open from around 10 A.M. until 6 P.M. The nearby Ladies Market in Tung Choi Street opens every afternoon. A wide range of ladies' jeans, shoes, other clothes, and accessories are for sale until about 10 P.M.

The other places of interest are actually in New Kowloon, part of the New Territories, but because they seem to be part of Kowloon, I will mention them here. The first is the **Lei Cheng Uk Museum,** which contains a tomb that is probably almost 2,000 years old. There is detailed information about the tomb and the funerary objects found inside, and an exhibition of Han dynasty (A.D. 25-220) agricultural techniques. The museum is on Tonkin Street, about a five-minute walk from the Cheung Sha Wan MTR Station. One station farther than this will take you close to the Tsui Museum of Art in Rediffusion House, 822 Lai Chi Kok Road. The collection has more than 2,000 pieces of Chinese art and a great ceramic collection of about 500 pieces on display. Admission is free and the museum is open 10 A.M. to 4:30 P.M. Monday to Saturday.

The **Wong Tai Sin Temple** is visited by more than three million worshippers annually and it provides visitors with an excellent insight into Chinese religious beliefs and practices. The main temple with its red pillars, golden roof, turquoise friezes, and yellow latticework is a good example of traditional Chinese temple architecture. Tables for offerings of fruit and joss sticks line the lower terrace where paper offerings are burned and prayers are made. Taps of blessed water are nearby and fortune-tellers ply their

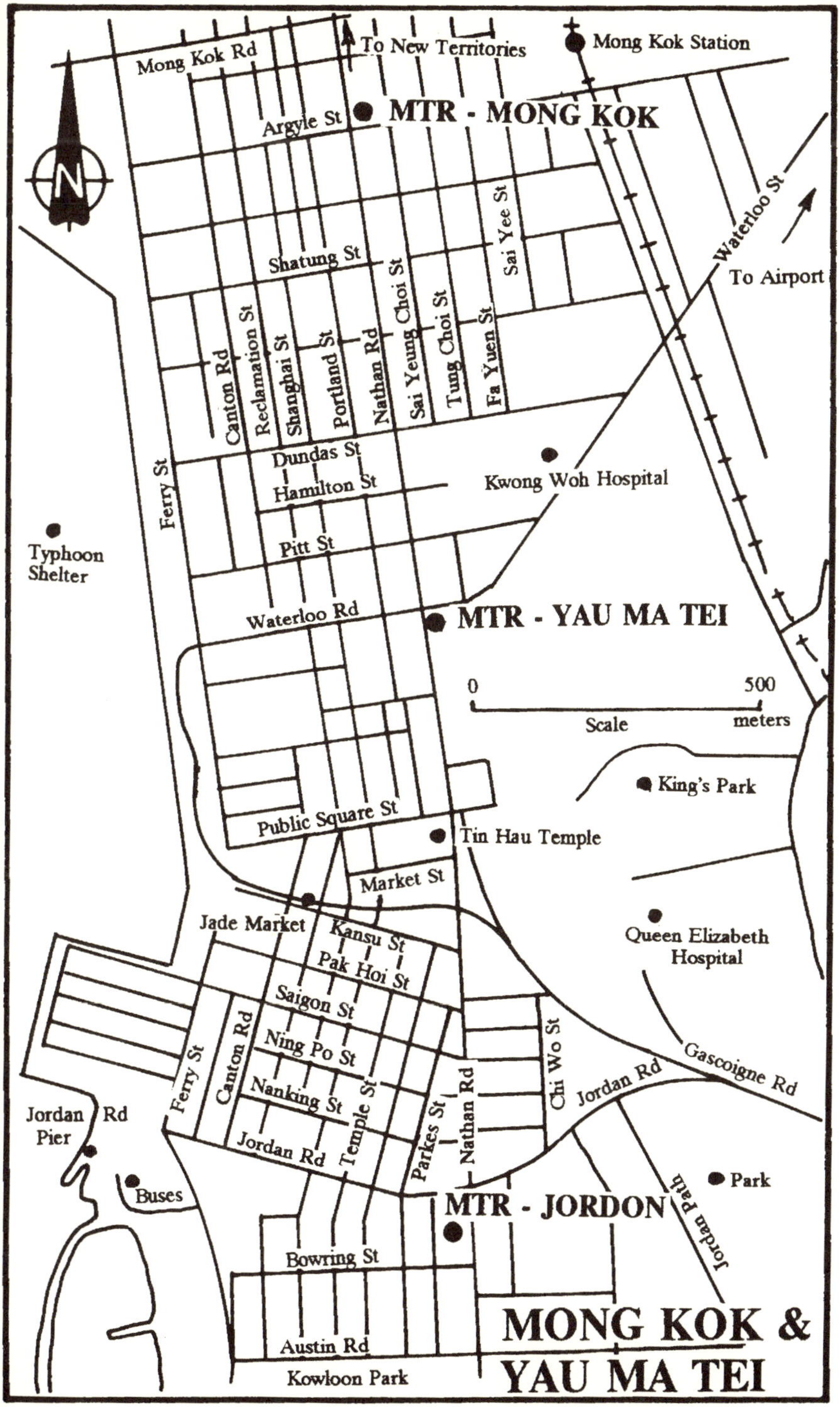

Mong Kok Rd
To New Territories
Mong Kok Station
Argyle St
MTR - MONG KOK
Waterloo St
To Airport
Shatung St
Sai Yee St
Canton Rd
Reclamation St
Shanghai St
Portland St
Nathan Rd
Sai Yeung Choi St
Tung Choi St
Fa Yuen St
Dundas St
Hamilton St
Kwong Woh Hospital
Ferry St
Typhoon Shelter
Pitt St
Waterloo Rd
MTR - YAU MA TEI
0
500
Scale
meters
King's Park
Public Square St
Tin Hau Temple
Market St
Jade Market
Kansu St
Pak Hoi St
Queen Elizabeth Hospital
Saigon St
Ning Po St
Nanking St
Ferry St
Canton Rd
Chi Wo St
Gascoigne Rd
Jordan Rd
Jordan Pier
Rd
Temple St
Parkes St
Nathan Rd
Jordan Rd
Buses
MTR - JORDON
Jordan Path
Park
Bowring St
Austin Rd
Kowloon Park
MONG KOK &
YAU MA TEI

trade. Despite the noise and activity, there is much respect, reverence, and faith here. The temple is open from 7 A.M. until 5 P.M. daily. A small donation is expected from visitors. It is easy to reach. Take the MTR to Wong Tai Sin Station, and follow the signs.

The **Sung Dynasty Village** tries to give a living museum experience of lifestyles during China's Sung dynasty (A.D. 960-1279). All of the "villagers" are dressed in period costume and some work in a series of pavilion shops displaying ancient crafts such as calligraphy, incense-stick manufacture, umbrella-making, and candy production. Samples can be purchased. There is a tea pavilion and a wine tavern, and dim sum is cooked and served on the riverside walkway. You will also find acrobats, fortune-telling, a monkey show, and kung fu displays. To top it off, you can visit a wax museum featuring many leading figures from Chinese history. Individual visitors are admitted daily from 10 A.M. to 8:30 P.M. Admission is HK$110 for adults and HK$60 for children. The No. 6A bus from the Star Ferry in Kowloon terminates close to the village.

It is worth visiting the rural, coastal village of **Lei Yue Mun.** It was from its boulder-edged cliffs in 1941 that the invading Japanese forces launched their attack on Hong Kong Island. Today, the fishing village is still characterized by a cluster of stilted buildings and it is known for its seafood restaurants and fishmonger stalls. Some of Lei Yue Mun's restaurants have terraces from which visitors can enjoy the sea breeze and appreciate the view. You take the MTR to Kwun Tong Station, then take bus 14C to its Sam Ka Tsuen terminus, then walk for five minutes around the headland.

7. Guided Tours

Many of the comments made in the Hong Kong Island chapter under this heading apply equally to Kowloon. Many of the tours listed in that chapter are available to visitors in Kowloon via a hotel pick-up service. Here I only list tours that have a substantial Kowloon content. It should be noted that most of these are also available to people staying on Hong Kong Island or the New Territories.

The **Kowloon and New Territories Tour** operates daily both in the morning and the afternoon. The route covers the urban and industrial areas of Kowloon and the scenic rural areas of the New Territories. Included are the busy Kwai Chung container terminal, Tsuen Wan, a beach at Castle Peak, a stop near the Chinese border, Tai Po, Shatin and the racecourse, and scenic Amah Rock. The cost is around HK$140.

The **Housing and Home Visit** tour is an opportunity to spend some time close to ordinary Hong Kong residents. The four-hour tour departs every Thursday morning and takes you inside public housing estates, model flats, markets, a nursery or kindergarten, one of the estate family flats, and the popular Wong Tai Sin Temple. The cost is around HK$200.

There are several three-hour tours to the Sung Dynasty Village. They depart around 10 A.M., 12:30 P.M., 3 P.M., and 5:30 P.M. The village is a replica of a city from the Sung dynasty. There are shops, houses, colorful cultural shows, a wedding parade, a monkey show, and demonstrations of Chinese folk arts. There is also a wax museum depicting famous figures from Chinese history. A meal or snack is served. The cost is from around HK$240 depending on the tour you take.

The **Open-Top Bus Tour/Pearl of the Orient** takes five hours and operates nightly. You depart Tsim Sha Tsui in an open-top bus to see the Yau Ma Tei typhoon shelter, Lung Cheung Road lookout, resettlement estates, and Nathan Road's "Golden Mile." This is followed by a waterborne buffet dinner with live music while cruising around Victoria Harbour on the *Pearl of the Orient*. The cost is around HK$440.

Kowloon by Night and Buffet Dinner Cruise is a variation of the previous offering. The tour begins with a predinner cocktail at a cozy bar, followed by a visit to the Temple Street night market with its street entertainment and hawker stalls. A boat is then boarded for a buffet dinner with live music and dancing. The nightly five-hour tour costs from around HK$375.

8. Culture

For a free introduction to Chinese opera, take yourself to Temple Street, where every evening, local troupes gather to reherse material on the pavement opposite the multistory parking garage.

See the culture sections in other chapters for further information.

9. Sports

For a complete understanding of all the sporting options open to the visitor, you also need to read the "sports" section of the Hong Kong Island chapter, the New Territories chapter, and the Outlying Islands chapter. There are, however, a number of sports opportunities in Kowloon and these are mentioned below.

Kowloon Park comes alive each morning just after dawn with mass displays of *t'ai chi ch'uan*. You are welcome to watch or join in. It is a personal, individual, beautiful ballet based on the idea that all life is change. The various postures are said to put the participant in touch with the rhythm of the universe and provide the gifts of inner peace and tranquility. If you wish to follow this interest more seriously, there are many classes at all levels at the YMCA International House, 22 Waterloo St. (Tel: 2771-9111). Classes are also held in *judo, tae kwon do, hung kuen,* and *hak kei do*. You could also contact the Hong Kong Chinese Martial Arts Association at 687 Nathan Rd. (Tel: 2394-4803).

Tennis courts are available in the Kowloon Tsai Park in North Kowloon (Tel: 2336-7878). The cost is around HK$30 depending on the time of the day. The same center also has squash courts. The Brunswick Bowling Centre, Energy Plaza, Mody Road, has modern bowling alleys.

Ice skating is available at the Laichikok Amusement Park (Tel: 2741-4281) next to the Sung Dynasty Village, and at the Whampoa Super Ice within Whampoa Gardens, Hung Hom (Tel: 2774-4899). A roller skating rink can be found at Telford Gardens (Tel: 2757-2211). The Kowloon Cricket Club plays in a park adjoining Austin Road.

10. Shopping

I urge you to read the shopping section of the Hong Kong Island chapter in conjunction with the following, because many of the general comments that were made there are equally applicable to Kowloon. In some ways Kowloon is an even better place to shop than Hong Kong Island because Tsim Sha Tsui is almost one huge shopping complex. On the other hand there are probably more blatant rip-offs in Kowloon than elsewhere, so beware. Here are a few pointers.

DEPARTMENT STORES

Duty Free Shoppers Hong Kong is very big here. There are outlets at 5 Hankow Rd. (Tel: 2721-2281); at Ocean Terminal in Harbour City (Tel: 2735-5111); at the China Ferry Terminal, 33 Canton Rd.; at 77 Mody Rd., Tsim Sha Tsui East; and at three locations within the international air terminal. Remember, though, that the only merchandise for sale that is liable for duty in Hong Kong is liquor and tobacco, so prices here are not necessarily better than anywhere else. There is, however, an excellent range, so it is well worth a visit.

Lane Crawford has two outlets: one at Manson House, 74 Nathan Rd. (Tel: 2721-9668); and the other in Ocean Terminal, Harbour City. Japanese stores are represented by **Isetan** in the Sheraton Hotel Shopping Mall (Tel: 2369-0111); **Tokyu** in the New World Centre, 24 Salisbury Rd. (Tel: 2722-0102); **Yaohan** at Whampoa Garden, Hung Hom (Tel: 2766-0338); and **Mitsukoshi** in Sun Plaza, 28 Canton Rd. (Tel: 2375-7222). **Mark's and Spencer** is in Ocean Centre, Harbour City (Tel: 2730-3163).

Several of the locally owned Chinese stores are here. **Dragon Seed** has an outlet in Albion Plaza, 2 Granville Rd. (Tel: 2723-6568), and a boutique

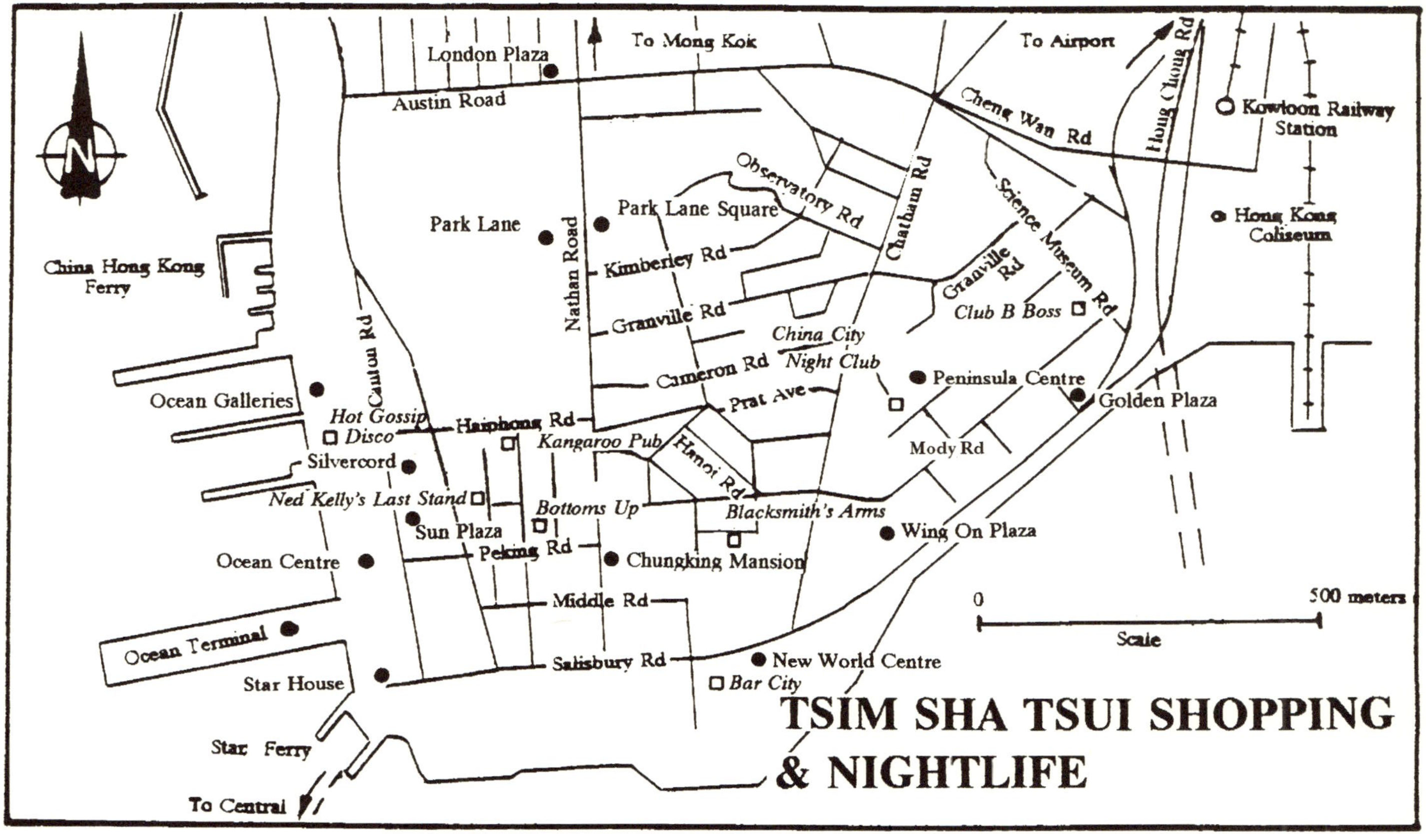
TSIM SHA TSUI SHOPPING
& NIGHTLIFE
N
London Plaza
To Mong Kok
To Airport
Austin Road
Cheng Wan Rd
Hong Chong Rd
Kowloon Railway
Station
Hong Kong
Coliseum
Observatory Rd
Chatham Rd
Science Museum Rd
Park Lane
Park Lane Square
Nathan Road
Kimberley Rd
Granville Rd
Granville Rd
Club B Boss
China Hong Kong
Ferry
China City
Night Club
Cameron Rd
Prat Ave
Peninsula Centre
Golden Plaza
Ocean Galleries
Canton Rd
Hot Gossip
Disco
Haiphong Rd
Kangaroo Pub
Hanoi Rd
Mody Rd
Silvercord
Ned Kelly's Last Stand
Bottoms Up
Blacksmith's Arms
Sun Plaza
Wing On Plaza
Peking Rd
Chungking Mansion
Ocean Centre
Middle Rd
0
500 meters
Scale
Ocean Terminal
Salisbury Rd
New World Centre
Star House
Bar City
Star Ferry
To Central

within the New World Centre. **The Sincere Company** has a store at 83 Argyle St., Mong Kok (Tel: 2394-0261). And **Wing On** stores can be found at 361 Nathan Rd., Yau Ma Tei (Tel: 2780-4341), and 62 Mody St., Tsim Sha Tsui East.

Finally there are the Chinese emporiums. At one time these only sold items made in China but these days they seem to have some other items as well. They are very big on arts and crafts and household goods. Try **The Chinese Merchandise Emporium** at 65 Argyle St., Mong Kok (Tel: 2395-3191); the **Chung Kiu Chinese Products Emporium** at 47 Shan Tung St., Mong Kok (Tel: 2780-2331); at 528 Nathan Rd., Yau Ma Tei; and at 17 Hankow Rd., Tsim Sha Tsui; **Friendship Stores** at 86 Canton Rd. (Tel: 2369-8202); and **Yue Hwa Chinese Products** at 301 Nathan Rd., Yau Ma Tei (Tel: 2384-0084), an excellent store; or there are other branches at 54 Nathan Rd. and 143 Nathan Rd. in the Park Lane Shopper's Boulevard.

SHOPPING MALLS

Harbour City used to lay claim to the title of the "largest shopping center in Asia" but other developments have reduced this to "one of the largest centers in Hong Kong." Certainly it is an amazing place with more than 500 shops and 50 restaurants. It is actually made up of several centers—Ocean Terminal, Ocean Centre, Ocean Galleries—that have been linked by walkways and escalators. It is easy to get lost but perhaps that is part of the fun. The complex stretches along Canton Road and incorporates or surrounds the three Omni hotels.

China Hong Kong City is at the northern end of Harbour City. This is the major terminal for ferries to China and there are growing opportunities for shoppers. The complex is still growing. On the same road, the **Silvercord Shopping Centre** is a good place to look for computers.

Elsewhere, the **New World Center,** between the Regent and New World hotels, has 250 stores and comes with the slogan "shop where the locals shop." The "locals" must have more money than I do if they shop here regularly, but it is a good place to browse and there are often sales to provide some bargains. Farther east, there are a number of complexes on Mody Street. These include **Wing On Plaza, Houston Centre, Tsim Sha Tsui Centre, Empire Centre,** and **Chinachem Golden Plaza.** These are stand-alone complexes, but it is not difficult to visit several of them within a few hours.

Finally there is **Chungking Mansion** back on Nathan Road. This is in the very heart of the "Golden Mile" and some people think it is great. I am not one of them. I find it too hot, too crowded, and many of the shopkeepers are too pushy. Fans of this place say it is a place for a bargain. I have never been so lucky, but it may be worth a try. It is next to the Holiday Inn Golden Mile.

INTERESTING SHOPPING AREAS

There are three areas worth identifying. The **Jade Market** is located under the fly-over near Kansu Street in Yau Ma Tei. This is a good place to pick up some small pieces as souvenirs. It is not the place to go if you are a serious buyer who knows little about the product. There are all varieties of jade with prices to match. It opens daily between 10 A.M. and 4 P.M.

Tung Choi Street in Mong Kok is often called "Ladies Market" because the area specializes in inexpensive local ladies' fashions, jewelry, shoes, and accessories. Stallholders setup around noon and operate until about 10:30 P.M. You reach here by MTR to Mong Kok Station then exit to Nelson Street.

Temple Street is Hong Kong's most popular night market. Hundreds of stalls set up at around 7 P.M. to sell clothing, watches, stationery, sunglasses, cassettes, luggage, and much more. Activity reaches a peak around 9 P.M., when it can get very crowded and customer service drops off sharply. Watch for pickpockets.

BEST BUYS

Art Works. I believe Hong Kong Island is better for antiques but the following places have some interesting art and art objects and some truly outstanding modern pieces.

Chinese Arts & Crafts—Silvercord Centre. Tel: 2375-0155.
　　　　　　—Star House, Salisbury Road. Tel: 2735-4061
　　　　　　—233 Nathan Rd. Tel: 730-0061.
Eileen Kershaw—Peninsula Hotel, Salisbury Road. Tel: 2366-4083.
Phoenix & Co.—66 Mody Rd., Tsim Sha Tsui. Tel: 2368-4808.
Tong-in Antique Gallery—5 Hankow Rd. Tel: 2369-1406.
Amazing Grace Elephant Co.—Ocean Centre, Harbour City. Tel: 2730-5455.
Welfare Handicrafts—Salisbury Road. Tel: 2366-6979.

Cameras and Photographic Equipment. Talk to the sole agents first then consider:

Broadway Photo Supply—731 Nathan Rd. Tel: 2394-3827.
　　　　　　—59 Hip Wo St., Kwun Tong. Tel: 2797-2952.
The Camera Shop—Ocean Terminal, Harbour City. Tel: 2730-9227.
Fujimage—Park Lane Shopping Centre, Nathan Road. Tel: 2368-4128.
Sunlight Photo Supplies—20 Mody Rd. Tel: 2366-6757.

Computers. There are dozens of computer shops in the Silvercord Centre, 30 Canton Rd. Browse around and please ask in several places for prices. In my very limited experience, I have found the following reasonably helpful:

Mastertech Automation—48 Lower ground floor. Tel: 2375-0699.

Mastor Technology—12 Lower ground floor. Tel: 2722-0188.

Furs. There are several factory outlets in Kowloon that claim to be substantially cheaper than the retail stores. Try these:

Asia Fur Co.—36 Man Yue St., Hung Hom. Tel: 2633-4287.
Deluxe Fur Salon—21 Man Lock St., Hung Hom. Tel: 2334-8725.
International Fur—1 Hok Cheung St., Hung Hom. Tel: 2334-2346.

Upmarket Clothing. Many of the top names are represented here.

Alfred Dunhill—Peninsula Hotel. Tel: 2368-7721
　　　　　　—Hyatt Regency Hotel. Tel: 2311-4448
Boutique Christian Dior—Peninsula Hotel. Tel: 2721-9370
Benetton—The Hong Kong Hotel, 3 Canton Rd. Tel: 2369-3510
　　　　—New World Centre, Salisbury Road. Tel: 2311-4328
Esprit—Park Lane, Nathan Road. Tel: 2739-0290
　　　—Ocean Galleries, Harbour City. Tel: 2735-6889
Etienne Aigner—Hyatt Regency Hotel. Tel: 2369-6236
Hermes Boutique—Peninsula Hotel. Tel: 2368-6739
Jaeger—The Regent Hotel. Tel: 2366-1901
Jojce Boutique—The Regent Hotel. Tel: 2368-7649
Lanvin—The Regent Hotel. Tel: 2721-5816
The Swank Shop—The Peninsula Hotel. Tel: 2721-5956
　　　　　　—Ocean Terminal, Harbour City. Tel: 2735-0842

Clothing Factory Outlets. The Kaiser Estate area of Hung Hom is crowded with outlets. It is just a matter of going from one to the other to find what you want. If you are a serious budget shopper, this is the place. If, on the other hand, you just want a few items, you can find several places in Tsim Sha Tsui that would suit your purpose. Here are a few listings:

Cava, Ltd.—Star House, 3 Salisbury Rd. Tel: 2735-1922.
Dorfit, Ltd.—71 Peking Rd., Tsim Sha Tsui. Tel: 2312-1013.
Ede Limited—37 Man Yue St., Hung Hom. Tel: 2334-4218.
Everview—38 Man Yue St., Hung Hom. Tel: 2764-0289.
Fashions of Seventh Ave.—9 Hok Yuen St., Hung Hom. Tel: 2764-4655.
Gat Design—21 Granville St., Tsim Sha Tsui. Tel: 2722-6287.
Mayeelok—Silvercord, 30 Canton Rd. Tel: 2375-0493.
Shoppers' World—17 Hankow Rd., Tsim Sha Tsui. Tel: 2376-1075.

One further option is to go to D & D Warehouse in the Gee Luen Chang Building at 11 Yuk Yat St., Kwa Wan, near Kai Tak Airport. On the third floor, this large, modern, high-tech space is decked out with chic clothes for working women. The look is based on clean lines, fine drape, and subtle colors. They accept credit cards.

Custom Tailoring. Kowloon is packed with tailors and there is considerable price competition. All tailors can copy an existing garment but many are not great at interpreting from a picture. Kwun Kee Tailor is by far the largest chain with multiple outlets in Mong Kok and Yau Ma Tei, and shops at 62 Cameron Rd., Tsim Sha Tsui (Tel: 2724-3987), and 67 Mody Rd., Tsim Sha Tsui East (Tel: 2723-0687). Jimmy Chen & Co. is an upmarket tailor with outlets in the Omni The Hong Kong Hotel (Tel: 2730-5045) and the Peninsula Hotel (Tel: 2722-1888). There are many "cheap" outlets in Chungking Mansion, 36 Nathan Rd.

Ceramics, Bone China, and Porcelain. Leading brands of Western bone china are claimed to be at least 50 percent lower than in the United States and Japan. Chinese porcelain is also a good buy with lamps, vases, and figurines being popular items. Dealers will dispatch items back home for you but it is advisable to take out "all-risks" insurance. You can even commission your own design at one of the porcelain factories. Try the following:

Ah Cow Factory—489 Castle Peak Rd., Lai Chi Kok. Tel: 2745-1511.
Art Universe—Royal Garden Hotel, 69 Mody Rd. Tel: 2369-2729.
Hunter's of Hong Kong—Peninsula Hotel. Tel: 2722-1169.
　　　　　　　　　—Kowloon Hotel. Tel: 2311-3596.
Noritake—Ocean Centre, Harbour City. Tel: 2736-2971.
Royal Copenhagen—Ocean Terminal, Ocean City. Tel: 2735-4321.
Waterford Wedgewood Trading—Peninsula Hotel. Tel: 2311-0681.

Jewelry. If you thought Hong Kong Island had plenty of jewelry stores, just wait until you see Kowloon. It is quite impossible for me to make recommendations. There are a few chains such as Chow Sang Sang Jewellery (Tel: 2730-3241), Chow Tai Fok (Tel: 2385-0047), Edelweiss (Tel: 2730-8950), Jewelry Kingdom (Tel: 2311-5937), and Tse Sui Luen Jewellery (Tel: 2739-6673). Then there are hundreds of individual outlets ranging from those in the top hotels to holes-in-the-wall in Mong Kok. There are also a few so-called factory outlets that could be worth trying. You should know something about precious stones and gold, however, before you make any large purchases. Try these:

Chaumont International—57 Peking Rd. Tel: 2368-7331.
Citygold—51 Man Yue St., Hung Hom. Tel: 2765-7650.
Heng Ngai—4 Hok Yuen St. East, Hung Hom. Tel: 2764-8922.
Lloyds—68 Sung Wong Toi Rd., Kowloon City. Tel: 2334-1331.
Way Shun Gems—21 Man Lok St., Hung Hom. Tel: 2330-6833.

Watches. Check the sole agents listed in the Hong Kong Island chapter. You could also visit one of the outlets of City Chain. You will have no trouble finding one because at last count there were 26 in Kowloon. Look in Nathan

Road, Harbour City, Mody Street, or telephone 2736-1011 for the nearest outlet to you.

Leather Goods. Try the markets for imitation leather goods, the streets between Nathan Road and Chatham Road for locally made goods, and the following for top quality items:

a.testoni—The Peninsula Hotel. Tel: 2368-8000.
Bally Boutique—Royal Garden Hotel. Tel: 2723-0811.
            —Regent Hotel. Tel: 2311-4366.
Chanel Boutique—Peninsula Hotel. Tel: 2368-6879.
Gucci—Sun Plaza, 28 Canton Rd. Tel: 2375-2023.
Hermes Boutique—Peninsula Hotel. Tel: 2368-6739.
Longchamp Co.—The Regent Hotel. Tel: 2721-6391.
Louis Vuitton—The Peninsula Hotel. Tel: 2366-3731.
Toyo Leather Ware—49 Carnarvon Rd. Tel: 2721-5403.

If you are seriously into leather, you should take a visit to the factory neighborhood of Kwun Tong. Here at Union Hing Yip Factory Building, 11th floor, 20 Hing Yip St., you will find Leather Concepts. This sells big-name designer leather goods for men and women. Prices are not low, but quality is tops and value is excellent. There are men's and women's jackets and coats, women's trousers, and handbags and accessories.

Optical Goods. There are 19 outlets of The Optical Shop in Kowloon, so you will easily find one of those. Try Nathan Road, Mody Road, Ocean City, or telephone 2736-0810. I have no particular recommendations.

11. Entertainment and Nightlife

You should read the entertainment and nightlife section of chapter 4 in conjuction with this section to get a better picture of the nighttime scene. What must be realized, however, is that this is now a bustling metropolis offering an expensive, but diverse, range of after-hours distractions catering to all tastes. From the pursuit of the artistic to the razzamatazz of the glitzy night spot, this throbbing city is fast gaining a reputation as a serious devotee of, and venue for, exciting, international-standard cultural and entertainment pursuits.

As you would expect, the major hotels have much to offer. The following are some of my personal favorites. The **Tartan Bar** at the Omni Marco Polo Hotel (Tel: 2736-0888) is unpretentious but there is a nice atmosphere. There is subdued live entertainment nightly. At the adjacent Omni Prince Hotel, **The Tavern** (Tel: 2736-1888) with its Victorian decor serves the same purpose but it has more of a party mood. Across on Nathan Road, the very popular **Chin Chin Bar** at the Hyatt Regency (Tel: 2311-1234) has a cozy atmosphere enhanced by singers in the evening, while **Nathans** is more upmarket with a pianist setting the mood for relaxation. Across the road at the Holiday Inn Golden Mile, **Baron's Tavern** (Tel: 2369-3111) is a spacious cocktail lounge that stays open until 3 A.M. At the Ambassador Hotel, **Point After** (Tel: 2366-6321) has trendy decor and karaoke singing, while **Someplace Else** at the Sheraton Hotel and Towers (Tel: 2369-1111) has exotic cocktails, live entertainment, filling Mexican food, and good fun, all at acceptable prices.

Moving towards Tsim Sha Tsui East, it is worth stopping off at the **Mezzanine Lounge** at the Regent Hotel (Tel: 2721-1211) to admire the view and take in the live music. Then you can visit the **Catwalk Nightspot** at the New World Hotel (Tel: 2369-4111) for a choice of Latin American music, disco sounds, or karaoke. The **Tiara Lounge** at the Kowloon Shangri-La Hotel (Tel: 2721-2111) has gentle music and dancing harbor lights, and you will find a similar atmosphere at **The Balcony** within the Royal Garden Hotel (Tel: 2721-5215), and the **Golden Carp Bar** at the Holiday Inn Harbour View (Tel: 2721-5161). **Le Rendezvous** at the Regal Kowloon Hotel (Tel: 2722-1818) is a smart, elegant room with a lively band that creates a party mood most evenings. Out at the Regal Airport Hotel, the **China Coast Pub** (Tel: 2718-0333), with its traditional English fare, darts, and billiards is a cheerful place.

Away from the hotels, Kowloon nightlife seems to have considerable Australian influence. **Ned Kelly's Last Stand** (Tel: 2366-0562), at 11A Ashley Rd., has cold beer, pub food, and great Dixieland jazz most evenings. **The Kangaroo Pub** (Tel: 312-00830), at 35 Haiphong Rd., has a range of beers, wood panelling, and a chatty atmosphere. **The Blacksmith's Arms** (Tel: 2369-6696), at 16 Minden Ave., substitutes British atmosphere for Australian. **Bottoms Up** (Tel: 2721-4509), a topless bar at 14 Hankow Rd., has an eye-catching sign and made it into an ancient James Bond movie, but it has seen better days. **Hot Gossip Disco** (Tel: 2730-6884) in Harbour City is one of the best boogie bars. **Amoeba** (Tel: 2376-0389) at 22 Ashley Rd. is currently Kowloon's hippest hangout with minimalist decor and rock music for the aspiring deaf.

There are several large hostess clubs in Kowloon that are best avoided if money is not unlimited. Most are aimed at the local rich Chinese market or visiting Japanese and Korean businessmen, but they will welcome anyone. Inside you find luxurious decor, luxurious hostesses, and luxurious prices. **Club B Boss** (Tel: 2369-2883), at 14 Science Museum Rd., claims to be the world's largest Japanese-style nightclub with more than 1,000 hostesses of many nationalities. The nearby **China City Nightclub** (Tel: 2723-3278), at 67 Mody Rd., and **Club Metropolitan** (Tel: 2311-1111), at 77 Mody Rd., have similar multimillion-dollar ambiance. **Club Deluxe** (Tel: 2721-0277) is not so expensive and welcomes couples to enjoy the music, waterfalls, and Filipino bands, as well as providing hostesses. This is in the New

World Office Building at 18 Salisbury Rd. In the basement of this same complex, you will find **Bar City** (Tel: 2369-8571), a complete entertainment center. The entry ticket with drink coupons allows you to wander between the various forms of entertainment. There is a high-tech disco, live bands in a Las Vegas-style setting, and Country and Western cabaret artists.

Kowloon has a number of cinema complexes. Harbour City Cinemas (Tel: 2735-6915) has English-language movies in good surroundings. The Space Museum (Tel: 2734-2722) shows a range of spectacular films.

12. The Kowloon Address List

Ambulance—St. John's	Tel: 2713-5555
Airlines—Cathay Pacific	
Reservations	Tel: 2747-1888
Flight Information	Tel: 2747-1234
—Dragonair, 33 Canton Rd.	
Reservations	Tel: 2590-1188
Flight Information	Tel: 2769-7728
Churches—St. Andrew's Anglican, 138 Nathan Rd.	Tel: 2367-1478
—Rosary Roman Catholic, 125 Chatham Rd. South	Tel: 2368-0980
—Kowloon Union, 4 Jordon Rd.	Tel: 2367-2585
Emergency—Police, fire, ambulance	Tel: 999
Hong Kong Tourist Association—General	Tel: 2801-7177
—Shopping	Tel: 2801-7278
Hospital—Queen Elizabeth, Wylie Road	Tel: 2710-2111
Public Transport—Kowloon-Canton Railway	Tel: 2602-7799
—Kowloon Motor Bus	Tel: 2745-4466
—Mass Transit Railway	Tel: 2750-0170
—Star Ferries	Tel: 2366-2576
Telephone Information—	Tel: 1081

6

The New Territories

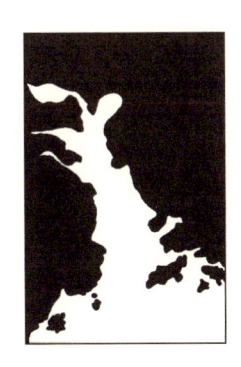

1. The General Picture

The largest land area of Hong Kong lies between Kowloon and the Chinese border. This area was leased by Britain for 99 years under the second Convention of Peking of 1898. It is called the New Territories. Actually, everything north of Boundary Street is included in this lease and should be called the New Territories, but in practice the name is used for the area north of the Kowloon Hills. This is the area that I have adopted in this chapter.

This area was long neglected, but with Hong Kong's growing population, it has seen considerable development in recent years. A "New Towns Program" has created skyscraper settlements in areas that were open fields a few years ago, and this has sent the population from half a million in 1970 to nearly two and a half million today. Fortunately, much of the countryside has been preserved within 21 country parks and nature reserves. The result is an area of scenic contrasts—hilly woodlands, sandy bays, ornate temples, bustling markets and town centers, isolated hamlets, and modern highways. The major towns (some with populations of many hundreds of thousands) are as modern as any towns on earth, yet there are areas where indigenous villages and fisherfolk observe traditions that are centuries old and present the visitor with fascinating images of ancient China and that lifestyle.

Most visitors to Hong Kong do not take the time to visit the New Territories. This is a pity because this area presents a different picture to others and you need to see them all to fully understand the success and magic of Hong Kong. Even one day is better than nothing; and even though you

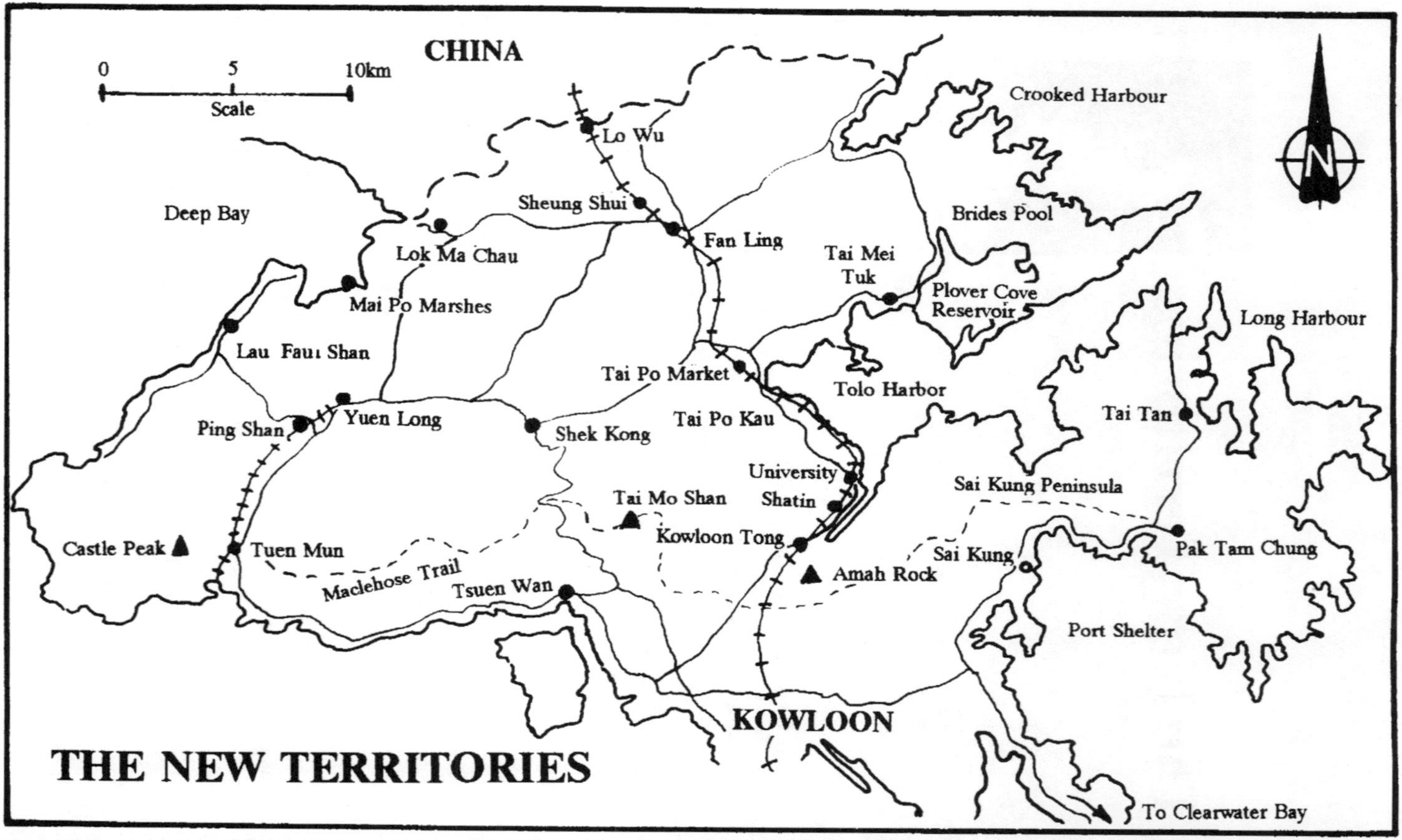
CHINA
0
5
10km
Scale
Deep Bay
Lo Wu
Sheung Shui
Fan Ling
Lok Ma Chau
Mai Po Marshes
Lau Fau Shan
Yuen Long
Ping Shan
Crooked Harbour
Brides Pool
Tai Mei Tuk
Plover Cove Reservoir
Long Harbour
Tai Po Market
Tolo Harbor
Tai Po Kau
Shek Kong
Tai Tan
University
Sai Kung Peninsula
Tai Mo Shan
Shatin
Kowloon Tong
Sai Kung
Pak Tam Chung
Amah Rock
Castle Peak
Tuen Mun
Maclehose Trail
Tsuen Wan
Port Shelter
KOWLOON
THE NEW TERRITORIES
To Clearwater Bay

A Chinese temple. (Courtesy of the Hong Kong Tourist Association)

cannot see all the points of interest in that time, you will have a much better appreciation of Hong Kong. Transportion to this area has dramatically improved in recent years. You can reach here by MTR, the electrified KCR, ferry, and hoverferry. There are even hotels for those who wish to stay here.

2. Getting There

It really depends on where you wish to go, whether you decide the MTR, the KCR, a bus, or a ferry will be best. The MTR line goes out in a northwest direction to the industrial and residential area of Tsuen Wan. The KCR line goes north, then northeast to Shatin, then northwest through Tai Po and Fan Ling to Sheung Shui. There is a hoverferry to Tuen Mun in the northwest of the New Territories from Blake Pier on Hong Kong Island. You can also reach here by No. 68M bus from Tsuen Wan, or by No. 68X bus all the way from Kowloon. It is very difficult to get a taxi from Kowloon or Hong Kong Island because they are not allowed to pick up again in the New Territories.

3. Local Transportation

Green-colored **taxis** are readily available in all the major towns. They operate with a HK$8 flag fall and 80 cents for every 200 meters. They will only pick up and set down in the New Territories. The **MTR** operates through Mei Foo, Lai King, Kwai Fong, Kwai Hing, and Tai Wo Hau to Tsuen Wan. The **Kowloon-Canton Railway** runs through Tai Wai, Shatin, Fo Tan, the Chinese University, Tai Po Market, Tai Wo, Fanling, Sheung Shui, and Lo Wu. You cannot go to Lo Wu on your own unless you have a visa to China because this is within the border-restricted zone.

There is a very modern and efficient **Light Rail Transit** system (LRT) linking the towns of Tuen Mun and Yuen Long. There are five lines in all with three of these departing from the hoverferry pier in Tuen Mun. Lines 610 and 611 are the ones that go all the way to Yuen Long. Fares are HK$3 to $4.30 and there are ticket vending machines at each stop but no turnstiles. The system operates from 5:30 A.M. to 12:30 A.M. daily.

There is an extensive network of **bus** routes, but it will take a while to work out how to travel the area by bus. Many of the services operate from or near the MTR stations at Tsuen Wan and Choi Hung, the KCR stations at Tai Po and Sheung Shui, or the LRT stations at Tuen Mun and Yuen Long. **Bicycles** can be rented at Shatin and Tai Po and probably at other centers.

4. The Hotel Scene

There are no hotels in the luxury or expensive categories in the New Territories but there are three excellent midmarket properties and some budget accommodation.

MEDIUM-PRICE HOTELS

The **Kowloon Panda Hotel** (Tel: 2409-1111) is a long way from Kowloon but obviously that name has more appeal than New Territories. The hotel is situated in Tsuen Wan and, with 1,026 rooms, is the largest hotel in Hong Kong. Facilities are good and it would demand a much higher tariff than its current HK$700 for a standard room, if it were in Kowloon or on Hong Kong Island. Rooms have remote-control TV with satellite reception and in-house movies, IDD telephone, refrigerator, and tea- and coffee-making facilities. There is a wide choice of restaurants and bars. The elegant Yung Yat Ting Restaurant serves traditional and nouveau Cantonese cuisine. The Yuet Loy Heen Restaurant serves Cantonese dim sum and seafood cuisine, family style.

You can enjoy a barbecue and drink at the Pool Deck after a workout at the gymnasium, or try Continental and Asian buffets at the Coffee Shop. Afternoon tea and cocktails are available in the Lobby Lounge, while the Chianti Ristorante Italiano specializes in pizzas and pastas. The Palmetto Lounge and Bar on the 30th floor has an international lunch buffet, and live entertainment in the evening. There is a business center, an outdoor pool, and a health club with sauna and massage. (Book with the hotel at 3 Tsuen Wah St., Tsuen Wan, New Territories, Hong Kong; Fax: 852-2409-1818.)

The **Regal Riverside** (Tel: 2649-7878) is the largest hotel in Shatin with 784 rooms and 44 suites. Rooms are spacious and well appointed and some have nice views over the surrounding town and countryside. Restaurant choice is extensive. My favorite is the Regal Seafood Restaurant, where authentic Cantonese cuisine and dim sum is offered in a traditional Chinese setting. The Asian Delights Authentic Thai Restaurant has some great spicy food as well as teppanyaki, while the Botania Cafe has light Western and international dishes in a nice setting overlooking the river or the pool terrace. Other choices are the 24-hour Boulevard Cafe for local and Western snacks and the Poolside Barbecue for after-sunset succulent steaks and seafood.

The Oasis Lobby Lounge is a good place to meet friends, while the Pool Terrace has a sunken bar for a refreshing drink. At night, the Carnival Bar has live music and the Cosmos Discotheque and Karaoke is Hong Kong's largest discotheque. The Topform Health Club has a good range of equipment. (Book with the hotel in the United States on 1-800-222-8888; in Canada on 1-800-233-9188; or at Tai Chung Kiu Road, Shatin, Hong Kong; Fax: 852-2637-4748.)

The **Royal Park Hotel** (Tel: 2601-2111) is another nice property in Shatin. It is situated close to Shatin city hall and not far from the MTR station. The 436 rooms and 12 suites have bay windows offering good views of Shatin and are well equipped for all your needs. Rates are from HK$1,020. There is a business center, an indoor/outdoor pool, and a fully equipped gymnasium. Restaurant choices include the Royal Park Chiu Chow Restaurant, the Fortune Lounge Seafood Restaurant on level 2, The Derby for all-day Western dining, the Sakurada Japanese Restaurant for lunch or dinner, and the Forget-Me-Not Lounge for a buffet lunch and evening live entertainment. (Book with the hotel at 8 Pak Hok Ting St., Shatin, Hong Kong; Fax: 852-2601-3666.)

BUDGET ACCOMMODATION

There are several YHA hostels where you can get a bed for less than HK$100. Unfortunately most are difficult to get to without walking. One that is quite isolated but is not too hard to reach is **Bradbury Hall** (Tel: 2328-2458) in Chek Keng. This is about as far east as you can go. There is a boat that goes here from near the Chinese University KCR station, but they are not very frequent. Alternatively you can get a No. 92 bus from near the Choi Hung MTR station to Sai Kung, then a No. 94 bus to Pak Tau Au. From here it is a 30-minute walk. At the other end of the Territory there is the **Beachside Hostel** (Tel: 2491-9179) at Ting Kau near Tsuen Wan. A private room with bath will cost around HK$160, while one without a bath is available for about HK$100. Dorm beds are around HK$40.

5. Dining and Restaurants

I must confess that I have never found any great restaurants in the New Territories. That is partly because I have never stayed in this area, but I suspect that there may not be too many that would rank as a gourmet highlight. The following are satisfactory.

Good Cantonese food is available in the major hotels. The **Fortune Lounge** at the Royal Park Hotel specializes in seafood dishes such as scallops stuffed with minced shrimp, and baked stuffed crab shells. It is open daily from 11 A.M. to midnight. The **Regal Seafood Restaurant** at the Regal Riverside Hotel serves similar fare together with Cantonese favorites. It is open from 11 A.M. to midnight. **Yuet Loy Heen** at the Kowloon Panda Hotel has Cantonese cuisine and a set-price menu from 7 P.M. to 9 P.M. offering unlimited servings of 26 dishes such as shark's fin with crabmeat. It is open from 7:30 A.M. to 11 P.M.

Outside the hotels there is some choice. In Tsuen Wan the **Holly Restaurant** (Tel: 2492-8165), in Lo Tak Court, 1 Cheong Tai St., is a local restaurant with an English menu. It has most of the popular Cantonese dishes at average prices. **The House of Canton Restaurant** (Tel: 2406-0868), at 7/F Riviera Plaza in Riviera Garden, Tsuen Wan, is another good choice. They have a rotating "special of the day," which is an excellent value. Try the crab with Singapore sauce or the lightly curried vegetables with Portuguese sauce.

The three-decked **Treasure Floating Restaurant** (Tel: 2637-7222) on the river at Shatin has plenty of atmosphere and a range of seafood dishes. The Japanese-style octopus snacks are popular. The **Flower Lounge Restaurant** (Tel: 2698-1168), in the huge New Town Plaza at Shatin, is an elegant place that has good-value set lunches and inexpensive dim sum. The open-air **Yucca de Lac Restaurant** (Tel: 2692-1835), at Ma Liu Shui just north of Shatin, has an extensive Chinese menu, a Western snack menu, and lovely views of Tolo Harbour. In Sai Kung, the **Fung Lum Restaurant** (Tel: 2792-6623) in the Siu Yat Building has a good reputation for seafood, chicken, and duck. Out on isolated Tap Mun Chou, which can be reached by ferry from Ma Liu Shui, the small **New Hon Kee Restaurant** (Tel: 2328-2428) serves some of the freshest and best seafood in Hong Kong. Another seafood favorite is the **Oi Man Restaurant** (Tel: 2472-1504), away out at isolated Lau Fau Shan on the northwest coast fronting Deep Bay.

Other cuisines are also available. The **Royal Park Chiu Chow Restaurant** in the Royal Park Hotel features the hearty and rich flavors of Chiu Chow cuisine. The roasted goose washed down with strong Chiu Chow tea is a favorite. The **Sakurada Restaurant** in the same hotel has traditional Japanese cuisine, including freshly prepared sushi and teppanyaki served in a bright atmosphere. Thai food is the specialty of the **Asian Delights Restaurant** in the Regal Riverside Hotel. There is a buffet and an à la carte menu. In the same hotel, the **Botania Cafe** overlooking the river has a good range of Western dishes and a very popular weekend buffet. **Chianti,** in the Kowloon Panda Hotel, is a delightful, relaxed restaurant with popular pasta dishes, pizzas, and a great fillet steak covered in Chianti and pepper sauce.

Outside the hotels, the cozy **Pizzeria Giovanni** (Tel: 2477-8935) on Lok Road at Yuen Long is well worth the visit. Listen to the Italian music and finish with a cappuccino. The American-style **Spaghetti House** (Tel: 2697-9009) in the Shatin New Town Plaza also has giant-sized sandwiches and chicken in a basket and will appeal to those visitors looking for a quick, simple meal. In the same shopping complex, you will find a Pizza Hut and other fast-food outlets. If you are into vegetarian food, then two restaurants in Tsuen Wan will appeal. The **Bodhi Restaurant** (Tel: 2415-0113), at 2 Tak Wah St., has beancurd, fungi, and bamboo shoot dishes as well as other Chinese vegetarian favorites. The restaurant is bright and clean, and there is no alcohol served. It is open from 11 A.M. to 11 P.M. The **Yuen Yuen Restaurant** (Tel: 2490-9882) is situated within the Yuen Yuen Institute, a Taoist temple complex at Sam Dip Tam. There are inexpensive mushroom, beancurd, and vegetable dishes served in a cheerful, bustling atmosphere. It is open from 11 A.M. to 6 P.M. As a complete contrast, there is the **Grilled Chicken King** (Tel: 2498-2405) at Tsu Wan Town Square. Malaysian food is available at the **Cosmo Restaurant** (Tel: 2650-7056) at 80 Kwong Fuk Rd., Tai Po Market.

6. Sight-seeing

The best way to see some of the New Territories in a short time is to take a tour. If you have longer or just wish to see a few areas, then there are some excellent sights to see and you can reach them all by public transportation. A good place to start is Tsuen Wan.

TSUEN WAN

You reach here by taking the MTR to the end of the line. One hundred years ago this area was a scattering of Hakka villages around a market town, with a population of around 3,000. Now the area is home to close to one million people but amazingly, old Hakka lifestyles still partly live on in nearby hillside hamlets. The town is not particularly appealing but you should at least see the **Sam Tung Uk Museum.** As you exit the station, you will see direction signs to the museum, which is about a five-minute walk away.

The museum is set in a restored 200-year-old walled Chan clan village. The eight houses display period furniture or exhibitions of various aspects of Hakka lifestyles. You can also see agricultural equipment, and special exhibitions are held in the hall off the walled village's rear lane. There are English captions and an orientation room to help visitors. Admission is free and the museum is open 9 A.M. to 4 P.M. daily, except Tuesday.

Another point of interest is the **Chuk Lam Sim Yuen,** a monastery and temple complex, about 20 minutes on foot from the MTR station, or a short taxi ride. This was founded in 1927 and it contains three of the largest "Precious Buddha" statues in Hong Kong. A little farther afield is the spectacular **Yeun Yeun Institute** temple complex dedicated to the three main religions practiced in Hong Kong—Buddhism, Taoism, and Confucianism. A replica of Beijing's "Temple of Heaven" is a big attraction. You reach here by taxi, or take No. 81 maxicab from Shiu Wo Street near the MTR station.

One of the big attractions of Tsuen Wan is the surrounding countryside. Hong Kong's highest peak, **Tai Mo Shan,** (957 meters) is nearby, and there are some good country parks and walking trails. It is worthwhile to visit **Tai Mo Shan Country Park.** Take a taxi or No. 51 bus from Tsuen Wan ferry terminal or MTR station to the park entrance just above the village of Chuen Lung. Near the entrance, there is a sign-posted Family Trail that offers good views and a one-kilometer, 30-minute hillside walk. It is also possible to walk to the summit along steep but surfaced Tai Mo Shan Road. The views of the Chinese coastline of Deep Bay are excellent on a clear day.

From this same point, it is possible to walk the 22-kilometer route to Tuen Mun along the **MacLehose Trail.** There is only one small village on this entire length and it is only recommended to serious, well-prepared walkers with a good map (map No. 2 of the Countryside series produced by the Hong Kong government). The trail generally follows the hilltops and goes by Tai Lam Reservoir. For those not into serious walking, it is best to return to Tsuen Wan and take the No. 68M bus from the MTR station to Tuen Mun. The road follows the coast and passes the huge seawater desalination plant at Lok An Pai.

TUEN MUN

This is another of the new towns but it has an ancient history. It was once an Imperial outpost guarding the eastern approaches to Deep Bay and the Pearl River estuary. Portuguese troups once occupied this area centuries ago. Now it is all high-rise housing estates. If you are arriving by bus from Tsuen Wan you will stop in the town center. If you have come direct from Central on the hoverferry you will arrive at a terminal some three kilometers away and will have to come to the center of town by route 506 of the

Light Rail Transit (LRT). The town center is modern, clean, and a bit sterile. Have a look at the Town Park and the huge Tuen Mun Town Plaza shopping center. There are plenty of eating places here if you are hungry.

Most points of interest are out of town. Butterfly Beach, a bit west of the hovercraft pier, is good for swimming. Castle Peak, a rugged mountain west of the town, can be climbed by the energetic and you are rewarded by great views. Everyone can enjoy the **Ching Chung Koon Temple.** When this was opened in 1949, it was a rural retreat. Now it is surrounded by high-rise housing. This huge Taoist temple is dedicated to Lu Sun Young, one of the Eight Immortals of Chinese mythology who rid the earth of many evils. The main hall contains lanterns from Beijing's Imperial Palace and many other treasures. The grounds have lotus ponds and a fine bonsai garden. Take the LRT to Ching Chung Station and walk across the road.

A little farther north you will find the **Miu Fat Buddhist Monastery.** This is considered by some to be one of the greatest temples in this part of Asia. Two spectacular dragons guard the entrance and inside it is decorated with more than 10,000 sculptures of Buddha as well as Chinese and Thai paintings. The monastery can be very busy at festival time but you are likely to see monks chanting and worshipping at any time. You reach here by taking the LRT to Lam Tei Station then walking for five minutes along a path to Castle Peak Road. Turn left and you will see the monastery.

If you keep heading north on the LRT for another five stations, you will reach Ping Shan and have the option of a side excursion to **Lau Fau Shan.** This is famous for its oyster beds and oyster restaurants. The shoreline is covered with millions of oyster shells and the small settlement has some appeal. From Ping Shan Station, you walk to the feeder bus stop and take No. 655 bus to Lau Fau Shan. You need to return the same way. When you get back to Ping Shan, you should visit the Kun Ting Study Hall on Ping Ha Road. This was built in 1870 by the Tang clan who began to settle this area in the thirteenth century. Originally the study hall provided facilities for both ancestral worship and education. Children were taught arts and classics with the aim of helping them pass the Imperial Civil Service examinations and hence become officials in the Qing administration. Restoration of the building was carried out in 1990. The nearby Tang Ancestral Hall was built about 700 years ago and is still used today.

Get back on the LRT and go to the end of the line at **Yuen Long.** This was a market town and a fishing center for many years, but now it is a rapidly developing industrial and dormitory town. The people here still honor Tin Hau, the goddess of the sea, seafarers, and fisherman, because of their seafaring ancestry, and this is the site for the most elaborate and colorful Tin Hau Festival celebration in Hong Kong. North of here, is the **Mai Po Marshes,** which are hard-up against the border with China. There is something hauntingly innocent about this area. Perhaps it is such a contrast to the more well known face of Hong Kong. In the morning light the marshes have a kind of pearly quality.

Our aim now is to reach the KCR line at Sheung Shui, so the best way to reach here is by No. 77K bus. As you head east, you go backward in time. The traffic thins and you can catch glimpses of Hakka women in black pajamalike suits working in the fields, their wide-brimmed, black-veiled hats keeping the insects at bay. In places, concrete is replaced by orchids and honeysuckle, jasmine and magnolia, and roaring jets give way to flapping butterflies.

At the moment we will only go as far as **Kam Tin.** This was the tenth-century settling place of the Tang clan, and today there are five walled villages in the area. The best known and most promoted is **Kat Hing Wai,** which was built during the late 1600s and is still inhabited by hundreds of people bearing the Tang name. The walled village was built to protect the inhabitants against tigers and roving gangsters and the moat, the six-meter-high walls, and four corner guardhouse towers with slit windows were quite effective for this purpose. The village has been extensively modernized inside and the two-meter-wide central lane leads past souvenir sellers. But it is well worth visiting, particularly when there are no tours around. You are expected to give a donation when you enter the village and you must negotiate a fee before taking photographs of the black-dressed women.

This is also the area for the **Friday Sek Kong Market.** It is an outdoor event that does not operate in bad weather. It spreads across a series of fields—one field will be a mixture of blue-and-white porcelain pieces, a zoo of plastic dinosaurs, and namebrand sports shirts at prices far less than any street market in Kowloon or on Hong Kong Island.

SHEUNG SHUI

This is a long-established market town being engulfed by the Fanling New Town. If you do not plan to visit China, you may still be interested to see the remarkable development that has recently occured in the Shenzhen Special Economic Zone just across the border. The best place to see this is the **Lok Ma Chau Lookout Point** a few kilometers west of Sheung Shui. There are restroom facilities and hawkers selling food and souvenirs. The best way to reach here is taxi from the Sheung Shui KCR station.

If history is important to you, then a visit to **San Tin** is a "must." This is the home base of the Man clan that migrated here about five centuries ago. The best place to go is the village of Fan Tin Tsuen. You can reach here by No. 76K bus from Sheung Shui. It is worth visiting the Man Lun-Fung Ancestral Hall, which is thought to have been built four hundred years ago. Not far away is Tai Fu Tai, a stately mansion built in 1865 by a senior clan member. The house is built of granite and traditional gray bricks and there is some fine decoration both inside and out.

TAI PO

We will now take the KCR back towards Kowloon, but only as far as Tai Po. This is now one of the booming new towns, but originally this was an ancient market town. These new towns have almost no identity of their own. They consist of rows of plastic housing buildings, each twenty or thirty stories high, and each full of the usual tensions and stresses of public tower-block living. They must be recognized, however, as fulfilling a very real need in Hong Kong, and the accommodation is almost universally far better than the residents knew before. The area's original inhabitants were Tanka boat people who were conscripted by the Imperial court as pearl fishermen a thousand years ago. Now, the area is home to many high-tech industries.

I suggest that you alight at the Tai Po Market station. You can walk to a number of attractions from here or you can rent a bicycle in this vicinity. This is also the starting point for trips to Plover Cove Reservoir and some country parks. The first place to go is the **Hong Kong Railway Museum,** a 15-minute-walk from the present station. This small, but pleasant museum is located in an old station that was originally built in 1913 in traditional Chinese architectural style. The station has been well restored and an exhibition gallery presents the history of the local railway system and the town as it was when the railway arrived. There is a collection of railway rolling stock from 1911. Admission is free and the museum is open daily, except Tuesday, from 9 A.M. until 3:50 P.M.

Not far from the railway museum is the **Man Mo Temple.** This restored building on Fu Shin Street is dedicated to the Taoist gods of war and literature. About a kilometer away on the other side of the river is the recently restored Tin Hau Temple, dedicated to Tin Hau, the patron goddess of fishermen. You find this on Ting Kok Road near the old Tai Po market.

Nature lovers will enjoy a visit to the Plover Cove Reservoir and the Tai Mei Tuk Visitors Center. You can reach here by taxi or No. 75K bus from Tai Po Market Station. The reservoir is interesting because it has been reclaimed from the sea. A dam was built across the mouth of a bay, the salt water was pumped out, then fresh water was brought in from China. The result is a 12-square-kilometer freshwater lake with its own ecosystem. There are youth hostels, barbecues, and picnic sites. They are quiet midweek but can be crowded on weekends. Information and advice is available from the visitors center on Bride's Pool Road. The five-kilometer-long Pat Sin Leng Nature Trail from here is a popular walk. It ends near Bride's Pool Waterfalls, which are attractive during summer months after rain has fallen.

You can rejoin the KCR and go to University station. The Chinese University is on a hillside adjacent to the station and it is very attractive. A free university bus runs through the campus at about 15-minute intervals. The best way to see the area is to take this uphill and then walk back to the station. The main attraction is the **Art Gallery** (Tel: 2609-7416), located in the Institute of Chinese Studies. There are visiting exhibitions and a permanent collection of 1,300 Cantonese paintings and calligraphic works, 300 Han and pre-Han dynasty bronze seals, and 400 jade flower carvings. Admission is free and it is open daily, except Sunday mornings and most public holidays, from 10 A.M. until 4:30 P.M.

SHATIN

It is two stops on the KCR from University to Shatin, another of the new towns. This has become a desirable place to live and it is also a popular place to visit. Hakka migrants settled here in the seventeenth century and some of their descendants still grow vegetables and flowers in the district. The top attraction here is the **Ten Thousand Buddhas Monastery.** It is close to the station but you need to negotiate 400 steps to reach the temple. On the way up the hill, you will pass the Thai-style Fat Wah Temple with its four-faced Buddha statue. The 10,000 Buddhas in the main temple (actually there are around 13,000) are stacked in shelves around all the temple walls. Each one is supposed to be in a slightly different pose. A nine-story pagoda and colorful statues stand in front of the temple. There are further temples higher up the hillside. The view from the temple is inspiring. Shatin is spread out below and there are great views towards the Lion Rock mountain range and the famous landmark of Amah Rock.

Back at valley level, the New Town Plaza is an extensive shopping and recreation center across the other side of the railway station. There is a huge range of shops with prices a bit lower than those in Kowloon and Hong Kong Island (so I am told by a local expert), plus an indoor swimming pool, roller-skating rink, and bowling alley. There is a regular free 20-minute performance by the center's illuminated, computer-controlled musical fountain.

The other feature out here of interest to some is the **Shatin Racecourse,** one of the most modern horse-racing facilities in the world. The course can accommodate 83,000 people and it often approaches this figure. During the racing season (September to June), meetings are held here or at Happy Valley on Hong Kong Island every weekend and Wednesday evenings. Visitors over 18 can show their passport and get admission badges to the Members' Enclosure at the track (Tel: 2837-8345 for details about the program). The eight-hectare Penfold Park located in the center of the course is a popular landscaped bird sanctuary and parkland when racing is not taking place. It is closed on Mondays and the day after public holidays.

One more section on the KCR brings us to Tai Wai Station. This is the closest station to the **Che Kung Temple** and **Tsang Tai Uk fortified village.** The temple is small and not greatly impressive but it can be busy on weekends and at festival times. It honors a great general who lived about one thousand years ago. There is a flower-decked Thai-style Buddhist shrine nearby. The nineteenth-century fortified village on Sha Kok Road is not far away. This was a stronghold of the Tsang clan and the architecture is similar to that found in Hakka settlements in China. There are four parallel rows and two side columns of houses forming an enclosed compound with a central courtyard.

SAI KUNG

The final areas to explore are the Sai Kung and Clearwater Bay peninsulas. These provide some of Hong Kong's finest scenery and most isolated areas. Much of the region is protected by country parks so this is a great place for walkers, swimmers, and other outdoor enthusiasts. From Tai Wai you reach here by KCR to Kowloon Tong Station (one section), then change to the MTR and go four sections to Choi Hung. From here there are buses to both peninsulas.

Bus No. 92 goes from Choi Hung MTR Station to the ancient fishing and harbor town of Sai Kung. On the way you will pass the huge Hebe Haven Marina Cove project and will wonder about my undeveloped comments on this area. Fortunately from here on the comment generally applies. The town of Sai Kung is seeing some changes but the town still retains much of its charm. You can wander around narrow back lanes filled with little shops and enjoy the seaside aroma of Port Shelter. There is the small Tin Hau Temple on Yi Chun Street, dedicated to the Taoist patroness of fishermen. There are several good seafood restaurants along the waterfront and a growing number of Western-style fast-food outlets and pubs. Sampan trips around Port Shelter and to some excellent beaches can be arranged at the main jetty.

From here you can travel farther east on the No. 94 bus to Pak Tam Chung. The bus departs every hour on the hour and the trip takes around 20 minutes. There is not much here but it is good to just wander around taking in the atmosphere. One place you must visit is the **Sai Kung Country Park Visitor Centre.** It contains a comprehensive exhibition of maps, models, photographs, and rural artifacts that illustrate the history, geography, and geology of the peninsula. You will be interested in the description of the High Dam Reservoir project and may then wish to visit the project. The reservoir is built in what was a sea channel. Dams were built at both ends and the sea water pumped out. Now it is a fresh water reservoir. There are good roads and trails in the area for walkers. The visitors center is open daily, except Tuesday, from 9:30 A.M. to 4:30 P.M. One thing to pick up from here is the Pak Tam Chung Nature Trail brochure. The trail starts a few hundred meters inside the park and is well worth walking. There are sign-posted markers along the 30-minute trail that tell you about the lifestyle of the early inhabitants of this area. One of the highlights is an old fortified village built in the midnineteenth century. The Wong family decendants abandoned their village in the 1960s, and later agreed to it being converted into what is now the **Sheung Yiu Folk Museum** (Tel: 2792-6365). The houses contain typical Hakka furnishings and there are display galleries for other interesting items. Admission is free and the museum is open daily, except Tuesday, from 9 A.M. to 4 P.M.

From Pak Tam Chung it is possible to go north by bus to Tai Tan and Wong Shek Pier. You will see some nice countryside and from the pier it is possible to get a ferry back to Ma Liu Shui near the Chinese University or across to Tap Mun Island, which some claim is the most interesting island in Hong Kong. (See chapter 7, "The Outlying Islands.")

CLEARWATER BAY

This is reached by No. 91 bus from Choi Hung MTR Station. The peninsula is a mountainous arm of land sheltering the eastern entrance to Victoria Harbour and the new town development on Junk Bay. The area is good for walkers, although many of the trails are quite strenuous. The bay itself is beautiful and it has one of the best beaches in Hong Kong. There are lifeguards, changing rooms, snack counters, and some children's waterchutes. Unfortunately, on a busy summer weekend, it is almost standing room only, so it is best to go midweek. The area has become popular with expatriate residents and you will see their mansions on the hillsides.

Clearwater Bay Country Park covers quite a large area of the peninsula and there are some exhilarating walks over Junk Peak. An easier walk is the 30-minute clifftop trek along Clearwater Bay Road Extension to the entrance to the Clearwater Bay Golf and Country Club. There are some lovely views of the sea and a small fishing village cove. From here there is a sign-posted walk to **Tin Hau Temple** in Joss House Bay. This is Hong Kong's oldest established temple, built on this site in 1266. The current buildings were extensively restored in 1962 but much of the old atmosphere remains. Beyond the traditional smoke and bell towers, there are two images of Tin Hau on a richly decorated altar. The raised forecourt contains further offering tables and smoke chambers. To the right of the temple, up a wooded path, there are 108 Chinese characters in a glass-enclosed rock inscription. These ideograms were carved in 1274.

7. Guided Tours

Please refer to the Guided Tours sections of chapters 4 and 5 for additional information on available tours within Hong Kong. The following have a major New Territories component.

The four-hour **Heritage Tour** departs Wednesday and Saturday mornings. It visits four sites of historical interest and also includes some interesting rural country. The tour allows time at the Leio Cheng Uk Han tomb and museum; the Sam Tung Uk Folk Museum; Tai Fu Tai, an opulent stately home; and Man Shek Tong Ancestral Hall. The cost is around HK$250.

The **Land Between Tour** operates daily, except Sundays. It offers a look at the bustling areas of Kowloon and the tranquility of the New Territories. You visit Hong Kong's highest mountain, Tai Mo Shan; a Buddhist temple; Luen Wo Market, a bird sanctuary at Luk Keng overlooking the Chinese border; and Sam Mun Tsai fishing village. A Chinese lunch is served, then the return journey is made via Shatin Racecourse and the Lion Rock tunnel. The six-hour tour costs around HK$275.

The **Sports and Recreation Tour** visits the luxurious Clearwater Bay Golf and Country Club on Sai Kung Peninsula. The eight-hour tour operates on Tuesdays and Fridays and includes lunch and admission; however, it does not include the cost of sports participation. Golf, tennis, squash, table tennis, and swimming are offered. Equipment can be rented or purchased in the Pro Shop, but you should take appropriate sportswear and shoes. The cost is around HK$300.

The **Come Horseracing Tour** was mentioned in the Hong Kong Island chapter. It is possible to take this tour to the spectacular Shatin Racecourse when meetings are being held there. Check with the HKTA (Tel: 2801-7177) for details about race days. The cost is around HK$450.

8. Culture

The cultural highlights have been covered in the sight-seeing section of this chapter and the culture section of chapter 4.

9. Sports

Sporting facilities other than golf and swimming are less well known here than on Hong Kong Island and in Kowloon.

The **Royal Hong Kong Golf Club** (Tel: 2670-1211) has three 18-hole courses at Fanling that can be reached by train from Kowloon. Visitors can play these courses on Monday through Friday. Green fees are around HK$650 per 18 holes, or HK$1,000 for the day. The courses are in fine condition. Visitors can play the course at the **Clearwater Bay Golf and Country Club,** but you will be charged HK$1,000 for 18 holes. Clubs can be rented for HK$100 and electric carts for HK$200. (Tel: 2719-2454).

Tennis courts are available at the **Hong Kong Sports Institute** in Shatin (Tel: 2605-1212). There is an ice-skating rink at the **Riviera Ice Chalet,**

Riviera Gardens, Tsuen Wan (Tel: 2415-7888). Horseback riding can be enjoyed at the **Hong Kong Riding Union** in Shatin (Tel: 2604-5111).

10. Shopping

Two of the largest shopping complexes in the city are located in the New Territories, but I know less about shopping here than in Kowloon or on Hong Kong Island. The fact is that most visitors will not do much shopping in the New Territories because they will not be in the area and will not take the effort to go there just for shopping. My Hong Kong contacts tell me that some things are cheaper here, but at the same time there will be less English spoken and less experience with what the visitor expects.

DEPARTMENT STORES

The Japanese **Yaohan** department store almost has a monopoly on things out here. There are major stores in the New Town Plaza, Shatin (Tel: 2697-9338), and the Tuen Mun Town Plaza (Tel: 2450-3338), and other branches at 2 Tai Hang St., Yuen Long, and within the Kowloon Panda Hotel, Tsuen Wan. There is a branch of **The China Products Company** at 264 Castle Peak Rd., Tsuen Wan (Tel: 2498-3363).

OTHER PLACES

The New Town Plaza at Shatin is a major shopping center with all the facilities you would expect. As well as Yaohan, there are branches of chains such as **Beleno** (Tel: 2603-0335), **Giordano** (Tel: 2922-9406), **Kwun Kee Tailor** (Tel: 2606-7168), **City Chain** (Tel: 2693-2437), and **The Optical Shop** (Tel: 2606-5999). Riviera Plaza at Tsuen Wan and Tuen Mun Town Plaza at Tuen Mun are two other important centers.

11. Entertainment and Nightlife

As in most cities, the outher suburbs are unlikely to be a great source of nightlife, and that is certainly the case in the New Territories. These are largely dormitory communities visited at night by very few tourists. The nighttime offerings that are around are aimed at the locals and are not geared for English-speaking foreigners.

Within the hotels there are a few possibilities. The Regal Riverside Hotel at Shatin has live music and cocktails in the colorful **Carnival Bar** (Tel: 2649-7878), and disco music and karaoke in the **Cosmos** until 3 A.M. Out at Tsuen Wan, the Kowloon Panda Hotel has two possibilities. The spacious, rooftop **Palmetto** cocktail and music lounge has happy hours from 5 P.M. and a six-piece band from 9 P.M. The amazingly named **Pandaoke Karaoke** lets you join friends in one of 42 private lounges with laser-disc players and drink service on hand. You can sing you heart out until 2 A.M.

There is a UA6 cinema complex at New Town Plaza, Shatin (Tel: 2698-0651). There are occasional concerts and other performances at the following;

Lut Sau Town Hall, Yuen Long. Tel: 2473-1393.
North District Town Hall, Sheung Shui. Tel: 2671-4400.
Shatin Town Hall, Shatin. Tel: 2694-2536.
Tai Po Civic Centre, Tai Po. Tel: 2665-4477.
Tsuen Wan Town Hall, Tsuen Wan. Tel: 2414-1355.
Tuen Mun Town Hall, Tuen Mun. Tel: 2452-7300.

12. The New Territories Address List

Airlines—Cathay Pacific	
Reservations	Tel: 2747-1888
Flight Information	Tel: 2747-1234
—Dragonair	
Reservations	Tel: 2590-1188
Flight Information	Tel: 2769-7728
Emergency—Police, fire, ambulance	Tel: 999
Hospital—Prince of Wales, Ngan Shing Street, Shatin	Tel: 2636-2211
Immigration—	Tel: 2824-6111
Police—crime hotline	Tel: 2527-7177
Public Transport—Hong Kong Ferry Co.	Tel: 2542-3082
—Kowloon-Canton Railway	Tel: 2602-7799
—Light Rail Transit	Tel: 2468-7788
—Mass Transit Railway	Tel: 2750-0170
Telephone Information—	Tel: 1081

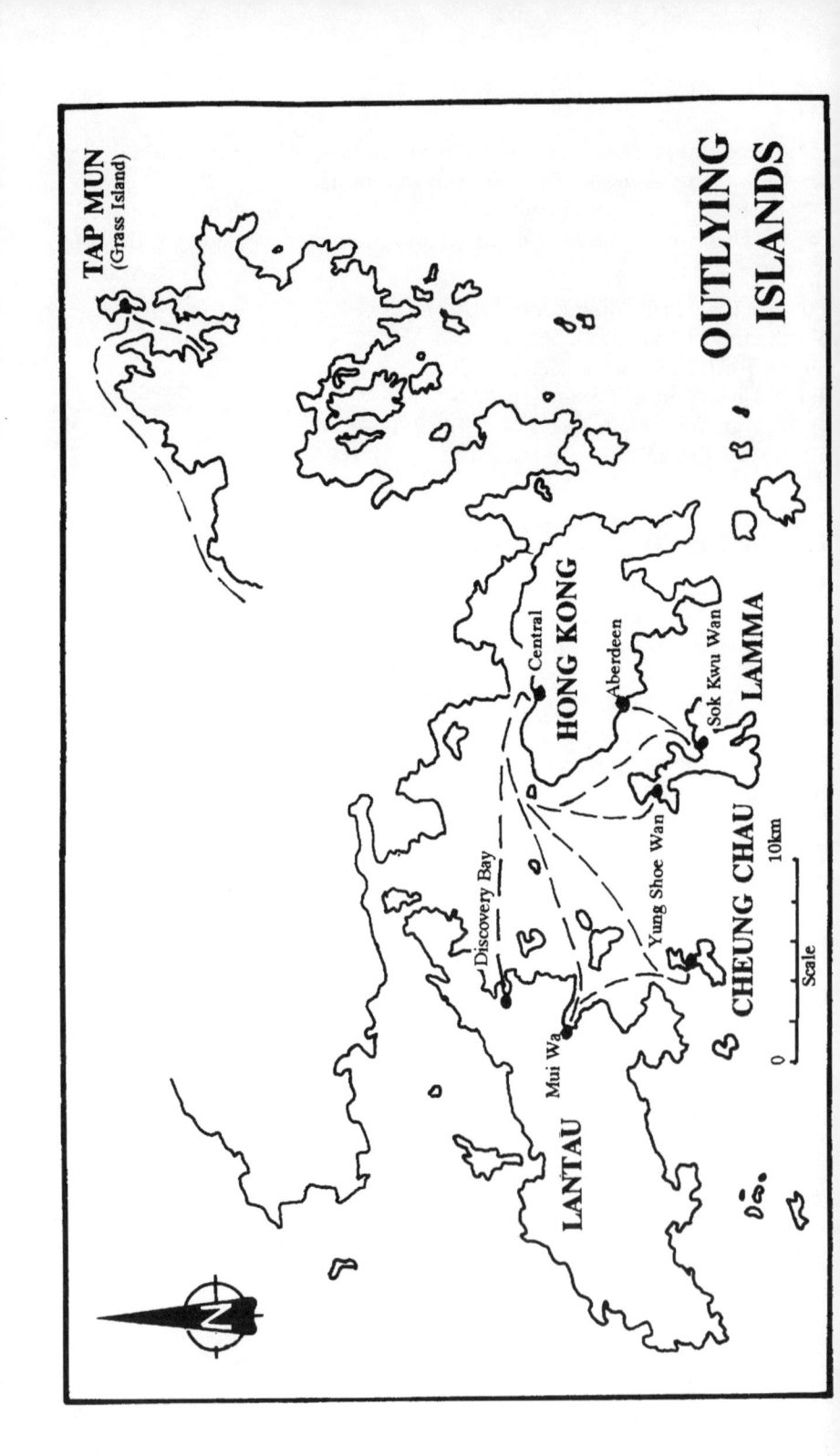

OUTLYING ISLANDS

7

The Outlying Islands

1. The General Picture

Many visitors to Hong Kong leave without ever visiting one of the outlying islands. They thus get a biased view of what Hong Kong is all about because they have missed one of the important elements of the Territory.

There are around 235 islands to chose from, but many of these are little more than small rocky outcrops. Most of the islands are uninhabited today but they were not always so. Until the 1960s, many had permanent fishing villages but now many of these are ghost towns with the people living on the mainland, looking for a "better" life.

There are four outlying islands that have particular interest to visitors. **Lantau Island** is the largest of all the islands. It is the only one with cars but it has remained substantially undeveloped until construction started recently on a new airport for Hong Kong. **Cheung Chau Island** is small but quite heavily populated and it is becoming a place to avoid on public holidays. **Lamma Island** is the least developed of the larger islands but it has a dedicated expatriate population that is there to escape the crowds of other areas. **Peng Chau Island** is small, quiet, but relatively developed. It is attracting new residents looking to escape the mainland rush.

Many of the outlying islands still have weekday-deserted beaches where breakers crash lazily on the shore and send a sheet of silver water skating across clean, ice-smooth sand. Some have casual restaurants where on tropical afternoons, dogs and old people sleep amongst the tables and chairs, on verandahs under the shade of spreading trees. In the cooler months, a fog can come across the water, misting out all sight of the adjacent high-rise concrete forests and providing a wonderful watercolor of a cool gray wash over sea and sky.

The **Hong Kong Ferry Co. (Holdings) Ltd.** operates scheduled ferry services to several islands, from piers in Central District on Hong Kong Island. A few other islands are served by small ferries either on a scheduled basis or on demand. Many of the remote islands are popular destinations for yachts and rental boats. Hong Kong residents like visiting the outlying islands on weekends, so it is generally better for visitors to go on weekdays. Weekend prices for island accommodation is double (or even more) the weekday cost.

2. Getting There

The main islands are served by ferries operated by the Hong Kong Ferry Co. (Holdings) Ltd. (Tel: 2542-3081). The ferries are clean, cheap, and comfortable during off-peak periods. Many have an air-conditioned top deck and all serve drinks and snacks. Trips to the major islands take from 45 to 60 minutes. Hovercraft also operate to some of the major islands. These

Sampans, used frequently to take short trips from Cheung Chau Island to its neighbor, Lantau, are tied up along the island's waterfront, waiting for hire. (Courtesy of the Hong Kong Tourist Association)

THE OUTLYING ISLANDS

take about half the time and cost twice the price of the ferries. Ferries leave from the Outlying Districts Services Pier or the Central Harbour Services Pier on Hong Kong Island. Most hovercraft leave from Government Pier. These are all adjacent to each other in Central District. On the ferries, return tickets can only be purchased for deluxe class. This is strongly recommended on weekends and public holidays.

3. Local Transportation

Lantau Island has taxis and buses; Lamma Island has bicycles to rent, and everywhere else you walk. *Kaidos,* small village ferries, are sometimes available, particularly on weekends.

4. The Hotel Scene

Good accommodation on the islands is in very short supply. The only hotel of note is the Warwick on Cheung Chau but there are other smaller and cheaper hotels, a few guesthouses and hostels, and a growing number of holiday units.

MEDIUM-PRICE HOTELS

The **Warwick Hotel** (Tel: 2981-0081) is a six-story, 70-room hotel on the beach at East Bay Cheung Chau Island. The rooms are all air-conditioned; have a private bath and shower; and have television, radio, and telephone. There is a restaurant, a snack bar, a swimming pool, and a discotheque. Rates start at around HK$1,000. (Book with the hotel at East Bay, Cheung Chau Island, Hong Kong; Fax: 852-2981-9174.)

The **Silvermine Bay Hotel** (Tel: 2984-8295) at Mui Wo on Lantau Island has 78 rooms from around HK$600. Rooms are fairly basic but they have private bathrooms, air conditioning, and telephone, TV, and refrigerator. There is a restaurant and a bar, a swimming pool, and a children's playground. Watersports are available on the beach. (Book with the hotel at Silvermine Bay, Mui Wo, Lantau Island, Hong Kong.)

BUDGET ACCOMMODATION

Accommodation can be booked on some of the outlying islands from a Holiday Flats booking office at the Central Harbour Services Pier, in Central District. You can also book at similar places on Cheung Chau Island and on Lantau Island.

On Cheung Chau, one of the best value places is **Star House** (Tel: 2981-2186) at 149 Tai Sun Bak St., about two blocks from the ferry pier. Basic rooms start at less than HK$200 on weekdays.

On Lamma, in Yung Shue Wan, the choice is between the **Man Lai Wah Hotel** (Tel: 2982-0220) with air-conditioned rooms and private bath on Main Street near the pier, or the nearby **Lamma Vacation House** (Tel: 2982-0427) at 29 Main St.

Lantau has the only real international-style dormitory budget accommodation. The choice is between the **Po Lin Monastery** (Tel: 2985-6854) at Ngong Ping, where a bed and three vegetarian meals cost around HK$200, or the **Trappist Haven Monastery** (Tel: 2987-6286) at Tai Shui Hong. Good accommodation is available at the **Sea Breeze Hotel** (Tel: 2984-7977) at Pui O Beach from around HK$300. A bit farther along this road, the **Cheung Sha Resort** has units that can accommodate up to six people from around HK$250. There are a number of similar places at Tong Fuk.

5. Dining and Restaurants

As you would imagine, seafood is the local specialty. There are good restaurants on all the main islands and seafood is not particularly expensive. Each of the islands also has a choice of Chinese restaurants and some Western fare.

Cheung Chau gives you a choice of the Warwick Hotel's **Bayview Chinese Restaurant** with its Chinese and Western dishes in air-conditioned surroundings, the **East Lake Restaurant** on Tung Wan Road, or a number of cheap sidewalk cafes on waterfront Praya Road. Depending on your mood and your purse, each will have appeal.

Lamma is a food lover's paradise and people come from Hong Kong Island just to eat at the waterfront restaurants. These restaurants are slowly moving upmarket so prices are no longer cheap. There is a big choice at both Yung Shue Wan and Sok Kwu Wan. Most have an English menu, accept credit cards, and serve Western wine. At Yung Shue Wan, the **Man Fung Seafood Restaurant** (Tel: 2982-1112) at 5 Main St., the **Lung Wah Seafood Restaurant** (Tel: 2982-0281) at 20 Main St., and **Lamcombe Seafood Restaurant** (Tel: 2982-0881) at 49 Main St. are all popular. All have sea views and a friendly atmosphere. Ferries bound for Sok Kwu Wan dock at a pretty harborside terrace. The al fresco seafood restaurants here are particularly appealing at night. They are casual, but the food and wine are excellent. Try the **Lamma Mandarin Seafood Restaurant** (Tel: 2982-8128) at 8 First St., or the **Peach Garden Seafood Restaurant** (Tel: 2982-8581) at No. 11. Both are open from 10 A.M. to 10 P.M.

On Lantau, many visitors like to try the vegetarian food provided at the **Po Lin Monastery** and the **Lantau Tea Gardens.** Elsewhere on the island, there is considerable choice. At Silvermine Bay, there are a cluster of open-air food stalls on Silvermine Road, not far from the ferry pier. The noodles here are excellent and prices are very reasonable. The **Silvermine Bay Restaurant** (Tel: 2984-8267) at 1 Chung Hau Rd. is more upmarket. The beach at Tong Fuk and Cheung Sha also has a good selection from which to choose.

6. Sight-seeing

All the outlying islands offer sight-seeing possibilities and it is difficult to say which is the most interesting. If you like crowds and activity, you will probably enjoy Cheung Chau the best. If restaurants are your thing, then Lamma would be your choice. Lantau is good for space and solitude while tiny Tap Mun Chau will take you back in time to a more relaxed world.

CHEUNG CHAU

This is the busiest of the islands. It has a permanent population of around 40,000 but this swells considerably on weekends when thousands of people visit from Hong Kong Island and Kowloon. There have been harbor reclamation and new housing projects constructed but there is still much of the "old" remaining for the visitor to see. The best way to explore the town is on foot, and if you wish to go farther afield you could consider the rental of a bicycle.

You arrive at the ferry pier in the middle of the main harbor. As you exit the pier, you will see a mapboard outlining the locations of places of interest on the island. Turn left onto the waterfront street (Praya Road) and wander along here until you come to the Pak Tai Temple. As you walk, look to the left and see the rows of junks lined up in the harbor. They are the homes of the remaining floating population of this fishing town. On the right, you will see a shop renting bicycles.

The **Pak Tai Temple** is one of the most important monuments on Cheung Chau. The temple was built in 1783 and is dedicated to Pak Tai, the sea god. The god's image wears a golden crown to commemorate the visit of Princess Margaret in 1966. Under the feet are a snake and a turtle, which symbolize his power over the sea and sea creatures. In front of the altar are statues of the martial gods, and they are flanked by two granite pillars carved with dragons. An iron sword from the Sung dynasty period, symbolizing good luck, is placed on the right side of the altar. The temple area is the site for the annual Bun Festival. (See the culture section of this chapter.)

As you exit the temple, look for Pak She Street, which runs parallel to Praya Road. This will take you back to the center of town. On the way, you will pass a brown building opposite No. 11, which is the home of a "tong" or district association. These organizations were originally formed by people who came from the same districts in China and they function as community

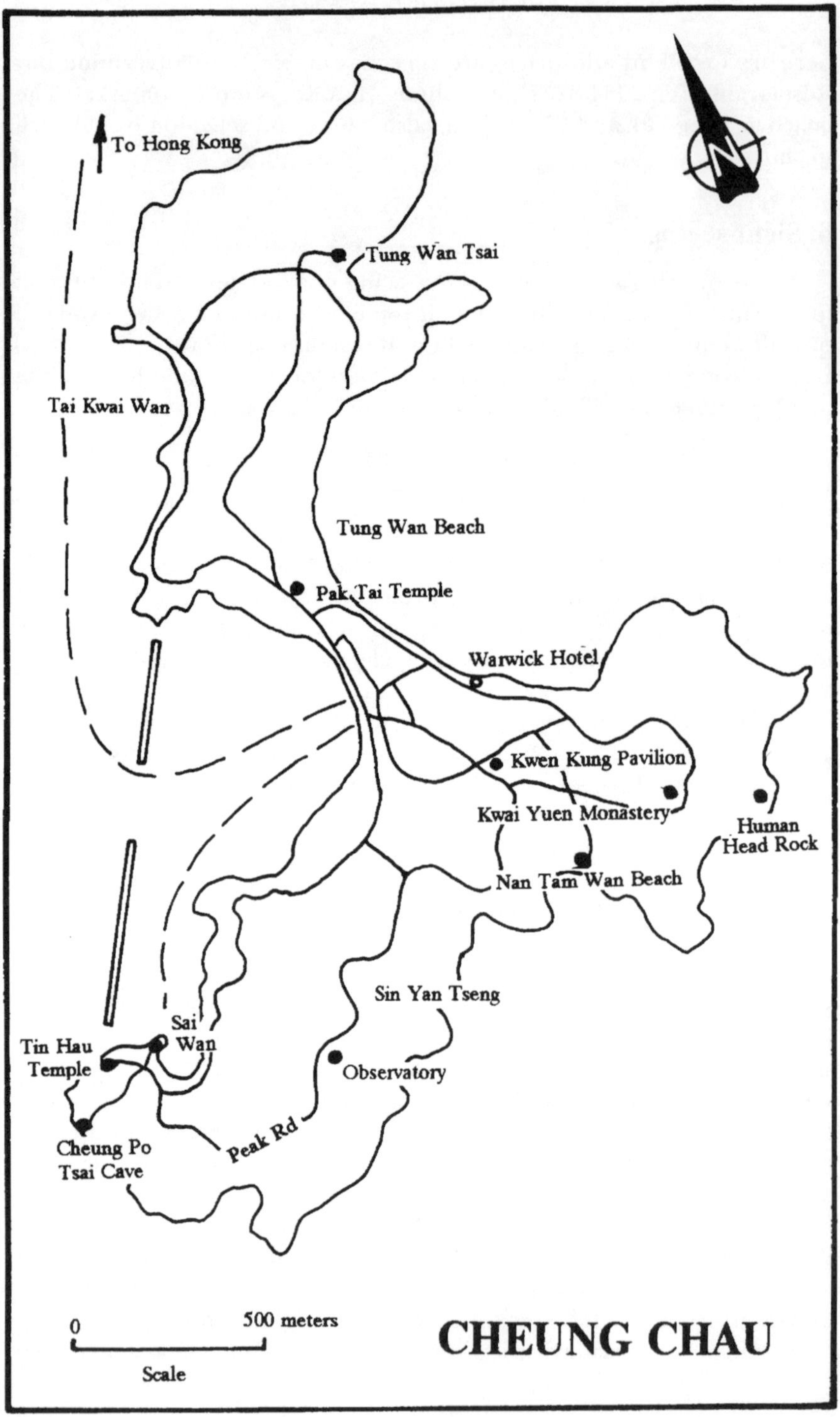
To Hong Kong
Tung Wan Tsai
Tai Kwai Wan
Tung Wan Beach
Pak Tai Temple
Warwick Hotel
Kwen Kung Pavilion
Kwai Yuen Monastery
Human
Head Rock
Nan Tam Wan Beach
Sin Yan Tseng
Sai
Wan
Tin Hau
Temple
Observatory
Peak Rd
Cheung Po
Tsai Cave
0
500 meters
Scale
CHEUNG CHAU

centers, mutual protection societies, and business co-operatives. At No. 25, there is a clinic of a Chinese orthopedic surgeon who combines surgical and orthopedic features to "straighten the bones." Herbal and massage treatments are also used.

Opposite No. 34, you will see the clinic of a Chinese doctor who uses diet, drugs, herbs, physical exercises, and acupuncture. At No. 47, there is a shop selling the famous Cheung Chau shrimp paste; and at No. 56, there is a Chinese bakery. At the corner of Kwok Man Road, there is a small street shrine to the earth god. Just walk a little to your left, then turn right into San Hing Street.

At No. 38, browse around inside the herbalist shop and see the different herbs displayed in big glass jars. At No. 68, there is an incense shop while at No. 80, you can buy a straw or bamboo hat as worn by the boat people. Opposite No. 105, there is a fresh produce market selling fish, seafood, poultry, meat, and local and imported fruit and vegetables.

You are now back close to the ferry pier but it is worth walking down Tung Wun Road towards the nice beach of Tun Wun. A short distance brings you to an old banyon "sacred tree." Some local people believe this tree is inhabited by the spirits of healing and fertility, and stones under the tree are worshipped. You pass a primary school, a restaurant, and a pub before you reach the beach. The Warwick Hotel can be seen on the right. Just below the hotel, you can see a bronze-age rock carving, made by unknown people about 2,500 years ago.

Elsewhere on the island, you can visit the small Kwum Yum Temple; the Kwai Yuem Monastery; the Kwan Kung Pavilion at the foot of Peak Road; the Cheung Po Tsai cave, which was once the treasury cave of the notorious pirate Cheung Po Tsai who had command of 40,000 men and several hundred ships; and the Sai Wan Tin Hau Temple. If you visit these last two places, you can catch a *kaido* (village ferry) back to the main ferry pier.

LAMMA

This is the nearest large island to Hong Kong City, but it is also the least developed of the major islands. The main village is Yung Shue Wan, on the northwest side of the island. Walking off the ferry pier into the village gives the visitor a touch of culture shock. You could almost be in a Mediterranean port. The pastel villas climb steep hills covered with flowering bougainvillea. There are several good restaurants here and tourism seems to be the main industry. You can see diners in open-doored restaurants or under shade umbrellas tucking into steamed prawns, baked crabs, and deep-fried squid, washed down by the pale golden San Miguel beer.

There is a small Tin Hau temple guarded by two stone lions at the southern end of the village. From here, there is a paved path that leads to Sok

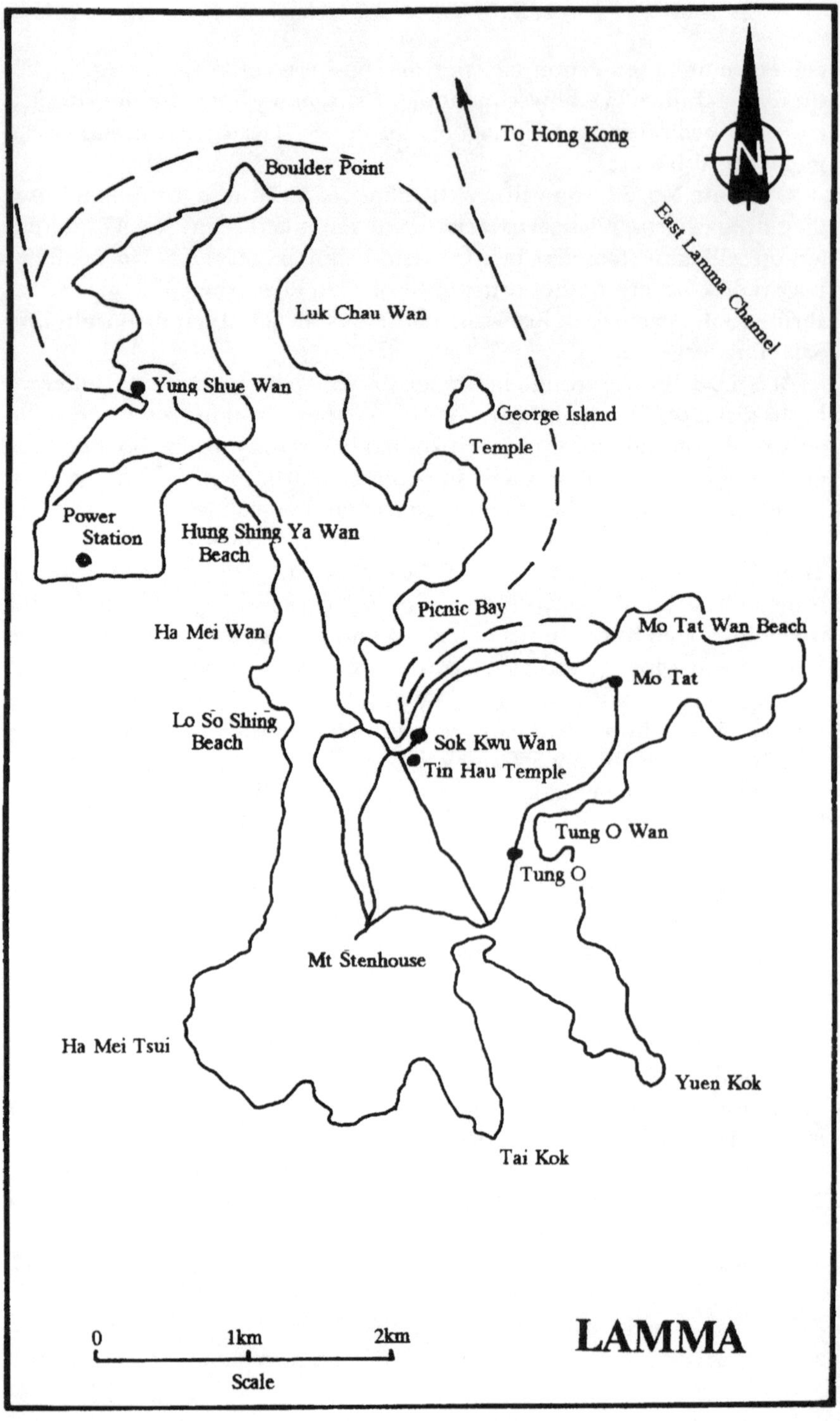
To Hong Kong
Boulder Point
East Lamma Channel
Luk Chau Wan
Yung Shue Wan
George Island
Temple
Power
Station
Hung Shing Ya Wan
Beach
Picnic Bay
Ha Mei Wan
Mo Tat Wan Beach
Mo Tat
Lo So Shing
Beach
Sok Kwu Wan
Tin Hau Temple
Tung O Wan
Tung O
Mt Stenhouse
Ha Mei Tsui
Yuen Kok
Tai Kok
0
1km
2km
Scale
LAMMA

Kwu Wan, the other village on the island. It passes through tiny clusters of family hamlets where old men still walk down regimented lines of vegetables with twin watering cans hanging from bamboo poles over their shoulders.

After a short while, you reach Hung Shing Ye beach, which is popular for windsurfing and swimming on weekends. The beach has lifeguards, changing facilities, restaurants, and accommodation, but it also has a huge coal-fired powerstation nearby and a bad reputation for dangerous marine stingers. There is a path that follows the coast to a small, pretty, undeveloped beach but the main path goes inland through grassland and rocks, then over a hill. From here you can look down on Sok Kwu Wan.

As you go down the hill, a path to the right goes across to Lo So Shing beach. This was once a major turtle egg-laying beach but the locals used to enjoy flipping the mother turtles over onto their backs when they came ashore, so now there are no more turtles. Instead, there are lifeguards and other "developed" facilities. Just outside Sok Kwu Wan, you will see a cave that was excavated during World War II by the Japanese as a depot for a flotilla of kamikaze torpedo boats that were eventually never used. There is a Tin Hau temple as you enter the village and some excellent waterfront restaurants near the ferry wharf. There are ferries from here to Hong Kong Island.

Lamma has a growing expatriate population fleeing the sky-high rents on Hong Kong Island. Many are of an artistic bent and they have pushed up the land prices and taken over many small fishermen's homes. The result is that you see two cultures—the newcomers sipping a Campari soda under the shade of a camphor tree while meters away, incense smoulders in a century-old shrine to a fisherman's god.

LANTAU

Until the last few years, Lantau had maintained an almost pristine environment. The island is nearly twice the size of Hong Kong Island, yet its population was less than 15,000. More than half the island is set aside as country park and several monasteries provided further retreat opportunities. Unfortunately this is all changing. First it was tourism but now it is a massive airport construction project that will change Lantau forever. If you want to see the old Lantau, you will have to be quick.

The ferry from Central will land you at Mui Wo (often known as Silvermine Bay). This is not a great place although there is a beach, some seafood restaurants, and several interesting walks. Most visitors will head for the bus that takes you to other parts of the island. Take bus No. 1 if you are going to Tai O, bus No. 2 for the Po Lin Monastery, and bus No. 3 for Tung Chung. Note that on weekends all buses are heavily used and it may take you considerable time to get around the island. The other option is to take

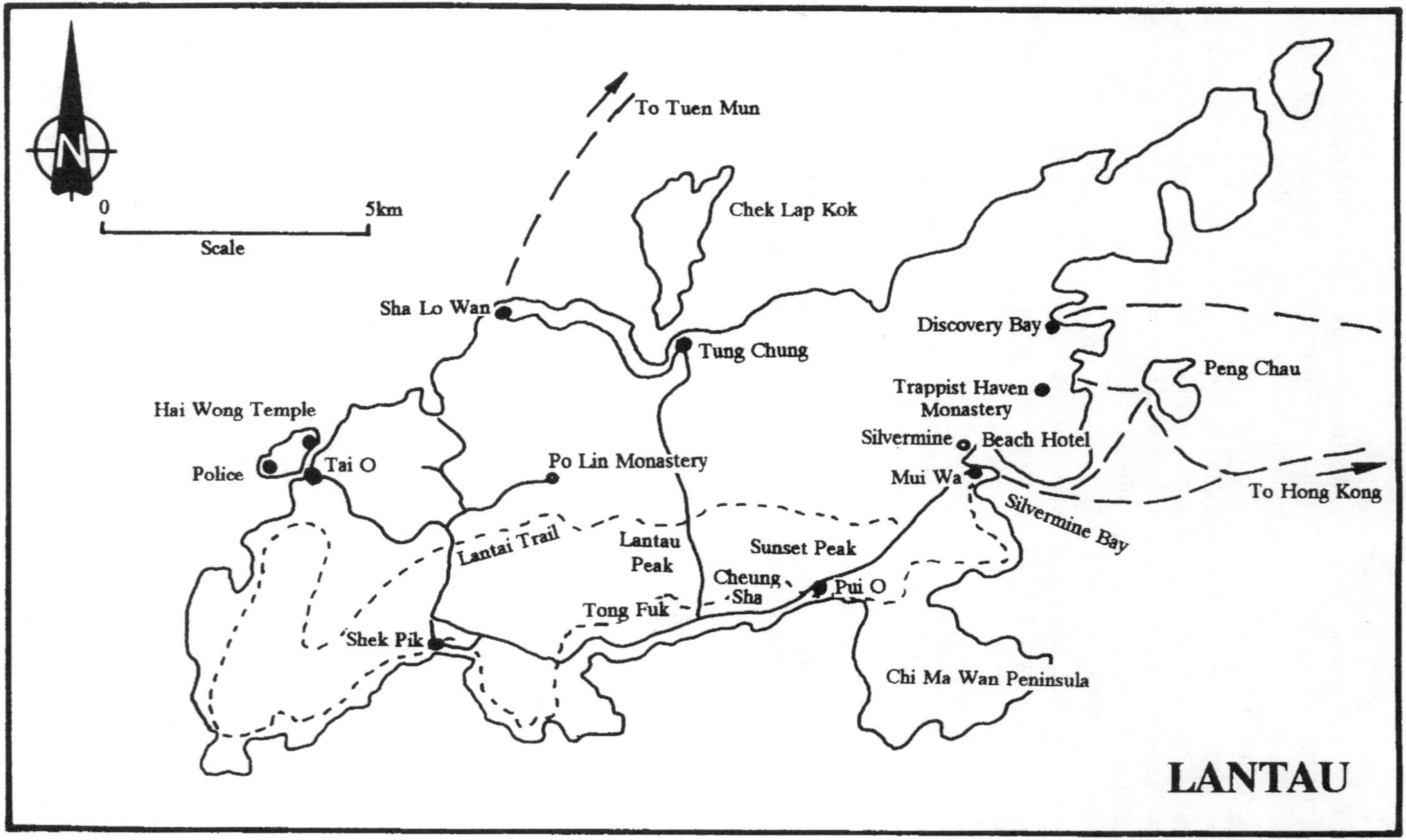
N
0
5km
Scale
To Tuen Mun
Chek Lap Kok
Sha Lo Wan
Tung Chung
Discovery Bay
Peng Chau
Trappist Haven
Monastery
Silvermine
Beach Hotel
Mui Wa
To Hong Kong
Silvermine Bay
Hai Wong Temple
Police
Tai O
Po Lin Monastery
Lantai Trail
Lantau
Peak
Sunset Peak
Cheung
Sha
Pui O
Tong Fuk
Shek Pik
Chi Ma Wan Peninsula
LANTAU

a taxi. From Mui Wo this is relatively easy but when you want to return from other parts of the island, it can prove to be almost impossible. Customer service is an unknown concept with Lantau taxi drivers!

Tai O is a large, rich village on the western end of the island. It was once an important trading and fishing port and during the 1980s it was the center of smuggling activities with China. This latter activity in electronic goods was very lucrative and you see it reflected in the modern homes that dot the village. Tai O is partly built on Lantau and partly on a small island just a few meters away. The two parts are linked by an ancient rope-drawn boat pulled by two old women and this is a popular photograph location.

There are two main temples in the village although neither is anything to get too excited about. The Kwan Tai Temple was originally built in 1748 to honor the god of war. It has a very old bronze bell. The Hau Wong Temple was built in 1699 to commemorate the last emperor of the Song dynasty who was pursued by the Mongols and fled to this place. The Sun Kit Drawbridge is another photographic opportunity.

The **Po Lin Monastery** is the feature of the island that most appeals to international visitors. This started as a place of retreat and the forty or so monks who live here still lead a spartan life. At the same time, the monks realize that they have a major visitor attraction on their hands and they have decided to exploit that. On weekends, it can be almost a carnival atmosphere as families invade with radios, children, and noisy enthusiasm. The main complex was started in the 1920s and was greatly expanded in the 1960s. The buildings are not particularly impressive but the 34-meter-high Buddha statue makes an impression on everyone. The Buddha is mounted on a pedestal copied from the Temple of Heaven in Beijing.

Visitors can take a vegetarian lunch of mushrooms, spring rolls, vegetables, and rice by buying a ticket at an office as you enter the monastery. Because this is a Buddhist monastery, visitors should dress conservatively and should not bring meat into the compound. You can stay overnight either here or at the adjacent Tea Gardens. The tea plantation does not appear to be thriving but you can sample the product in the cafe. If you so wish, you can also take a horseride.

The 70-kilometer Lantau Trail is a serious walker's delight. It runs the length of the island along the mountain tops from near Mui Wo, then returns along the coast. The two most interesting sections of the trail are probably those between the Po Lin Monastery and Mui Wo (about 15 kilometers and seven hours), and the southwest section between Tai O and Shek Pik (about 12 kilometers and 4 hours). The first walk is only for the fit and energetic because the path goes up and over Lantau Peak (934 meters), Sunset Peak (820 meters), and you have the option of Lin Fa Shan Peak (756 meters). The second walk is mainly level and you visit several nice beaches and have some good coastal scenery.

Asia's largest outdoor bronze Buddha gazes serenely out to sea. The Buddha is situated on a hillside above the Po Lin Monastery on Hong Kong's Lantau Island. (Courtesy of the Hong Kong Tourist Association)

THE OUTLYING ISLANDS

The area between Pui O and Tong Fuk has become a popular beach region. Several of the beaches have lifeguards from April to October and there are changing rooms, food stalls, restaurants, and accommodation. It is a 20-minute bus ride back to Mui Wo.

North from Mui Wo you can visit the Trappist Haven Monastery, which is run by an austere order of the Roman Catholic church. The monks have all taken a vow of silence and visitors are expected to keep their radios turned off and speak quietly. The path from Mui Wo goes up and over some hills and there are good views from the top. The monastery runs a dairy farm and visitors can buy the fresh product for a refreshing break. You can overnight here or take a *kaido* to Peng Chau Island. There is a mountain road to the Discovery Bay luxury condominium development and from here there are high-speed ferries back to Hong Kong Island.

If you have travelled to **Peng Chau Island,** you will find that this is a small but fairly developed island. It is positively crowded after empty Lantau. There are no cars on the island and you can see all the sights by walking around for an hour. There are some shops displaying hand-painted porcelain and locally made furniture. The 200-year-old Tin Hau Temple is worth a quick visit. Ferries and hoverferries operate back to Hong Kong Island.

The final outlying island worth visiting is **Tap Mun Chau.** This is northeast of Hong Kong Island and is reached by ferry from the New Territories. The island is visited for its quiet laid-back atmosphere, so it is best to go midweek. There is a ferry from Ma Liu Shui, a few minutes walk from University KCR Station or you can catch a *kaido* from Wong Shek Pier near Tai Tan. The island was once a thriving community but now the population is mainly old and numbers just 300. There are several fish farms in the bay and this is the major industry. You will see old women sorting abalone and sea urchins and you can get some excellent seafood at the New Hon Kee restaurant. There is a small temple to the goddess Tin Hau. It is worthwhile walking over the grassy hills to the cliffs on the far side of the island. Illegal immigrants from China used to arrive on these shores but today it is just the swell rolling in from the ocean. There is a small guesthouse if you wish to stay overnight.

7. Guided Tours

Please read the guided tours sections of chapters 4 and 5 for a complete understanding of the tours available to Hong Kong visitors. The following tours have a substantial Outlying Islands content.

The **Cheung Chau Island Tour** is a four-hour morning tour that operates daily, except Sundays. You cruise through bustling Victoria Harbour

On Peng Chau Island, the goddess Tin Hau sits on the altar in the temple dedicated to her worship. The temple was built in 1792, and, as the protector of all fisherfolk, she is very much revered on this island. (Courtesy of the Hong Kong Tourist Association)

THE OUTLYING ISLANDS 183

then have time to see some of the sights on Cheung Island. The cost is around HK$200.

The **Lantau Island Monastery Tour** operates daily, except Sunday. The seven-hour tour takes you to the largest island in Hong Kong, where a bus provides access to Cheung Sha beach, Tai O fishing village, and Po Lin Monastery. A vegetarian lunch is served at the monastery. The cost is around HK$350.

8. Culture

The main points about Hong Kong culture have been covered in previous chapters but special mention should be made of the Bun Festival that is held on Cheung Chau in May. The festival is unique to this island and its origin is not really clear. There is a procession and other festivities.

9. Sports

Beaches are the main attraction. A number of beaches on Cheung Chau, Lamma, and Lantau have been gazetted under the care of the Urban Council and have lifeguards, changing facilities, barbecues, and other facilities. Windsurfing facilities are available at Tung Wan beach on Cheung Chau and at Silvermine Beach on Lantau.

There is a nice golf course at the Discovery Bay Golf Club (Tel: 987-7273) on Lantau Island. This is reached by hoverferry from Blake Pier in Central on Hong Kong Island. Green fees for a nonmember are HK$600 on weekdays with club rental HK$150 and electric carts HK$200. Visitors are not allowed on weekends or public holidays.

10. Shopping

There are no major shopping facilities on the Outlying Islands and little to buy of interest to a visitor.

11. Entertainment and Nightlife

Other than restaurants and a few offerings from the small number of hotels, there is little nightlife on the Outlying Islands of interest to visitors.

12. The Outlying Islands Address List

Airlines—Cathay Pacific
        Reservations   Tel: 2747-1888
        Flight Information   Tel: 2745-1234

    —Dragonair
        Reservations   Tel: 2590-1188
        Flight Information   Tel: 2769-7728
Emergency—   Tel: 999
Hong Kong Tourist Association—   Tel: 2807-6543
Public Transport—Hong Kong Ferry Company   Tel: 2542-3082
Samaritans—A friend in need   Tel: 2834-3333
Telephone Information—   Tel: 1081
International Direct Dialing—   Tel: 001
Operator Assisted Calls—   Tel: 010
Typhoon Information—   Tel: 2835-1473
Utilities—Hong Kong Electric Company   Tel: 2555-4000
    —Water Supply Department   Tel: 2811-0788

Macau

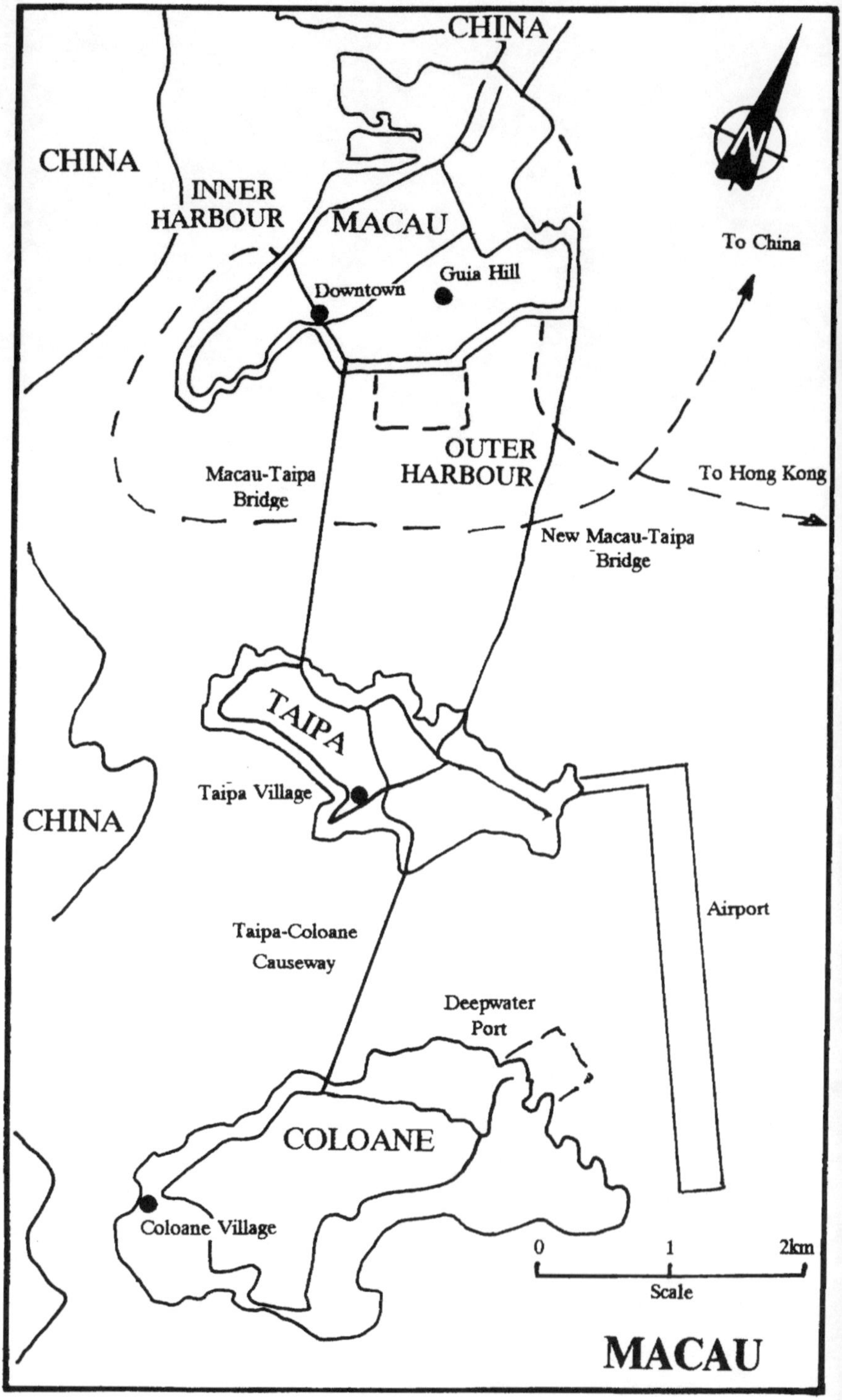
CHINA
CHINA
INNER HARBOUR
MACAU
Guia Hill
Downtown
To China
OUTER HARBOUR
Macau-Taipa Bridge
To Hong Kong
New Macau-Taipa Bridge
TAIPA
Taipa Village
CHINA
Airport
Taipa-Coloane Causeway
Deepwater Port
COLOANE
Coloane Village
0
1
2km
Scale
MACAU

8
The Land, Life, and People of Macau

Macau is only 60 kilometers from Hong Kong yet its history has made it a very different place. It is a strange blend of European and Chinese influences, modern development, and ancient cultures. It is the oldest surviving European settlement in Asia, yet ninety-five percent of the population is Chinese. In a way, it is a living museum, but then there is the hustle and bustle of construction of an airport, a port, and high-rise buildings; and you could be forgiven if you thought it was an outpost of Hong Kong. It is a curious place that somehow manages to be familiar and welcoming, whether you come from the East or the West. It is well worth a visit.

Geography

Macau is on the southeast coast of China around latitude 22 north and longitude 113 east. It is about 60 kilometers southwest of Hong Kong Island and about 140 kilometers from Canton (Guangzhou), China.

The territory is small with a land area of only 17.5 square kilometers; however, this is growing due to land reclamation. It consists of a peninsula on which is built the city of Macau, and the islands of Taipa and Coloane. At the extreme northern end of the peninsula, there is a border gate with China. Taipa is joined to the peninsula by two bridges, and Coloane is connected to Taipa with a causeway. The new airport is on reclaimed land at one end of Taipa.

Climate

The climate is similar to Hong Kong—warm to hot—although there are significant climatic variations during the year. January to March is considered the winter and it can be cold and cloudy, but it is often sunny. In April, the humidity starts to build up, and from May to September it is hot and humid with rain and tropical storms. October to mid-December is sunny and warm and this is probably the best climate for visitors.

The monthly mean temperature ranges from 15 to 28 degrees Celsius (59 to 83 degrees Fahrenheit) while the humidity varies from 50 percent to 82 percent. Rainfall averages around 2,000 mm with May, June, and August being the wettest months.

Cotton clothing is recommended for the summer while sweaters and jackets are needed at times during the evening for the rest of the year. For a short period in winter, sweaters are needed during the day, and an umbrella is useful anytime.

History

The Macau area seems to have been unimportant to China until the arrival of the Portuguese in 1513. The Portuguese had first landed in India in 1498 and had become aware of the enormous potential in trade with Asia. Some time later a strategy was devised to create a series of Portuguese ports that would enable this trade to be developed. The Portuguese captured Goa in India in 1510, and Malacca on the Malayan peninsula in 1511. They then set out to establish trade with the then almost unknown Chinese.

Initially, the contact did not work out well, but in 1556 the Portuguese made an agreement with some Canton officials to rent a small peninsula that had two natural harbors, and so Macau was founded. It then grew rapidly as a trade center as the Portuguese developed a profitable network of trade between China, Japan, Malaya, and India, then eventually to Europe. They had a virtual monopoly on this trade and huge profits were made. Some of the money ended up in Portugal but much of it remained in Macau, so the city prospered.

Macau also served as a base for Christian missionaries planning to convert Japan and China to Christianity. This activity provided the city with some of its most glorious, and controversial, moments in its history. The interests of traders and missionaries often clashed and the local Portuguese administration was often less than enthusiastic about the missionaries "meddling in Chinese affairs."

Late in the sixteenth century, Portugal's power started to slide. In 1580, the Spanish occupied Portugal, and soon after, the Dutch expanded their influence into the Asian region. The Dutch tried to invade Macau five times in the seventeenth century but each time they were repulsed. The Dutch did, however, capture Malacca from the Portuguese and this robbed Macau of a lifeline. At around the same time, the Japanese reacted against the missionaries that were operating in the country and closed the country to foreign trade. This devastated the trade routes that the Portuguese had built, and China found that it was unable to export or import the things that it wanted. In disgust, China closed the port of Canton to the Portuguese and for 100 years Macau languished.

From the mideighteenth century, Macau grew again as the French, Dutch, Scandinavians, Spanish, and Americans increased their trade with China. During this period, Macau became the summer residence of the major traders who were required by the Chinese to leave their factories in Canton to await the opening of the next trading season. For a time the city prospered but there were ongoing disputes between the Portuguese, the Chinese, and then the British. The British dealt Macau a major blow in 1841 when they settled in Hong Kong, just 60 kilometers to the northeast. Immediately the economic importance of Macau collapsed and it has never returned to the same heights.

The Macau governor was forced to introduce licenced gambling in the 1860s to help keep the colony financially solvent. Politically, the Portuguese managed to sign a treaty with China in 1887 that effectively recognized Portugal's sovereignty over Macau. Dispite this, Macau turned into something of a backwater for forty years until the Sino-Japanese War erupted in the 1930s. At this time the population swelled to 500,000 and it rose even higher during World War II when many Europeans took refuge here. Japan decided to respect Portugal's neutrality and did not invade Macau. More refugees arrived when the Communists took power in China in 1949. In 1966, Macau was invaded by Chinese Red Guards during the Cultural Revolution, but the Chinese government backed off when the Portuguese threatened to walk away from Macau.

Macau, however, is heading for a major change. After the 20th of December 1999, Macau becomes a Special Economic Region of China. Under the terms of the Sino-Portuguese pact, Macau is to enjoy a "high level of autonomy" for fifty years in all matters except defense and foreign affairs. Only time will tell if this is successful.

The Government

There is almost a secrecy about the government of Macau. It is as though no one wants to talk about it. Even its status is a bit of a mystery. It suits both China and Portugal to say that Macau is a piece of Chinese territory currently under Portuguese administration. It is administered by a governor appointed by the president of Portugal and he in turn appoints seven undersecretaries. There is also a legislative assembly with 23 members and this elects a president. In addition there are two mayors: one for the peninsula and one for the two islands. Just how much influence China has at present is a moot point. China has a Hong Kong and Macau Affairs Office that is taking a stance on many issues. Many believe that nothing happens in Macau these days without the blessing of China. If this is the case, then perhaps there will be little change in 1999.

The Economy

To a large extent Macau lives on tourism and gambling. Around eight million visitors descend on Macau each year and 80 percent of these are Chinese from Hong Kong who are coming for the gambling. While licensed gambling commenced in the 1860s, it was not until 1934 that casino gambling was introduced. Today, the licensed gambling is all controlled by a private syndicate called the *Sociedade de Turismo e Diversoes de Macau* (STDM) headed by Mr. Stanley Ho, and it provides about a half of the government's revenue. The government is convinced that tourism will continue to thrive and it is currently spending something like US$750 million on an international airport on reclaimed land on the east side of Taipa Island. STDM also has a stake in the airport, the deep-water port, the major reclamation areas, and many property developments.

Macau has a small but growing number of light industries. These are mainly in the textile and clothing sector and they are staffed in part by Chinese workers who cross the border daily from Zhuhai. Wages are considerably lower than in Hong Kong and this is encouraging some overseas investment in labor-intensive industries. The country is a duty-free area and the maximum taxation rate is fifteen percent.

Macau sees a future in developing export-oriented industries based on the relatively low wages, and it also hopes to become an export port for goods from China. Because it has no natural deep-water harbor, it has gone ahead and developed a port on the northeast edge of Coloane Island that handles containers, oil, and other cargo. In association with this and the airport, the new bridge from Taipa Island to the peninsula and the associated ring road around Macau City will ease traffic congestion and provide a good road connection to China.

The economy is rapidly becoming integrated with the adjacent Special Economic Zone in China and a new freeway is under construction to Canton. While some long-term residents are not enthusiastic about all these changes, there is no doubt that the economy will benefit and the change is inevitable.

The People

The population is estimated at 460,000 with about 95 percent Chinese,

3 percent Portuguese and other Europeans, and 2 percent from other regions. Most live on the peninsula in one of the most densely populated places on earth but the government is encouraging the development of high-rise Taipa City on Taipa Island for future population increases.

There has been surprisingly little assimilation between the Portuguese and the Chinese despite 400 years of contact. Most Portuguese cannot speak Chinese and vice versa. Mixed marriages are not unheard of but Eurasians are not a significant force in Macau.

Taoism and Buddhism are the major religions for the Chinese population, while the European population is primarily Roman Catholic. The Catholic Church has significant influence in Macau and has been successful in converting some Chinese to this faith.

Language

Portuguese and Chinese are the two official languages. The majority of the population speaks Cantonese as the language of choice. English is generally used in trade, tourism, and commerce. As a short-time visitor, you will have no major language problems if you only speak English.

Because, however, many signs and maps are still in Portuguese, it may help to know the following words:

alley	—beco
avenue	—avenida
beach	—praia
bridge	—ponte
building	—edificio
bus stop	—paragem
church	—igreja
guesthouse	—hospedaria
inn	—pousada
island	—ilha
market	—mercado
museum	—museu
police station	—esquadra da policia
post office	—correio
restaurant	—restaurante or *casa de pasto*
road	—estrada
street	—rua

Culture and Lifestyle

The culture of the Chinese majority is almost indistinguishable from that found in Hong Kong. The small Portuguese population, however, has a completely different culture based on Western influences and this can still be seen in many parts of Macau. The most interesting thing for the visitor is when the two cultures merge. You see this with food—one of the highlights of any visit to Macau. There is also some indication of it in modern art, drama, and dance. It also affects other aspects of life. Macau is far safer than most Western cities and walking around at night is generally no problem. At the same time you will receive many stares if you appear on the popular beaches in the latest bikini from Europe.

Food and Drink

Macau is a great place to find good restaurants at prices significantly cheaper than their Hong Kong equivalent. There are various cuisines available but naturally Portuguese, Chinese, and Macanese (Macau-born Portuguese and Eurasians) predominate. Traditional dishes from Portugal include *bacalhau,* the country's beloved cod fish, served baked, grilled, stewed, or boiled. Wines are one of the real treats of Macau. Portuguese and other table wines can be bought in supermarkets at a fraction of the price in most Asian countries.

All the Chinese favorites are readily obtainable and the ingredients come fresh from the Chinese farms on the Pearl River Delta. Dim sum is popular and easy to find. The most popular dishes include *har kau* (steamed shrimp dumplings), *shui mai* (dumplings filled with pork and shrimp), and *tsuen guen* (spring rolls filled with pork, chicken, mushroom, and bean sprouts).

Macanese food includes some of the spicy dishes the Portuguese learned about on their visits to Africa and south Asia. Macau's most popular dishes include African and Goanese chicken, and piquant prawns, all baked or grilled with peppers and chillies. Also popular is the Brazilian *feijoadas,* a stew made from pork, potatoes, kidney beans, cabbage, and spicy sausage. To accompany the meal, Macau's bakers make Asia's best Continental bread rolls.

Unlike quick Cantonese stir-fry cooking, Macanese food inclines towards slow simmering, which produces rich and aromatic gravies ideal for serving with rice or boiled potatoes, or to be mopped up by chunks of crusty Portuguese rolls.

Festivals

Macau celebrates many of the traditional Chinese festivals, then adds some Christian ones as well. The principal festivals in the first half of the year are Chinese New Year in late January or early February; the Procession of our

THE LAND, LIFE, AND PEOPLE OF MACAU

Lord of Passos in late February or March, on the weekend forty days before Easter, in the evening from St. Augustine's Church to the Macau Cathedral, then the next afternoon from the Cathedral to St. Augustine's; the Ching Ming Festival (Chinese All Souls Day) in April; Easter; the A-Ma Festival, Macau's most personal Chinese festival held with color and activity at the A-Ma Temple in April; the Feast of the Bathing of Lord Buddha in May; the Procession of Our Lady of Fatima in May from the Santa Domingo church to Penha church; the Dragon Boat Festival in June; the Feast of Kuan Tai; the Feast of Na Cha; and the Feast of St. John the Baptist, the saint of Macau, all in June.

In the second half of the year there are the Mid-Autumn Festival in September; the Festival of Ancestors (Chung Yeung) in October; All Saints and All Souls in November; the Macau Grand Prix in November; the Feast of the Immaculate Conception in early December, and Christmas. More details of some of these festivals can be found in chapter 3.

The following are the public holidays currently taken in Macau:

New Year's Day—January 1
Chinese New Year—3 days in late January or early February
Ching Ming Festival—early April
Easter—3 days in late March or in April
Liberty Day—April 25
Labor Day—May 1
Day of Portugal—June 10
Dragon Boat Festival—June
Feast of St. John the Baptist—June 24
Mid-Autumn Festival—September
Republic Day—October 5
Festival of Ancestors—October
All Saints Day and All Souls Day—November 1, 2
Independence Day of Portugal—December 1
Immaculate Conception Day—December 8
Christmas Eve and Christmas Day—December 24, 25

Accommodations

Prices and difficulty with accommodation vary throughout the week and the year. Weekdays during the low season (January to Easter) is the time to look for bargains. Weekdays at other times of the year will not be too bad, but weekends are an entirely different matter. Room prices rise substantially at some places on all weekends and when an event such as the Macau Grand Prix in November is on, rooms can be impossible to obtain.

Really cheap accommodation is almost impossible to find but midmarket and top-class accommodation is readily available most times, at prices substantially less than Hong Kong. Most hotels are on the peninsula.

Health and Safety

Macau has a similar situation to Hong Kong. In terms of violent crime, Macau is safer than most Western cities. Pickpocketing can be a problem in crowded places such as casinos and ferry terminals, so you need to take sensible precautions.

There are two large hospitals providing full facilities. One is government-run, the other private with government subsidy. The health and disease problems that you encounter in much of Asia are less common here. Water is treated and chlorinated and according to officials, it is safe to drink. Bottled water is readily available.

9

Macau—Mainland and Islands

1. The General Picture

Many visitors to Hong Kong do not take the time to see Macau, and of those that do, most only make it a day trip. That is a pity because this tiny Portuguese outpost is a curious mixture of East and West quite different from Hong Kong. It is a city of gambling, new high-rise buildings and extensive construction activity tempered by a slightly slower pace of life; a love of good food and wine; narrow, cobbled side streets; Baroque churches; and restored Colonial villas.

Ten years ago, Macau was a desultory, decaying city with a lack of hope—so very different from its chaotic, capitalist neighbor, Hong Kong. A visit at that time was like winding the clock back a half-century in time. Some writers still picture Macau like that today, but the reality is that those days are gone forever.

The new airport, scheduled to open in 1996, is about to make Macau more accessible to the world; and tourism and general business is on the rise. While much of the old-world "European" attraction of Macau has disappeared in recent years as the territory has pursued a new "development" philosophy, new hotels, casinos, and other entertainment and cultural developments are offering the visitor new reasons for visiting and staying that one extra day. Unfortunately, with the frenzied reclamation, mountains being shaved to give way to development, and the sprouting of pink, green, and yellow faceless buildings, Macau has done itself few favors recently in the eyes of most tourists.

There are experiences in Macau that you cannot have in Hong Kong or China, however, so that is ample reason for me to go there. I suggest that you will find plenty of interest for a three-day stay; but even if you can only spare one day, it is worthwhile making the trip. If possible, avoid the weekends because at that time thousands of Hong Kong residents visit and things become quite crowded and more expensive.

2. Getting There

Most people arrive in Macau by sea from Hong Kong. Although the distance is 60 kilometers, the trip can be made in one hour. There are several different types of craft to choose from. The jetfoils are my choice, although others prefer the hoverferries, the jetcats, or the high-speed ferries.

Jetfoils depart from Hong Kong at about 15-minute intervals during the 7 A.M. to 8 P.M. period, then they operate about a half-hourly service until midnight, and then several other sailings during the night. In Hong Kong, most sailings depart from the Shun Tak Center wharf on Connaught Road, Central, on Hong Kong Island. Some jetfoil, jetcat, and hoverferry services are now operating from the China Ferry Terminal in Tsim Sha Tsui, Kowloon.

Boeing jetfoils take 55 minutes for the run between Hong Kong and Macau.

The jetfoils are operated by the Far East Hydrofoil Co. Ltd. (Tel: 859-3333). **Jumbocats** are operated by the Hong Kong Macau Hydrofoil Co. Ltd. (Tel: 521-8302). **Hoverferries** have basically been replaced by **catarmarans** and these are operated by the Hong Kong and Yaumati Ferry Co. Ltd. (Tel: 542-3081). Hong Kong Hi-Speed Ferries, Ltd., operate large ferries that take 90 minutes to make the crossing (Tel: 815-3043).

It is wise to book your return ticket in advance because at times the seats are in great demand and particular sailings may be full. Jetfoil and jumbocat tickets can be bought up to 28 days in advance at Shun Tak Center and through Ticketmate outlets in the Causeway Bay, Tsim Sha Tsui, Jordan, Mongkok, Kwun Tong, Wanchai, and Tsuen Wan MTR stations. If you buy a ticket other than at the pier, double check that you know where the ship departs from. You need to arrive 30 minutes before departure to allow for customs and immigration. Fares are higher on weekends and at night than on weekdays. The ticket price includes departure tax from both Hong Kong and Macau.

If time is critical to you and money is not, it is possible to take an East Asia Airlines **helicopter** from Shun Tak Center to the new ferry terminal in Macau. Travel time is about 20 minutes and the cost is around HK$1,100 one-way. Flight details are available from Hong Kong, Tel: 2859-3359 or from Macau, Tel: 573-066.

From China, you can walk across the border to Macau between 7 A.M. and 12 P.M. You can also take a direct bus from Guangzhou (Canton), but this is sometimes delayed at the border so some travellers prefer to take the bus from Guangzhou to the border, walk across, and take a Macau taxi to their accommodation. A further option is an overnight ferry from Zhoutouzui Wharf in Guangzhou to Macau. The major hotels in Guangzhou sell tickets for this service.

3. Local Transportation

Taxis are readily available and the cost is reasonable. There are two types—black with cream-colored roof, and all yellow. It makes no difference which you take. The charge is M$7 flagfall and the first 1,500 meters, then M$0.90 for every subsequent 250 meters. There are also waiting time and luggage charges. For the islands there is an additional charge of M$5 for Taipa and M$10 for Coloane. Unfortunately, many taxi drivers have only very basic English language ability so it is useful to have a map or the address written in Chinese before you head out.

Pedicabs are a slower and more romantic way of getting around but they are hardly suitable for Macau's heavy peak-hour traffic. You must negotiate a fare for the particular trip or you can rent by the hour. Again English is a problem so you may not end up where you expect, but the ride will be fun. Expect to pay about M$50 for an hour and do not ask the driver to take you up some of the steep streets to the hilltops. You will find pedicabs at the ferry terminal and along Rua da Praia Grande.

For the budget-minded, the **city bus** is an option. A single trip will cost M$2.00 and there is a good network. It helps to have a good map with English and Chinese names so that you can show the driver where you wish to go. From the ferry terminal a bus No. 3, 3A, 12, 28A, or 28C will take you downtown to the Lisboa Hotel area. Bus 28A will also take you across to Taipa Island. From the Lisboa Hotel area you can walk to many points of interest. Bus No.s 11, 21, 21A, 28A, 33, and 38 go from the city to Taipa Island (fare M$2.50), and 21 and 21A continue on to Coloane (fare M$3.20 to the village, M$4 to Hac Sa). You need the exact fare because change is not given.

There are several companies renting **mokes**—small jeeplike vehicles. These cost around M$300 a day and drivers must be over 21 years of age and hold a valid International Driving Licence. Try Avis at the Mandarin Oriental (Tel: 336-789) or the mokes at the New Century Hotel (Tel: 831-212). Chauffeur-driven cars are also available.

Bicycles are a good way to explore the islands and they are available for rent from shops at Taipa Village. Note that they are not allowed on the Macau–Taipa bridges.

4. The Hotel Scene

Macau has had a small hotel building boom in recent years, but it is still often hard to get a room. During the summer period much of the upmarket and midmarket accommodation is fully booked, even on weekdays. Weekends at any time of the year are a problem. This is despite the fact that many Macau visitors do not overnight here at all. Last year nearly eight million people visited Macau but less than two million actually stayed overnight.

EXPENSIVE HOTELS

My two favorites in this category are both small and old. Somehow this seems to fit the character of Macau. Top of the heap is the **Bela Vista** (Tel: 965-333), which has 8 magnificent rooms and suites in a building that is more than 100 years old. The six-million-dollar (in U.S. currency) restoration of this building has produced something that is truly beautiful. It has been refurbished in the style of a luxurious Portuguese family home. You can dine in the charming restaurant or out on the verandah overlooking Praia Grande Bay. There is an adjacent bar ideal for lunchtime cocktails or a relaxing nightcap. The lobby, magnificent staircase, and cozy upstairs

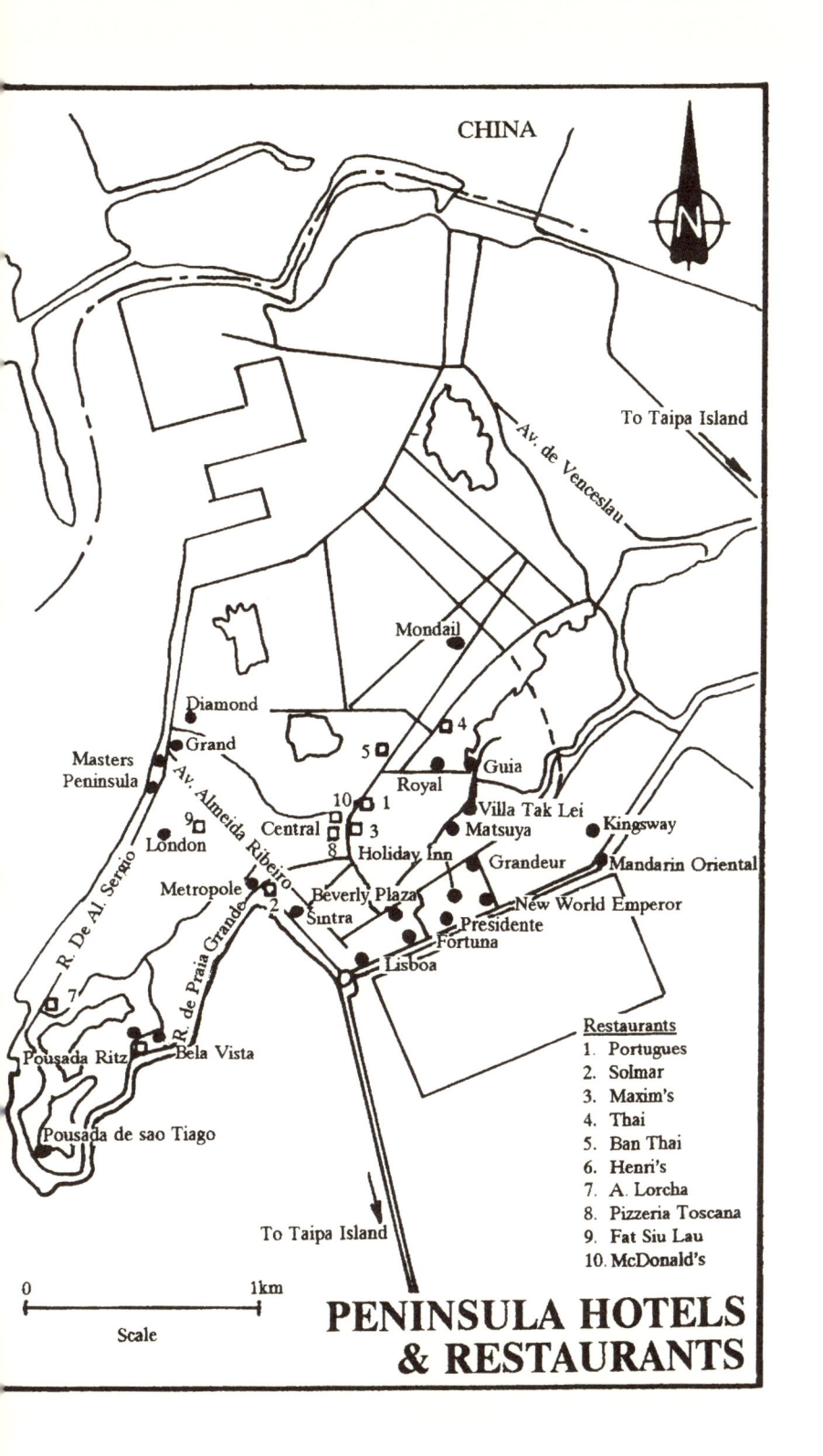

PENINSULA HOTELS & RESTAURANTS

CHINA

To Taipa Island

Av. de Venceslau

Mondail

Diamond

Grand

Masters Peninsula

Av. Almeida Ribeiro

4

5

Royal

Guia

10

Central

1

3

Villa Tak Lei

Matsuya

Kingsway

London

8

Holiday Inn

Grandeur

9

Metropole

Beverly Plaza

Mandarin Oriental

R. De Al. Sergio

2

Sintra

Presidente

New World Emperor

R. de Praia Grande

Fortuna

Lisboa

7

Pousada Ritz

Bela Vista

Pousada de sao Tiago

To Taipa Island

Restaurants
1. Portugues
2. Solmar
3. Maxim's
4. Thai
5. Ban Thai
6. Henri's
7. A. Lorcha
8. Pizzeria Toscana
9. Fat Siu Lau
10. McDonald's

Scale 0 — 1km

lounge are outstanding. Guests are entitled to use the health club facilities of the Mandarin Oriental Hotel. At M$1,900 for the cheapest room, and rising to M$4,400 for the Bela Vista suite, it is certainly not cheap; but it simply reeks with class and it is a wonderful value when compared with what you would pay in Hong Kong. (Book with the hotel at 8 Rua do Comendador Kou Ho Neng, Macau; Fax: 853-965-588.)

My other favorite is the **Pousada de Sao Tiago** (Tel: 378-111), 23 rooms, all elegantly decorated in carved dark mahogany wood, blue-and-white Iberian tiles, and pink marble. This is situated on the very southern tip of the peninsula overlooking the harbor within the old fortress, Fortaleza de S. Tiago da Barra. The transformation has been carried out brilliantly and has received much praise. There are three restaurants serving Portuguese and European food, a bar, and a swimming pool and terrace. Room rates start at around M$1,200. (Book with the hotel at Avenida da Republica, Macau; Fax: 853-552-170.) It is a great place for a late afternoon drink.

The third recommendation started out as a small property, but it has recently grown dramatically with the opening of the new wing. It cannot lay claim to a long history, however. The **Pousada Ritz** (Tel: 339-955), 160 rooms, is modern and swanky. It has a Cantonese restaurant called the Lijinxuan; the Restaurant Amigo for European cuisine; a bar; indoor, heated swimming pool; beauty parlor; florist; sauna and massage; billiard room; tennis court; squash court; and small shopping arcade. Room rates start at around M$1,100. (Book with the hotel at Rua da Boa Vista, Macau; Fax: 853-317-826.)

Of the major hotels, the **Mandarin Oriental** (Tel: 567-888), 438 rooms, has the best reputation on the peninsula. I find the external architecture fairly mundane, but it has a wonderful lobby, the whole hotel has been beautifully decorated, and it has the famous Mandarin service that will impress most guests. The facilities are extensive. There is a choice of four restaurants. The Dynasty is a fine Cantonese restaurant; the Cafe Girassol serves European and home-style Macanese specialties; Mezzaluna offers casually elegant dining in an Italian style; and the Poolside Terrace has light snacks. The popular Bar da Guia themes the annual Macau Grand Prix and is open until 1 A.M. The hotel has an outdoor swimming pool, two squash courts, two tennis courts, gymnasium, business center, casino, shopping arcade, and nightly live entertainment. Room rates start at around M$1,100. (Book with the hotel at P.O. Box 3016, Macau; Fax: 853-594-589.)

The **Hotel Royal** (Tel: 552-222), 380 rooms, is another relatively new luxury hotel with all the necessary facilities. It is located on the hill not far from the Guia Lighthouse. The Vasco da Gama room is a fine European restaurant; the Ginza Teppanyaki serves Japanese food; while the Royal Canton has Chinese cuisine. The hotel has a shopping arcade, the Lucky Star

Pousada de Sao Tiago, Macau.

Hotel Lisboa—main entrance and tower.

Japanese karaoke lounge, an indoor swimming pool, a gymnasium, and sauna and massage. Room rates start at M$750. (Book with the hotel at Estrada da Vitoria, Macau; Fax: 853-563-008.)

The final mainland hotel in this category is the flamboyant **Hotel Lisboa** (Tel: 377-666), 1,050 rooms, and Macau's largest hotel. On first sight it is difficult to take this place seriously, but actually it is quite a fine hotel once you get inside. Apart from the large 24-hour casino, there are plenty of other facilities, including a shopping arcade; a swimming pool; sauna and massage; eleven restaurants serving Portuguese, European, Chinese, Japanese, Korean, and Thai food; and six bars and lounges. Room rates start at around M$750. (Book with the hotel at P.O. Box 85, Macau; Fax: 853-567-193.)

In my mind, three of the best large hotels are on the islands. They suffer somewhat by not being within walking distance of the main sight-seeing attractions, but as compensation they have space and great facilities. The **Hyatt Regency** on Taipa Island (Tel: 831-234), 353 rooms, is a fine property that has been around for about ten years. While it is used extensively by business people, it has the relaxed atmosphere of a resort. This is emphasized by the adjacent Taipa Island Resort, which is open to hotel guests, with its huge outdoor, heated swimming pool; the fitness center with spa, sauna, and massage facilities; four tennis courts with lighting for night use; two squash courts; a volleyball court; a gymnasium; and an indoor games' room. The hotel has an upmarket casino and there are Portuguese, Cantonese, and Macanese restaurants; a coffee shop; and a bar. Regular transfers to the ferry terminal and city are provided. Room rates start at M$990. (Book with the Hyatt Group or direct with the hotel at 2 Estrada Almirante Marques Esparteiro, Taipa Island, Macau; Fax: 853-830-195.)

The **New Century** (Tel: 831-111), 598 rooms, is the newest of the island luxury hotels. It has a grand lobby and all the other facilities you would expect from a five-star hotel. There are restaurants serving Cantonese, Western, Japanese, and Mediterranean food. There is a lobby lounge, a poolside bar, and a karaoke/disco lounge. Sporting facilities include a large outdoor pool, two tennis courts, two squash courts, a fitness and aerobics club, five snooker tables, table tennis, games' room, and massage. The hotel has a business center and the largest shopping arcade in Macau. Room rates start at M$1,050. The hotel also has some two- and three-bedroom serviced apartments that are extremely attractive and well priced from M$19,000 a month. (Book with the hotel at Estrada Almirante Marques Esparteiro, Taipa Island, Macau; Fax: 853-832-222.)

Then there is the **Westin Resort** (Tel: 871-111), 208 rooms, on Coloane Island. The eight-story property terraces up the hillside, providing each large room with an ocean view. There is a Cantonese restaurant and an all-day cafe, three lounges and bars, two outdoor swimming pools, eight tennis courts, and a health club equipped with an indoor pool, whirlpool, sauna, and massage. The hotel is directly linked to the Macau Golf and Country Club with its 18-hole course. Room rates start at M$1,200. (Book with Westin Resorts in North America on Tel: 1-800-228-3000; in Australia, Tel: 1-800-222-944; in the United Kingdom, Tel: 0-800-282-565; or direct with the hotel at Estrada de Hac Sa, Ilha de Coloane, Macau; Fax: 853-871-122.)

Back on the peninsula, the **Holiday Inn** (Tel: 783-333), 435 rooms, falls into the bottom end of this category. The standard rooms are perfectly acceptable; but if you want more, the executive floor for business travellers offers a private executive club lounge. The hotel has a Cantonese and an Italian restaurant and a cafe serving international food. The Lounge has high tea and piano music, and there is a heated pool, a gymnasium, and a casino. Room rates start at M$800. (Book with the Holiday Inn network or direct with the hotel at Rua Pequim, Ed Yee Chan Kok, 8-B, Macau; Fax: 853-782-321.)

Another excellent property is the **New World Emperor Hotel** (Tel: 781-888), 405 rooms. I recently stayed here and was impressed by the service and facilities. The rooms are large and well appointed; the Cantonese restaurant and the international-style coffee shop have excellent food at reasonable prices; the nightclub is one of the hottest spots in town; and the location is convenient. Although the hotel is only about two years old, an upgrade of facilities is already underway. All in all, I rate this highly and with room rates from M$780, it is a good value. I would happily return here. (Book with New World Hotels International in North America on Tel: 800-538-8882, or direct with the hotel at Rua de Xangai, Macau; Fax: 853-782-287.)

MEDIUM-PRICE HOTELS

My favorite hotel in this category is probably the **Hotel Guia** (Tel: 513-888), 89 rooms. The hotel is located on Guia Hill below the historic Guia Lighthouse. The atrium lobby is attractive and the rooms are well appointed. There is a Chinese restaurant and a small coffee shop on the lobby floor. The Guia Disco Nightclub is in the basement. Room rates start at M$470. (Book with the hotel at 1 Estrada do Engenheiro Trigo, Macau; Fax: 853-559-822.)

A hotel of an entirely different sort is the large and modern **Beverley Plaza** (Tel: 782-288), 300 large rooms. This is located close to the Lisboa casino in the main commercial area. The hotel has several shops, a business center, a bar, and two restaurants. Room prices are from M$700. (Book with the hotel at Avenida do Dr. Rodrigo Rodrigues, Macau; Fax: 853-780-684.) **The Fortuna** (Tel: 786-333), 368 rooms, is similar but has more entertainment facilities. Rooms cost from M$750. (Book with the hotel at 15

Rua de Cantao, Macau; Fax: 853-786-363.) A third property of similar standard is the **Kingsway** (Tel: 702-888), 410 rooms, from M$650. There is a shopping arcade, restaurants, bars, nightclub, sauna, and casino. (Book at Rua de Gonzaga Gomes, Macau; Fax: 853-702-828.) Then there is the **Hotel Presidente** (Tel: 553-888), 330 rooms, in a good location opposite the new convention center. The hotel has a Western and a Korean restaurant, a lobby lounge, a sauna, the Skylight disco/nightclub, and nice rooms. Rates start at M$660. (Book with the hotel at Avenida da Amizade, Macau; Fax: 853-552-735.)

If you enjoy smaller hotels, the **Matsuya** (Tel: 575-466), 47 rooms, would be a good choice. It is on the way up Guia Hill but is within walking distance of many points of interest. There is a bar, a dining room, and a cafe. Room rates start at M$330. (Book with the hotel at 5 Estrada de S. Francisco, Macau; Fax: 853-568-080.) An alternative is the **Metropole** (Tel: 388-166), 112 rooms, in a very central location. There is a Chinese restaurant-nightclub, a Western restaurant, a fast-food outlet, and a shop for basic necessities. Room rates are from M$460. (Book at 63 Rua da Praia Grande, Macau; Fax: 853-330-890.) Over next to the floating casino, the **Macau Masters Hotel** (Tel: 937-572) is in a similar category. Some rooms look across the river into China while others have poor views. There is a coffee shop and restaurant that serve Chinese and Western food and a small bar. The hotel is popular with the Hong Kong gamblers who play at the adjacent casino. Room rates are from M$400. (Book at the hotel at 162 Rua das Lorchas, Macau; Fax: 853-937-565.)

On Coloane Island, the **Pousada de Coloane** (Tel: 882-143), 22 rooms, provides a quiet atmosphere overlooking the beach. There is a swimming pool, a children's playground, an open terrace garden, a bar, and a restaurant featuring Portuguese food and wine. It would make a nice hideaway during a hectic Asian visit. Room rates start at around M$550. (Book with the hotel at Praia de Cheoc Van, Coloane Island, Macau; Fax: 853-882-251.)

Downmarket from these places you could try the **Peninsula** (Tel: 318-899). This is a well-run, clean, modern building with room rates from M$350 single and M$400 double. There is a restaurant and sauna. You find it on Rua das Lorchas, just north of the floating casino on the Inner Harbour. In the same area, the **Hotel Grand** (Tel: 921-111) at 146 Avenida Almeida Ribeiro has single rooms from M$260 and doubles from M$330. Also in this area is the excellent **Diamond Hotel** (Tel: 923-118), 20 rooms, at 11 Rua Nova do Comercio. The place is new and clean, but when I visited there was no one available who could speak English. Room rates are around M$300. The **Hotel London** (Tel: 937-761), 46 rooms, is a few blocks to the south overlooking a small square at 4 Praca Ponte e Horta. Double rooms are available from M$230. Across town on Estrada Sao Francisco, the **Villa**

Tak Lei (Tel: 577-484) has air-conditioned rooms with TV and telephone from M$300.

BUDGET ACCOMMODATION

There are two main areas to look for low-cost accommodation. The first is the area around the floating casino, on the west side of the peninsula. There are many options here in small villas and guesthouses, but the standard varies from passable to awful, so you need to do your own inspection. Try along Rua das Lorchas, on Rua do Gamboa, and on some of the small side streets. Rooms are available in this area from M$60 but you do not get much for this price.

The second area is more upmarket and will appeal more to some people. It roughly covers the region bounded by Rua da Praia Grande, Avendia D Joao IV, and Avenida do Doutor Mario Soares, and is on the eastern side of the peninsula. Room rates here start at around M$100 on weekdays.

5. Dining and Restaurants

Macau is a great place to find excellent little restaurants tucked away down narrow alleys. Some have authentic Portuguese food while others specialize in Macanese, Chinese, Thai, Japanese, or Vietnamese. My usual policy is to eat the cuisine of the country I am visiting, and in this case that would be Chinese, but I strongly recommend that you have at least one Portuguese or Macanese meal, because it is unique in Asia and because it is so good. Service tends to be more genteel than in Hong Kong and no one seems to mind if you settle in with a nice bottle of Portuguese wine. On the islands, it is even possible to find a place where conversation is punctuated by the rhythmic breaking of the waves on the beach and mumurs of the breeze in the nearby Casuarinas.

Here is a selection of my favorites that serve Portuguese or Macanese dishes.

A Lorcha (Tel: 313-193) is a bit out of the way but it is worth finding. It is on the southwest tip of the peninsula near the A-Ma Temple, at 289 Rua do Almirante Sergio. Although it is unpretentious, the food is some of the best in the city. There are also some interesting Chinese dishes. The only place to rival this one for food at reasonable prices is the equally out of the way **Riquexo** (Tel: 565-655), at 69 Avenida Sidonia Pais on the northern side of Guia Hill. This opens for lunch (12-3 P.M.) and dinner (6-9 P.M.). Many of the dishes are home-cooked and brought to the restaurant each day.

Back closer to the center of town at 16 Rua do Campo, **Portugues** (Tel: 375-445) has an excellent reputation for fine food, good atmosphere, and reasonable prices. It stays open much later than most Macau restaurants, so it is a good "fall-back" place if you are running late. **Henri's** (Tel: 556-251), also called Henri's Galley, at 4 Avenida da Republica is famous for its African chicken and its spicy prawns. It opens for lunch and dinner and serves some good Portuguese wines and brandies.

Similar comments can be made about **Solmar** (Tel: 574-391) at 11 Rua da Praia Grande. It claims to be "the most popular restaurant in town." The cozy **Restaurante Jardin Do Mar** (Tel: 303-008), at Rua Nova A Guia No 9, near the Royal Hotel, has timber beams, tasty food, and folk singing nightly from 8 P.M. I had an excellent, reasonably priced meal in the small **Estrela Do Mar** (Tel: 322-074) at Travessa do Paiva No. 11 off the Rua da Praia Grande, near Government House. The **Tai Pan Restaurant** (Tel: 526-979), at 12C Avenida Ouvidor Arriaga near the center of the peninsula, is famous for its fiery devil crab but there is much more to be savored from an extensive menu. It is said that the fresh squid in a sauce of olive oil, vinegar, and parsley is the best in town. I can recommend the seafood rice. Finally there is **Fat Siu Lau** (Tel: 573-585), at 64 Rua da Felicidade, back over towards the floating casino. The area has a well-patronized nightlife, and the restaurant is open until around 1:30 A.M.

Taipa Island is a good location for restaurants. The Hyatt Regency Hotel has two restaurants that qualify as outstanding. The first is **Alfonso's** (Tel: 821-234), which features superb Portuguese food, great seafood, and tasty Portuguese breads. There is a Sunday buffet that is very popular. Also at the Hyatt is the **Flamingo,** in a pavilion overlooking a delightful pond. The atmosphere is marvelous and the food excellent.

Within Taipa village, there are at least three restaurants worth trying for Macanese food. The **Panda** (Tel: 827-338), at 4 Rua Direita Carlos Eugenio, advertises heavily and is probably the best known. Its Portuguese chicken, curry crab, and spicy prawns are all excellent. Close-by is the well known **Pinocchio** (Tel: 827-128), at 4 Rua de Sol, where spicy fish and fowl are served in what once was a delightful, shady courtyard. **Galo** (Tel: 827-318), at 47 Rua do Cunha in the same part of the village, may have the best food of the three and the atmosphere is cozy and pleasant.

You should also check out the **Restaurant and Pub Bee Vee** (Tel: 812-288), located in the old control tower at the Taipa end of the original Macau–Taipa bridge. The restaurant is owned by an old manager of the Bela Vista Hotel and some of the atmosphere of the hotel can be felt here. The pub, with a clasic bar of gleaming brass and burnished teak, is on the ground floor. Outside is a courtyard that becomes a sidewalk cafe in summer. The casually elegant restaurant, with its menu containing all of the old Bela Vista favorites, is on the upper floor.

Within the hotels there are some excellent restaurants. I like the **Grille Fortaleza** (Tel: 378-111) at the Pousada da Sao Tiago on the Avenida de

Republica for a really big night out in a grand atmosphere. **The Amigo** (Tel: 339-955) at the Pousada Ritz at 2 Rua de Boa Vista is another special, intimate place for a special evening. Neither of these places is cheap. **A Galera** (Tel: 577-666) at the Hotel Lisboa is a nice grill room with live music and reasonably high prices. The **Vasco da Gama** (Tel: 552-222) at the Royal Hotel has some unusual Portuguese dishes and a pleasant, relaxed atmosphere.

When it comes to Chinese food, again there are some good choices. You can eat very cheaply at the street stalls, with a little more style at some of the outdoor restaurants, then in a variety of places—at some of the Orient's finest eateries. There are two good food street markets, called *dai pai dong*, one by the sports field at the side of the Hotel Lisboa on Rua da Escola Commercial, and the other up near the China border close to the Lotus Temple. You can eat at these places at almost any time by pointing to the steaming pans of noodles and whatever you fancy of the green vegetables and nuggets of meat. Sit on a tiny stool at a rickety table and take your chopsticks from the communal box. The experience and the food are just great. The area near the floating casino is good for outdoor restaurants.

Upmarket from these, are places such as **Long Kei** (Tel: 573-970), at 7 Largo do Senado, which has little atmosphere but great food. The **Tong Kong** (Tel: 937-575) at 32 Rua da Caldiera specializes in seafood and Hakka cuisine at reasonable prices. The **Jade Garden** (Tel: 710-203) at 35 Rua Dr Pedro Lobo is part of the Hong Kong chain that specializes in Cantonese food and dim sum. Quite a deal of choice is offered at the **Jai Alai Casino Regent Food Center** (Tel: 725-222) at Palacio de Pelota Basca. The midnight dim sum has a big reputation if you enjoy eating at this time of the day.

A further step up is the **Fook Lam Moon** (Tel: 786-622) at 259 Avenida Dr. Mario Soares. This is a branch of one of Hong Kong's top Cantonese restaurants and this outlet upholds the reputation. It is very good and quite pricy. The **Regal Riverside Seafood Restaurant** (Tel: 517-171) at 124 Rua de Luis G Gomes is another place with a big reputation. You will find the **456 Shanghai Restaurant** (Tel: 388-404), at the Lisboa Hotel; and the Dynasty (Tel: 567-888), at the Mandarin Oriental Hotel, in the same category. None of these is likely to disappoint.

Other restaurants with different cuisines include the **Leong Un** (Tel: 827-387), at 46 Rua de Cunha, Taipa Island; and the **Pizzeria Toscana** (Tel: 372-855), at 28 Rua da Formosa, near Rua do Campo, both for good filling Italian food; and the **Thai** (Tel: 573288), at 27A Rua Abreu Nunes, or the **Rung Nok Thai** at 21A Rua do Brandoa, for some of the hottest Thai food around. Korean food is available at the **Korean Restaurant** (Tel: 569-039) at the Hotel Presidente, and authentic Japanese food is available at the **Ginza** (Tel: 552-222) in the Royal Hotel. The **Tee Jei Kitchen** (Tel: 827-103) is a good Indian tandoori restaurant at Estrada Nova on Taipa Island.

For those who cannot live without them, there are pizzas at **Pizza Hut** within the Hotel Lisboa, Big Macs at **McDonald's** at 17 Rua do Campo opposite Portugues Restaurant and at three other locations in town, and great breakfasts and "goodies" at **Maxim's Cake Shop** just across the road and at several other locations in town.

6. Sight-seeing

Macau is best encountered at an intimate level. It is by wandering around that you come across the almost hidden paradoxes and idiosyncrasies that still make this such an enduring visitor place. Just by glancing at the architecture on the few remaining old buildings, for instance, you can see the cultural compromises of East and West that determine a colonaded, Iberian-style building should be embellished with a pitched Chinese roof and a row of dragons guarding the front steps.

It is possible to see most of peninsula Macau's attractions in a day by walking and taking the bus to the more distant points. I would start my sight-seeing at the ruins of **St. Paul's Church.** This was probably designed by an Italian Jesuit in the early seventeenth century and built with the assistance of Japanese Christian artisans who had fled from feudal persecution in Japan. A cornerstone shows a date of 1602. The magnificent building overlooked the old walls of the city of Macau and it was described as "the greatest monument to Christianity in all the Eastern lands." During a typhoon in 1835, the church caught fire and burned to the ground—leaving only the facade and the staircase that you see today.

The facade is topped by a cross and below this there are three tiers with niches containing bronze statues that were cast in Macau. At the top is a figure of a dove, representing the Holy Spirit. Below is a statue of the Infant Jesus. The center of the third tier is a statue of the Virgin Mary surrounded by angels and flowers. The forth tier contains niches with statues of four Jesuit saints, and below these on the ground level are the three doors to the church. When I last visited, a museum was under construction behind the facade.

Close-by is the **Cidadel of Sao Paulo do Monte.** This was built by the Jesuits about the same time as St. Paul's. It formed the strong central point of the old city wall. Today it is used as an observatory and it provides excellent views of the city and adjacent areas of China. Open hours are 7 A.M. to 6 P.M. daily and there is a tourist information desk there. The fort's moment of glory came in 1622 when the Dutch attempted to invade Macau and a cannon ball fired from the fort is said to have blown up a Dutch ship, thus bringing the battle to an end.

From the church and the fort, you can walk down the cobblestone and

PENINSULA MACAU

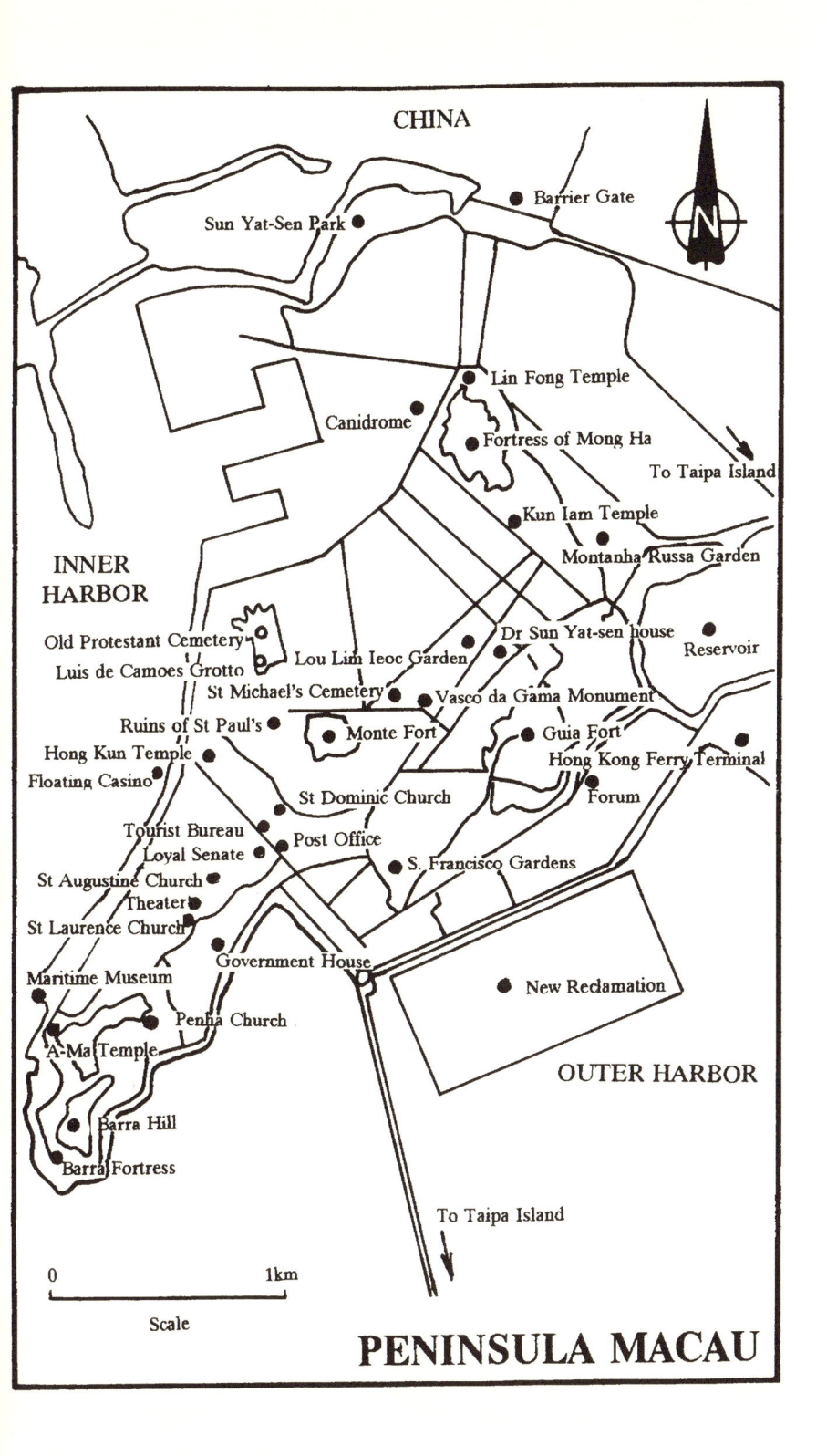

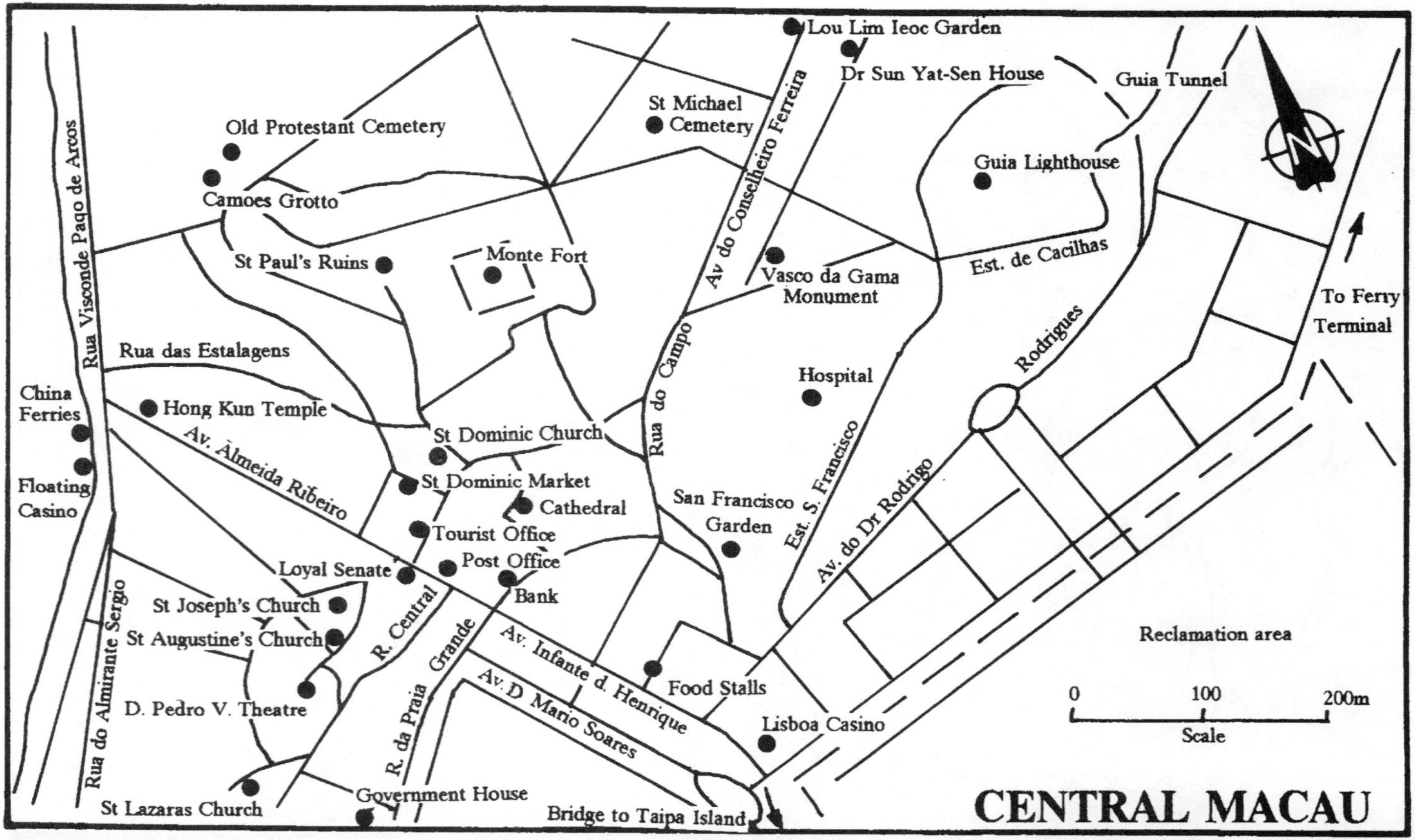
CENTRAL MACAU
Lou Lim Ieoc Garden
Dr Sun Yat-Sen House
Guia Tunnel
St Michael Cemetery
Old Protestant Cemetery
Guia Lighthouse
Camoes Grotto
Av do Conselheiro Ferreira
Est. de Cacilhas
St Paul's Ruins
Monte Fort
Vasco da Gama Monument
To Ferry Terminal
Rodrigues
Rua Visconde Paqo de Arcos
Rua das Estalagens
Hospital
China Ferries
Hong Kun Temple
St Dominic Church
Rua do Campo
Est. S. Francisco
Av. Almeida Ribeiro
St Dominic Market
Av. do Dr Rodrigo
Floating Casino
Cathedral
San Francisco Garden
Tourist Office
Post Office
Loyal Senate
Bank
St Joseph's Church
R. Central
St Augustine's Church
Av. Infante d. Henrique
Reclamation area
R. da Praia Grande
Rua do Almirante Sergio
Food Stalls
D. Pedro V. Theatre
Av. D Mario Soares
Lisboa Casino
0
100
200m
Scale
Government House
St Lazaras Church
Bridge to Taipa Island

tiled streets to the Avenida Almeida Ribeiro. On the way you pass busy shops; the seventeenth-century **St. Domingos Church,** considered to be the most attractive of the Baroque churches; the St. Domingos market; Food City; the Tourist Office painted in traditional mustard yellow; the grey Central Post Office; and the lovely fountain. Straight ahead, is the **Leal Senado** (Loyal Senate), which was built in 1784 and is the best example of traditional Portuguese architecture in Macau. This building has a long history of involvement in political events, first by representatives of the Chinese Ming dynasty and Portuguese officials for trade talks, then as a venue for the local Portuguese community to debate home politics. Today, it is the home of the Municipal Council. Inside, the lower walls are decorated with attractive blue-and-white Portuguese tiles, while there are several historic stone carvings in an interior courtyard. There is an archive, open 1 P.M.-7 P.M. daily, on the second floor with documents dating back to 1820.

If you now walk west, you will pass through the old city center with its jewelers, goldsmiths, and watch shops. Many of the buildings here were built in the first two decades of this century and they are worth special attention. The Hotel Central was one of the smart places to be in the 1920s and 1930s. Venture into the side streets and you seem to go back in time. You will find many small restaurants here and stalls selling cured beef, pork strips, sesame and almond cakes, and other Chinese delicacies. It is a great place to wander around and find your own special memories. If you go far enough, you will eventually reach the Inner Harbour and the **Floating Casino.** The casino is often very crowded but it is worth a quick look. This area is good for evening sidewalk dining.

You can now walk, or take the bus (No. 11 or 21A), to the **Temple of A-Ma.** This was built about five centuries ago and is considered to be the oldest in Macau. It is said that when the Portuguese first landed on the peninsula and asked the name of the place, they were told it was A-Ma-Gao meaning Bay of A-Ma. The Portuguese shortened this to Ma-Gao and so the present name was derived. According to legend, A-Ma was a poor but beautiful young woman who could calm the seas and protect the fishermen. The temple is built on the spot where she supposedly landed in Macau before walking to the top of nearby Barra Hill and ascending into heaven. The temple today is actually a series of shrines, some dedicated to A-Ma and others to Kun Iam, the goddess of mercy and queen of heaven.

Across the street from the temple is the excellent **Maritime Museum** that focuses on Portuguese and Chinese maritime links. It also exhibits the East Asian seafaring traditions, historic accounts of various explorers, models, pictures, and a small aquarium. It is open 10 A.M-5:30 P.M. daily except Tuesday, with admission of M$5, except Sunday when it is free.

Continue south along Rua da Barra to the **Barra Fortress,** which was built in the seventeenth century and had a great strategic importance in defending the city from sea attack. Today it houses the Pousada de Sao Tiago Hotel and is well worth a visit. Close-by is the **Gate of Understanding,** a 40-meter-tall monument opened in 1993 to honor Sino-Portuguese relations.

Follow the Avenida da Republica around the tip of the peninsula until you come to the pink **Governor's Residence,** built in the nineteenth century. Now climb the hill through the swish residential area to **Penha Church** and the Bishop's Residence. The church was originally founded in 1622 by the crew and passengers of a Portuguese ship that had narrowly escaped capture by Dutch raiders. It was completely rebuilt in 1837. The chapel is open daily from 9 A.M. until 4 P.M. and the site affords good views over the city and harbor, and the nearby towns in China. As you come down the hill, detour slightly to visit the beautiful Hotel Bela Vista, then continue along Rua da Praia Grande to the nineteenth-century, pink **Government House.** This area once fronted the ocean and was extremely attractive. Unfortunately reclamation activities have destroyed the area and the artificial lakes, which have now been built to restore water to the area after strong public protests, are only a faint reminder of the real thing.

Up the hill from Government House is **St. Laurence Church** with its twin square towers. The present church dates from the midnineteenth century but was built on the site of a much older chapel. As you walk along Rua

The Government House—typical Portuguese architecture.

Central, the church and seminary of **St. Joseph** is on your left. You can visit the nineteenth-century church by walking through the seminary and across the courtyard. One of the things of interest to some is the arm bone of St. Francis Xavier, which is enshrined in a silver reliquary. The bone was originally shipped to Japan because of Xavier's association with that country, but when it was refused entry it was brought to Macau and was in St. Paul's until after the fire.

St. Augustine Church is slightly farther on. It has foundations dating from the late sixteenth century but the main church is from the early nineteenth century. By continuing along Rua Central or Calcada Tronco Velho, you will be back at the Leal Senado.

GO NORTH

The northern part of the peninsula also has many points of interest but they are not conducive to an easy circular walk. I suggest you could try the following and use two buses to help ease the distance. Start at the back of the Hotel Lisboa and look at the Portuguese-style **Military Club** built in 1872. Behind this is a military museum that is open daily from 2 P.M. to 5 P.M. Now head up Estrada de S. Francisco for a good view over the newer parts of the city. Continue past the Guia Hotel to the top of **Guia Hill**. This is a tranquil place where you can relax amid large trees, fine lawns, and pleasant gardens. A fort was built on this the highest point in Macau in 1637 and today it contains a chapel, a lighthouse, and a tourist information desk and coffee bar. The lighthouse was built in 1865 and is the oldest on the China coast. It is opens to visitors from 9 A.M. to 5:30 P.M. and is well worth a visit.

As you walk down the hill again, turn right at the Guia Hotel and go down past the Royal Hotel. This will take you to a small park and the **Vasco da Gama Monument**. Vasco da Gama was the first European to sail around the Cape of Good Hope and reach India and Asia. The monument recognizes this achievement. Not far from here, you can visit **St. Michael Cemetery** to see the beautiful tombs that are works of art.

Four blocks north of here on Avenida do Conselheiro Ferreira de Almeida, is the delightful **Lou Lim Ieok Gardens**. This is the most Chinese of Macau's gardens and it was built by a wealthy Chinese merchant in the nineteenth century. The garden is modeled in the Suzhou-style and it consists of large ponds, groves of bamboo, traditional Chinese-style rocks, grottoes, twisting pathways, flowering bushes, and towering trees. There is a nine-turn zigzag bridge, which is supposed to be able to stop evil spirits, leading to a large pavilion built in the pseudo-Victorian style of the Ching Dynasty. There is also a flamboyant Western-style house. The gardens are open daily from 6 A.M. to 10 P.M. and there is a small admission charge.

The **Memorial House of Dr. Sun Yat-sen** is only one block away. The house was built in 1918 to house relics of the founder of the modern Chinese Republic. Dr. Sun Yat-sen was born in a nearby Chinese town and he practiced medicine in Macau for some years. When he left, his first wife and family stayed behind and continued to live in Macau. Sun and his associates were responsible for the overthrow of the last Chinese dynasty in 1911. The house is open daily, except Tuesdays, from 10 A.M. to 1 P.M. and also on weekends between 3 P.M. and 5 P.M.

It is a short, pleasant walk from here to the **Kun Iam Temple** on Avenida do Coronel Mesquita. This was built some 360 years ago and it is the largest, and probably the richest, temple in Macau. There is a huge entrance gate and you will notice the roofs are clustered with porcelain figures. The main temple consists of three altars on ascending levels. The first is dedicated to Buddha and three large bold lacquer images. The second is dedicated to the enlightened Buddha, and the third is dedicated to the goddess of mercy and gold lacquer figures of the eighteen wisemen of China. One of them is believed to be Marco Polo.

In the garden beside the temple, there is a round stone table on which the first Sino-American Treaty was signed in 1844 by the United States minister, Caleb Cushing, and the Viceroy of Canton, Ki Ying. Nearby is the marble statue of a monk in an ornate pavilion. Farther into the garden there is the remains of the "lover's tree." According to legend, two lovers who had been forbidden to marry committed suicide in a love pact. From their burial place, two trees eventually emerged and over the years they intertwined into one. The temple is open from 7 A.M. to 6 P.M. daily. The **Garden of Montanha Russa** occupies a heavily wooded hill close-by. This is one of the quietest retreats in Macau. There is a small restaurant serving Portuguese dishes.

Now walk northwest along Coronel Mesquita, turn right at Avenida do Almirante Lacerda and go past the Canidrome (dog racing track) to the **Lotus Temple (Lin Fung Miu).** This is an ancient place that probably existed before the arrival of the Portuguese. It is not spectacular but it is interesting to see the shrines dedicated to Kun Iam, to A-Ma, and to Kuanti, the god of war. The facade is famous for its intricate clay bas-relief, carved in the nineteenth century and depicting stories from history and mythology. The ceilings of the temple are particularly fine with black beams and exposed white tiles. Stone lions guard the entrance.

Walk along Avenida Artur Tamagnini Barbosa from here to the next point of interest—the **Border Gate with China.** Nowadays the border between Macau and China is a busy check point for two-way traffic of tourists, business people, and traders and shoppers; however, it used to be part of the inpenetrable Bamboo Curtain between Macau and the rest of the world. In those days it was forbidden to take photographs at the century-old stone gateway that marked the Macau side of the border. Now, however, visitors who do not cross into the bustling town of Gongbei can photograph it from the vantage point of Sun Yat-sen Park. There are landscaped gardens including a fung shui forest of trees that are believed to bring good luck, ponds, and a children's playground. Photographers are everywhere. Near the old gate itself, there is a small park with a pond and some beautiful murals.

Even enthusiastic walkers are encouraged to take a No. 16 bus along Rua da Ribeira do Patane to the next point of interest. You need to get out at Rua do Tarrafeiro. From here it is a short walk to the **Camoes Garden and Grotto.** Legend has it that Luis de Camoes, Portugal's greatest poet, spent part of his exile in Macau when it was first settled in 1557, although the evidence of this is very sketchy. A heroic bust of the poet stands in a natural rocky alcove in the wooded gardens. The bust faces a wall of stone panels inscribed with poetry by and about Camoes. The gardens are a pleasant, popular place with the local Chinese and you will usually see old people and families talking, playing games, and enjoying the shade. There are good views from the hilltop. Take a look at the 1770s house that has been beautifully restored by the Orient Foundation. On the main floor there is a museum of Chinese antiquities and Colonial relics, while the lower floor is devoted to an art gallery and a small auditorium. During the late eighteenth and early nineteenth centuries, this was the rented home of the British East India Company, where merchant princes held court and ambassadors stayed en route to Beijing in their quest to interest the emperors in trade.

The adjacent, beautifully maintained **Protestant Cemetery** is worth a brief look. This is the resting place of numerous non-Portuguese who lived in or visited Macau over the centuries. Under Roman Catholic law it was forbidden for Protestants to be buried on Catholic ground and this meant all of Macau within the old city walls. Outside the walls was nominally China, but the Chinese did not want their land desecrated by foreigners, so the Protestants were left with a major problem. It was finally solved when the British East India Company provided land for this cemetery. There are several well-known names represented, including Churchill; Morrison, who was the first Protestant missionary to China; and Chinnery, who is noted for his brilliant portraits of Macau and its people from the early nineteenth century. Others include opium traders, sailors, teachers, adventurers, and wives and children who succumbed to the rigors of the East. The nearby **St. Anthony Church** is a fairly recent building on the site of three previous churches, all of which have burned down. A short walk brings you back to the ruins of St. Paul's.

TAIPA ISLAND

Taipa has an entirely different character from the heavily developed peninsula. Despite massive recent development at the airport site and at

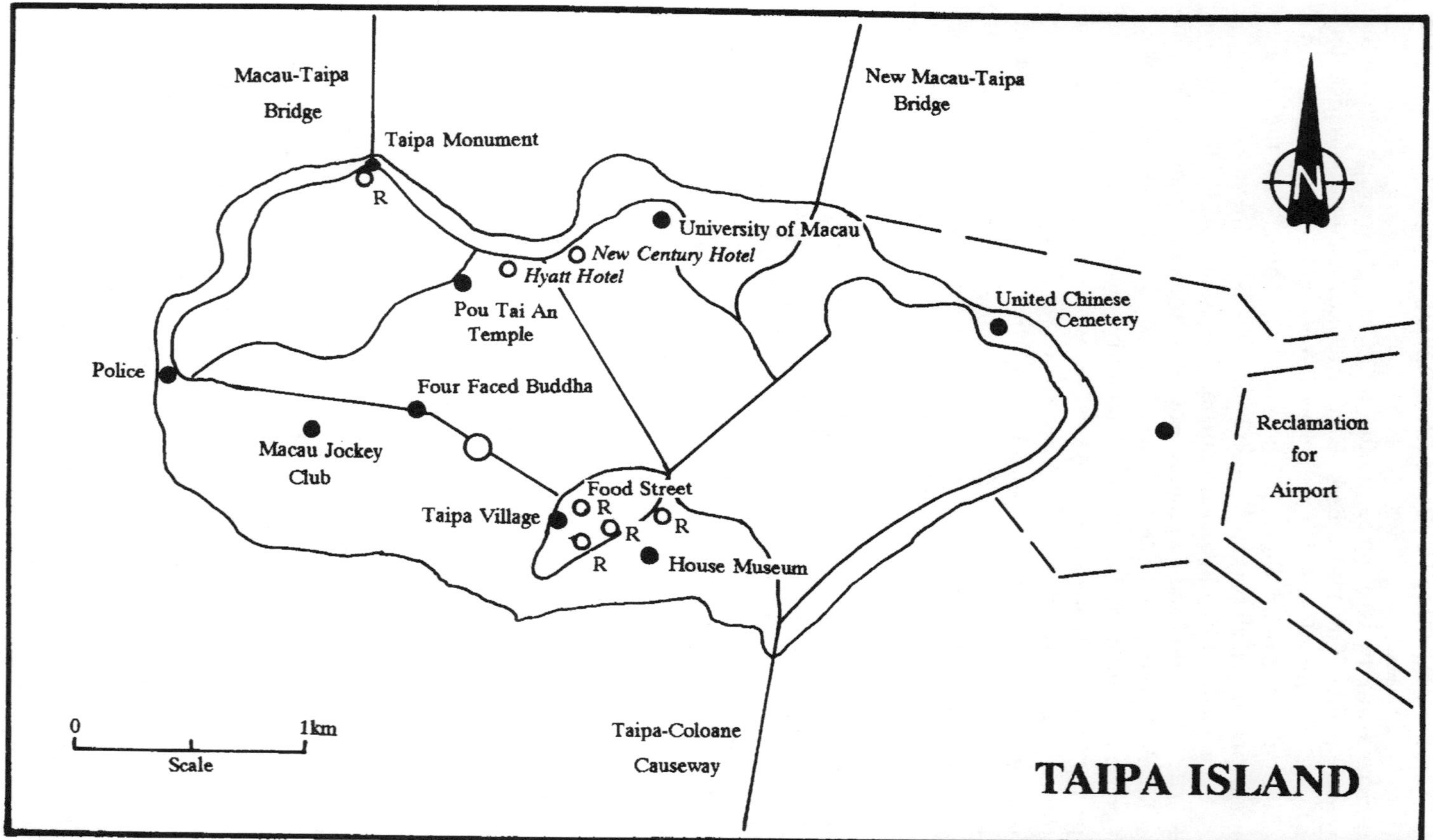

Macau-Taipa Bridge
Taipa Monument
R
New Macau-Taipa Bridge
N
University of Macau
New Century Hotel
Hyatt Hotel
Pou Tai An Temple
United Chinese Cemetery
Police
Four Faced Buddha
Macau Jockey Club
Reclamation for Airport
Food Street
Taipa Village
R
R
R
R
House Museum
0
1km
Scale
Taipa-Coloane Causeway
TAIPA ISLAND

Taipa City, there are still some areas that have a rural feel. Fortunately, Taipa Village has been able to retain much of its attraction, so it is a good place to wander around both during the day and at night.

Some hundreds of years ago, Taipa was actually two islands, but siltation over the years has caused them to join. The same siltation, with a little help from man, is slowly connecting Taipa to Coloane, the other island of Macau. It was only two decades ago that Taipa's main claim to fame was its fireworks factories. These have now closed down, although you can still walk through the remains of one of them in the village. Taipa now has two five-star hotels, the most expensive residential apartments in Macau, a huge residential development, many restaurants, some nightclubs, a horse-racing track, and even casinos. Taipa is now joined to the mainland by two bridges. The first was opened in 1974 and the second in 1994.

The two major hotels are near the end of the old bridge on the major bus route from the city. Close-by is the **University of Macau** on a hill overlooking the sea. The buildings are not particularly attractive but it is worth looking around. There are undergraduate and postgraduate courses in the arts, sciences, and business plus special Chinese and Portuguese studies. One of the most popular adult courses recently has been Modern Chinese Legal Procedure, which is taught by experts from Beijing.

Below the university, you will find the **United Chinese Cemetery.** This is built on a very attractive site and you should stop for a short visit. The Chinese believe that everyone must endure purgatory before entering paradise, so they do all they can to ease the souls of their ancestors. One way is to select a site using the principles of *fung shui,* the geometric system that is used to determine the right position for a temple, a house, and even office furniture. The ideal cemetery location is to back onto a hill, which is the home of guardian dragons, and face the open sea or a valley, preferably away from the north, where evil spirits live. The site for this cemetery is ideal and it is shared by Buddhists, Taoists, and Confucians. There are some very interesting statues of gods of the other world, and some nice pavilions. You will often see people praying and picnicking at family graves.

If you would like to see how a Macanese family lived in the early part of this century, go to Taipa's old praia waterfront. Unfortunately, the water has long retreated but one of the houses has been restored with European period furniture and ornaments, together with Chinese carpets and furnishings carefully copied from pictures of the time. The museum has captured the atmosphere of a leisurely, genteel era and a unique bicultural community. It is open daily except Mondays from 9:30 A.M. to 1 P.M. and from 3 P.M to 5:30 P.M. The nearby century-old Our Lady of Carmel Church probably has little interest to most visitors but the nicely maintained **Carmel Garden,** with its vine-covered gazebo, fountains, and stone benches, is very attractive. The main part of Taipa Village is a good place to wander around. There are several old temples, no-longer used firecracker factories, Chinese shophouses, colonial Portuguese offices, and great restaurants.

Adjacent to the village is the Macau Jockey Club where horse racing is held regularly, the new residential development of Taipa City, and a Thai-style Four-Faced-Buddha statue. The **Pou Tai Un Temple,** which provides vegetarian meals to visitors from its homegrown gardens, is back behind the Hyatt Hotel. This temple is still growing and new buildings with yellow-tiled roofs, vividly painted carved wooden eaves, and ornate balconies stand overlooking older prayer halls. The small **Pak Tai Temple** with its interesting carvings and statues is in Taipa Village. Bicycles can be rented in the village for those who enjoy this method of sight-seeing.

COLOANE ISLAND

Coloane is a larger, less-developed island. The island has some good beaches and these are very popular on summer weekends. There are a couple of good walking trails for hikers. The island also has an interesting Chinese temple, a junk-building yard near Coloane Village, the yellow-and-white Portuguese chapel of St. Francis Xavier, and the beautifully tiled roofed Tam Kong Temple, whose unusual attraction is a whalebone carved into a model of a ship complete with a wooden dragon head and crew. There are also some nice embroided banners.

Coloane Park on the west side of the island is worth a visit. The twenty hectare site features extensive gardens, ponds, and a large walk-in aviary. The aviary has a high net roof over a patch of natural woodland and more than 200 species of birds live here. You will see rare Palawan peacocks, white-crowned pheasants, and many more. Outside, Australian black swans make their home on a man-made lake, which is surrounded by botanical gardens containing tropical flowers, Chinese plants, and fragrant herbs. Picnic and camping areas are available, barbecue facilities are provided, and there is a good Western restaurant. The gardens are open from 9 A.M. until dusk. You can reach here on a No. 21A bus at a fare of M$4.00 from peninsula Macau.

Coloane Village has some interest. This originated as a fishing village but now tourism is probably more important. It is just a stone's throw from here to China and there is some trade and two-way crossing for shopping and business. You will see a small police-and-customs post at the wharf that attempts to control this to some extent. North of the pier are the remains of several junk builders' yards and also a few that are still operating. The classic Chinese junk, with its batwing sails seems to belong to another age. Nowadays the fishermen use motors instead of sails and the basic shape of the boats is changing as fewer fishing families live on their junks. There

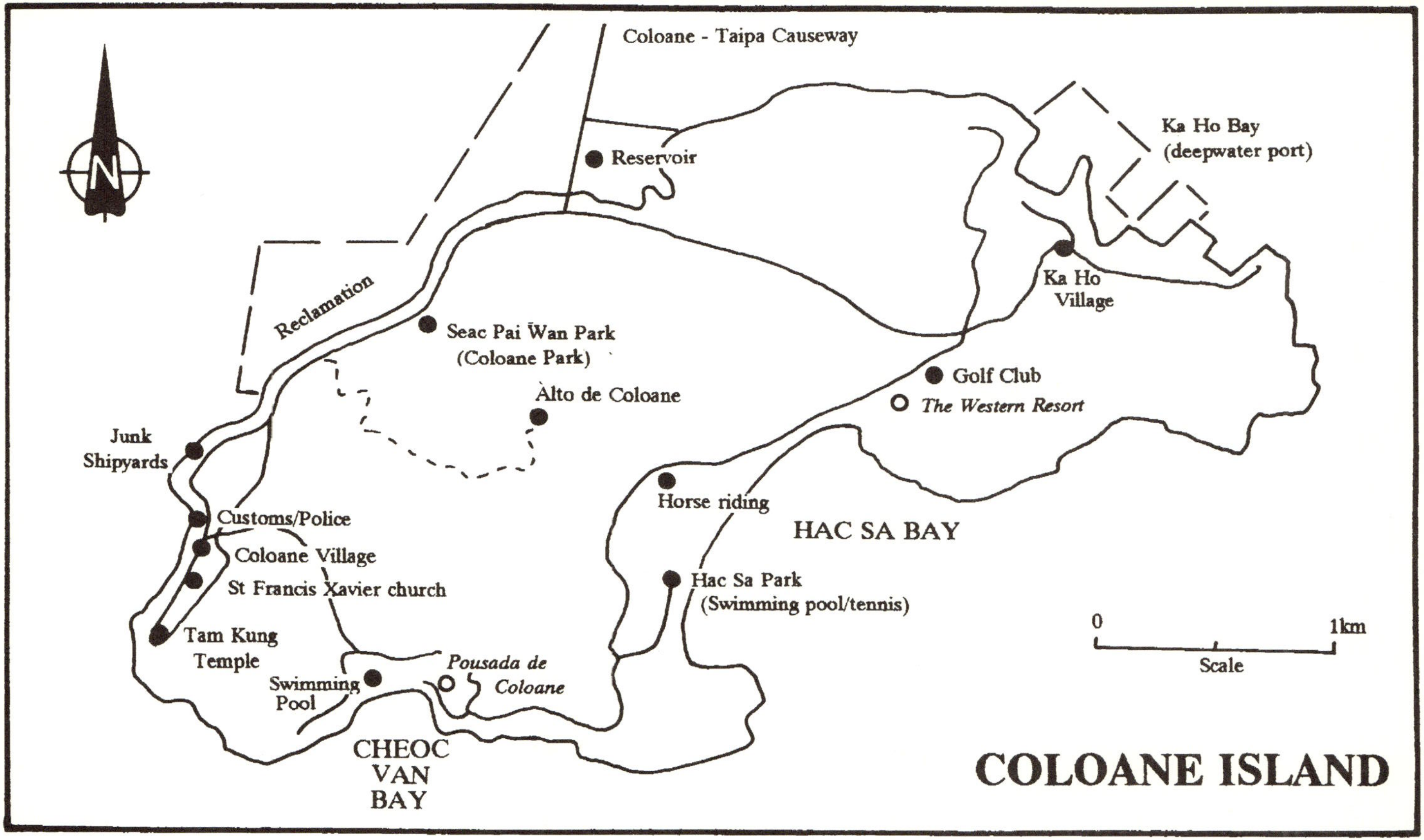

COLOANE ISLAND

are still a few yards here where junks are constructed just as they were a century or more ago, by craftsmen who learned from their fathers. The boats are built without formal plans and the sturdy planks are still shaped over an open fire. You are welcome to enter the yards where you see some activity.

Elsewhere in the village you can visit the **Chapel of St. Francis Xavier,** which was built about 70 years ago to honor the saint who died on nearby Shang Ch'an Island, after being on a mission to Japan. It follows a classic Portuguese style with a cream-and-white facade and bell tower. Many Japanese come here to pay their respects to the saint and to the many Japanese Christians who were martyred in Nagasaki in 1597. There are three small Chinese temples and several restaurants.

No one goes to Macau because of its beaches, but it is nice to know that they are there if you have the need for some sun, sand, and sea. The two main beaches are **Cheoc Van** and **Hac Sa** on the southern and eastern sides of the island. The water at both beaches is often an ochre color rather than a nice blue, due to the silt from the Pearl River, but in fact the water is safe for swimming. Canoeing and windsurfing equipment is available for rent. Each of the beaches has a park associated with it. Cheoc Van Park has a large irregular swimming pool, a restaurant and bar, and changing rooms. It is open from 8 A.M. until 9 P.M. on weekdays and until midnight on weekends. The Hac Sa Sports and Recreation complex has an olympic-size swimming pool, a children's pool, a rink for roller skating and roller hockey, a space for flying model airplanes, a multipurpose sports field, a minigolf course, a children's playground, and places for picnics and barbecues. It is open 8 A.M. to 9 P.M. on weekdays and until midnight on weekends. Use of the pool costs M$10 for adults.

7. Guided Tours

If you are just paying a one-day visit to Macau, a guided tour is essential if you are to make the most of the day. Even if you are staying longer, a half-day tour is a great orientation for later exploring.

There are two basic tours available in Macau. The first is a three-hour **City Tour** that usually includes the Barrier Gate, the Kun Iam Temple, the Ruins of St. Paul's, Guia Lighthouse, the Leal Senado, the Lou Lim Ieoc Garden, Penha Church, A-Ma Temple, and the Maritime Museum. Other points of interest such as Monte Fort, Sun Yat-sen House, and the Camoes Garden are included depending on the time of the year and the traffic and weather conditions. The cost of this tour in an air-conditioned coach is around M$130. By limousine it is around M$150 per hour.

The second is a two-hour **Islands Tour** that includes Taipa Village, a view of the new airport, a stop at the Chinese Cemetery, the Four-Faced-Buddha Shrine, the Macau Jockey Club, Coloane Village, a junk builder, and the two main beaches on Coloane. This costs around M$90.

An alternative is to tour in a colorful replica of a 1920s English bus, called a **Tour Machine**. These are equipped with air conditioning and leather upholstery, and they seat up to nine passengers. They operate on fixed routes with stops at visitor attractions on the way. They can also be rented by the hour with a driver to explore Macau or China. For reservations call Avis at the Mandarin Oriental (Tel: 336-789) or International Tourism (Tel: 975-183 in Macau or 2541-2011 in Hong Kong).

The border between Macau and China has been open to foreign tourists for fifteen years and there are large numbers of foreigners visiting China on one-day trips. Macau agents and the China Travel Service in Macau operate air-conditioned coaches and handle visa applications. There are two standard tours, both including a visit to Cuiheng, the birthplace of Dr. Sun Yat-sen. The **Zhongshan Tour** also takes in the Zhongshan Hot Springs Resort; lunch at Shiqi, the county capital; and a visit to a local village. The **Zhuhai Tour** includes a visit to Shijingshan Tourist Center, lunch, and a visit to the fishing village of Xiangzhou. Other longer tours are available from some tour operators in Macau.

You can see Macau from an entirely different perspective by renting an ultralight aircraft and pilot. You will feel like one of those magnificent men in their flying machines. Photographers will get some great shots (for bookings, Tel: 782-216).

I have only had limited experience with Macau tour operators but I must say that those I have dealt with recently have been good. I make a special commendation for Eric Chang of International Tourism, who faithfully corresponded by fax, and on one occasion telephoned me, while I was dealing with him long distance; he made arrangements that would bring no monetary rewards to the company. This company would certainly be a good place to start. It has its own cars and air-conditioned coaches, and guides that speak English, Cantonese, and Mandarin. (Contact International Tourism at 9B Travessa do Padre Narciso, Macau; Fax: 853-974-072.)

8. Culture

You can start your cultural experience early in the morning by taking a stroll to Monte Fort, Guia Hill, or one of Macau's gardens. Here you will see men "walking" their small songbirds in delicate bamboo cages. After they both have enjoyed the morning air, the men take their birds to a teahouse to show off their bird's singing ability to fellow enthusiasts. You will sometimes see a man hang his bird's cage on a tree branch while he joins others in *t'ai chi ch'uan* exercises that are said to tone up both body and mind for the day ahead.

Later in the day, if you happen to be in Leal Senado Square with a Chinese companion, you can seek future guidance from a sidewalk fortuneteller. They will offer to read your palm, face, or head to advise you what is in store for you later in your life. Unfortunately, none seem to speak English.

Macau has lost much of its old Colonial architecture over the past twenty years, but a few prize examples remain. The Leal Senado, the General Post Office, the wonderful Dom Pedro V Theatre, the Governor's House, and Government House are all good examples of buildings with a glorious past and, hopefully, an assured future. There are also a series of old mansions along Avenida do Conselheiro Ferreira de Almeida that have been saved from the wrecker's clutches and renovated for use as a library, national archives, and offices for the education department. These buildings date from the early 1920s and feature arcades of elegant arches, flat roofs with carved pediments, high shuttered windows, and interior patios.

If you happen to be in Macau when there is a performance at the gemlike **Dom Pedro Theater,** I urge you to attend. The theater was built in 1859 and it was once the stage for international opera companies and famous soloists from around the world. Then it fell into disuse and at one time it was extensively renovated without too much care for the past. Today the small auditorium, with stalls and balcony, has been faithfully restored to host local and international performers. It is a masterpiece.

I have mentioned before about the availability of cheap Portuguese wine in Macau, but for the adventurous drinker, Chinese wines can be a new experience. They are made from rice, sorghum, fruit, and assorted other ingredients and they vary considerably in quality, price, and effect. You can find wine shops with their ancient fermenting vats in many parts of the city. Look out, too, for the shops selling wine with whole snakes in the bottles. Remember, the Cantonese say "Yum sing" as they down their drinks.

The lion dance is a Chinese way of celebrating. You will usually see a lion dance performed during a traditional Chinese festival, but it also occurs at other occasions such as the opening of a new building or a new business. If you happen to be in Macau on a Sunday, the Tourist Office organizes a half-hour dance at Barra Square from 10:30 to 11 A.M. If you like this kind of thing, Chinese dances are performed by students in front of the St. Paul's facade from 11 to 11:30 A.M. on Sundays.

There are many museums in Macau that provide you with opportunities to see some of the local culture. In the sight-seeing section of this chapter, mention was made of several of these including the Leal Senado, the Maritime Museum, the Dr. Sun Yat-sen House, and the Taipa House Museum. In addition to these, you can visit the Post Office Museum, housed in the

General Post Office in the center of the city, and the Historic Archives in one of the old mansions in Avenida do Conselheiro Ferreira de Almeida.

The **Post Office Museum** contains displays of stamps, postal equipment, the studio of Macau's first radio station, a 1930s automatic telephone exchange, and photographs of such events as the territory's first airmail delivery by Pan Am flying boat in 1937. The museum is open weekdays from 3 to 5 P.M. The **Historic Archives** contains letters, books, and manuscripts pertaining to Portugal's exploration and Macau's relations with Europe, China, Japan, and southeast Asia from a wide variety of government, civic, ecclesiastic, and private sources. There are items dating from 1587. There is a small military museum in the Sao Francisco Barracks that is open 2 to 5 P.M. daily.

The **Grand Prix Museum** is in the CAT building next to the Macau Forum near the ferry terminal. Included are such names as Ayrton Senna, Michael Schumacher, and David Coulthard, all of whom raced in Macau. Models of their cars are on display. There is also a replica of the first winner more than forty years ago, a TR2. The Motor Cycle Grand Prix, which began in 1967, has its own area. There is a 1:1,000 scale relief map of the circuit with lights to indicate points of interest. The Macau Government Tourist Office has been able to find television footage of some of the earliest races and this is shown in the appropriate displays. Films are also shown on a giant video wall.

9. Sports

Macau has reasonable sporting facilities for both players and spectators.

Horse racing is the big sport and the facilities at the Macau Jockey Club on Taipa Island are excellent. There are day races begining at 2 P.M., twilight meetings from 3:30 P.M. and night meetings from 7:30 P.M. A giant matrix screen shows the odds and close-ups of the action. The four-story grandstand has air-conditioned boxes, restaurants, and a small casino, as well as ample betting windows. Entrance for visitors is M$20 and the minimum bet is M$10. There are free bus transfers between the track and the Hotel Lisboa on race days. For further information Tel: 821-188. The racing season is from September to June.

Greyhound racing is also popular. This is held year-round at the Canidrome near the China border. Meetings are held Tuesdays, Thursdays, Saturdays, or Sundays with more than 300 dogs taking part each day. There are two grandstands, a VIP lounge, and a coffee shop. It is the only such facility in Asia and is very popular. Races are broadcast over radio and TV and there are several off-course betting facilities.

Motor racing fever hits Macau each November when the city hosts the annual Grand Prix for Formula Three cars, motorcycles, and production cars. The road circuit rivals Monaco and includes the winding roads on Guia Hill and the straightaway along the Outer Harbor. Many famous names have driven here since the event was first staged in 1953.

There is only one **golf** course in Macau and that is the Macau Golf and Country Club adjacent to the Westin Resort on Coloane Island. The 18-hole course is of championship design and is quite spectacular. It can get very crowded on weekends.

Tennis and **squash** are available at several hotels. The facilities at the Hyatt Regency, the Mandarin Oriental, the Westin, and the New Century are available.

Ice skating and **Ten Pin Bowling** are both available at the Future Bright Amusement Park on Praca de Luis Camoes. Swimming and windsurfing are available at Cheoc Van and Hac Sa beaches. The Macau Forum is a regular venue for roller-skate hockey, table tennis, and athletics.

The **Macau International Marathon** takes place on the first Sunday of December and it is the most important athletic event in the Territory. Further information and entry forms are available from the Macau Sports Institute, Tel: 580-762 or Fax: 853-343-708.

10. Shopping

Macau is a free port and many items are available at duty-free prices and no sales tax. Macau's most popular buys are jewelry, gold, antiques, and porcelain. Most of the **jewelry** shops are concentrated on Avenida do Infante D Henrique and its continuation, Avenida Almeida Ribeiro. Major credit cards are accepted by all these retailers. Most of the gold is 24 carat, which the Chinese buy for investment. You will see the daily gold price displayed in the stores. It is recorded in *tael,* which is equivalent to 1.2 troy ounces or 37.799 grams. This fixes the price for solid gold items. You should haggle a bit for jewelry containing gems. It is important to get a receipt with a full description of all the items you have bought.

When shopping for antiques, it is better to patronize recommended shops rather than street stalls. You will not find any treasures from the souvenir stalls at the Border Gate, St. Paul's Ruins, or Penha Hill. Better to look along Rua das Estalagens or Rua Nossa Senhora do Amparo between Avenida Almeida Ribeiro and St. Paul's. You will not discover a priceless Ming vase or Shang bronze, but there are some interesting items anyway. Most date from the Ching dynasty and include snuffboxes, porcelain, and furniture. Sometimes you will find old coins, simple Ming bowls, and older items that have been smuggled out of China. Of course, some of the items are not genuine, but even these can be good buys because of the excellent craftsmanship.

Knitted-ware and locally made clothes are available at the street stalls and shops near St. Domingos market close to Senate Square. You need to bargain but prices can be very reasonable.

Tobacco and **alcohol** are cheaper in Macau than they are in Hong Kong. Portuguese wines, port, and brandy in particular are excellent buys. The top table wines are very good.

Electric gadgetry and **watches** are also good buys but you are likely to find a better range in Hong Kong. Prices seem to be little different. Make sure that you get an international warranty card.

For a unique souvenir, you can have a personal *"chop"* or seal made from soapstone. Many small shops specialize in these seals, which have been used for centuries in China. The shopkeeper will help you choose the Chinese character to represent your name, which will be carved on the seal. It is sold in a box or purse, with a small ink pad.

The main shopping center for visitors is in the Avenida Almeida Ribeiro, St. Domingos market, Rua Palha, Rua S. Domingos, Rua Pedro Nolasco da Silva, Rua do Campo area.

The following are a few places to get you started:

Antiques—The Antique House, 11 Av. Coronel Mesquita
          Hong Hap, 133 Av. Almeida Ribeiro
Arts & Crafts—Kin Seng Porcelain, 24 Rua Sao Paulo
          Perola do Oriente, 32 Av. do C. Ferr. Almeida
          Va Yun, Rua Estalagens (for Chinese birdcages)
Gold & Jewelry—Chow Sang Sang, 58 Av. Almeida Ribeiro
          Tai Fung, 36 Av. Almeida Ribeiro
Books—Livraria Portuguesa, 18 Rua do S. Domingos
          Portuguese Bookshop, Rua Pedro Nolasco da Silva
Department Stores—Nam Kwong, 1 Av. Almeida Ribeiro
          Yaohan, Av. Amizade (near ferry terminal)
Fashion Clothing—Benetton, 22 Dr Pedro Jose Lobo
          The Mandarin Oriental and Lisboa Hotels
          Toni Benar, 27 Rua da Praia Grande
Pharmacies—Farmacia Popular, Largo do Senado

11. Entertainment and Nightlife

For many people, the casinos of Macau are the only entertainment that they need. There is, however, quite a deal more to Macau than these. Sauna and massage is very big and some of these places offer more. The girls are mainly from Thailand and this helps explain why there are so many Thai restaurants here. Then there are the pubs, the lounges, the discos, and the nightclubs. There is little regular theater or classical music, but you can often see an English-language movie at the Cineteatro on Rua Santa Clara.

Macau has nine casinos, all operated under Government franchise by the Sociedade da Turismo e Diversoes de Macau (STDM). With the exception of the casino at the racetrack, all casinos operate around the clock. Rules are standard in all halls. They offer established Western games and long popular Eastern games of chance. The casinos also have a glittering array of slot machines, called "hungry tigers." There are notices in the casinos at each entrance, reminding players that they should only commit what they can afford to lose. Baccarat is the most popular game in all the casinos with nearly two thirds of the tables devoted to this passion. The next favorite is blackjack, then *dai siu*. Roulette is not popular.

Frankly, I find the Macau casinos unexciting places. They are often very crowded, the dealers are downright rude, no one ever attempts a smile, and the facilities are very basic. Compared to most casinos around the world, they are dismal. It is not even interesting to watch the Chinese gamble. They are obsessive, but they play in a lackluster, emotionless fashion. Despite this, the casinos turn over huge amounts of money and continue to draw people from all over Asia. Most players take the whole thing very seriously and go to great lengths to place their bets, turn over the cards, and sit, all in a lucky way. The minimum bet is HK$20 but at some of tables it is considerably higher. This is not the place for a casual flutter. Visitors under 18 are not allowed, and photography is strictly banned. About half have a dress code.

The **Lisboa Casino** is the largest and busiest in town. There are hundreds of slot machines and dozens of blackjack tables. The big spenders head for the more exclusive baccarat areas, while the less affluent crowd around the tables where the traditional Chinese games of *dai siu* (big and small), *fantan* (the button game), and *pai-kao* (Chinese dominoes) are played. Bets wagered in the VIP Golden Palace range from US$5,000 to US$100,000.

The **Macau Palace** is more commonly known as the "floating casino." It is situated on a converted twin-deck ferry moored to the shore in the Inner Harbor. Any romantic notions you may have of Mississippi-type riverboat glamour will be quickly dispelled. It is crowded, smoky, windowless, and unglamorous. The same can be said for the **Kam Pek Casino,** housed in a renovated building in the main street close to the Inner Harbor. This is more a neighborhood casino than the others.

Then there is the **Jai Alai Casino** housed in what used to be the jai alai stadium. The casino draws big crowds partly because it is near the ferry terminal. If you are going to Macau to gamble, there is no way you want to see anything! The **Casino Victoria** is a small gambling room in the grandstand of the Macau Jockey Club on Taipa Island. It is open on race days from 11 A.M. to 3 P.M.

The remaining casinos are attached to hotels and they are generally more upmarket. The one at the Hyatt Hotel is the longest established and in some ways is the most exclusive. The elegant casino at the Mandarin Oriental is at the top of the hotel's grand staircase. The **Kingsway Hotel Casino** is dazzling with chrome-trimmed furnishings, while the **Holiday Inn Casino** opened the day I left the Territory so it remains an unknown entity.

Macau is surprisingly short on **small pubs** where you can relax with a drink without being hassled. The only ones that I know of are the Talker Bar, opposite the Kum Iam Temple in Av. do Coronel Mesquita, the Snyper Bar, opposite the Royal Hotel, the China Pop Bar at 47A Beco do Sal in the south part of the peninsula, and a recently opened bar opposite Pizzeria Toscana in Rua Formosa. Within the hotels, Oskar's Bar at the Holiday Inn has a computerized dart board, a CD jukebox, and table games; there is a nice, intimate but lively bar at the Hyatt; the Bar de Guia at the Mandarin Oriental captures some of the excitment of the Grand Prix; and the bars at the Bela Vista and the Pousada de Sao Tiago are great places for a cocktail at any hour. Prince Galaxie at the New Century Hotel is a bar with 1950s decoration that has live music most nights.

There are several **nightclubs** that feature soft lights, sweet music, and charming hostesses. Naturally these are male-orientated places but some are happy for you to bring your own partner. I have had no experience at these myself but Macau friends recommend China City (Tel: 726-633) at the Jai Alai Palace, the Ritz Nightclub (Tel: 726-622) at the same location, the Thai Palace Nightclub (Tel: 596-633) at 75 Rua da Praia Grande, and the Golden Time Nightclub (Tel: 596-666) in the same building. These places generally feature live music from Filipino groups. They can be very expensive for the unwary.

The popular **discos** are the Skylight (Tel: 780-923) at the Hotel Presidente, which has a dance show by overseas troupes: the Hotel Mondail Disco; The Moulin Rouge Disco at the New World Emperor Hotel; and the Guia Disco Nightclub at the Hotel Guia. Generally there is a cover charge of between M$60 and M$200 at these places depending on the night. It usually includes one or two drinks. There is a popular karaoke lounge at the Hotel Royal and folk singing at the restaurant Jardin Do Mar.

The **Crazy Paris Show** is described as sexy yet sophisticated, risqué but not raunchy, and it is Macau's longest running show. In the tradition of the classic Parisian revue, a cast of Western girls illustrate the striptease with dance, acrobatics, and imaginative tableaux. The French choreographer creates a new program every few months. Shows are staged at 8 P.M. and 9:30 P.M. nightly at the Mona Lisa Hall at the Lisboa Hotel, and there is an 11 P.M. show on Saturdays. The ticket price is M$150.

There are hotel saunas and massage available to the public at the Hotel Lisboa, the Hotel Sintra, the Presidente Hotel, the Hotel Royal, and the Hotel New World Emperor.

12. The Macau Address List

Bank—Banco National, 2 Av. Almeida Ribeino	Tel: 376-644
Bus Station—Transmac, 2 Est. Harg Ilha Verde	Tel: 271-122
Doctor—Alfredo Ritchie, 24A R. Pedro Nolasco da Silva	Tel: 373-766
Emergency—	Tel: 999
Hospital—St. Januario, Calcada Visc. S. Januanio	Tel: 577-199
Pharmacy—Farmacia Popular, Largo do Senado	Tel: 566-568
Police—Av. Dr. Rodrigo Rodrigues	Tel: 577-199
Post Office—Largo do Senado	Tel: 574-491
Taxi—Vang Iek Radio Taxi Company, Lisng Um Bld 1	Tel: 519-519
Telephone Inquiries—English	Tel: 185
Time—	Tel: 140
Tourist Office—Largo do Senado	Tel: 315-566
Travel Agency—H. Nolasco, Av. Almeida Ribeino	Tel: 572-418

China—The Pearl River Delta

10

The Land, Life, and People of the Pearl River Delta

Both Hong Kong and Macau border the Chinese Province of Guangdong, the home of the Cantonese people. These are the people you find in Chinatowns throughout the world. The capital of Guangdong Province is Guangzhou (Canton), the largest city in southern China and the most accessible major center in China.

Geography

Guangdong Province is part of the Zhongnan Region of China. It occupies only about 2 percent of China's land area but the Pearl River Delta is one of the richest and most important areas in the whole country. The delta supports a huge population in Guangzhou and other centers, and is one of the regions that is crucial for China's so-called Economic Miracle.

Guangzhou is remote from Beijing, the Chinese capital (2,300 km), so it has a reasonable amount of independence and is more outlooking than any other part of the country. The Pearl River provides the basis for a good trade and transport system and this is directed towards Hong Kong and the outside world rather than Beijing and northern China.

The delta region is generally flat and low-lying, but there are some hills and mountain ranges. Because of the huge growth that is occurring in this area and the desire for flat land for development of factories and housing estates, large areas are being filled, leveled, and turned into environmental disasters. Hills are bulldozed, rich agricultural land is being filled, and important waterways and swamp areas are being lost.

Climate

The climate within the Pearl River Delta is similar to Hong Kong and Macau—cool in winter and hot and humid in summer. As you move farther inland, the temperature changes are more pronounced.

Cotton clothing is recommended for summer while sweaters and jackets are needed during the winter. If you are planning to travel farther north in China during winter, be aware that temperatures can plunge below zero at times.

Guangzhou receives around 1,750 mm of rain each year, so the area is usually lush and green. Rainfall is concentrated during the April to September period, with June being the wettest month. At this time, a light raincoat is very useful.

History

There is evidence that primitive man lived in China some 500,000 years ago. The skull of a so-called Peking Man from this period was discovered near Beijing in 1929.

Little is known, however, of human development in this area until the twenty-first century B.C. Around 2205 B.C. was the start of the Shang dynasty and records of daily life and literature have been found from this period. The Shangs were replaced by the Zhou dynasty in 1122 B.C. It was during this period that the casting of iron was discovered and this led China to become one of the most advanced areas in the world at this time. This was also the time that the Taoist and Confucianist philosophies evolved and these have had a major influence on Chinese thinking until the present day.

These dynasties were based in northern China and little is known about this period in the south. It is assumed, however, that settlements in the south were scattered and the population was tribal and predominantly aboriginal.

The area we know today as China was first more or less united under Qin Shihuang in 221 B.C. He ascended the throne at the age of 13 and is called "the first exalted emperor." In this period the first town was established at what is now Guangzhou.

Qin Shihuang made monumental changes to Chinese society. He abolished the fuedal system and established a new order of society that was to last for 2,000 years. He set up a central government and established a system of imperial examinations that dramatically raised the level of education and culture. The written language was standardized, a system of weights and measures was established, and he commenced a form of currency. Communications were improved with roads and canals established between the capital and outlying areas.

At the same time Qin Shihuang was known for his tyranny. He is said to have killed hundreds of scholars because their views were different from his. He also destroyed the records of great teachers such as Confucius and Mencius, and what is read today has been rewritten by scholars from memory. One of the most important discoveries of modern times was made in 1974 when a vault was uncovered containing 6,000 terracotta warriors in full uniform and battle formation protecting Qin Shihuang's nearby tomb.

The Han dynasty (206 B.C. to A.D. 220) was established after the overthrow of Qin Shihuang. During this period the Chinese empire stretched from Afghanistan to Korea and from Mongolia to Vietnam. The Silk Road was established and contacts were made with central and western Asia and even with Rome. Trade flourished and China was opened to other cultures. Buddhism was introduced from India, a new style of writing was introduced, and there were notable advances in science and technology, including the invention of paper.

Guangzhou developed during this period into an outward-looking trading town. Indian traders came here, and there is evidence that it was visited by the Romans. When the Han dynasty collapsed, the Guangzhou region became almost an autonomous country. Progress continued but there was constant strife with adjacent separate kingdoms. In other parts of the country, the nomadic tribes from the north gained some territory and the areas to the east and west were lost.

In A.D. 618, the Tang dynasty reunified China; and central Asia, Korea, and northern Vietnam again came under Chinese control. Developments were made in agriculture, the country's administration was run by the best scholars, Chinese arts and literature flourished, and the art of printing was developed. Guangzhou continued as a trading port with regular visits from Arab traders. It had a sizeable trade with the Middle East and southeast Asia.

Several other dynasties followed the Tangs but none achieved the same heights of glory. Gradually influence was lost over the more outlying parts of the Empire. To counter this, Chinese emigration was encouraged to these areas in the twelfth century and the native tribes were killed, isolated into small areas, or pushed south into areas such as Laos, Thailand, and Hainan Island. Trade and contact with the outside world largely stopped. Guangzhou grew during this period, but it retained an independent focus as it was so far from the center of power in Nanjing. It was not until the rule of the second Ming emperor, Yong Le (1405-1433), that China again took much interest in the wider world. During his rule several enormous maritime expeditions made contact with many parts of Asia and Africa, but it appears that they were not particularly impressed by what they found and discontinued the contacts.

Initial contact with modern European nations began in the early sixteenth century. The Portuguese arrived at the mouth of the Pearl River in 1513 but their attempts to gain a trading base on the China coast met with little success. It was not until 1557 that the Portuguese and some Cantonese officials made an agreement allowing Portugal to rent a small peninsula of land now known as Macau.

Next came the Jesuits and they were allowed to establish themselves at Zhaoqing, a town northwest of Guangzhou, and later in Beijing. The British arrived in the seventeenth century and the government opened Guangzhou to them in 1685. The Europeans came to buy goods such as tea, silk, and porcelain but they had little to sell China in return once the Japanese silver trade was closed off to them. In order to balance the trade, the British hit on the idea of opium. The Chinese Imperial Government (Qing dynasty) tried to ban its sale but corrupt officials and merchants did nothing to stop it.

This lead to the Opium Wars of the nineteenth century, which the Chinese lost. The British and the Chinese initially agreed to the Convention of Chuan Bi, then later to the Treaty of Nanking, but disputes and fighting continued. The Treaty of Tientsin was signed, which allowed the British to establish diplomatic representation in China, but even this was not the end of the fighting. In 1859, a combined French and British force marched on Peking and the Convention of Peking was forced on the Chinese. At the same time a rebel movement had started in Guangdong and this lead to the antidynastic Taiping Revolution, which substantially weakened the authority of the Qing dynasty.

By the late nineteenth century, China was under considerable pressure from several Western countries and Japan as these nations started to occupy land and establish growing influence with sections of the Chinese population. Secret societies were being established to bring down the Qing dynasty and in 1905 several of these merged to form the Alliance for Chinese Revolution under the leadership of Dr. Sun Yat-sen, who was from a village south of Guangzhou.

The Qing dynasty collapsed in 1911 when there was an army coup in central China and many of the southern provinces gave support to the Sun Yat-sen alliance. On January 1, 1912, Sun Yat-sen was proclaimed president of the Chinese Republic. In reality Sun Yat-sen controlled little more than some of the southern provinces. Most of the rest of the country was controlled by local military warlords left over from the Qing dynasty. Dr. Sun Yat-sen was also handicapped by not having a strong political base or an army, so he set out to build his power base.

By 1921, several Marxist groups had banded together to form the Chinese Communist Party and Sun Yat-sen had established a strong base in Guangzhou where he had set up a government made up of surviving members of the Kuomintang, the party that emerged as the major force after the fall of the Qing dynasty. A possible confrontation was emerging between these forces, so Sun Yat-sen established a shaky alliance based on the need to establish an army to defeat the northern warlords. The National Revolutionary Army was under the command of Chiang Kai-shek.

Dr. Sun Yat-sen died in 1925 and Chiang Kai-shek took over. He launched a military campaign in 1927 to subdue the northern warlords but at the same time he took the opportunity to attack the Communists and his enemies within the Kuomintang. In Shanghai, he launched a surprise attack and wiped out the Communists within the city. This was followed by massacres in Guangzhou, Nanchang, and other places. By mid-1928, Chiang Kai-shek was in control of the country and he set up a national government in Nanjing. The Communists were driven into the mountains and were constantly persecuted.

The Japanese, meanwhile, had been eyeing China and in the 1930s they made a move into eastern China. For a while Chiang Kai-shek kept fighting the Communists but when a full-scale war with the Japanese broke out in 1937, he was forced to join forces with the Communists against their common enemy. The Japanese, however, proved to be too stong and they occupied China until 1945. When the Japanese left, civil war broke out between the Kuomintang and the Communists. By 1950 the Communists had won and the Kuomintang fled to Taiwan to form the Republic of China.

On October 1, 1949, Mao Zedong (Tse-tung) declared the founding of the People's Republic of China, and the Communist Party of China set out to establish a new political and social system. Industries were taken over by the government and peasants formed co-operatives to help each other. The economy started to recover and Mao Zedong pushed further ahead with his plan. In 1959 he launched a campaign known as the Great Leap Forward. The entire countryside was divided into communes with about 5,000 households each. Privacy and individual choice was eliminated. Everyone ate in communal halls, children were looked after in boarding schools, and people worked in fields and factories doing what the party ordered.

Initially both crop and factory production rose, but the peasants were being driven to exhaustion. Suddenly agriculture production dipped and floods and drought drove the country into famine. Many people starved to death and Mao was forced to take a back seat in the organization. In 1966, urged on by his wife, Jiang Qing, Mao tried to regain control with the launch of the Cultural Revolution. Mao called on the Chinese to rebel against the "four olds"—old ideas, old culture, old habits, and old customs. He was supported by a group of radical young people called the Red Guard, who went on a rampage of destruction and humiliation.

Books were burned; relics destroyed; temples were torn down; the homes of intellectuals were invaded and smashed; and the people were killed, thrown into prison, or sent to the countryside to do manual work.

The Revolution soon got out of hand and troops were used to recreate some law and order. Enormous damage was done to the economy and China's reputation in the world. When Mao died in 1976, the Cultural Revolution came to an end. In a power stuggle that followed, Deng Xiaoping emerged as a leader and he introduced many economic and social changes. He opened up the country to foreign travellers, established Special Economic Zones for development, and started the long process back toward allowing some individuality.

The process appears to have become almost irreversible. It can be seen most clearly in Guangzhou, where economic capitalism has become the goal of many. Free enterprise, private business, and individualism have been embraced by a significant section of the population and this region is dragging the rest of China into the capitalist age. Freedom has not kept pace with this change and the world was horrified when the People's Liberation Army killed hundreds of unarmed students who were demonstrating for democracy in Tiananmen Square in 1989. Again China's international reputation was severely damaged and cynicism of the ruling old guard remains deep even today.

The Government

The workings of the Chinese government are not well known outside a group within the Communist party, but it is possible to put some things together. China is a one-party state and the highest authority rests with the Standing Committee of the Communist party. Below this is the Central Committee, consisting of provincial leaders and less senior members of the central party.

The National People's Congress is the highest organization of state power in China. It has the power to amend the constitution and make laws. It elects the president, vice-president, and other senior position holders. The Congress is made up of representatives or deputies from all regions of China. Members are elected every five years and they meet once a year in Beijing. They are all Communist party members.

The State Council is the highest authority in administration. It enforces the laws and decisions of the National People's Congress and has the power to adopt administrative measures and issue orders. Overall responsibility for the Council lies with the Premier (Prime Minister). Ministries, State Commissions, and some Special Agencies report to the State Council.

Under the central government, China is divided into a number of provinces, regions, and municipalities. Each of these is divided into cities, counties, and towns. At the lowest level there are the residents' committees, which manage public welfare, settle disputes, see that state rules are observed and implemented, and keep an eye on all citizens. In parallel to these are the work units *(danwei)* that control most Chinese from the day they start work until they die. No major personal decisions can be made without consulting a work unit. A couple planning to marry must get the approval of the work unit first. The work unit must give approval to travel or for a change in job. Members must attend meetings when ordered and housing, salaries, mail, ration coupons, heating subsidies, and so on have been traditionally controlled by these organizations.

Times are changing, however, and particularly in areas like Guangzhou. Foreign companies are employing more labor and capitalism appears to be further advanced, so the work unit has lost much of its importance. In fact we are probably witnessing the end to some of the extraordinary control that the Communist party has been able to exercise over people's lives. The rising middle class is less inclined to be so tightly controlled and already the cracks in the system are showing. The next ten years will be extremely interesting.

The Economy

When the Communists took power in 1950, all private enterprises were confiscated and turned over to the government. At the same time China largely isolated itself from the economies of the rest of the world. During the disastrous Cultural Revolution of the 1960s and 1970s, all basic forms of free enterprise, such as simple street stalls and markets were abolished. Intellectuals were killed or sent to do manual work in the country, thus depriving the country of managers and people with high technical skills. By the mid-1970s the economy was heading towards collapse as agricultural production plummeted and factories produced shoddy items that nobody could afford.

The country was probably saved from civil war and economic collapse by the death of Mao in 1976 and the reversal of the Cultural Revolution policies. The so-called Gang of Four, led by Mao's wife, were arrested and imprisoned and the policy of isolation was reversed. Under the direction of Deng Xiaoping, China opened its doors to foreign trade and investments. Special Economic Zones were set up where foreign investors were encouraged to build factories and operate businesses. Most of these were in the Guangdong area because of its proximity to Hong Kong and Macau.

With the new economic policy, Chinese for the first time in many years could own small businesses. In Guangdong, this has been enthusiastically embraced and today the sidewalks and markets are crowded with small capitalist entrepreneurs. The government is still trying to reconcile the conflict between Socialist theory and the reality of the free market; but in the meantime, China is continuing to move toward a capitalist economy.

All this has not been without its problems. Many party officials and others with influence have made a fortune from the new system. You see palatial homes, expensive foreign cars, and conspicuous consumption everywhere in Guangdong. At the same time, unemployment has become a problem as unprofitable state-run enterprises are being forced to shed unproductive workers. Many of these people are not suited to the new industries that are appearing, so they have little hope of future employment. In many cases the only option is to try and start a small roadside business offering basic goods and services.

Another problem is urban drift. With travel restrictions partly lifted, Chinese peasants are flooding to the cities to look for a better life. Many arrive without a job or a place to stay and are forced to stay on the streets. People still need a residence permit before they can rent an apartment or get a job, and authorities are reluctant to issue these to everyone who applies because the existing infrastructure cannot cope with the influx. Guangzhou and the Special Economic Zones are particularly favored areas so there are special problems here. Around Guangzhou Railway Station, you can see many people camping out at night because they have nowhere to go. There are beggars on the streets and crime is on the increase. The Special Economic Zones have become almost different countries with foreigners needing passports to enter and the Chinese requiring special permits, which are only issued to those with a confirmed job or those with the ability to bribe an official. Corruption has increased dramatically in recent years and is now almost endemic in some areas.

Despite these problems, the Chinese economy is growing rapidly. The Pearl Delta area is leading the rest of the country and, in fact, some people believe that this area is growing too rapidly. Whether this can be controlled or not is difficult to say. Some outsiders perceive that local officials in this area are almost ignoring directives from Beijing and it appears that there is little central officials can do about it. There are significant social and environmental concerns about what is happening, but there is little doubt that the Pearl Delta area is far more prosperous and people are less controlled than in the rest of the country. It is a fascinating mixture of successes, failures, and curious results coming from new policies, as China struggles to enter the modern world.

The People

Twenty percent or 1.2 billion of the world's population lives in China. About six percent of this lives in Guangdong province. Overpopulation has been a problem in China for many years but the present chronic problems were caused by Mao Zedong, who believed that more population

Mother and child.

meant more production and consequently urged the people to have as many children as possible "for the good of the country." Although the cities are bursting at the seams, 80 percent of the population still lives in the countryside, giving China the greatest number of farmers in the world.

China's main ethnic group is the Han Chinese, who originated in the river valleys of eastern China. They number more than one billion and represent 95 percent of the population. In the Pearl Delta they represent more than 98 percent of the population. Throughout the country there are 55 other ethnic groups and they occupy more than 50 percent of China's total land area. The biggest minority is the Zhuangs, with 13.5 million people. In the Pearl Delta there are some Miao and Li people.

China's population continues to grow by some 20 million people a year despite the existance of a strict birth control policy since 1982. The legal marriage age for men is 22 and for women it is 20. City dwellers are limited to one child per couple, then there are stiff penalties for having more. Couples in the countryside can have two if their first child is a daughter. This is a reflection of the fact that China is still a male-dominated society and sons are valued much more highly than daughters.

Poverty, wars, and rebellions have encouraged many Chinese to leave their country in search of a better life. Many have left from the Pearl Delta region and have settled in Hong Kong, other Asian countries, and around the world. They are collectively known as Hua Qiao. There are some 32 million Hua Qiao around the world. Many of these have been opposed to the Communist regime and have continued to practice customs and traditions that are discouraged in China. In recent years, the Chinese government has encouraged these people to visit China and many have made visits to their hometowns to make donations to build schools, hospitals, and public buildings.

Religion

Religious freedom disappeared when the Communists came to power, and during the Cultural Revolution all forms of religious activity were harshly suppressed. Monks, priests, and nuns were killed or imprisoned; and churches and temples were ransacked, destroyed, or turned into factories and warehouses. The result is that the majority of Chinese today are atheist.

In the last ten years or so, there has been a religious revival of sorts. Some monks and priests have been allowed to reopen their church or temple and some buildings have even been restored by the state. The 1982 Constitution guarantees religious freedom, but there is still some reluctance by many to openly practice the old ways.

Christianity and Islam have made little inroads into China. Chinese who admit to having a religion are more likely to practice a mixture of Taoist and Confucian philosophies and Buddist beliefs. Older Chinese are often superstitious due to the Taoist belief in keeping harmony with nature and the universe. If good luck can be brought to a major event, it will be. The younger generation is taught by the authorities to be less superstitious and this leads to some family problems at times.

Hong Kong remains a far better place to see Chinese religious beliefs than the Pearl Delta.

Language

Cantonese is still the most popular dialect in the Pearl Delta, but Mandarin, or Putonghua, is the official language. Putonghua is based on the Beijing dialect, which is a variation of the Northern dialect. It is taught in schools throughout China. Chinese from different areas of China cannot communicate in their own dialect, however, the written form of all the dialects is the same.

Putonghua has a limited range of sounds but these are expanded by four tones that are used to distinguish words from each other. Most Westerners find tonal languages difficult to master. It is more difficult because most non-Chinese find the written language totally incomprehensible. To help overcome this problem, the Chinese in 1958 adopted a system known as Pinyin as a method of writing their language in the Roman alphabet. It was thought initially that this might eventually take the place of Chinese characters, but this now looks unlikely particularly since a form of simplified script writing was adopted in 1964. Pinyin is the reason some names have changed in English. Peking became Beijing, Mao Tse-tung became Mao Zedong and so on.

There are more than 50,000 words in Chinese script but only about 3,000 are in common use. It is common practice to see Chinese people reach for the dictionary to look up a word. There are 11 basic strokes and Chinese words are written in a proper sequence of strokes. The simplest word has only one stroke while the most complicated has 30. Chinese take their handwriting seriously as it reflects on their upbringing and character. The style of handwriting often determines whether a letter is read or put aside.

Here are a few Mandarin words to help you while you are in China.

Numbers

one	—yi
two	—liang
three	—san
four	—si
five	—wu
six	—liu
seven	—qi
eight	—ba
nine	—jiu
ten	—shi
eleven	—shi yi
twelve	—shi liang
one hundred	—yi bai
one thousand	—yi qian

Useful Words and Phrases

thank you	—xiexie
How are you?	—ni hao
help	—jiuming a
How much does it cost?	—duoshao qian
I'm sick	—Wo sheng bing
I'm lost	—Wo mi lu
I want to go to . . .	—Wo yao qu . . .
train station	—huoche zhan
airport	—feijichang

bus station	—changtu qiche zhan
bank	—yinhang
tourist hotel	—jiudian
hospital	—yiyuan
taxi	—chuzu che
post office	—you ju

Food

steamed rice	—bai fan
noodles	—mian
fried noodles	—chao mien
soup	—tang
chicken	—ji rou
duck	—ya rou
fish	—yu
vegetables	—shu cai
water	—kai shui
beer	—pi jiu
tea	—cha

Culture and Lifestyle

The Chinese attitude towards life is still influenced by Confucian ethics, which teach people to respect each other. This may come as a surprise to a visitor who has just been brushed aside in the rush to board a bus, but it certainly holds true with personal relationships. The Chinese will go through all means not to embarrass another person they know. They never say "no" to any request and rarely outwardly disagree with anything. They have been brought up to mask their feelings, often by laughing or smiling. When two Chinese get to know each other, they have established relations. They are then obliged to do each other favors.

Life for most Chinese again revolves around the family despite the Cultural Revolution attempt to downgrade this institution. It is common to find three generations living together in the city and in the country it can extend to include uncles, aunts, numerous cousins, and so on. The oldest member in the family is looked on as a person of wisdom and his opinion is highly valued. Old people are well looked after and respected even if they are ill or bed-ridden. The family hierarchy is carefully preserved and each member of the family knows where he or she stands.

Adult Chinese usually live with their parents until the time they marry. Upon marriage, the woman moves into the man's parents' home. They will then live in the parents' home until their death. In the past, marriages were often arranged by parents, but now couples choose whom they want to marry. They must then seek the approval of their work unit and if approval is given, they can register the event. Previously marriages were elaborate affairs but now there is a simple civil ceremony. Wedding couples in the city then often hold a dinner for family and friends.

Most Chinese homes are small and simply furnished. The Chinese take pride in neatness, and houses and apartments are seldom messy. Some homes in the country are built around a courtyard with no external windows. Inside there is a kitchen, a living room, and several bedrooms. Toilet facilities are often outside and shared between families. Similar houses exist in the cities, but they are then usually shared by several families. City homes seldom have bathrooms and most companies provide shower facilities for staff. In the Pearl Delta area, Hong Kong interests have constructed many Western self-contained houses and these are in great demand by the newly rich.

Most people wear Western-style clothes. In the north, Mao suits are still popular but you see little of this in the Pearl Delta. During the Cultural Revolution, everyone wore this uniform but now young people are interested in modern Western and Hong Kong fashions, and women are returning to the traditional long, slim dresses with slits up the side for after-dark wear.

The Chinese have a title for every member of the household. This came about because historically the Chinese family was an extended one with several generations living together. A Chinese person is never asked how many brothers and sisters he has, but how many are older and younger than he is. Elder brothers, elder sisters, younger brothers, and younger sisters all have different names. So too, do each maternal and paternal grandparent and each aunt and uncle.

Outside the family, Chinese of all ages are known by their surname. Often *xiao*, meaning "little," is used as a prefix for younger people and *lao*, meaning "old," is put in front of the surname of a middle-aged person to show respect for his or her age and experience when you are addressing somebody you know. In formal address to males, the surname is put before *xiansheng*, meaning "mister." Strangers are often addressed as *tongzhi*, or "comrade."

Food and Drink

The daily activity that gives the Chinese the most pleasure is eating. "Have you eaten yet?" is often used as a greeting. It is often said that if it moves, the Chinese will eat it. Certainly there is a recipe for almost every animal and every part of the body. It was probably poverty that drove the Chinese to make the best use of an animal. Stir-frying food by cutting it into small pieces so that it cooks quickly and saves precious firewood was developed for the same reason.

The Chinese cook food on burners fueled by either firewood or gas. The kitchen holds little else but a cleaver, a wok, a soup ladle, and chopsticks. The cleaver can prepare most foods, while the wok is an all-purpose cooking utensil. The best woks are made of cast-iron; but it is common to find them in stainless steel, aluminium, or a nonstick material.

Rice is so important to a Chinese that *fan* means both cooked rice and a meal. Rice is treated with utmost respect. Every spilled grain is swept up, cleaned, and cooked. Rice is eaten at most meals. Chopsticks are used to eat rice and all other foods except soup. In the past, chopsticks were made from silver, ivory, jade, bone, or wood. Today they are mainly wood, bamboo, or plastic. There is no rule as to how they should be used, except that they should not cross.

Cantonese cuisine is the best known form of Chinese food outside of China. The Cantonese are known to be very fussy about the freshness of the ingredients. Dishes are never overcooked and flavors are seldom masked with overpowering sauces. Vegetables are lightly stir-fried or blanched in hot water and dressed with oyster sauce. The Cantonese are also famous for their soups and their egg noodles, which are eaten with a dumpling soup or topped with red-roasted meats. They also have exotic tastes in meat. Snake is made into a soup while dog is roasted or stewed. Hard-to-find iguanas are preciously suspended in wine and taken in small quantities for their tonic effect. Dried pieces of crocodile meat are made into a soup, while bears' paws are lovingly braised and served to very important guests. Other delicacies are bird's nests, sharks' fins, and camels' noses.

Noodles, or *mien*, come in all shapes, sizes, and lengths. Noodles are made from wheat or rice. In the south, egg is added to the wheat dough. Sometimes a few drops of alkaline water are added to give the noodles a slightly bitter taste. Noodles in the south can be round or flat and can be as thick as spaghetti, or as fine as hair. They are fried plain or crispy, topped with a hearty sauce of shrimp and pork, or added to a rich soup. Long noodles symbolize a long life and are served at birthday celebrations.

Breakfast is usually rice gruel made from leftover rice or broken pieces of grains. In the Pearl Delta region, pieces of meat and an egg are often added to make a tasty congee. It is eaten with a variety of pickled vegetables or pieces of salty, fermented bean curd. Dinner is the main meal of the day and it is usually eaten around 6 P.M. Family members sit around a table filled with a soup; one or two dishes of vegetables; and a main dish of fish, poultry, or pork. Everyone has a bowl of rice, and each helps himself to whatever he wants from the common dishes.

Do not be surprised if a Chinese eats noisily at the table. It is not considered bad manners to slurp soup. It is disrespectful to use chopsticks as drumsticks or to point with them during a conversation. It is perfectly all right to put bones and other scraps on the table rather than the edge of your bowl.

Local wines are popular, but they are not usually used during meals. Chinese wines are made from rice, sorghum, millet, or grapes. The most popular are made from rice and they come as white, yellow, and burning. Some are drunk warm in small cups. Beer has become popular, particularly, in the cities. Different regions have their own brands and in the Pearl Delta area, imported beer has become popular with the middle-class.

Tea is the most important beverage in all parts of China. It is drunk at all times of the day as a drink and for medicinal purposes. The Chinese believe it stimulates the digestive system, nervous system, and heart and reduces the harmful effects of smoking and alcohol. There are basically three types of tea: green, red, and oolong. Sometimes jasmine flowers are added in the fermentation process of green or oolong tea to perfume it.

Food prices are cheap in the markets, reasonable in many small restaurants, tolerable in the hotels and many of the "name" restaurants, and outlandish in a few upmarket places.

Festivals

The Chinese calendar is basically an agricultural one that follows the moon and divides the year into twelve lunar months. The Chinese use the lunar calendar to mark most of their festivals and some of the older generation use the Chinese one more than the Western one; however, the Western calendar is adopted for daily use. China has one of the fewest public holidays in the world, so some of the festivals are not holidays.

Lunar New Year, or the **Spring Festival,** is the most important festival for the Chinese. It is usually between late January and late February. The Chinese believe that the year must begin with a good start, so everything to ensure good fortune is done. Spring cleaning of houses is undertaken, homes are decorated with symbols of good luck, new clothes are bought, rice bins are filled, quarrels are mended, and debts are paid. Children make a special effort to be home with their parents on New Year's Eve, as the reunion dinner is the most important event of the preparations. At midnight, firecrackers are set off to scare away any evil spirits and house lights are turned on to chase away bad luck. On the first day of the New Year, people dress in their new clothes and visit relatives. Nothing unpleasant is allowed to happen on this day. Celebrations last for two weeks, although most people are back at work by the fourth day. On the fifteenth day, a lantern festival is held to end the celebrations.

The **Qingming Festival** is held in early Spring. This is the day the Chinese remember their dead ancestors. Visits are made to cemeteries to sweep

At Chinese New Year it is a tradition that the house should be filled with flowers and plants. These are grown to bloom just at the right time—a difficult feat as Chinese New Year occurs in the cooler months of January or February.

tombs and pay respect to the departed. This is not necessarily a solemn day, and it often becomes a family outing with a picnic at the tomb.

The **Duanwu Festival,** or **Dragon Boat Festival,** is held on the fifth day of the fifth lunar month. It remembers a patriotic poet who drowned himself because his state was overrun by conquerers. Villagers rushed to the river and threw rice dumplings into the water to stop the fish from eating his body. Then they spent days in boats trying to find the body. To remember this day, dragon boat races are held and rice dumplings are eaten.

The **Zhongqiu Festival** is when the Chinese celebrate midautumn on the fifteenth day of the eighth lunar month. This is when the moon is at its fullest and brightest, the weather is at its best, and mooncakes made of thin pastry filled with sweet mashed lotus seeds are eaten and given as gifts.

National Day is October 1, and celebrations are held throughout the country. The first two days in October are public holidays.

The Arts

Many of the art styles of China developed in the Tang dynasty (A.D. 618–907), when artistic expression reached a peak. In the seventh century, a white clay was discovered along the banks of the Yellow River. This clay was used to produce white porcelain pieces that over the years became so refined that they were thin and translucent. The most popular of these were the blue-and-white pieces from the Ming period and these became so famous in the West that they were called "China," after their place of origin.

The art of carving was also refined. Classic pieces are of ivory and jade and some of the detail is extremely fine. Hopefully ivory is no longer used. Cloisonné is another popular art form. Enamel paint is used on thin plates that are then soldered onto metal bases.

Painting is a traditional art form that remains popular today. There are five main subjects: human figures, landscapes, flowers and trees, birds and animals, and fish and insects. Paintings are usually done on silk or on an absorbent paper made of bamboo pulp. Many famous artists specialize in painting just one subject. Many complete a painting in a short time and then paint the same subject again and again until the desired effect is achieved. Brush strokes are important to a painting and so is the attempt to catch the spirit of the subject.

Calligraphy is often used to complete a Chinese painting, but it is also used on its own. It is much more than handwriting—it is an art in its own right. Calligraphers traditionally write poems, couplets, or proverbs, which are hung on walls. The Chinese have placed great importance on good calligraphy and for 1,300 years, a scholar's handwriting carried great weight in his score in the civil service examination. Even today, some poets will take as much pride in the writing as in the content of their poems.

Embroidery was first used with the invention of the silk thread and it has been refined over the years by women who wanted to wear something more than plain cloth. Embroidery decorates clothes, shoes, fans, purses, and hair accessories. It is also used on altar cloths, flags, banners, and wall hangings. Some embroideries are not unlike Chinese landscape paintings. Elaborate pieces can take years to do and are often worked on by more than one person. Guangdong is one of the most well known embroidery areas in China and it has its own designs and style.

Papercuts are an art form that was developed by country women. Patterns can be regular, symmetrical, repeated patterns; or complicated designs with birds, animals, flowers, and so on. The resultant designs are often used to decorate the house during festive seasons. They are stuck on lanterns, windows, doors, and walls. For these occassions, the designs are often of good luck, longevity, and health symbols. Designs are sometimes handed down from generation to generation and designs differ from village to village.

Opera is an art form quite different from the others we have mentioned. It started out as street performances where gongs, cymbals, and drums were used to attract an audience. Each region of China has its own style of opera. Some stress singing, others acrobatics or dancing. They are still performed in the open in the street or in parks. A performance can last several hours with whole families turning up and leaving at different times. Sometimes spectators stand up and join in the chorus. Costumes are bright, colorful, and elaborate. Most characters wear long, flowing robes and some wear splendid headdresses. Stage makeup is as fascinating as the costumes with actors coloring their faces according to the roles they play. Chinese literature, of which the operatic drama is a part, has a 3,000-year history and is one of the major literary heritages of the world.

Music is an important part of opera and in major performances, an orchestra with Chinese instruments is assembled. Some of the more unusual instruments are the ertu, a fiddle with two strings played with a bow made of bamboo and horsehair; the pipa, a four-string lute that is held upright and is strummed or plucked; and the guzheng, a large zither with 18 to 21 strings that is played like a harp. In ancient times, playing the guzheng was considered a status symbol.

Acrobatics has been a performing art in China for 22 centuries. It started out as a means of livelihood for farmers during the winter months and this is why the props used are often household items like crockery and furniture. These objects are often tossed in the air or piled precariously on top of each other. Balancing acts on bicycles, chairs, and large urns are also common.

Art is also important in Chinese architecture. Chinese buildings have distinctive roofs and structures that make them different from other buildings. They also often have elaborate ornamentation. In important buildings, there are paintings of dragons and auspicious flowers and plants decorating ceilings, pillars, and walls. Doors are often painted red for good luck and have rows of nine gold studs running vertically and horizontally. Glazed tiles are used extensively in many buildings to add color and texture.

Accommodations

When China first opened its doors to Western visitors, there were only a small number of hotels where visitors were allowed to stay. That number has slowly grown over the years until now there is good choice in the upper and middle parts of the market. The budget end is much more restrictive, with the authorities claiming that the restrictions are for the safety of foreigners. Just what the restrictions are, and what they are for is very difficult to determine; but the fact remains that there are hotels in which many visitors would be prepared to stay, but that refuse to accept them and claim that they are not allowed to have foreign guests. I have had personal experience of that on my most recent visit.

The good news is that Pearl Delta hotels are excellent value when compared to Hong Kong, and some of the better properties are catching up to the rest of Asia when it comes to service. Unfortunately, the same cannot be said for most of the others. Cheaper midmarket hotels have rooms from around US$30 and these will often be large, clean, and well appointed. For this price you will have your own bathroom and air conditioning, TV, and a telephone. Someone at the front desk will speak English, but most of the other staff will not. For an extra US$25 you will get additional facilities and perhaps some better service.

Upmarket hotels start at around US$100 a night. The facilities will be equivalent to a three- to four-star hotel in the West. You can expect good restaurants, some sports facilities, and some entertainment. From around US$125, you enter the realm of the five-star hotel. Some of these provide facilities that would cost twice this in Hong Kong. Many of these are managed by international chains and they have introduced a service concept that was unknown in China until recently. Here the guest actually matters.

Health and Safety

There are some health problems when travelling in southern China but they are insignificant compared to some other countries. Likewise with safety. China generally is safer than many Western countries; and although there is more crime in Guangzhou than many other parts, it is still safe to walk around most areas in the day and at night.

Diarrhea afflicts many China visitors but generally it is not serious and will disappear quickly. It can be caused by the water or by unfamiliar food. As a precaution, it is best not to drink the water from the tap. Most hotels will provide flasks of boiled water or tea in the rooms. Avoid spicy or oily food for the first few days of your visit if you are prone to have diarrhea problems. If you do catch travellers' diarrhea, try switching to a simple diet of white rice, boiled eggs, bananas, and yogurt for a few meals and drink plenty of fluids to avoid dehydration. If the diarrhea persists for more than a few days, see a doctor.

Another problem faced by travellers in the colder months is the "China flu." For some reason China seems to contain some of the most severe strains of influenza you will find anywhere. Most Chinese in the cities seem to suffer from it during winter, so it is difficult for visitors to remain unaffected. It is made worse by the Chinese habit of spitting everywhere. In many cases it develops into bronchitis and at that point it is probably a good idea to go for the antibiotics. Unfortunately these are not always readily available in China, so you might consider taking some with you for emergency use. Remember that medical advice is to always finish a full course of antibiotics, and that is usually at least five days.

Malaria, hepatitis, tuberculosis, AIDS, and other diseases are found in

China and you should be aware of them. In fact it is an excellent idea to talk to your physician about this before you leave home. My experience is that you should not become paranoid about these health risks, but at the same time it makes sense to take simple precautions. Why get bitten by mosquitoes that may be carrying malaria when it is relatively simple to avoid being bitten? Why risk AIDS or hepatitis when sexual abstinence and avoidance of contaminated needles eliminates the problem?

Herbal medicine is an area that some visitors will be interested in investigating. I have had little personal experience with this but I have spoken to many people who believe that this can be very valuable in some instances. Quite clearly Chinese herbal doctors cannot cure every disease. A visit to a hospital quickly proves that. There is some evidence, however, that there are effective herbal treatments for sore throats, general pain, asthma, migraines, and so on, for some people. An added bonus is that most short-term herbal treatments seem to have few side effects. Despite this, it would be foolish to start self-treatment without a visit to a doctor.

The other Chinese treatment of interest to many is acupuncture. Again the question is often asked, "does it work?" The answer is difficult to determine. It probably depends on the condition being treated, the skill of the acupuncturist, and the belief of the patient. At worst, acupuncture is probably harmless, but you should not forget that AIDS and hepatitis can be spread easily by contaminated needles. It would be wise to insist that the acupuncturist use new needles even if this costs more. This system has been used for generations, so it cannot be just dismissed as useless. Some surgical operations have been carried out using acupuncture as an anesthetic with good results. It will be a long time, however, before we see this as a common procedure.

It is generally conceded that the Pearl Delta area has little violent crime against foreigners. This is partly because the area is densely populated and there are usually people (and police) on the streets and other places that are frequented by visitors. The crowds and "rich" visitors from Hong Kong and overseas have, however, attracted gangs of pickpockets and these often target foreigners in crowded places. As everywhere else, it is wise to keep your passport, wallet, and other valuables well hidden away out of reach. Crowded buses and train stations are favorite places for pickpockets, so beware.

Some years ago, it was very unusual to see a Western woman travelling alone in China and anyone that did ran into problems with accommodation and other things. That appears to be in the past, so if you wear conservative clothes and blend into the local scene, you are unlikely to strike any problems. Expect to be stared at if you wear anything too revealing or unconventional.

11

Guangzhou and the Pearl River Delta

1. The General Picture

Guangzhou occupies a strategic position on the Pearl River Delta, about 120 kilometers northwest of Hong Kong. The city is one of the oldest in China; and it is the largest city in the south, with a population of about 3.5 million. It is the capital of the important Guangdong Province, which occupies about 2.2 percent of China's land area. Its importance to the economy is far more significant than this, however. For more than 1,000 years, this was one of the main gateways for trade with China and it remains an important port and business center.

Lately, some decidedly Western comforts have been added to the total Chinese picture, so visiting has become more attractive to many tourists and business people. The once pale and gray city has become much more colorful. Bright yellow, pale green, and shocking pink now contrast with the once ubiquitous drab gray and blue Mao suits that were worn by the whole population.

Guangzhou is an attractive subtropical city, on the banks of the Pearl River. It enjoys an abundant rainfall and a mild climate and its parks and gardens remain green all year. Many of the roads are lined with evergreen trees, and flowers are grown for display in many parks. In China it is known as the Flower City.

The city has a 2,800-year history, but little remains from past centuries. At one time it was surrounded by an eight-meter-high wall, about 16 kilometers in length, and there were many canals throughout the area. You see almost

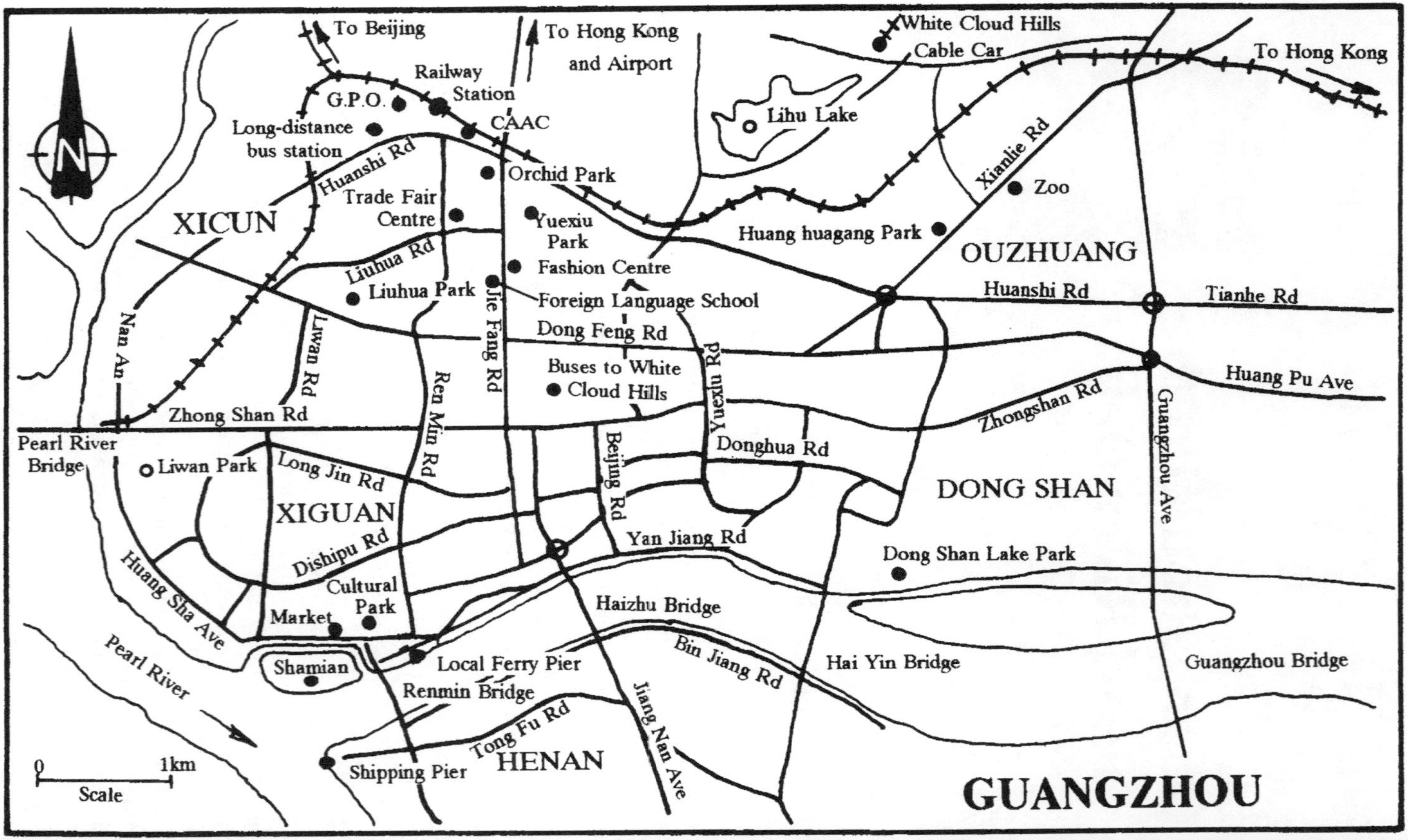
GUANGZHOU
To Beijing
To Hong Kong
and Airport
White Cloud Hills
Cable Car
To Hong Kong
Railway
Station
G.P.O.
CAAC
Long-distance
bus station
Lihu Lake
Huanshi Rd
Orchid Park
Xianlie Rd
Zoo
Trade Fair
Centre
Yuexiu
Park
XICUN
Huang huagang Park
OUZHUANG
Liuhua Rd
Fashion Centre
Liuhua Park
Jie Fang Rd
Foreign Language School
Huanshi Rd
Tianhe Rd
Nan An
Liwan Rd
Dong Feng Rd
Ren Min Rd
Buses to White
Cloud Hills
Yuexiu Rd
Huang Pu Ave
Zhong Shan Rd
Zhongshan Rd
Guangzhou Ave
Pearl River
Bridge
Liwan Park
Long Jin Rd
Beijing Rd
Donghua Rd
DONG SHAN
XIGUAN
Yan Jiang Rd
Dishipu Rd
Dong Shan Lake Park
Huang Sha Ave
Cultural
Park
Haizhu Bridge
Market
Pearl River
Shamian
Local Ferry Pier
Bin Jiang Rd
Hai Yin Bridge
Guangzhou Bridge
Renmin Bridge
Jiang Nan Ave
Tong Fu Rd
HENAN
0
1km
Scale
Shipping Pier

no evidence of this today. The major thoroughfares of Jiefang Lu (Liberation Road) and Zhongshan Lu divided the old city and ran to the major gates in the walls. These roads are now traffic-choked, wide boulevards serving the outlying suburbs.

A visitor is likely to be initially confused with the layout of the city. There is no clear city center and many roads are not straight, so it is difficult to know your direction of travel. Hotels tend to be concentrated into three widely dispersed areas, so it is important that you select the correct location if you are visiting on business. Sight-seeing attractions are found throughout the area so you will do quite a deal of travelling if you hope to see them all.

The south bank of the Pearl River was once considered an undesirable area, but this started to change with the construction of the first river bridge in 1932. Now there are five bridges in the main city and the southern side of the river has developed into a major industrial and residential neighborhood. Nevertheless, it has limited tourist interest and you would do well to concentrate your sight-seeing activities on the north bank.

It will take a minimum of three days to cover the major points of interest, and a week is not too long to do the city justice. As you become more familiar with it, you will find more and more things of interest during both day and night. It is too sprawling to cover by foot, but there are areas where you will enjoy wandering around, taking in the sights and sounds of a thriving urban area going through another major economic adjustment. You somehow get the feeling that Guangzhou is enjoying its new opportunity to embrace capitalism.

2. Getting There

Guangzhou has a major international airport, so it is possible to fly there from many places. There are regular flights from Hong Kong, and direct services by well-known international airlines from Bangkok, Singapore, and Malaysia. CAAC, and other Chinese carriers also serve the city, but many foreign travellers tend to shun these because of poor service and a fear about safety.

There is a rail line connecting Hong Kong with Guangzhou and there are a growing number of international services between the two cities. These take around three hours. If you do not catch one of these, you will be forced to walk across the border from Lo Wu Station in Hong Kong to Shenzhen in China and take another train from there to Guangzhou. Some of these trains only go as far as the East Guangzhou station and this is likely to be a long way from your final destination.

There is no rail line to Macau at present, but there are buses that connect the two cities. From Macau, some travellers prefer to walk across the border then catch a bus in Zhuhai to Guangzhou. This trip takes about four hours in normal circumstances.

There are government-run and private **buses** from Shenzhen to Guangzhou. The private buses are air-conditioned and provide the best service, and these depart from near the Shenzhen railway station. The drivers will like to be paid in Hong Kong dollars. The trip from here currently takes about four hours, but when the new freeway is fully open, it will be quicker.

Ferries connect Hong Kong and Guangzhou, and Macau and Guangzhou, although this latter service *may not* last. The jetcat from Hong Kong takes three hours. It departs from the China Hong Kong ferry terminal in Kowloon and arrives at the Zhoutouzui Wharf in Guangzhou. There is also an overnight **slow ferry** that does the same trip. It is best to buy tickets for both of these services in advance at the China Hong Kong ferry terminal. The service from Macau departs from a wharf near the floating casino and arrives at Zhoutouzui Wharf in Guangzhou.

3. Local Transportation

Guangzhou City sprawls over 93 square kilometers and the sight-seeing attractions are scattered so that walking between them is not practical. Fortunately, there is a good network of public transport and taxis are available. Heavy traffic and a lack of English speakers, however, can make travel around the city a frustrating experience at times.

Taxis are found outside the hotels, transport terminals, and shopping centers. They may also be hailed in the street. They are equipped with meters and in my experience, the drivers will use them. Taxi drivers do not speak English, so you will have to have your destination written in Chinese. Taxi fares are reasonable, but at times you will get caught in traffic and your journey will take much longer than you expect. It is possible to rent a taxi by the hour and this is not a bad method of sight-seeing if you are in a small group. You must negotiate a fare before you depart and have the places you wish to see written on a piece of paper in Chinese. Your hotel may help with negotiations.

Bicycles are available for rent from some hotels and stores in the city. In some circumstances this can be a good way to see the city. I am told that some visitors have had their rental bicycles stolen and this obviously involves inconvenience, time, and money; so a safety chain could be a good investment. Most tourist attractions have bicycle parks where an attendant will supervise proceedings for a small fee.

There is an extensive network of **buses** and **electric trolley buses** that you can use. Each has a number but there are no English names. At peak periods they are very crowded, but at other times they are practical to use. Buses have conductors who cannot speak English so you will need a map or address in Chinese in order to buy the correct ticket. Chinese maps with bus routes are available in some hotels.

4. The Hotel Scene

Hotels are significantly cheaper in Guangzhou than they are in Hong Kong, and they are also cheaper than in Macau. The best hotels are very good, both in service and facilities. You will often find you can get something done in the hotel that was impossible elsewhere.

EXPENSIVE HOTELS

I have decided to classify hotels as expensive if their base rate is US$100 or more. The following fall into this category.

The **White Swan** (Tel: 888-6968) is one of Guangzhou's favorites. It has a riverfront location on Shamian Island and some rooms have great river views. The hotel has been there long enough to develop some poise and character so it is a very pleasant place to stay. Rooms are about standard for this type of property but surprisingly they lack hair dryers. They are equipped with satellite TV, so you can keep up with the latest world news, sports, and music.

The hotel has a vast, impressive lobby with a waterfall at one end. On several levels there are nine restaurants, bars with music, a shopping arcade, 24-hour money exchange service, a post office, and a 24-hour business center for faxes, telex, and cables. Outside there are two swimming pools, eight flood-lit tennis courts, squash, golf driving range, health club, and sauna and massage. Major credit cards are accepted. Room rates are US$100 for standard and US$120 for deluxe rooms. During the **Canton Trade Fair** time, these rise to US$220 and US$250 respectively. (Book with any Leading Hotels of the World office, or direct with the hotel at 1 Southern St., Shamian Island, Guangzhou, China; Fax: 8620-886-1188.)

The **Guangdong International Hotel** (Tel: 331-1888) is in one of the newest and most striking buildings in Guangzhou. This is in an entirely different area of the city from the White Swan and, personally, I don't find it as attractive; but it is closer to some of the major businesses and sight-seeing attractions. The lobby is glamorous but a little complicated, and it is a surprise to see that McDonald's is the most prominent restaurant. As you discover more about the hotel, you will find that there is in fact a fine choice of the world's cuisine from Cantonese, Sichuan, Huai Yang, and Japanese to classic Western in other outlets.

There is an executive floor for business travellers, with a complimentary breakfast and international newspapers. Deluxe suites have a personal fax machine and a personal butler. Sporting facilities include swimming, tennis, billiards, bowling, a gymnasium, and sauna and massage. There are shops, hairdressing salon, and an outdoor garden. Room rates are Standard US$115, executive US$150, deluxe suite US$175. (Book with the hotel at 339 Huanshi Dong Rd., Guangzhou, China; Fax: 8620-331-3490.)

The **Dong Fang Hotel** (Tel: 666-9900), 1,300 rooms, is a fine hotel with more of a Chinese feel to it than some of the other properties. This is in the third major hotel area near the Trade Center and not far from the railway station. Although it is not old, everything here is slightly dated; it is as if the hotel needs some modernizing, at least in its fittings. The main buildings are built around a garden and this is quite lovely. Unfortunately, there are not many places where you can sit by yourself and enjoy it. As you would expect of a hotel of this size, there is a wide range of facilities and restaurants. The hotel has some single rooms that help reduce the price. Room rates are standard single US$80, standard double US$100, deluxe double US$110. (Book with the hotel at 120 Liuhua Rd., Guangzhou, China; Fax: 8620-666-2775.)

Almost next door is the **China Hotel** (Tel: 666-6888), 1,017 rooms and suites. This gleaming high-rise is operated by New World Hotels International and there is a positive attitude toward service with a smile. It is something that you do not always receive in China. The rooms are what you would expect, and some have good views over the park. Try and get one on this side. Room facilities are very adequate. There are 17 restaurants and bars, and 24-hour room service. Food Street, on the ground floor, has a selection of stalls serving various Asian specialties at reasonable prices and is well worth trying. The Hasty Tasty Fast Food Shop on the ground floor has a good selection of unremarkable Western fast food. Some of the other restaurants are very upmarket.

The hotel has a good choice of sports and entertainment. There is a swimming pool, tennis courts, tenpin bowling, a gymnasium, a health center, sauna and massage, karaoke, the Catwalk music lounge, a disco, a shopping arcade, and a reader's lounge. Other facilities include a post office, a bank, a hairdresser, a travel service, and a ticket booking office. Room rates are around US$120, while small suites are US$145. (Book with the New World Hotel organization, or directly with the hotel at Liuhua Road, Guangzhou 510015, China; Fax: 8620-667-7014.)

The **Garden Hotel** (Tel: 333-8989), more than 1,000 rooms, is back in the same area as the Guangdong International. I have never stayed here, but the hotel seems to have a nice feel. The huge lobby combines modern design with some magnificent Chinese works of art and treasures to produce a unique ambiance that you will not forget quickly. Rooms are typical for this type of property. Some of the restaurants are stunning. The Connoisseur lives up to its name with fine French food. The rooftop revolving Carousel Restaurant has a good seafood buffet, and the Peach Blossom is a Cantonese restaurant in traditional imperial surroundings. There are many more options.

The grounds provide space for a swimming pool, two tennis courts, two squash courts, a snooker and pool hall, and a health club with gymnasium, sauna/steam bath, and massage. Other facilities include a shopping arcade, bank, post office, money exchange, hair and beauty salon, children's playground, tour service, and taxi service. Room rates are standard double US$105, deluxe US$115. (Book with the hotel at 368 Huanshi Rd., Guangzhou, China; Fax: 8620-335-0467.)

The final recommendation in this category is the **Holiday Inn City Center** (Tel: 776-6999), 431 rooms, in the same area as the Garden Hotel. This is a smaller property, but it does not lack facilities and it has all the efficiency of an international Holiday Inn. All rooms have either a king-size bed or two double beds and there is a high ratio of suites or executive floor rooms. The three executive floors have a lounge where complimentary breakfast is served. A business center offers full secretarial and translation services.

Dining and entertaining facilities include a Cantonese restaurant, a Chaozhou restaurant, a Western restaurant, a self-service food street with ten specialty stalls, an Art Deco noodle shop, a casual cafe overlooking a waterfall, a discotheque, and a 500-seat cinema. There is a pool and a health club, exchange facilities, 24-hour room service, nonsmoking floors, and handicapped rooms. Rates are superior US$110, deluxe US$120, balcony US$130, and executive US$160. (Book with the Holiday Inn organization or direct with the hotel at 28 Guangming Rd., Guangzhou, China; Fax: 8620-775-3126.)

MEDIUM-PRICE HOTELS

The midrange covers the price range of US$30 to US$99. There appear to be two categories at either end of the range and not so much in the middle.

At the top end, the **Landmark Hotel** (Tel: 335-5988), 900 rooms, is a new hotel beside the Pearl River, near Haizhu Bridge. The 39-story building provides some excellent views of the city and it is situated in a good position for public transport. Rooms are well appointed and there are deluxe and suite floors for those who need more. Business travellers will appreciate the studio rooms that can be converted into offices during the day. There are four major restaurants—Parkview for Cantonese food, Chiu Chou City for Chiu Chou food, the Sidewalk Cafe for intercontinental fare, and the Landmark Club for Western cuisine. I expect that by the time you read this, there will be a swimming pool, health club, gymnasium, tennis court, badminton court, more restaurants, a post office, and a duty-free shop. These facilities may also convert this hotel into the expensive category. Current room rates are standard US$85, superior US$95, and deluxe room US$115. (Book with the hotel at Qiao Guang Road, Guangzhou 510115, China; Fax: 8620- 333-6197.)

The **Furama Hotel** (Tel: 886-3288), 360 rooms, is only about half a kilometer away. It is a modern building in the center of the old part of Guangzhou and is surrounded by shopping, restaurants, and nightlife. The rooms are up to international standard and the service is fine. The Furama Palace offers Cantonese cuisine, the Tiffany Coffee House has a selection of international food, while the Food Street has dishes drawn from China and southeast Asia. Club 28 on the 28th floor is a lounge, disco, and karaoke venue with excellent views over the city. There is a business center, bank, beauty salon, and florist, but there are no specific sports facilities. There are scheduled free shuttle transfers to the airport and railway station. Standard room rates are US$80 and suites are US$130. (Book with the hotel at 316 Changdi Rd., Guangzhou, China; Fax: 8620-886-3388.)

The **China Merchants Hotel** (Tel: 668-1988), 240 rooms, is a similar hotel in another part of the city near the trade center, opposite Liu Hua Park, and only 800 meters from the railway station. The rooms are furnished to international standard and there are good Western and Cantonese restaurants. Recreational outlets include a bar, billiard room, health club, and karaoke. The hotel has a small shopping arcade, a business center, and a beauty salon. Room rates are superior US$75, deluxe US$85, and suite US$140. (Book with the hotel at 111-8 Liuhua Rd., Guangzhou, China; Fax: 8620-666-2680.)

The **Hotel Equatorial** (Tel: 667-2888), 300 rooms, is close-by. Standard room rates are US$75, deluxe are US$90, and suites are US$150. There are two restaurants—Western and Cantonese, a food alley, shopping arcade, and business center. A nightclub helps the evening pass quickly. (Book with the hotel at 931 Renmin Rd., Guangzhou, China; Fax: 8620-667- 2582.)

Just up the road from here is the **Liuhua Hotel** (Tel: 668-8800), 750 rooms, the nearest hotel to the Guangzhou railway station. The hotel is a bit dated and it is downmarket from the previous listings, but the facilities are good and the price is attractive. There are ten suites decorated in Chinese, English, French, and Latin American national styles, and these are very attractive. There is a business center and a conference center. There are numerous restaurants including the Jufulou seafood hot pot restaurant, a Western restaurant, a coffee shop, and a fast-food outlet. The Dream Of Flower karaoke operates each night. You can pick up your personal needs in the shopping arcade, the bank, or the bookshop. Room rates are from

US$45 to US$70 for doubles. (Book with the hotel at 194 Huanshixi Rd., Guangzhou, China; Fax: 8620-666-7828.)

The other hotel of note in this area, is the **Friendship Hotel** (Tel: 667-9898), 200 rooms, which belongs to the Guangdong Arts Center. The modern hotel is very popular with Chinese business visitors, but it appears that foreigners are not so numerous except at Fair time. All rooms have TV, refrigerator, IDD telephone, and attached bathroom. There are a number of well-appointed suites that are very attractive. The hotel has Western and Chinese cuisines, a cake shop, business center, Friendship theater, and a small shopping center. Room rates start at around US$40, and suites are US$90. (Book with the hotel at 698 Renmin Bei Rd., Guangzhou, China; Fax: 8620-667-8653.)

The **Bai Yun Hotel** (Tel: 333-3998), 700 rooms, is a 34-story building in the same area as the Garden Hotel. This is one of the quieter areas of the city and is within walking distance of Yuexiu Park, one of the city's major attractions. The hotel has undergone renovation in recent years so that now the rooms are modern and well furnished. There are more than 20 dining outlets to choose from, including a lounge at the rooftop garden. The first floor has a store, a health center, a barber shop, a beauty salon, sauna and massage, a bank, a bookshop, a post office, and a business center. Room rates start at US$60 and rise to the presidential suite at US$1,500. (Book with the hotel at 367 Huanshi Dong Rd., Guangzhou, China; Fax: 8620-333-6498.)

We now go back across town to where we started the hotel section. Shamian Island has become a popular location for hotels, and many of the older properties have been renovated and upgraded. The **Pearl Inn** (Tel: 888-8238) reopened mid-1994 as an excellent midrange hotel. The rooms are very attractive, the higher ones have nice views, and there is a good restaurant that carries on a long tradition. It may be a reopening special but room rates are currently from US$50. (Book with the hotel at Shamian Nanjie, Shamian Island, Guangzhou, China.)

The long-established **Guangdong Victory Hotel** (Tel: 886-2622) has recently opened a newly renovated building in the block adjacent to the original hotel. At the same time the older building has had a facelift so that now this is a very attractive property and one that I can thoroughly recommend. The restaurant on the ground floor of the original building remains extremely popular with good reason. The renovated building has a good Western restaurant. Standard rooms in the original building are from US$30, while in the renovated building they are US$45. Deluxe rooms are US$60 and the presidential suite can be had for US$400. (Book with the hotel at 53 Shamian St. North, Guangzhou, China; Fax: 8620-886-1062.)

The **Shamian Hotel** (Tel: 888-8124) is a final choice. This is one place that has not been upgraded so the rooms are available from US$30. The hotel is not great, but you can get all the benefits of this lovely location and many of the benefits of the White Swan Hotel, if you stay here. (Book with the hotel at 50 Shamian Nanjie, Guangzhou, China; Fax: 8620- 886-1068.)

BUDGET ACCOMMODATION

There is only one really budget place for Western visitors that I can recommend. That is the **Guangzhou Youth Hostel** (Tel: 888-4298) on Shamian Island. It is on the corner opposite the White Swan and has the benefit of this location. Beds in the dormitories cost US$10, 12, and 14. A single room can cost as little as US$13, and a double is US$24. Self-contained doubles are US$32. There is a small restaurant, and an international telephone service.

The old **Aiqun Hotel** (Tel: 886-6668) has been in existence since 1937 but it has recently been renovated and the accommodation is now very pleasant. This is an excellent location right on the river and in the heart of the older, thriving part of the city. Transport and shopping are right at your doorstep. The rooms are quite good, although the standard rooms are smaller than in many modern hotels. Fittings are way above budget quality. There are ten restaurants serving a variety of Cantonese, other Chinese regional foods, and Western cuisine, including a revolving restaurant called the Turning Hall. There is karaoke, a dancing hall, a beauty salon, a shop, and a foreign exchange counter. Room rates start at a very reasonable US$20 for a single and US$25 for a double. A suite can be had for US$35. (Book with the hotel at 113 Yanyiang Xi Rd., Guangzhou, China; Fax: 8620-888-3519.)

The **Dong Ya Hotel** (Tel: 888-2373), 175 rooms, is close-by although it is not on the river. This is a hotel that was established in 1914, but which has recently been renovated. The reception area is not great but the rooms are quite pleasant. Rooms have air conditioning, TV, and telephone. There are three Chinese and Western restaurants, a large conference hall, and a shopping arcade. Room rates start at US$20 for a single, and US$25 for a double. Better rooms are US$30. (Book with the hotel at 320 Changti Rd., Guangzhou 510120, China.)

The **Tianhe Hotel** (Tel: 551-2138), 88 rooms, is a nice property in an out-of-the-way location. That explains the price compared to the facilities. The rooms are small but reasonably fitted out, and there are restaurant choices ranging from a coffee lounge, the Tian He Palace for Cantonese food, the Seasonal Hot Pot City restaurant, Food Street, and a Timmy's fast-food restaurant on the ground floor. There is a karaoke room, a beauty salon, a business center, and travel booking office. Room prices start at a low US$25 and rise to US$35 for a suite. (Book with the hotel at Shipai Gangding Tianhe Rd., Guangzhou 510630, China; Fax: 8620-551-0803.)

5. Dining and Restaurants

As you would expect, Guangzhou has an enormous range of restaurants serving mainly Cantonese food. When it comes to listing them, the difficulty is in knowing where to start, so I have restricted myself to those I have recently sampled or inspected. It is likely that you will discover many more that are just as good, as you wander the streets of the city.

The Dishipu Road area just north of the Qingping Market is a happy hunting ground for restaurants. The best known restaurant here is the **Guangzhou** (Tel: 888-8388) on the corner of Wenchang Road. This has existed for more than seventy years and was once considered to be the top restaurant in the city. Times change and new places appear, but Guangzhou has managed to remain popular to the point where reservations are sometimes necessary. Little English is spoken but the management is friendly and you will almost certainly get a good meal. It tends to be expensive, so be careful what you order.

On the same road you could also try **Tou Tou Jiu** (Tel: 881-6111), at No. 10, and the **Lian Xiang Restaurant** (Tel: 881- 3388) just down the street. Both are very popular with wealthy locals and they have tapped into the tour group trade. The food is good and the choice is large. Again prices tend to be high. If you want something fast and cheap, try **Fairwood Fast Food** to the east of the Guangzhou, or **McDonald's** to the west. Both are a hit with the younger, affluent population, and English is spoken and understood.

Hidden away on one of the small side roads is the **Snake Restaurant** (Tel: 888-2517) at 43 Jianglan Rd. It is a bit hard to find, but if you fancy snake for dinner, it is worth perservering. Jianglan runs parallel to Dishipu Road and is about two or three streets south. You will find it by the snakes in the window. This place has existed for about eighty years and it continues a tradition of snake eating that has lasted for centuries. The Chinese believe that snake is good for the body, particularly the circulation system. In my experience you feel distinctly warm after eating snake, so perhaps this is an indication that the Chinese are correct. I tend to think it is better not to know what else is in some of the recipes.

If you walk east, you will come to Renmin Road. Along here and around the corner in Yanjiang Road, restaurants are everywhere. The **Yan Yan** is just off Renmin at the foot of the pedestrian overpass. This is good for fish and for roast suckling pig. Closer to the corner is **Cafe de Coral,** and across the other side of the street is the **Fu Cheng Restaurant. Ocean City Restaurant** is almost next to the local ferry terminal. It has fast food on the ground floor and two levels of main restaurant above. The large **Datong Restaurant** (Tel: 888-8447) is almost on the corner. This has several floors of eating areas and there is an almost endless choice of dishes. It is open all day and

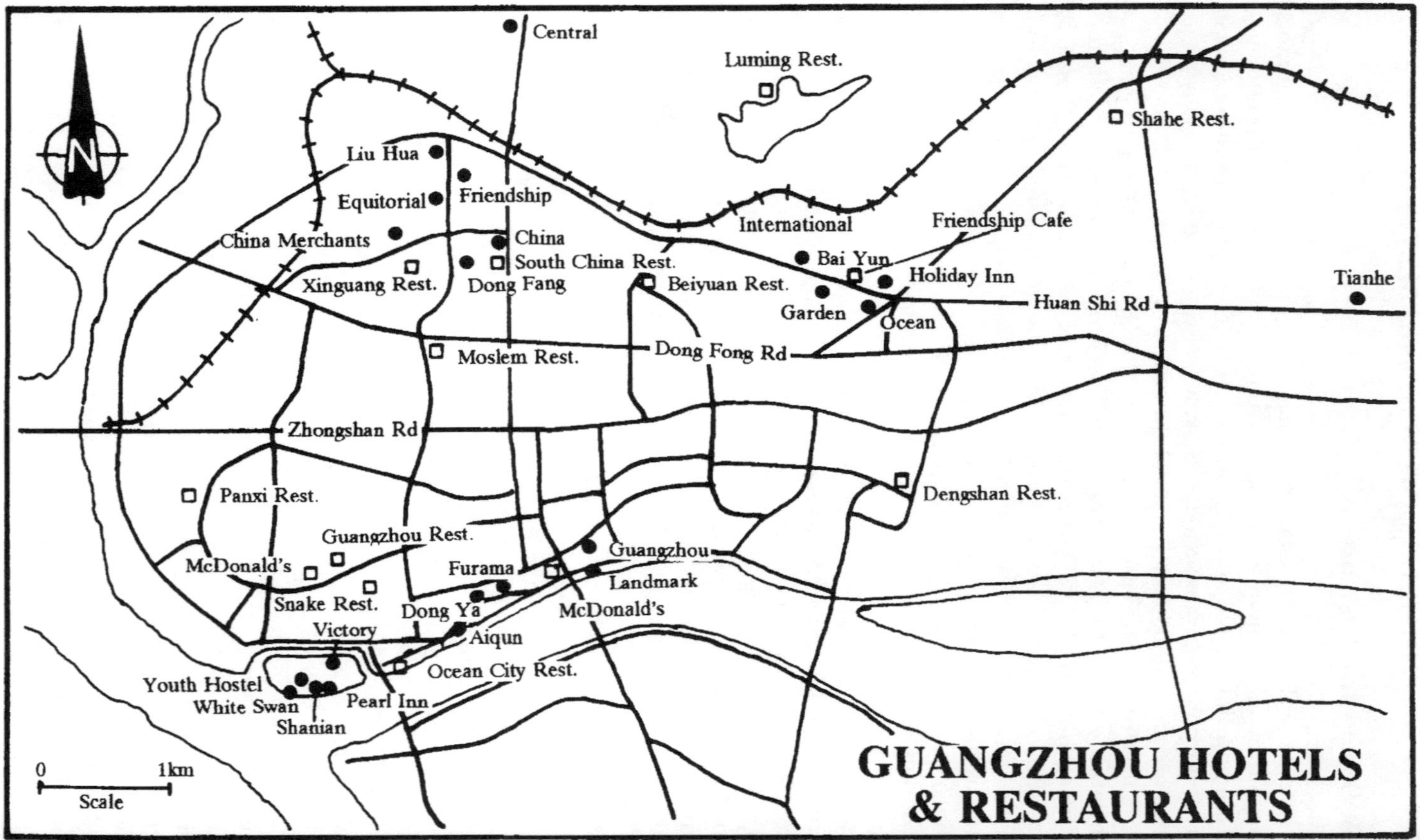
N
Central
Luming Rest.
Shahe Rest.
Liu Hua
Friendship
Equitorial
China Merchants
China
South China Rest.
Xinguang Rest.
Dong Fang
International
Friendship Cafe
Bai Yun
Holiday Inn
Beiyuan Rest.
Garden
Ocean
Huan Shi Rd
Tianhe
Moslem Rest.
Dong Fong Rd
Zhongshan Rd
Panxi Rest.
Dengshan Rest.
Guangzhou Rest.
McDonald's
Guangzhou
Furama
Landmark
Snake Rest.
Dong Ya
McDonald's
Victory
Aiqun
Ocean City Rest.
Youth Hostel
White Swan
Pearl Inn
Shanian
0
1km
Scale
GUANGZHOU HOTELS
& RESTAURANTS

is reasonably priced. The best idea is to walk around, look at a few menus, and make your own choice. All tend to be good.

Some of the hotels in this area have good restaurants. The revolving restaurant at the top of the Aiqun has quite good food and a great view. The **Dragon and Phoenix** in the Dong Ya serves excellent Chinese food. The Furama Palace has upmarket Cantonese cuisine.

As a contrast, the small **Pizza Den** has offerings from US$1.50, and there are many street food stalls offering almost anything that moves as an instant meal. This will cost even less.

Going farther east, there is a nice little "no name" restaurant with tables on the sidewalk; they will produce an English menu when pushed. Closeby is a **KFC** outlet for the best fried chicken in the area. The **Sheng Ji** restaurant is another choice or if you go farther you will find another McDonald's, by the traffic circle at the end of the Haizhu Bridge. The park outside the Landmark Hotel has more stalls for cheap noodles and rice, while inside the hotel, the **Landmark Club** has some of the best Western food around.

Shamian Island is also a happy hunting ground for the gourmet. Apart from the excellent restaurants at the White Swan Hotel, there is the excellent **Victory Restaurant** (highly recommended) on the corner of Shamian Dajie and Shamian 4-Jie, the restaurant in the Pearl Inn, and the Western restaurant in the recently opened section of the Guangdong Victory Hotel. Apart from the hotels, there is the very popular **Li Qin Restaurant** opposite the Victory, another Cantonese place just around the corner in Shamian Dajie, the **Lucy's Bar and Cafe** in Shamian Park, and another restaurant with no English name on Shamian Beijie between the two sections of the Victory Hotel. Best of all is the **Victory Cake Shop,** which has a wonderful selection of sweet delights at the best prices in town.

The **Xinguang Garden Restaurant** (Tel: 668-8928) is probably the most expensive place in town. It is situated in the center of a lake in Liuhua Park and is reached by decorative boat. I have never eaten here because I have been put off by stories of the prices, but those that have say it is a great experience. There is a wide choice of cuisine—Italian, Korean, French, Japanese, Chinese, and a rumored price tag of around US$300 for two. Check this with the locals before you go.

The **South China Restaurant,** in Jie Fang Road near the China Hotel, is not far from here. This is one of several popular, large, reasonably priced Cantonese restaurants that are found throughout the city. Another in the same category is the **Ocean Palace** near the Classical High Learning Academy. These restaurants cater mainly for local business people and wealthy families, and you will find that the food is good and the choice is vast. While you are in this area, look at the **Hasty Tasty Food Shop** at the China Hotel for Western-style fast food and pastries. Another place worth trying, if you are in the area, is the Friendship Cafe near the **Friendship Store** on Huan Shi Road.

Five other places have been recommended to me but I have not had the chance to try them myself. **Panxi Restaurant** (Tel: 881-5955), in Liwanhu Park on the western side of the city, is claimed to be the largest restaurant in the city. It is well known for its dim sum, which is served at all meals, and for its dumplings, although the menu is far wider than that. The **Muslim Restaurant** (Tel: 888-8991) on Zhong Shan Road at Renmin Road has been around for many years but the overpass has not added to its appeal. I'm told the food is good. I know nothing about the others apart from their names—**Beiyuan Restaurant** (Tel: 333-3365) at the big traffic circle on Yuexie Road at Xiaobei Road; **Dongshan Restaurant** on Nonglin Road in the east of the city; and **Luming Restaurant** in Luhu Park in the north. Readers who try them may like to give me some comments.

6. Sight-seeing

Guangzhou is a large sprawling city. Fortunately many of the major tourist attractions are reasonably close together in the area to the south of the main railway station. This is a good place to start your sight-seeing.

Yuexiu Park is the largest and most interesting park in the city. It is a good place to walk around as there is much to see and there are good roads and walking tracks to follow. This is the site of the large, impressive **Sculpture of the Five Rams,** which is the symbol of Guangzhou. Legend has it that long ago, five celestial beings came to the city riding through the air on rams. They carried five stems of rice, which they presented to the people with the claim that the area would be free from famine forever. The site for this event is said to be the Five Genies Temple (or Five Celestial Shrine), which is some distance from the park. The statue is much visited and photographed. It is a steep climb to the hilltop, so in hot weather the drinks stall does big business.

In the same general area of the park, you will find the **Guangzhou Museum,** housed in the Zhenhai Tower. The Tower was built in 1380 and was part of the old city wall. Today, this is one of only a few places where there is any evidence of this 15-kilometer-long wall that protected the city for centuries. The museum was established in 1929 and was one of the first in China. It contains a great number of historic relics and documents that show that this area has been populated for at least 5,000 years. The first town, called Panyu, was built here in the third century B.C. During the Tang and Song dynasties, Guangzhou became a major port known widely throughout the world. For two thousand years, it has been the political, economic, and cultural center of southern China. The city has been the cradle of revolution

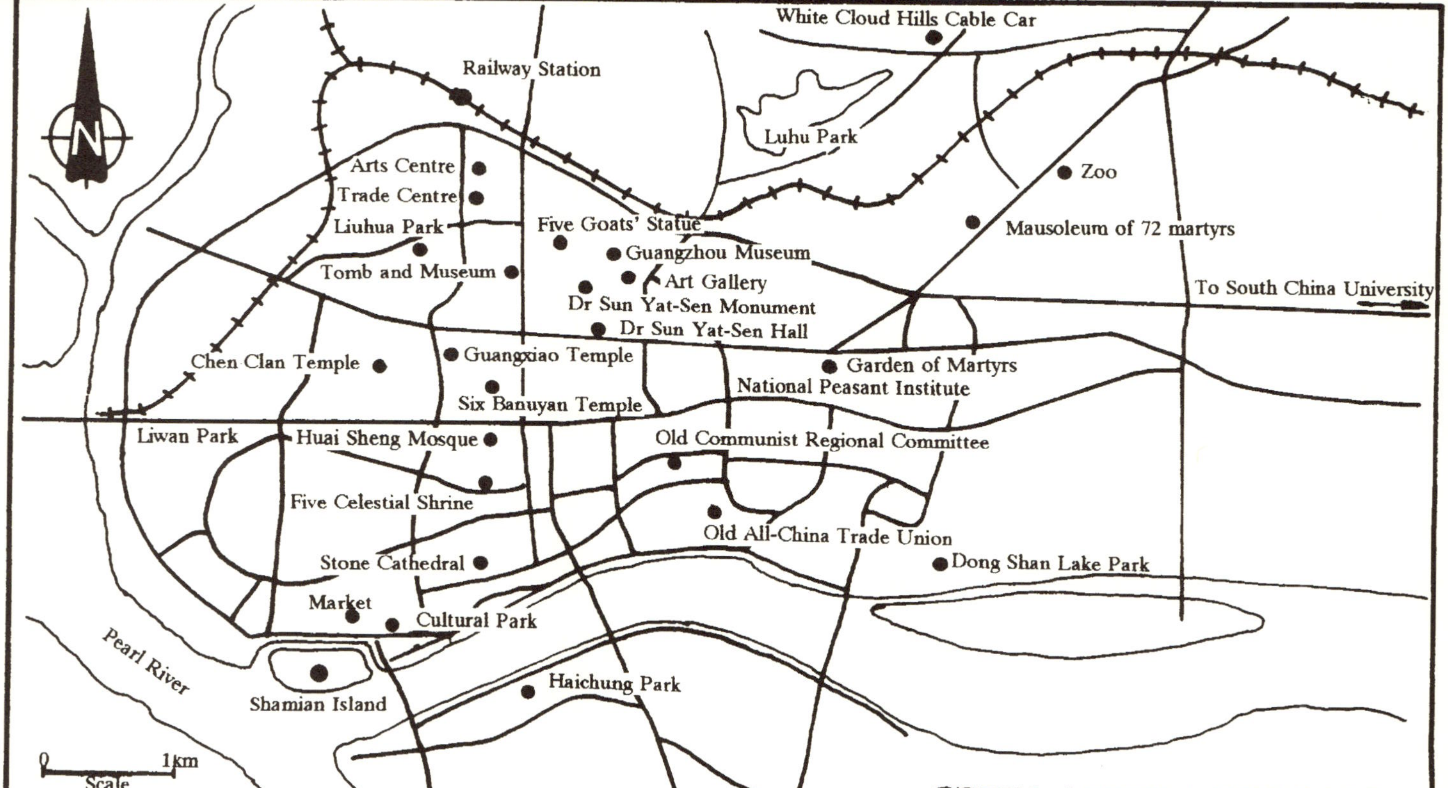

CITY ATTRACTIONS

in modern times. The Taiping Heavenly Kingdom Uprising, the Reform Movement of 1898, and the Revolution of 1911 all stemmed from Guangzhou. While at the museum, do not miss the ancient steles and iron cannons on display outside the building.

The park has several other places worth seeing. The **Monument to Dr. Sun Yat-sen** is a granite obelisk that provides a good view from the top. The **Guangzhou Art Gallery** is housed in a building next to the old wall. The 40,000-seat **People's Stadium** is a large venue for soccer and other outdoor sports, while there is also a swimming pool, indoor sports' ground, badminton courts, and two lakes for boating.

There are three attractions close-by that are outside the park. First there is the **Orchid Garden.** This is beautiful in summer when there are more than a hundred varieties on display. There is a lake and a tearoom and a nice atmosphere. Opposite the southern end of the park is the excellent **Museum of the Western Han Dynasty, Mausoleum of the Nanyue King.** The modern museum is built on the site of the tomb of the second king of the Nanyue Kingdom. You can visit the tomb for a small fee and there are many artifacts and English explanations in the museum. Do not miss it.

The third site is the spectacular **Dr. Sun Yat-sen Memorial Hall** on Dong Feng Road. This was built in 1930 on the site of the residence used by Sun Yat-sen when he became the president of the Republic of China. The spectacular Chinese-style, octagonal building houses a large auditorium seating around 3,000. Visitors can wander around and even go on to the stage to see some of the items of interest. It is surrounded by lawns and gardens and there is a souvenir shop with some excellent, but highly priced, paintings and arts and crafts.

You now have to move to other parts of the city to continue with your sight-seeing. Head south across Dong Feng Road and you will reach **Guangxiao Temple** on Hongshu Road. This has been the site of a temple for 1,600 years, although the present buildings are from the seventeenth century. This is a very important temple for some Buddhists and it is interesting to see as a tourist. The grounds are attractive and there are always people around, but it does not feel as if you are being overwhelmed by other sightseers.

Not far from here is the very interesting **Six Banyan Temple.** This has become a major tourist attraction, so at times you will share it with several busloads of other tourists. It seems that this has been a temple site for around 1,500 years, but none of the present buildings date from that time. The temple was given its name in the twelfth century by Su Dong Po, a famous calligrapher. He was so impressed by the temple and the six banyan trees in the courtyard that he scripted two large characters for six banyans. Within the compound you will find several temples and shrines. One houses

Dr. Sun Yat-sen Memorial Hall. (Courtesy of the China Service Tourist Company)

Guangxiao Temple. (Courtesy of the China Service Tourist Company)

three large Buddha statues while another has a statue of the monk, Hui Neng, who was worshipped here 1,000 years ago. The highlight for most visitors is the 57-meter-high, octagonal **Flower Pagoda.** You can climb to the top of this and have great views of the compound and the wider city.

Off to the west, is another attraction. During the days of the dynasties, entry into the elite world was dependent on passing a nationwide examination set by the authorities in Beijing. Several Chinese clans established schools so that their families could study and pass these examinations and so gain power within the establishment. The Chen clan established their **Classical Learning Academy** in Guangzhou in 1890. Now it is a folk and arts museum, and a very interesting place to visit. The Academy comprises nineteen buildings and a number of courtyards. All the buildings are decorated with stone carvings, wood carvings, brick carvings, ceramic sculptures, and iron castings. The result is most impressive. It is a paradise for photographers and visitors interested in sculpture and casting.

Still going south, the **Huai Sheng Mosque** is on Guangta Road to the east of Ren Min Road. It is believed that the first building to be erected on this site was in the seventh century when the first Muslim missionary to China established a mosque here. The present buildings are reasonably modern. Inside the compound is a smooth minaret of unusual design.

It is a kilometer farther south to the **Stone House Cathedral,** or the Sacred Heart Church, on Yide Road. This is an imitation of a European Gothic cathedral designed by a French architect in the second half of the nineteenth century. The area was leased to the French after the second Opium War and the signing of the Sino-French Tianjin Treaty. Construction took almost twenty-five years, with many of the interior items coming from France. The church was closed for some time but it now has masses each Sunday.

The area to the east and west of Ren Min Nan Road is the best place to look at Guangzhou's eclectic architecture. Many buildings date from the turn of the century or the twenties and thirties, and were built by rich Chinese returning from overseas. They imitated the styles of the West or mixed these styles with traditional Chinese architecture. Since Art Deco was in vogue at that time, Guangzhou has splendid examples of this style. In this area, you will probably see more Art Deco facades, more Ionic columns, more gables and pediments than anywhere else in China. Often they are viewed through the twisted trunks of ancient banyan trees.

There are several interesting places west of Ren Min Nan Road. The **Cultural Park** on Liu Er San Road is a combination garden, fun fair, museum, and entertainment complex. There are some excellent flower displays at various times of the year. You have to pay admission to enter but it is worth dropping in, particularly in the evening, when you might catch a Chinese opera, film show, or acrobatic display.

It is just a short walk to the **Qingping Free Market.** This started in 1979

A craftsman hand carving a stone lion statue.

when private enterprise was once again allowed in China. It has now developed into the largest and most prosperous market in the city. There is a wide range of goods on sale—meat, game, poultry, vegetables, fruit, flowers, bonsai, souvenirs, and antiques. You will be fascinated, or horrified, at the variety of live animals that are available here, all intended for the table. There are monkeys, snakes, lizards, tortoises, owls, frogs, dogs, raccoons, and so on. The market operates from about 6 A.M. to 7 P.M.

Across the other side of Liu Er San Road is **Shamian Island.** This is perhaps the most attractive section of Guangzhou, with the whole island still having much European color and atmosphere. It is a great place to explore at night because of its hotels, restaurants, and nightlife, all attractively lit amid lawns and trees. The island was little more than a sandspit when foreign traders were given permission to set up their warehouses here some 250 years ago. The island became a British and French concession after the Opium Wars and this is when many of the Colonial-style buildings were built. The White Swan Hotel and the American Consulate have prime riverfront positions and there are two churches, several hotels, restaurants, some night spots, two parks, and residential buildings on other parts of the island. You should not miss a visit here.

There are at least two other places that should not be missed. The **Mausoleum of the 72 Martyrs** is on Yellow Flower Hill on Xianli Road in the northeast part of the city. This was built in memory of the victims of the unsuccessful insurrection of April 1911. The uprising had been planned by a group of Chinese organizations led by Sun Yat-sen that opposed the Qing dynasty. Although this attempt failed, the Qing dynasty collapsed in October 1911 and a Republic of China was declared. The main memorial was built in 1918 with money collected from Chinese people around the world. The surrounding gardens are very attractive and several hours can be spent wandering around. There are food and souvenir stalls and a nice lake.

The **Memorial Garden to the Martyrs** is south of here on Zhong Shan Road. During 1927, communists in various parts of China staged uprisings against the Chiang Kai-shek government. These were suppressed by the Kuomintang troops, with the loss of many lives. The present government claims that around 6,000 people died in Guangzhou and that this site was one of the execution grounds. The garden is attractive with pavilions, broad paths, a lake, and nicely arranged flower gardens.

Enthusiasts and political students may wish to visit some of the other sites, but they will have limited appeal to most visitors. A few years ago, the government was giving great emphasis to the Peasant Movement Institute where early members of the Communist party were trained; to the original site of the Regional Committee of the Communist Party in Guangzhou; and to the original site of the All-China Federation of Trade Unions. Now these hardly rate a mention as far as most visitors are concerned.

It is appropriate to mention the **Canton Trade Fair** at this point. This is actually known as the Chinese Export Commodities Fair and it is of vital interest to business people conducting trade with China. The fair is held twice a year in April and October and it is the biggest event in the city. During the fair, hotel prices skyrocket and transportation can be a problem. If you are not visiting the fair, you should avoid Guangzhou during this period. For interest, you can see the exhibition hall at the corner of Ren Min Road and Liu Hua Road.

The **White Cloud Hills** is a popular area on the northern outskirts of the city. This is a large area of park, forest, and some development that is attractive if you need to get away from the crowds of the city. Buses operate from a terminal just to the west of Children's Park in the central city or you can take a taxi to the cable station at the bottom of the hills. The highest point in the hills is only about 380 meters high and this is difficult to reach, but nevertheless there are some good views on a clear day from several locations, including the well-known Cheng Precipice. The hills have many walking trails, tearooms for rest breaks, and some lawns and garden areas. The latest attraction is a large bird sanctuary near the top station of the cable car.

There are two amusement parks in the general direction of the hills. The Oriental Amusement Park (Dong Fang) has been updated recently with a huge new roller coaster and other attractions. It is being heavily promoted but has more appeal to the locals than visitors. Farther out, the Nanhu Amusement Park is similar, but the area is much more picturesque and during the week it is pleasant to sit by the side of the lake.

SOUTHEAST TO SHENZHEN

Guangzhou is linked to Shenzhen and Hong Kong by railway and highway. This corridor is being developed rapidly, often with total disregard for the environment, and with insufficient planning and infrastructure development. In some ways this area appears to be almost out of control, as rich agricultural land and attractive hills are being transformed into flat dust bowls with endless factories and residential developments, some of which are clearly not being used. Parts of the region are an environmental disaster but some people are becoming instant millionaires in the process. I assume they will leave here as soon as they can.

The new super-highway was not fully open when I last visited but large sections were being used. This has halved the travel time between Guangzhou and Shenzhen and means you can do the trip in about two hours. The main toll road, which has tollbooths at regular intervals, goes through Zen Cheng, a dreary industrial center; Guongchen; and the slightly more attractive Dongguan. Tourists are unlikely to want to stay in any of these places but they may be convenient for business people with interests in this region. Hotels, restaurants, and nightlife have improved dramatically in recent years. In Dongguan, try the large Royal Garden Hotel or the smaller and cheaper Jade Hotel. The huge Palace Nightclub is currently one of the "in" places in town.

An alternate route, which involves a major ferry crossing and the possibility of major delays, is via **Lotus Mountain** and Humen. Lotus Mountain is an interesting place well worth a visit. This was originally a quarry several hundred years ago but it has eroded and revegetated to the point that it looks quite natural. Over the years, pathways have been cut into the cliffs and pagodas and pavilions have been built. The result today is a huge rock garden with walks, good views over the Pearl River, gorges, lotus ponds, restaurants, and accommodation options. You can reach here by boat from Tianzi Pier near the Landmark Hotel in Guangzhou, by bus from near the Guangzhou railway station, or on organized day tours.

Humen is a small city on the east bank of the Pearl River. In 1839 the Commissioner of Canton, Lin Zexu, decided to try to stop the opium trade. His forces surrounded the British in Guangzhou and forced them to hand over 20,000 bags of opium, which were publicly destroyed in Humen. This lead to the first Opium War and to the establishment of Hong Kong. The destruction of the opium is commemorated at a fine museum at Bogue Fort in Humen. This is the only major attraction here.

Shenzhen is an amazing place. It is the nearest Chinese city to Hong Kong and it copies its neighbor at every opportunity. The surrounding area is called a Special Economic Zone, where China plays at capitalism. Since it was created in 1980, this zone has boomed in an amazing way. There is more construction underway here than anywhere else I have ever seen. It has brought with it many problems, but Chinese people are lining up in droves to move here. The problem has become so acute that the Chinese authorities have been forced to erect a major fence on the northern boundary of the zone and install check points where foreigners have to produce passports and locals special permits before they are allowed into the area.

Much of the development is fueled by Hong Kong money taking advantage of the relatively cheap land and labor costs. Developers have also erected several luxury resorts that attract Hong Kong people on weekends. Downtown Shenzhen is almost indistinguishable from the Hong Kong New Towns. High-rise hotels, office blocks, and sparkling shopping centers are thronged with people. The roads are crowded with luxury cars and few bicycles. Hong Kong dollars is the currency of choice. You need to remind yourself at regular intervals that this is actually China. It is about as different from the small inland rural villages as you could possibly imagine. This, of course, is one of its problems. It is creating two Chinas.

Shenzhen is actually the name of three different identities—the city adjacent to the Hong Kong border; the Special Economic Zone, which is roughly an area 40 kilometers by 8 kilometers; and the district that extends well outside the S.E.Z. The city has some interesting buildings, such as the International Trade Center, the Tain An International Center, the railway station, and some of the hotels. The railway station has a tourist information center; the Tain An Center has good shopping, including a Dickson Store and a branch of the exclusive Harvey Nichols from Knightsbridge, England. There are several parks, but these will have limited tourist appeal.

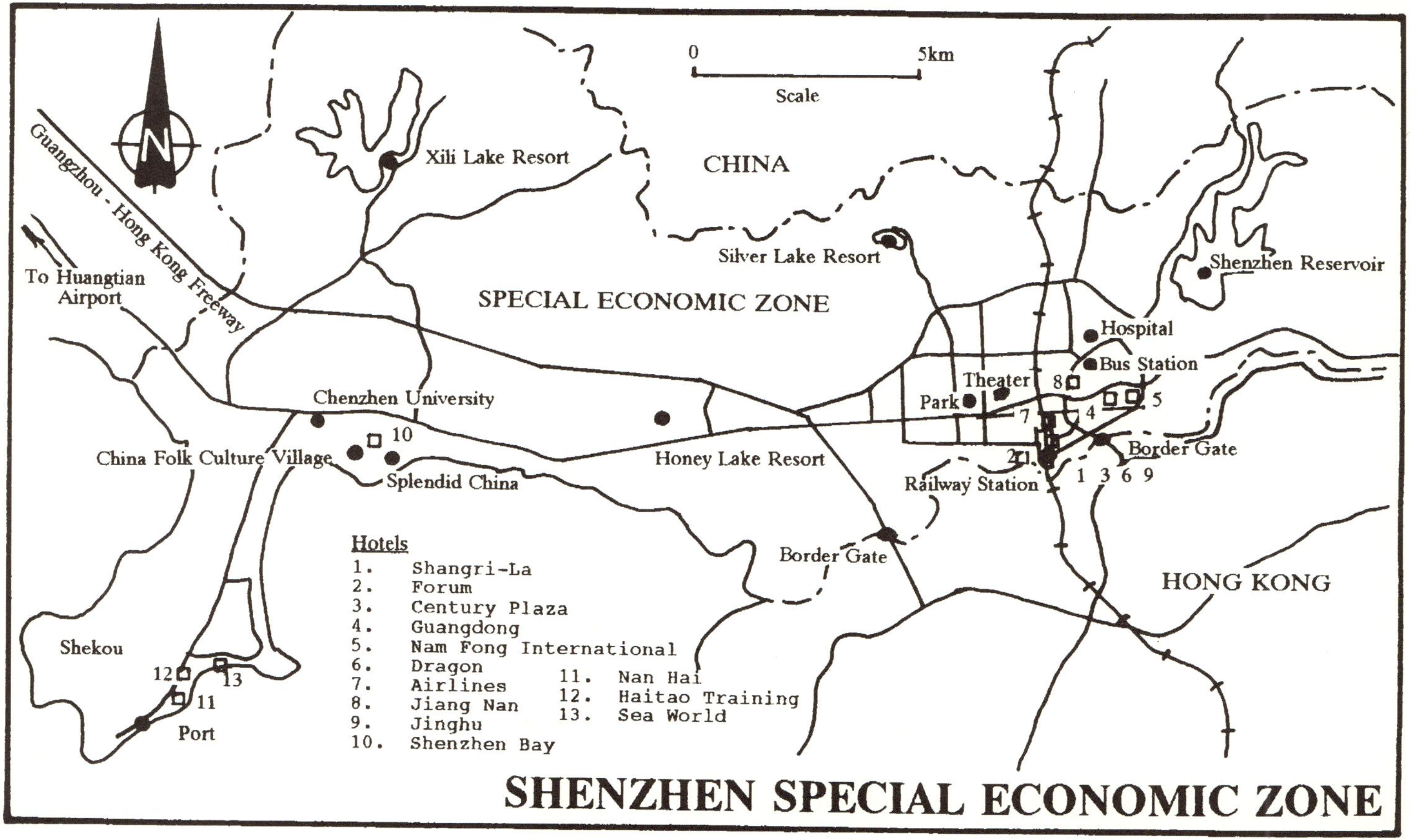
N
0
5km
Scale
CHINA
Xili Lake Resort
Guangzhou - Hong Kong Freeway
To Huangtian Airport
Silver Lake Resort
Shenzhen Reservoir
SPECIAL ECONOMIC ZONE
Hospital
Bus Station
Theater
Park
Chenzhen University
China Folk Culture Village
Splendid China
Honey Lake Resort
Border Gate
Railway Station
Border Gate
HONG KONG
Shekou
Port
Hotels
1. Shangri-La
2. Forum
3. Century Plaza
4. Guangdong
5. Nam Fong International
6. Dragon
7. Airlines
8. Jiang Nan
9. Jinghu
10. Shenzhen Bay
11. Nan Hai
12. Haitao Training
13. Sea World
SHENZHEN SPECIAL ECONOMIC ZONE

There are several top-quality hotels that will be welcomed by business people. Top of the heap is the classy **Shangri-La Hotel** (Tel: 233-0888), 553 rooms, near the railway station. This has four bars and restaurants, including the revolving Tiara Restaurant, where an excellent buffet is served with the panoramic view. There is an executive horizon floor with its own check-in facilities and a lounge serving cocktails. Other facilities include a business center with multilingual staff and Shenzhen's finest health club with outdoor pool and smart gymnasium surrounded by gardens. Room rates start at single HK$950 and double HK$1,100. (Book with the Shangri-La organization in the United States and Canada, Tel: 1-800-942-5050; in the United Kingdom, Tel: 81-747-8485; in Australia, Tel: 1-800-222-448, or fax the hotel on 86-755-223-9878.)

Next in line is the **Forum Hotel** (Tel: 558-6333), 541 rooms, operated by Inter-Contenental Hotels. This is a fine international hotel with excellent facilities including three specialist restaurants, two bars, a business center, an outdoor swimming pool, and health club. Room rates are from HK$730. (Book with Intercontinental Hotels in the United States and Canada on Tel: 1-800-327-0200; in the United Kingdom, Tel: 0-345-581-444; in Australia, 1-800-221-335; or fax the hotel on 86755-556-1700.) The 428-room **Century Plaza Hotel** (Tel: 222-0888) is in a similar category. Choose from the Jade Garden; Miyako, a Japanese restaurant; the Century Chaozhou Restaurant; or Seasons for Western and Asian food. There are two bars, a business center, a disco, and an executive floor. Room rates are from HK$740. (Book with the hotel at Kin Chit Road, Shenzhen; Fax: 86755-223-4060.)

The Landmark Hotel (Tel: 217-2288), 351 rooms, is the newest hotel to open in the city. It has a pool; health center; lounge bar; Cantonese, Chiu Chow, and Western restaurants; a business center; entertainment center; and executive floors. Room rates are from US$130. (Book with the hotel at 2 Nanhu Rd., Shenzhen; Fax: 86755-229-0473.)

There are several other places with good facilities and lower prices. The **Guang Dong Hotel** (Tel: 222-8339), 207 rooms, has nice rooms with all facilities; a business center; and Cantonese, Japanese, and Western restaurants. It also has a nightclub, a health center, and a shopping arcade. Room prices are a good value from HK$430. (Book with the hotel at Shennan Road East; Fax: 86755-223-4560.) You will find the **Nam Fong International Hotel** (Tel: 225-6728), 250 rooms, on the same road but a few blocks farther east. Facilities and prices are almost identical to the Guang Dong. One thing that distinguishes this hotel is the interior decoration of some of the restaurants and bars. See for yourself and make up your own mind. (Book with the hotel at Shennan Road East; Fax: 86755-225-6936.)

The **Dragon Hotel** (Tel: 222-9228) is situated within the modern railway station. The rooms are good and there are two restaurants, a nightclub, and a karaoke room. This would be an ideal location if you were travelling between Guangzhou and Hong Kong by train and wanted a break in Shenzhen. Room rates start at HK$340. (Book with the hotel on Fax: 86755-220-5664.) Perhaps the **Airlines Hotel** (Tel: 223-7999), at 130 Shennan Rd. East, is the best value in town at the moment. Room prices start at HK$280. Rooms are a little small, but they have all the facilities and there are three restaurants and a nightclub. There is an air ticket booking office in the hotel and coaches to and from the airport. (Book on Fax: 86755-223-7866.)

Going slightly downmarket, we come to the attractive **Jiang Nan Hotel** (Tel: 222-8182), 100 rooms. This is slightly away from the center of town but is still within walking distance of the shopping area. Rooms are acceptable and there are restaurants, a business center, and a nightclub/karaoke center. Try the bodysonic music massage chairs. Room prices start at HK$270. (Book with the hotel at 18 Dongmen C Rd.; Fax: 86755-220-2557.) The **Jinghu Hotel,** on Ren Min Nan Road not far from the railway station, has some single rooms at around HK$150 for those travelling alone.

The downtown area has several restaurants, but none are a particularly good value. Food Street, which runs off Shennan Dong Road almost opposite the Guang Dong Hotel, and Cunfeng Road east of Ren Min are two good locations for lower-priced restaurants. There is a McDonald's close to Food Street and another about two kilometers east on Shennan Zhong Road.

If you have no business interests in Shenzhen, there are still two good reasons to visit. The first is the **China Folk Culture Villages** and the second is **Splendid China**. In 1995, these will be joined by **Splendid World.** All are along Shennan Road about 15 kilometers west of downtown. I must confess that I went to the Culture Villages (Tel: 660-1106) expecting little. "This is a large tourist center where folk arts, culture and architecture of China's various nationalities are assembled in one area," says the tourist literature. I read this to mean "boring." I was wrong. I came away quite impressed. There are small villages where you can see something of the lifestyle of China's ethnic nationalities. There are song and dance performances by professional artists and there is some stunning architecture. You need several hours to appreciate this large attraction.

Splendid China is operated by the same company as a separate but adjacent attraction. It claims to be the world's largest miniature scenic spot, and this could be correct. Certainly it takes several hours to wind your way around one-fifteenth scale models of many of China's highlights. You see everything from the Great Wall, through life-size Terracotta Figures of horses and soldiers from the Qinling Mausoleum, to the Potala Palace of Tibet and the Stone Forest of southwest China. I found Splendid China very interesting but somewhat cold, particularly after the people-orientated Cultural Villages. I would do them in reverse order next time.

The other attraction to some people (particularly those from Hong Kong) is the resorts that have been built in the area. The only one that I have stayed in is the **Shenzhen Bay Hotel** (Tel: 660-0111), 308 rooms, next to the Cultural Villages. This is a modern property with good restaurants and a large outdoor area with wave pool, massage pool, swimming pool, and tennis courts. It hardly rates as one of the world's great resorts, however. Room rates are from HK$550. (Book with the hotel on Fax: 86755-660-0139.) **Honey Lake Country Club** (Tel: 674-5061) is a few kilometers back towards Shenzhen downtown. It is being heavily promoted in Hong Kong as a getaway location but I do not think it is particularly great. There is a huge, run-down amusement park as part of the development, complete with several roller coasters, go-cart track, castle, and monorail. Room rates are from HK$240 weekdays and HK$350 on weekends. The **Xiameisha Beach Resort** to the east of downtown has its supporters and this is the best beach in the area; however, do not expect a tropical paradise. None of these places will have great appeal to international visitors.

The town of **Shekou** is perhaps worth a quick look. This is a place that has gone from a small settlement to a booming town in just ten years. It is the main port for the region and a growing industrial zone. There are fast ferry connections to both Hong Kong Central and Kowloon (about 45 minutes). Moored near the town center is a ship called the *Minghua*, now used as the Sea World Hotel, restaurant, and nightclub. Closer to the Ferry Terminal is the **Haitao Training Hotel** (Tel: 668-1688), 35 rooms, from HK$380. It has a good Chinese restaurant. Close-by is the five-star **Nan Hai Hotel** (Tel: 669-2888), 396 rooms. The approach to the hotel is narrow and crowded but once inside, the facilities are excellent. The rooms are modern and well kept. The Penthouse Grill Room, the Hai Xu Chinese restaurant, and the coffee shop offer a good food choice. The Club Tropicana is a popular night venue. Room rates are from HK$500 single and HK$700 double. (Book with the hotel on Fax: 86755-669-2440.) The town has several good restaurants including the Casablanca Italian restaurant and the Pattaya Thai Restaurant.

SOUTH TO ZHUHAI

There are several roads to the south of Guangzhou. One leads to Foshan (about 30 kilometers) and then on to the Xiqiao Hills. **Foshan** is a market town and a trade, religious, and handicraft center. It is still a good place to buy pottery, cast-metal souvenirs, silk, and papercuttings. Foshan is famous for its **Ancestors' Temple.** The present building dates from about A.D. 1400 and is built entirely of timber without the use of nails. The temple contains a large bronze statue of the Northern or Black Emperor, a god who rules over water and everything in it. In the courtyard there is a pool with a statue of a turtle. There are various other old items in the temple and adjacent buildings.

The **Xiqiao Hills** are about 40 kilometers outside town. There are caves, waterfalls, and rocky peaks. There are several interesting old villages on the higher areas that can be reached by stone paths. There will be few other foreigners here but you will be welcome to wander around. Buses are available from the Foshan bus station or there are tours from Guangzhou.

Foshan has a good selection of accommodations, including the upmarket Foshan Hotel and the equally fancy Golden City Hotel, both close to Ancestors' Temple. The high-rise Rotating Palace Hotel is north of here near the center of town, while the much cheaper Pearl River Hotel is just across the street.

There is a road from here to **Shunde,** or an alternative road direct from Guangzhou. The Shunde area was once considered an attractive location because of its hills and country atmosphere, but both are rapidly disappearing. I do not know why international visitors would choose to stay here but if you do, the well-run Century Hotel (Tel: 293-333), 262 rooms, provides good luxury accommodation in a resort setting for HK$500 a night. There is a direct ferry service to Hong Kong from Shunde that takes 135 minutes.

The next major point on your route south is **Zhongshan City,** sometimes called **Shiqi,** about 85 kilometers from Guangzhou. This is another industrial city experiencing rapid growth. Although this is touted as the hometown of Dr. Sun Yat-sen, there is little tourist interest here. The large modern hotels you see in the city are catering to business people with interests in the area. As you pass through, it is worth stopping to see the **Sun Yat-sen Memorial Hall** and to visit forested Zhongshan Park with its pagoda. The attractive Fu Hua Hotel (Tel: 861-338), 400 rooms, has a central position overlooking the Qi Jiang River and two large floating restaurants. The rooms are good and there are restaurant options, a bank, shopping arcade, swimming pool, bowling alley, sauna, disco, health club, and garden. Rates are from HK$460. (Book with the hotel on Fax: 867-654-861-862.) The nearby Zhongshan International Hotel (Tel: 873-388), 369 rooms, is almost a carbon copy of facilities and price. As well as the same recreational facilities, both have revolving restaurants and business facilities. (Book with the hotel on Fax: 867-654-861-862.) Zhongshan City has direct jetcat services with Hong Kong. It takes about 105 minutes for the trip.

The old home of Dr. Sun Yat-sen is in **Cuiheng** town, about 15 kilometers southeast of Zhongshan City. This is a big deal to the Chinese; the first time I went there I expected to be let down. I was not. Subsequent visits have proved that this place is interesting and worth a visit. Dr. Sun Yat-sen is China's most famous revolutionary. He was born on this site in 1866, but not in this house. The museum is well presented and you see some interesting memorabilia as you wander around the house. Adjacent buildings house an extension of the museum, where there are other things of interest.

Sun Yat-sen is widely regarded as the father of modern China. He dedicated much of his life to the overthrow of the Qing dynasty and the establishment of a republic based on Western democratic principles, and so he spent much of his life in exile. He briefly served as the first president of the Republic of China but died of cancer in 1925 without being convinced that he had yet achieved his complete goal. In a recorded speech in 1924 he said, "If, by following the way and doctrine of the three principles of the people, we devote ourselves to the salvation of our country with one heart and one mind, we can certainly turn China from weakness to strength and from poverty to richness. She will then keep up with the big powers in the world today."

It is twenty kilometers from here to the **Chung Shan Hot Spring Resort** (Tel: 683-888), with its rooms and villas. This is a popular low-rise resort set amongst rock gardens and lakes. All rooms and villas are adequately equipped and there is running spring water in all the bathrooms. Facilities include a good, well-priced Chinese restaurant, a Western restaurant, a pool, tennis courts, and a disco. The adjacent Arnold Palmer-designed Chung Shan Golf Course is one of the best in China. It has its own proshop, clubhouse, sauna, and tennis courts. Rooms are from HK$220. (Book with the hotel on Fax: 867-654- 683-333.)

Not far south of here, you enter the **Zhuhai Special Economic Zone.** There is frantic development here just as there is in Shenzhen, but overall it is a more relaxed place than Shenzhen and you can actually enjoy yourself while you wander around. You will find that there are beaches, parks, and a good atmosphere; and the prices are less than in either Hong Kong or Macau. As you come in from the north, you will arrive first at an area known as **Xiangzhou** district. This is where you first encounter the beach, but you will be better off travelling a little farther to Jida district.

The **Jida** district has nice beaches, parks, and resorts and direct ferry connections to Hong Kong and Shenzhen. The beach at Haibin Park has been developed for visitors and is very popular on weekends. The **Zhonglu Hotel** (Tel: 332-208) within the park is a bit run-down but rates are attractive from HK$160. Just west of here is an area known as **Shi Ching Shan Tourist Centre.** This provides a hotel, shopping facilities, parks and gardens, sporting facilities, and walking opportunities. The hotel (Tel: 333-518) is at the base of Rocky Scenery Hill. If you climb to the top, through massive granite boulders, you are rewarded with excellent views over Zhuhai and on to Macau. There is boating on the lake, a golf course, tennis courts, and a shooting range. The hotel has a pool, business center, two restaurants, and a discotheque. Room rates are from HK$300.

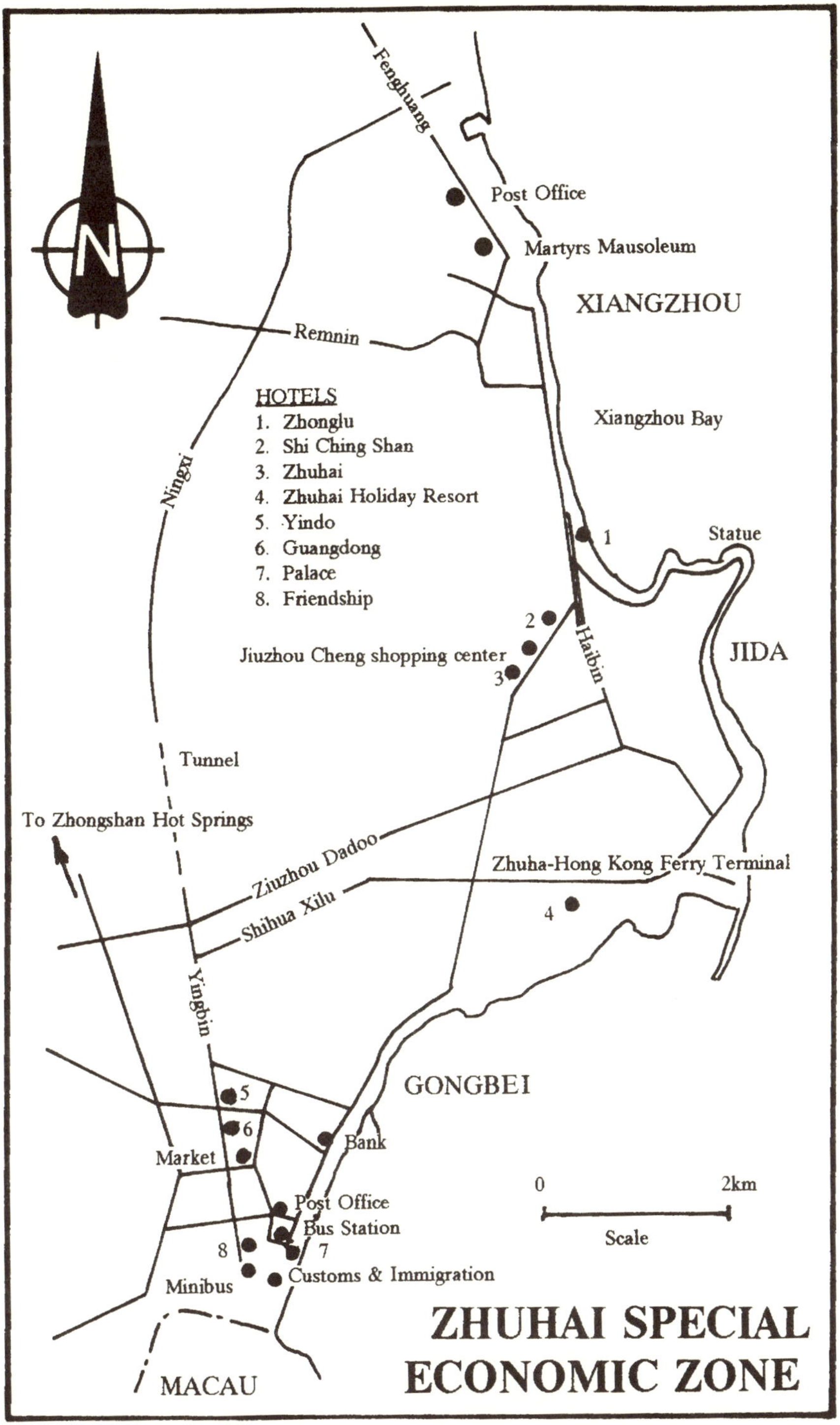

Fenghuang
Post Office
Martyrs Mausoleum
XIANGZHOU
Remnin
HOTELS
1. Zhonglu
2. Shi Ching Shan
3. Zhuhai
4. Zhuhai Holiday Resort
5. Yindo
6. Guangdong
7. Palace
8. Friendship
Xiangzhou Bay
Ningxi
Statue
Haibin
Jiuzhou Cheng shopping center
JIDA
Tunnel
To Zhongshan Hot Springs
Ziuzhou Dadoo
Zhuha-Hong Kong Ferry Terminal
Shihua Xilu
Yingbin
GONGBEI
Bank
Market
Post Office
Bus Station
0
2km
Scale
Customs & Immigration
Minibus
MACAU
ZHUHAI SPECIAL ECONOMIC ZONE

A short distance south is the distinctive Jiuzhou Cheng shopping center. This has grand architecture, terraces, lakes, and courtyards but I suspect it has seen better days. Shopping will have little appeal here but it is worth a quick look for its atmosphere. Next door is the low-rise **Zhuhai Hotel** (Tel: 333-718), 340 rooms and 6 villas. This is a well-run property built around lovely gardens and lakes. There is a pool, tennis court, billiard room, sauna, gymnasium, business center, two restaurants, karaoke, and a shopping mall. Room rates are from HK$400.

There is a nice drive around the coast to the **Zhuhai Holiday Resort**. You pass some small beaches, interesting rocky areas, and a sea statue that is drawing locals and visitors for photographs. The Resort Hotel (Tel: 332-038), 363 rooms and 87 villas, is on a large beachfront site. The facilities are extensive and on a summer weekend the place really swings. Midweek in winter is a different story. There are two restaurants, a coffee shop, bars, disco, bowling center, billiards, sauna and massage, tennis, swimming pool, roller-skating ground, horseback riding, shooting, archery. go-cart racing, and boating. Room rates are from HK$410, with villas from HK$1,380. Direct ferry services to Hong Kong are available from the adjacent harbor.

It is just a short drive to the **Gongbei** district, adjacent to the Macau border. This area has many restaurants and shops and is a good area to explore before you leave China. You will notice that many Macau people come here to shop because prices are lower than across the border. There is some nightlife here and some visitors may like to see the market. In the last three years, several top quality hotels have appeared in this area. They are primarily aiming at the business but it could be a good idea to spend a night here before crossing into Macau.

Three excellent hotels are the swanky **Yindo** (Tel: 883-388), 319 rooms; the equally impressive **Guangdong** (Tel: 888-128), 309 rooms; and the slightly older **Gongbei Palace** (Tel: 886-833). The Palace is on the waterfront but there is no beach, so there is little to pick between them for position. The Yindo has a fine range of sporting facilities, including swimming pool, bowling center, tennis, gymnasium, and minigolf. All have restaurants and nightlife. (Book with the hotels on Yindo, Fax: 86756-883-311; Guangdong, Fax: 86756-885-063; and Palace, Fax: 86756-885-686.) For something a bit downmarket, the Friendship Hotel, at the border gate, has rooms from around HK$120. There is an excellent food street behind the Yindo Hotel.

From here it is over the border to Macau.

7. Guided Tours

I have found it difficult to find independent tour operators in Guangzhou, outside those operating in the major hotels. Most people end up using the hotel tour company for their sight-seeing. Typical tours are half-day and full-day tours of the city, day tours to Foshan and to Lotus Mountain, and a two-day tour to Zhaoqing.

A typical half-day tour visits the Chen Clan Temple, the Qingping Market, Dr. Sun Yat-sen Memorial Hall, and the Guangzhou Museum. This costs around HK$170.

A day tour will do this, then add the Five Rams statue, a jade carving factory, the Six Banyan Temple, and the Mausoleum of the 72 Martyrs. This costs around HK$350.

The one-day, out-of-town tours cost around HK$400. The two-day trip to Zhaoqing, which includes a visit to the Seven-Star Crags, Dinghu Mountain, Qing Yun Temple, Feishui Waterfall, and overnight at the Songtao Hotel, is around HK$800. Trips will operate with as few as two passengers.

8. Culture

Every tourist visit to China that contains any element of organized sight-seeing, will automatically contain some cultural element. The Chinese government is obsessed with showing visitors collective farms, kindergartens, model villages, and so forth even though most visitors are not the slightest bit interested in these things, which have even become outdated in China. In most cases these visits are meaningless and have little to do with current Chinese life.

Up until recently there was also a push to try and immerse visitors in the political history of the Communist party, but this seems to have become less mandatory as touring options have opened up. Maybe officials have realized that visitors are interested in understanding the culture and life of China, but that they turn off when it is forced on them.

Most visits to tourist attractions in Guangzhou are a history and culture experience. Visitors who arrive without knowing about Dr. Sun Yat-sen will leave with a fair idea of his life, work, and principles just by visiting his home in Cuiheng, his memorial in Yuexiu Park, and his Memorial Hall on Dong Feng Road. Those with no knowledge of twentieth-century Chinese history will know much after visiting the Memorial Garden to the Martyrs, the Mausoleum of the 72 Martyrs, and the Chen Clan Temple.

The culture of modern China can be best seen on the streets. Walk through the **Qingping Market,** see the luxury cars on the streets, understand that there are restaurants in the city that no ordinary Westerner could ever afford, be surprised at the number of beggars on the sidewalks, see the homeless camped out on the square in front of the railway station, walk through the shopping centers and marvel at the range of goods available, watch as gleaming skyscrapers replace crumbling tenements. China cannot be conveniently packaged as poor, repressed, or whatever. It is a complex society coming to grips with the realities of the world. In the process some people are becoming millionaires, some are suffering, some are losing their power, and new power groups are emerging.

But all the old ways are not being rejected. Visit one of the temples and you will see young and old praying together. There is a renewed interest in the old history of the country. There is some evidence too, that the civil rights so dear to Dr. Sun Yat-sen are slowly returning.

There are one or two practical cultural items that are worth mentioning. Public toilets are available at railway stations, in some parks, and in public buildings but few have English signs and none provide toilet paper. Most have squat toilets (a porcelain slab with a hole in the middle but no seat) and most do not have cubicles. The first time you enter one of these rooms most visitors get quite a shock and many head straight for the door. The answer is to use the major hotels where you will find paper, Western toilet bowls, and privacy cubicles.

It appears that the Chinese have different concepts of public manners than many people from the West. Standing in line for tickets or to board a bus is unknown. It appears to be the survival of the fittest and foreigners will have to adopt this attitude if they are using public transportation. Littering is commonplace. You will see families dumping rubbish from upper floor windows in apartment blocks. The streets, parks, and tourist attractions are littered with all kinds of rubbish, which is sometimes collected by sweepers and cleaners. Watch for half-open manholes as you walk down the streets. The lids are removed so that restaurants and shopowners can dump their waste into the underground drainage system. Much of this ends up in the river. Spitting is also a common occurrence, so be careful where you walk.

9. Sports

Table tennis, basketball, and volleyball are the favorite sports in China and the Chinese produce many of the world champions in these sports. Seats to major games are very popular. This doesn't mean, however, that facilities for the general public are good even in these sports. For visitors who want to partake in sporting activities, the situation is even worse. There are no great opportunities to participate in sporting activities in Guangzhou outside the hotels. Some parks have public facilities for tennis, badminton, and table tennis but these are rarely used by foreigners. There are some public swimming pools, including a large complex in Yuexiu Park, but again it is very rare to see visitors there.

The luxury hotels have good facilities. Many have large swimming pools, tennis courts, bowling centers, health clubs, billiards, sauna, and massage.

Some will allow visitors to pay to use these facilities even though they may not be staying in the hotel.

There are golf courses in Shenzhen and Zhuhai.

In city parks you will see men seated on low stools in deep concentration over a chessboard. They are playing elephant chess or *weiqi,* both strategy boardgames. Elephant chess has been played for 1,300 years. Chess pieces include cannons, elephants, cavalry, infantry, and chariots, with a fortress in which the king and his counselors are entrenched. The two halves of the board are separated by the Yellow River. *Weiqi* has been around for even longer. It is played on a grid board marked with 19 vertical and 19 horizontal lines with 181 black and 180 white flat, round counters. Players mark out their own territory and then try to capture the other's territory and men. It is considered to be the most complicated boardgame in the world because of the high number of possible moves.

You will be able to see, but will have difficulty in participating in, martial art practice and classes. There are three major types practiced in Guangzhou. *Taijiquan,* or "shadow boxing," has been used since the seventh century, originally in self-defense. It is known for its smooth, graceful, circular movements that are combined with deep breathing and concentration. If it is performed correctly, you will end up in a light sweat and all limbs and internal organs will have been exercised. *Qigong* is a form of deep-breathing exercise that aims to regulate the mind, body, and breath to achieve longevity. It can be used to increase strength and decrease pain and its adherents claim success in controlling high blood pressure, heart disease, and aches and pains. It can stimulate the nervous system and increase blood circulation. *Wushu,* or kung fu, is used as a form of self-defense and as physical exercise. There are several different forms with Chinese boxing, as seen in kung fu movies, the most popular.

10. Shopping

Frankly I have not had a lot of luck with shopping in China. When I want a specific clothing item, I find that I cannot get the size, or the style is twenty years out of date, or the colors are limited to red and orange. Fortunately that is changing with the appearance of stores such as the Giordano chain, which is bringing Hong Kong variety and prices to the region.

There are a few department stores in Guangzhou that have a reasonable range and fixed prices. The largest of these is the **Nan Fung** (Tel: 888-8133), which runs between Yan Jiang Road and Liu'ersan Road near the river and Shamian Island. In this same area you can also try the **Landmark Department Store.** In Dishipu Road, there are several smaller stores such as the **Fortune Duck Department Store,** and on Zhong Shan Road there is the **Zhong Shan Wula Department Store.** Farther north there are two **Friendship Stores**—one near the Baiyun Hotel (Tel: 333- 6628) and the other near the China Hotel. The department stores usually accept international credit cards.

Many major hotels have attached shopping centers and there are some other areas where shopping is king. The best places are near the intersection of Zhong Shan Road and Beijing Road, Dishipu and Xiajiu roads north of the Qingping Market, and the area around the China Hotel. In this last area, it is worth checking out the Century City Shopping Center in Ren Min Road and the Fashion Center in Jie Fang Road. These days, you can actually find chic boutiques with loud music, hot floodlights, and scented air. Their merchandise includes dresses from Japan, perfume from Paris, and lipstick from London—all courtesy of Hong Kong. Surprisingly, you will also find things with the label, "Made in Taiwan, Republic of China."

What you as a visitor will actually want to buy in these places is a bit more difficult. Some suggestions include art materials and Chinese antiques, but please be aware that there are more fakes than genuine items; there are kites for wall hangings or for use, paper cuts, jade if you like it and know what you are doing, paintings, down jackets, stamps and coins if you are a collector, childrens' clothing, and personalized seals. Whatever you buy, you should carefully check it before you hand over your money. If it is clothing, check that the zipper works or that there are no missing buttons. Actually operate any electrical item. Defective goods are common, so the shop will accept this action without a problem.

There are a few night markets appearing around the city where you can pick up some souvenir items. You will need to bargain vigorously at these places but you may find something you like. I was asked to buy a Chinese silk dressing robe when I made a recent trip to Guangzhou. After trying all the department stores and markets, I finally realized that this was not something the local Chinese use. I ended up buying it, after much bargaining, in a souvenir store near a major hotel at exactly the same price as I would have paid in Hong Kong.

There are three other stores worth checking out if you are into cultural items. These are the Guangdong Provincial Cultural Relics Collection at 296 Ren Min Beilu (Tel: 666-2819), the Guangzhou Cultural Relics Collection at 146 Wende Rd. (Tel: 333-0175), and the Guangzhou Tourist Arts and Crafts Store at 284 Changdi Damalu (Tel: 888-2877).

11. Entertainment and Nightlife

Most visitors stick to the offerings in the hotels—music lounges, bars, discos, dancing halls, and massage. These are not expensive by Hong Kong standards and they are perceived as being safe. Because the major hotels are scattered over a wide area, it is not common for visitors to go to hotels other than where they are staying. For this reason there is a great similarity between what is offered at different places. I have no particular recommendation as to which is the best lounge, bar, disco, or massage.

Outside the hotels there is a growing choice, as some young people enter the new middle class and want entertainment outlets for themselves. Walk along Yan Jiang Road, Changdi Dama Road, and Liu'erson Road near the Cultural Park and you will find places like the Cherry Karaoke and Night Club, Gentlemen Night Club, and Ding Tong Dancing Hall. These places have English speakers at the front door but when you are inside, you may not find it so good. At some, you will see modern China dancing to the flashing lights and hard rock of the disco beat. Perhaps these are the sons and daughters of the 1960s Red Guards who campaigned so brutally against anything from the West.

The Cultural Park is worth visiting at night. There are often performances on the center stage. If you are lucky you will see visiting troops of acrobats, dancers, or opera stars.

12. The Guangzhou Address List

Airlines—CAAC, 181 Huanshi Rd.	Tel: 666-1803
Airport—	Tel: 666-6123
Bank of China—91 Chang Di Rd.	Tel: 334-0998
Books—Foreign Language Bookstore, 326 Beijing Rd.	
—The Bookshop, 276 Beijing Rd.	Tel: 333-4499
Consulates—Japan, Garden Hotel Tower	Tel: 333-8999
—Thailand, White Swan Hotel	Tel: 888-6968
—U.S.A., 1 Shamian Nanjie	Tel: 888-8911
Drug Store—278 Beijing Rd.	Tel: 333-1555
Hospitals—People's, 602 Ren Min Rd.	Tel: 333-3090
—Sun Yat-sen, 107 Yan Jiang Rd.	Tel: 888-2012
Police—863 Jie Fang Rd.	Tel: 333-1060
Post Office—G.P.O., by railway station	
Railway station—	Tel: 666-1789
Tourist Info.—CITS, 179 Huanshi Rd.	Tel: 667-7151
Zhoutouzui port—	Tel: 444-8218

Index

A-Ma Temple (Macau), 20, 211
Aberdeen (Hong Kong), 45, 90-95, 98
Acupuncture, 250
Airlines, 25, 26
Antiques, 106, 224, 225
Architecture, 56-58
Arts Festival, 62
Aw Boon Haw Gardens (Hong Kong), 93

Bars, 111, 149, 227
Bicycles, 154, 198, 254
Birthday of Confucius, 63
Birthday of Lord Buddha, 62
Birthday of Lu Pau, 63
Buddhism, 52
Bus, 27, 72, 153, 154, 198, 254
Business cards, 56
Business hours, 34

Camoes Garden (Macau), 215
Canton (China), 46, 47, 51, 58, 113, 116, 136, 187, 189, 197, 231
Canton Trade Fair, 255, 270
Casinos (Macau), 225
Cathay Pacific Airways, 25, 36, 111, 150, 167, 183
Causeway Bay (Hong Kong), 45, 64, 72, 77, 93, 101, 103, 105
Central District (Hong Kong), 27, 64, 67, 68, 72, 77, 86-90, 101, 103, 118, 276
Chiang Kai-shek, 235
Charles Elliot, 47
Chek Lap Kok Airport, 26, 115, 177
Cheoc Van Beach (Macau), 220
Cheung Chau Bun Festival, 62, 173, 183
Cheung Chau Island (Hong Kong), 62, 169, 173-75, 181
China, 15-18, 21-23, 26, 28-35, 37, 45-48, 50, 54, 56, 58, 113, 115, 136, 187-89, 196, 229-85
China Folk Culture Village, 20, 275
China Gate (Macau), 214
Ching Chung Koon Temple (Hong Kong), 159
Ching Ming Festival, 62, 193
Chung Yeung Festival, 63
Churches, 53, 112, 150
Cidadel of Sao Paulo (Macau), 208
Cinemas, 111, 167
Clearwater Bay (Hong Kong), 164
Climate, 27, 46, 65, 188, 232
Coloane Island (Macau), 187, 190, 197, 202, 218
Confucianism, 53
Consulates, 33
Country Parks (Hong Kong), 69, 151, 158, 163, 164

287

Cuiheng (China), 221
Culture, 98, 141, 165, 191, 221, 242, 247, 281
Customs, 33, 34

Day of Portugul, 193
Deng Xiaoping, 236
Dr. Sun Yat-sen, 213, 221, 222, 234, 266, 277, 278, 281, 282
Dom Pedro Theatre (Macau), 222
Dragon Boat Festival, 62, 246
Dongguan (China), 271

Electricity, 30

Ferries, 26, 27, 69, 113, 153, 170, 171, 197, 254
Food, 58, 60, 80-86, 128-33, 156, 157, 172, 173, 192, 205-8, 243, 261-64
Food Festival, 62
Foshan, 18, 20, 276, 281
Foshan Ancesters' Temple, 18, 20, 276
Fung Pin Shan Museum (Hong Kong), 91

Gambling, 99, 195
Golf, 100, 165, 183, 224, 283
Gongbei (China), 280
Guangdong, 18, 20, 50, 60, 231, 237, 238, 251
Guangzhou, 17, 20, 21, 25-29, 32, 58, 60, 113, 116, 187, 197, 231, 233, 238, 257-85
Guangzhou Museum, 264, 281
Guia Hill (Macau), 213

Hac Sa Beach (Macau), 220
Happy Valley (Hong Kong), 45, 71, 93, 97
Happy Valley racecourse, 20, 93, 99, 100, 162
Harbour City (Hong Kong), 120, 136, 144
Herbal Medicine, 250
Hillside Escalator (Hong Kong), 72, 90
History, 46, 48, 51, 67, 188, 189, 232, 251
Hong Kong, 15, 16, 18, 21, 22, 23, 25, 26, 27, 28, 29, 30, 31, 32, 33, 34, 35, 37, 38, 45-184, 187, 189, 192, 195, 196, 205, 231, 240, 251, 253, 254, 271, 272
Hong Kong Airport, 26, 49, 69, 115
Hong Kong Arts Centre, 91
Hong Kong Convention and Exhibition Centre, 91
Hong Kong Cultural Centre, 133
Hong Kong Festival, 63
Hong Kong Island, 29, 45-47, 50, 51, 63, 64, 67-112, 118, 133, 142, 153, 187
Hong Kong Park, 89
Hong Kong Railway Museum, 116, 161
Hong Kong Science Museum, 136
Hong Kong Tourist Association (HKTA), 35, 62, 64, 96, 112, 115, 150, 184

Hospitals, 112, 150, 167, 192, 228, 285
Hotels, 64, 72-80, 118-28, 154-56, 193, 198-205, 248, 255-60, 274
Humen, 20, 271, 272
Hungry Ghosts Festival, 63

Jade Market (Hong Kong), 137, 145
Jetfoils, 196
Jewelry, 108, 147, 224, 225
Jida (China), 278

Kennedy Town (Hong Kong), 63, 67, 71
Kowloon (Hong Kong), 27, 29, 45, 46, 48, 50, 51, 64, 69, 73, 113-50, 151, 276
Kowloon-Canton Railway, 27, 26, 113, 116, 153, 154
Kun Iam Temple (Macau), 214

Lamma Island (Hong Kong), 169, 171, 175-77
Language, 54, 56, 197, 240
Lantau Island (Hong Kong), 20, 46, 52, 169, 171, 177-81
Lau Fau Shan (Hong Kong), 159
Leal Senado (Macau), 211
Lei Chung Uk Museum (Hong Kong), 138
Lei Yue Mun (Hong Kong), 140
Light Rail Transit (Hong Kong), 154, 159
Lin Zexu, 47
Lok Ma Chau Lookout Point (Hong Kong), 160
Lotus Mountain (China), 271, 281
Lotus Temple (Macau), 214
Lou Lim Ieok Gardens (Macau), 213

Macau, 15, 16, 18, 21-23, 25, 26, 28-35, 37, 46, 50, 69, 115, 116, 185-228, 231, 253, 280
Macau airport, 26, 28-29, 195
Macau Grand Prix, 223
Macau Jockey Club, 223
MacLehose Trail, (Hong Kong), 158
Mai Po Marshes, 18, 159
Maiden's Festival, 63
Mail, 28, 29
Mao Zedong, 235, 237, 238, 241
Mass Transit Railway (Hong Kong), 68, 71, 72, 113, 116, 153, 154
Man Mo Temple (Hong Kong), 90, 161
Mausoleum of the 72 Martyrs (China), 270, 281
Memorial Garden to the Martyrs (China), 270, 281
Mid-Autumn Festival, 63, 193
Middle Kingdom (Hong Kong), 95
Miu Fat Buddhist Monastery (Hong Kong), 159
Money, 30, 31
Mong Kok (Hong Kong), 138, 145
Museum of Tea Ware (Hong Kong), 89

New Territories (Hong Kong), 16, 45, 46, 48, 50-52, 113, 138, 140, 151-67
News media, 36
Newspapers, 36, 37
Nightlife, 109, 148, 166, 225, 284
Noon Day Gun (Hong Kong), 93

Ocean Park (Hong Kong), 18, 45, 94, 97
Opium, 20, 47, 234, 272
Outlying Islands (Hong Kong), 45, 46, 52, 169-84

Pacific Place (Hong Kong), 75, 103
Packing, 28
Pak Tai Temple (Hong Kong), 173
Passports, 32, 33, 238
Pataca (Macau), 30
Peak tram (Hong Kong), 71, 72, 94
Pearl River Delta, 17, 18, 22, 25, 26, 32, 192, 229-85
Peng Chau Island (Hong Kong), 169, 181
Penha Church (Macau), 210
Peninsula Hotel (Hong Kong), 118, 124, 135
Plover Creek Reservoir (Hong Kong), 161
Po Lin Monastery, 20, 52, 179
Possession Street (Hong Kong), 90

Prices, 31, 32
Protestant Cemetery (Macau), 215
Pubs, 110, 149, 227

Qi Shan, 47
Qingming Festival, 245
Quingping Market (China), 261, 268, 281

Radio, 37
Railways, 27
Religion, 52, 53, 54
Rental cars, 27
Repulse Bay (Hong Kong), 68, 95
Restaurants, 80-86, 128-33, 156, 157, 172, 173, 205-8, 261, 264

Safety, 34
Sai Kung (Hong Kong), 163
St. John's Cathedral (Hong Kong), 89
St. Paul's Church (Macau), 20, 208
Sam Tung Uk Museum (Hong Kong), 157
Sculpture of the Five Rams, 264, 281
Shamian Island (China), 255, 259, 263, 269
Shatin (Hong Kong), 52, 153, 154, 155, 162
Shatin racecourse, 100, 116, 140, 162, 165
Shek O Beach (Hong Kong), 69, 100

INDEX

Shekou, 27, 69, 276
Shenzhen, 20, 25, 26, 33, 253, 254, 271-76, 283
Shopping, 100-109, 142-48, 166, 224, 283
Shueng Shiu (Hong Kong), 160
Shunde (China), 277
Six Banyan Temple (China), 266, 281
Skybus, 115
Space Museum (Hong Kong), 133
Special Economic Zones, 17, 20, 27, 32, 189, 230, 272, 278
Splendid China, 20, 272
Spring Lantern Festival, 62
Stanley (Hong Kong), 68, 95, 97, 105
Star Ferry, 18, 69, 72, 86, 113, 118, 120, 133, 136
Statue Square (Hong Kong), 86
STDM *(Sociedade de Turismo e Diversoes de Macau)* (Macau), 190, 226
Stone House Cathedral (China), 268
Sung Dynasty Village (Hong Kong), 140, 141

Tai Mo Shin (Hong Kong), 158
Tai O (Hong Kong), 179
Tai Po (Hong Kong), 161
Tailoring, 108, 147
Taipa Island (Macau), 187, 190, 197, 202, 206, 215-18
Tam Kung Festival, 62
Taoism, 52, 53
Tap Mun Chau (Hong Kong), 181

Taxis, 56, 69, 71, 153, 154, 197, 254
Telephone, 23, 28, 29
Television, 37
Temperature, 27, 30, 46, 188
Temple Street Market (Hong Kong), 137, 141, 145
Ten Thousand Buddhas Monastery (Hong Kong), 162
Tennis, 99, 152, 165, 224, 282
Tin Hau Festival, 62
Tipping, 32
Tourism, 50, 53
Tourist information, 35
Tramway (Hong Kong), 68, 71
Transportation, 25, 26, 68, 69, 112, 115, 116, 118, 150, 167, 170, 171, 196-98, 253
Travel agents, 22, 23
Tsim Sha Tsui (Hong Kong), 29, 45, 74, 113, 118, 133, 136, 141, 142
Tsim Sha Tsui East, 64, 122, 136, 149
Tsuen Wan (Hong Kong), 153, 154, 155, 157, 158
Tuen Mun (Hong Kong), 154, 158-60
Typhoons, 27, 28, 46, 184

United Chinese Cemeteries (Macau), 217

Victoria Harbour (Hong Kong), 69, 97, 115, 136, 141
Victoria Peak (Hong Kong), 16, 45, 50, 68, 69, 72, 94

Visas, 32, 33

Walking trails, 69, 96, 158, 163, 177, 179
Wanchai (Hong Kong), 45, 64, 91, 93, 101, 105, 118
Western (Hong Kong), 67, 77, 90, 91
White Cloud Hills (China), 271
Wong Tai Sin Temple (Hong Kong), 138

Xiqiao Hills (China), 277

Yau Ma Tei (Hong Kong), 136, 138
Yuan (China), 30, 31
Yuen Long (Hong Kong), 154, 159
Yuexiu Park (China), 264, 281

Zhongqui Festival, 246
Zhongshan (China), 277
Zhuhai, 25, 27, 190, 221, 254, 278, 283
Zoological Gardens (Hong Kong), 89

OTHER MAVERICK GUIDES

MAVERICK GUIDE TO MALAYSIA AND SINGAPORE
All New 2nd Edition
By Len Rutledge

Rutledge walked the major city streets, drove thousands of miles to the hill resorts, historic centers, and beaches of peninsular Malaysia, traveled to exotic island paradises, and tramped the jungles of Borneo to provide an exciting insider's account of the traditions, cultures, and modern lifestyles. Essential reading for anyone interested in this region.

488 pp. 5½ x 8½
Photos Maps Index
ISBN: 0-88289-990-2 $14.95 pb

MAVERICK GUIDE TO VIETNAM, LAOS, AND CAMBODIA
By Len Rutledge

Helpful hints on the laws and customs, lessons on the languages, and valuable tips on housing, food, and entertainment. Visitors can sight-see the temples in Cambodia, hike Lao highlands, or shop in Hanoi and Ho Chi Minh City.

392 pp. 5½ x 8½
Color photos Maps Index
ISBN: 0-88289-923-6 $17.95 pb

OTHER MAVERICK GUIDES

MAVERICK GUIDE TO THAILAND: 2nd Edition
By Len Rutledge
Full of festivals, daily music, drama, literary events, and some of the finest restaurants in the world, modern Thailand accommodates five million annual visitors with ease. Rutledge tells how to get there, describes the land and life of the people, and includes details on hotels, dining, sight-seeing, tours, sports, shopping, and entertainment.

384 pp. 5½ x 8½ Photos
Color maps Index
ISBN: 0-88289-942-2 $15.95 pb

THE MAVERICK GUIDE TO BALI AND JAVA: 2nd Edition
By Don Turner
Presents essential travel information to the tourist as well as business travelers in the familiar Maverick format. Turner explains the weather, geography, flora and fauna, local food and flavorings and useful phrases to help you get by.

As always, the finest accommodations and eating establishments are listed as well as the more budget-priced options so the traveler has the ultimate choice. Maps are included in addition to tables that measure distances between cities.

312 pp. 5½ x 8½
Photos Maps Index
ISBN: 1-56554-052-2 $14.95 pb

Please tell us about your trip to Hong Kong,
Macau, and South China.
(This page can be folded to make an envelope.)

Place your check or money order inside this envelope. Please do not send cash through the mail.

FOLD

FOLD HERE. FASTEN LIP ON FRONT WITH CLEAR TAPE.

Please fasten sides with clear tape.

Please fasten sides with clear tape.

FOLD HERE

RE: 1st edition, Hong Kong

Place first class postage here

THE MAVERICK GUIDES
Pelican Publishing Company
1101 Monroe Street
P.O. Box 3110
Gretna, Louisiana 70054